# Locational Analysis in Human Geography

Second Edition

Volume I

For Brenda, Margaret, and Val

# Locational Models

GF
50
H33
1977b
v.1

**Peter Haggett**
Professor of Urban and Regional Geography, University of Bristol

**Andrew D. Cliff**
University Lecturer in Geography and Fellow of Christ's College, Cambridge

**Allan Frey**
Senior Lecturer in Geography, University of Bristol

Copyright © Peter Haggett, Andrew Cliff and Allan Frey 1977

First published 1977 by
Edward Arnold (Publishers) Ltd
25 Hill Street, London W1X 8LL

The first edition of
Locational Analysis in Human Geography
© Peter Haggett 1965
was first published in 1965 by
Edward Arnold (Publishers) Ltd
and reprinted 1966; 1967; 1968; 1969; 1970; 1971.

ISBN Cloth 0 7131 5899 9
vol. I paper 0 7131 (Chapters 1–7) 5955 3
vol. II paper 0 7131 (Chapters 8–16) 5956 1

All rights reserved. No part of this publication may be reproduced, stored in a retrieval system, or transmitted in any form or by any means, electronic, photocopying, recording or otherwise, without the prior permission of Edward Arnold (Publishers) Ltd.

This book is published in two editions. The paperback edition is sold subject to the condition that it shall not, by way of trade or otherwise, be lent, re-sold, hired out or otherwise circulated without the publisher's prior consent in any form of binding or cover other than that in which it is published and without a similar condition including this condition being imposed upon any subsequent purchaser.

Filmset by Keyspools Limited, Golborne, Lancs.
Printed in Great Britain by J. W. Arrowsmith Ltd., Bristol

# Contents

| | Page |
|---|---|
| Contents[1] | v |
| Preface | ix |
| Acknowledgements | xiii |

**Volume I: Locational Models**

| | |
|---|---|
| **1 On Geography** | 1 |
| 1.1 Introduction | 1 |
| 1.2 Geography: the internal dialogue | 2 |
| 1.3 Geography: external relations | 10 |
| 1.4 Trends in geography | 12 |
| 1.5 Conclusions | 24 |
| **Part One: Models of Locational Structure** | 25 |
| **2 Interaction** | 26 |
| 2.1 Introduction | 26 |
| 2.2 Interaction and spatial form | 26 |
| 2.3 Elementary interaction models | 30 |
| 2.4 Interpretation of model components | 33 |
| 2.5 Maximum entropy models | 40 |
| 2.6 Interaction fields | 47 |
| 2.7 Interaction territories | 55 |
| 2.8 Conclusions | 63 |
| **3 Networks** | 64 |
| 3.1 Introduction | 64 |
| 3.2 Location of routes | 64 |
| 3.3 Network location | 69 |
| 3.4 Routes through networks | 76 |
| 3.5 Empirical studies of network structure | 86 |
| 3.6 Conclusions | 96 |

[1] A detailed contents list appears at the beginning of each of the chapters. Starred sections (*) indicate areas which demand a fuller statistical background than is assumed in the remainder of the book.

**4** **Nodes** 97
4.1 Introduction 97
4.2 Settlement patterns 97
4.3 Size distribution of settlements 110
4.4 Changes over time 121
4.5 Relationship between size and spacing of settlements 126
4.6 Impulse transmission between urban areas 132
4.7 Conclusions 138

**5** **Hierarchies** 139
5.1 Introduction 139
5.2 Functional hierarchies of settlements 139
5.3 Periodic and evolving settlement hierarchies 153
5.4 Specialized centres within the hierarchy 161
5.5 Hierarchic distortion due to agglomeration 170
5.6 Hierarchic distortion due to resource localization 177
5.7 Conclusions 189

**6** **Surfaces** 191
6.1 Introduction 191
6.2 Surfaces and gradients 192
6.3 Movement-minimization models: statement 199
6.4 Movement-minimization models: evaluation 207
6.5 Distortion of regular gradients 211
6.6 Surface change over time 222
6.7 Conclusions 230

**7** **Diffusion** 231
7.1 Introduction 231
7.2 The Hägerstrand model 234
7.3 The logistic curve 238
7.4 Central place diffusion 240
7.5 Diffusion barriers and corridors 242
7.6 Goodness-of-fit of diffusion models with reality 244
7.7 Epidemic models* 247
7.8 Conclusions 257

**References and author index** 559

**Further reading** 594

**Subject index** 597

## Volume II: Locational Methods

**Part Two: Methods of Locational Analysis** 259

**8 Data Collecting** 260
8.1 Introduction 260
8.2 Geographical populations 261
8.3 Spatial sampling procedures 267
8.4 Data coverage problems 282
8.5 Conclusions 290

**9 Map Description** 291
9.1 Introduction 291
9.2 Mapping and measurement levels 291
9.3 Single component maps 293
9.4 Multicomponent maps 301
9.5 Probability mapping 306
9.6 The shape of map distributions 309
9.7 Maps as graphs 313
9.8 Co-ordinate systems for map data 324
9.9 Conclusions 328

**10 Hypothesis Testing** 329
10.1 Introduction 329
10.2 Spatial independence: the problem 329
10.3 Spatial independence: solutions 336
10.4 Spatial stationarity 342
10.5 Normality 345
10.6 Irregular collecting areas 348
10.7 Conclusions 352

**11 Spatial Autocorrelation** 353
11.1 Introduction 353
11.2 Concepts of autocorrelation 354
11.3 Testing for autocorrelation* 356
11.4 Autocorrelation in regression 360
11.5 Autocorrelation and correlogram analysis 367
11.6 Autocorrelation and hypothesis testing* 374
11.7 Conclusions 377

**12 Scale Components** 378
12.1 Introduction 378
12.2 Polynomial trend surface analysis 379
12.3 Analysis of variance* 384
12.4 Fourier and spectral analysis 390
12.5 Space-time spectral analysis 406
12.6 Conclusions 413

**13** **Point Patterns** 414
13.1 Introduction 414
13.2 Quadrat counts, I: Probability distributions 415
13.3 Quadrat counts, II: Selection criteria 422
13.4 Quadrat counts, III: A regional example 430
13.5 Polygon techniques 436
13.6 Distance-based methods 439
13.7 Conclusions 446

**Part Three: Regional Applications** 449

**14** **Region Building** 450
14.1 Introduction 450
14.2 The regional concept 450
14.3 Regions as combinatorial problems 460
14.4 Regions as assignment problems 465
14.5 Regions as districting problems 477
14.6 Nodal regions as graphs 485
14.7 Conclusions 490

**15** **Allocating** 491
15.1 Introduction 491
15.2 The transportation problem 492
15.3 The transportation algorithm 497
15.4 Extensions of the transportation problem 505
15.5 Further programming models* 510
15.6 Conclusions 515

**16** **Forecasting** 517
16.1 Introduction 517
16.2 The basic space-time autoregressive model (STAR) 518
16.3 Integrated space-time models (STIMA and STARIMAR) 522
16.4 Model identification* 525
16.5 Parameter variation over time and space* 534
16.6 Purely spatial forecasting* 539
16.7 Conclusions 540

**Postscript** 541

**Appendix**
1 Glossary of notation 543
2 Statistical tables 551

**References and author index** 559

**Further reading** 594

**Subject index** 597

# Preface to the Second Edition

Locational studies have changed over the last fifteen years in ways hardly foreseen when the first edition[1] was being written. Then, geography stood on the edge of changes in both emphasis and style which came, in the mid-1960s, to be bundled together as yet another 'new' geography of the sort which periodically besets the discipline. The times were those of J. F. Kennedy's New Frontier; universities and their individual subjects were expanding; the mood was optimistic. Perhaps individual disciplines catch the feeling of society as a whole, for now the mid-1970s find geography in a more sombre mood. The first edition described itself as 'a report from an active battlefront'. Even with three authors, rather than one, peering through the smoke, the lines of development remain as hard to see. But, if we retain the military metaphor, then the cavalry charge described in the early 1960s seems now to have slowed to grinding trench warfare. To be sure, the current geographer is better armed but he faces a tougher battle. As capabilities rise, so too do expectations, and certain locational problems are now revealed as starkly difficult. To overcome them will take much more time and effort and a higher order of application than had been imagined a decade or so ago.

As with any architectural renovation, the present book is an odd blend of old and new. Retained is the basic distinction between locational concepts

[1] Few books are more exasperating than those which refuse to die gracefully! Since the first edition of this book was written, dozens of more substantive works on locational analysis by other pens have been published. Thus it was the expectation (even hope) of the original author that the first edition of this book would be the only one. Left unchanged and unrevised it might be expected to slip peacefully from the bookshelves, to be recalled—if at all—as a nostalgic 'period piece'. Unpredictably, the book stubbornly refused to go out of print and although outdated was translated into an increasing number of foreign languages. Given soaring printing costs, to revise a few points here and there and to update references would have added hugely to the published costs of any 'new' version, while doing little to come to terms with the changes in human geography as a whole. A more radical revision was called for. I was fortunate in that, at a time when my own timetable was having to be drastically curtailed, two of my colleagues (both then at Bristol) agreed to help with the task. Andrew Cliff took especial interest in the sections concerned with formal statistical and mathematical modelling (especially Chapters 7, 10–13, 15–16), while Allan Frey concentrated on methodological and conceptual questions. Without their efforts and enthusiastic cooperation, a second edition would have remained long unwritten. It is our joint view of locational analysis and its role in human geography that this second edition now presents.

P.H.

(Part One), and ways of testing and extending them (Part Two); added is a concern with regional applications (Part Three). Within Part One, the spatial format—from 'flows' to 'surfaces'—is maintained, and a new chapter on diffusion has been added. Part Two is heavily revised and contains much new material to allow a fuller examination of the statistical models needed in locational analysis. Part Three extends the work of the first edition on region building by considering optimization and forecasting methods. Given the increasing importance of regional planning at present, we would expect greater emphasis to be given to Part Three in any future revisions. Decisions on whether to retain or to dispense with old favourites in the material contained in the first edition caused occasional heart searching. Inevitably, what was seen as 'sound timber' by the original author, sometimes appeared as 'dry rot' to his colleagues. But we were agreed that many of the debates on the philosophy of geography (for example, on exceptionalism, the place of quantification in the subject, and the neglect of the geometric tradition) had now grown stale. New issues, like the value of a phenomenological approach and the radical role of science, have taken their place in Chapter 1. Likewise, the notion of a natural scale of geographical magnitude (the G-scale of the first edition) has been revised to bring the scale into line with Haggett (1965a).

Inevitably, problems of what to cut out were incomparably more difficult than what to include. We were tempted to add the subtitle 'a macrogeographical approach', to the book's main title to indicate the emphasis we squarely place on aggregate behaviour patterns and macroscale geographical phenomena. Major developments in human microgeography—in space/time trajectories, in perception, and in the theory of decision making—have taken place over the last decade, associated particularly with the research of workers such as Torsten Hägerstrand, Yi-Fu Tuan and Julian Wolpert. We debated whether or not to include an extended treatment of such material in this edition. In the end, the pressures of space and our consciousness of the fact that others could write with more authority in this area, restricted us to very limited cross-references. We view this work in microgeography with optimism, and look forward to the enrichment it promises for the somewhat formal areas of aggregate model building reported here.

Given its restricted compass, the book will be seen by some critics as narrow and positivist in its philosophy. Certainly, the Neyman–Pearson, rather than the Bayesian, approach to statistical analysis is followed in Part Two, where the emphasis is on the critical and sceptical scrutiny of locational ideas. Where these notions of human spatial organization come from remains a matter of intuition and imagination, and research on the topics reported in Part One leaves plenty of scope for creativity. Together, Parts One and Two form the two halves of Medawar's (1969) hypothetic-deductive method, still the conventional approach to most scientific problem solving. If this 'cycle' of construction and testing seems too academic, then in Part Three we begin to consider the utility of ideas in terms of their regional applications.

Throughout, our joint aim has been to direct this second edition, like the first, to the audience we know best—the second and third year undergraduate at an English university. Most of the chapters are thus based on lecture and classroom material. However, many locational models are now part of the English school curriculum, while statistical methods form an essential part of the first and second year geography undergraduate's training. A higher level of mathematical understanding is therefore assumed than was the case with the first edition. Important textbooks like those of King (1969b) and Wilson and Kirkby (1975) are now available, and we expect undergraduates to be familiar with these basic works. Sections in the book which are of greater statistical or mathematical difficulty have been starred and it is suggested that they could be omitted at a first reading. A glossary of notation appears at the end of the book which summarises the main notational conventions used, and a small selection of statistical tables is also included. Our hope is that the book may prove useful to the reader wanting a general outline of locational analysis while, at the same time, containing enough challenging material to attract those wishing to pursue study at greater depth.

Acknowledgement was paid in the first edition to a number of sources of help. These debts incurred by the original author have been compounded over the intervening years and remain heavier than ever, especially in both Cambridge and the West Country. All three of us have also benefitted from generous help on both sides of the Atlantic during periods of research or teaching in other institutions. We have also gained from critical comments by the editors of translated versions of the first edition, especially from the French (Philippe Pinchemel), German (Dietrich Bartels), and Russian editions (Yuri Medvedkov and Mark Bandman). Three other acknowledgements are in order. First, to Keith Ord of the Statistics Department at Warwick University, goes a special word for his unstinting advice and help with the more mathematical sections of the book. Second, we are grateful to our publisher, Edward Arnold, and to their Geography Editor, John Davey, not only for support in producing this volume, but for innovative leads given in geography publishing in this country. Third, we wish to thank Arin Bayraktaroglu and Sue Flint in the Statistics Laboratory at Cambridge, whose continued good humour enabled them to survive the typing of a lengthy manuscript made no easier by three varieties of handwriting, standardized only in illegibility.

Our children now span the age range from diapers, through pop music, to latch keys. It was not in their nature to suffer in silence while this edition was being hammered out at home, but we appreciated the occasional demodulation. That these brief episodes occurred at all was due, as always, to the three whose names grace an earlier page. We dedicate this book to them with affection.

Chew Magna, Somerset
Bonfire Night, 1975.

Peter Haggett
Andrew Cliff
Allan Frey

*Note:* The paperback edition of this book is presented in two volumes. These are self-contained and may be used individually. So that they may be read and used together, cross-references from volume I to volume II and vice versa are retained, and both volumes contain complete Contents pages, References and Indexes. The pagination of volume II continues from volume I. There is thus a jump in pagination between the final chapter of the latter and the References.

# Acknowledgements

The authors and publishers gratefully acknowledge permission received from the following to modify and make use of copyright material in diagrams and tables:[1]

Full citations to books, journals and authors may be found in the references; sources of material are given in the captions.

American Geographical Society for figs 6.18, 6.19; American Statistical Association for fig. 9.8 and table 9.1; Association of American Geographers for figs 4.11(b), 6.23, 9.20, 9.21, 13.15, 13.16 and tables 9.9, 15.2; Cambridge University Press for figs 2.9, 2.10, 2.12, 4.2, 4.3, 8.5, 8.9, 8.10, 11.5, 11.7, 11.16, 12.2, 12.3, 14.7, 14.8, 14.9, 15.3 and tables 2.4, 2.5, 14.4, 14.5; Centre for Urban and Community Studies, University of Toronto for fig. 3.15; Clark University for table 6.5; Colston Research Society, University of Bristol, for figs 12.26, 12.27; Department of the Navy, Arlington, Va. for fig. 14.3; to the Escher Foundation, Collection Haags Gemeentemuseum, the Hague for fig. 1.5; Dr P. Fores for fig. 9.24; W. C. Found for table 6.8; Geografiska Annaler for figs 5.13, 9.16, 9.17 and table 9.3; Charles Griffin & Co. Ltd for fig. 13.6 and tables 7.2, 8.5, 8.6, 10.5, 13.2, 13.3; Güven Gülöksüz for fig. 4.11(c); Harper & Row Inc. for fig. 1.3 and tables 1.1, 8.4; Heinemann Educational Books Ltd for fig. 9.6; Holden-Day Inc. for fig. 12.13(c) and (d); Institute of British Geographers for figs 1.4, 6.10, 16.3 and tables 10.2, 10.3, 16.1; Johns Hopkins University Press for table 8.7; Journal of Asian Studies for fig. 5.14; Liber Grafiska Map Service Division for fig. 7.2; Methuen & Co. Ltd for fig. 4.16; Northwestern University Press for fig. 7.4; Ohio State University for figs 4.20, 5.6, 12.5, 12.14, 12.15, 12.16 and 16.1; Oliver and Boyd, Dr F. Yates, the literary executor of the late Sir Ronald Fisher and the McGraw-Hill International Book Co. for statistical tables; Operations Research Society of America for fig. 14.18; Oxford University Press for fig. 14.1; Pergamon Press Ltd for figs 2.6, 6.20, 14.14 and tables 4.6, 4.9; Pion Ltd for figs 7.9, 11.2, 12.6, 12.12, 13.1, 13.2, 13.3 and tables 10.1, 10.4, 11.2, 11.4, 13.1; Pitman & Sons, London and Dr Frederick Croxton for fig. 8.2; Prentice-Hall Inc. for figs 6.3, 6.22, 15.7; J. N. Rayner and R. G. Golledge for figs 12.17, 12.18, 12.19, 12.20(a), 12.21, 12.23; Royal Statistical Society for table 14.6; R. S. Spooner for fig. 4.21; P. J. Taylor for table 2.1; University of

[1] Numbers refer to figures and tables in this book.

Chicago Press for fig. 10.5; University of Minnesota Press for fig. 7.8; University of Washington Press for fig. 14.21; James E. Vance Jr. for fig. 2.11; Wayne State University Press for fig. 14.20; John Wiley & Sons Inc. for table 12.1; Yale Law Journal Company and Fred B. Rothman & Co. for fig. 14.19.

Acknowledgement is also made to the copyright holders in the figures below which have been redrawn or modified from the first edition:

The American Association of Petroleum Geologists for fig. 12.1; The American Geographical Society for figs 3.21, 3.23, 4.10, 4.18 and 4.19; The Association of American Geographers for figs 1.9, 2.7, 6.14, 6.15, 6.21, 8.12, 9.2, 10.9 and 14.15; Department of Regional Science, University of Pennsylvania for figs 3.20, 5.3, 14.22 and 14.23; *Economic Geography* for figs 2.21, 5.1 and 6.11, The Free Press, Glencoe, for fig. 10.8; *Geografiska Annaler*, Sweden, for fig. 4.6; C. W. K. Gleerup Publishers, Sweden, for figs 2.3, 2.5, 3.8, 4.7, 5.11, 5.18, 5.19 and 7.1; K. A. Gunawardena for fig. 5.1; Hafner Publishing Co. for figs 2.2 and 4.10; Holt, Rinehart & Winston Inc for fig. 14.16; Hutchinson & Co. Ltd for figs 3.9 and 6.5; The Institute of British Geographers for figs 12.1 and 14.4; *Liverpool and Manchester Geological Journal* for fig. 8.3; The Ministry of Transport for figs 2.10 and 3.10; MIT Press and the author for figs 2.20, 5.9 and 5.26; Thomas Nelson & Sons Ltd and the editors for fig. 9.22; Peat, Marwich, Caywood, Schiller & Co. for figs 3.6 and 3.17; Princeton University Press for figs 3.4 and 3.18; *Professional Geographer* for figs 5.2, 9.3, 13.10 and 14.17; *Przeglad Geograficzny* for figs 14.12 and 14.13; Regional Science Research Institute for figs 9.11 and 15.2; The Research Center in Economic Development and Cultural Change, Chicago, for figs 4.12 and 4.13; The Royal Geographical Society for figs 8.6 and 12.4; The State University of Iowa, Dept. of Geography, for fig. 5.22; *Tijdschrift voor Economische en Sociale Geografie* for figs 4.2 and 7.1; *The Times* and T. H. Hollingsworth for fig. 2.21; The University of Chicago Press for figs 2.2, 3.16, 3.19, 3.20, 3.22, 6.16, 6.17, 9.12, 9.13, 9.14 and 9.15; The University of Michigan for fig. 7.7; The University of Michigan Press for figs 4.3, 4.4, 5.17 and 6.4; The University of Toronto Press for fig. 2.13; University of Wales Press for fig. 9.7; The US Conservation Foundation and the authors for fig. 8.11; The US Department of Agriculture for figs 8.3, 8.4 and 8.10; Yale University Press for figs 2.14, 2.16, 3.2, 3.3, 4.17, 5.4 and 5.10.

# 1 On Geography

1.1 **Introduction.** 1.2 **Geography: The Internal Dialogue:** 1[1] Definitions and traditions; 2 Locational traditions and spatial concepts; 3 Ecological traditions and system concepts; 4 Regional traditions and scale concepts. 1.3 **Geography: External Relations.** 1.4 **Trends in Geography:** 1 Paradigm shifts within geography; 2 Model building and quantification; 3 Deterministic and probabilistic explanation; 4 Positivism and phenomenology; 5 Geography as critical science. 1.5 **Conclusions.**

## 1.1 Introduction

The objectives of this book are (1) to describe the ordered ways in which the aggregate patterns of human geography are arranged in space (Part One); (2) to show by what methods these patterns may be detected (Part Two); and (3) to suggest how such information may be used in an applied regional context (Part Three). It can be argued, however, that order (and chaos too) lie in the eye of the beholder. Thus, if we ask of a given region whether its settlements are arranged in some predictable sequence, or if its land use zones are concentric, or if its growth is cyclical, then the answer depends largely upon what we are prepared to look for, and what we are prepared to accept as order. In Sigwart's words 'That there is more order in the world than appears at first sight is not discovered *till the order is looked for*' (Hanson, 1958, p. 204). Chorley (1962) has drawn attention to Postan's lively illustration of this problem as it afflicted Newton, newly struck on the head by an apple: 'Had he asked himself the obvious question: why did that particular apple choose that unrepeatable instant to fall on that unique head, he might have written the history of an apple. Instead of which he asked himself why apples fell and produced the theory of gravitation. The decision was not the apple's but Newton's' (Postan, 1948, p. 406).

It seemed essential, therefore, that we preface the main parts of this book by a chapter in which we set out the geographical viewpoints and biases of the authors. Geographical writing, like any other, inevitably reflects the assumptions and experiences of the writers. Some of this inevitable bias in our treatment of human geography will be very readily apparent. It is, for example,

[1] In the text third-order sections are fully numbered as 1.2.1, 1.2.2, etc. In the chapter heading summaries throughout the book these headings are referred to by their final digit only.

based largely on research carried out in the Western world, particularly northwest Europe and the Americas: neither the Soviet nor Afro-Asian sources have been fully tapped—the former by reason of language barriers and the latter on account of the relative scarcity of research. However, having said this, we note that, increasingly, the translation of work in journals like *Soviet Geography*, or invited reviews like those of Nishioka (1975) in *Progress in Geography*, is opening windows on research in other languages and social contexts that promises to be of increasing significance in interpreting the patterns of human geography.

A second apparent source of bias is towards the use of quantitative, rather than qualitative, analysis. This, too, may be rationalized in terms of the fundamental need for improved definition in geographical work. The historian of geography's development will look back on the 1960s as a decade of 'mathematical extravaganza', albeit one shared with other social sciences at various times in their growth. Wilson and Kirkby's *Mathematics for geographers and planners* (1975) represents a milestone in this trend, and we assume that readers of this book will be familiar with the main methods outlined there. Along with this quantitative emphasis goes a concern for theory-building at the aggregate or macrogeographical level.

Thus, in this first chapter, we examine in more detail some of the assumptions upon which the other chapters are based. To do this, we look at geography's internal structure, its external relations, and certain ongoing trends that are changing both.

## 1.2 Geography: The Internal Dialogue

### 1.2.1 *Definitions and traditions*

Geography has had a separate and recognizable existence as an academic subject for over two thousand years. Even before its formal teaching by the Greeks, the basic curiosity of man to know what lay 'over the hill' must have led to a passing on of experience and conjecture as to the form of the earth's surface. The subsequent history of geography has exemplified the basic need for organized knowledge about the earth's surface. The widening knowledge of the Great Age of Discovery led on to the nineteenth-century growth of the great exploring societies (like the Royal Geographical Society founded in London in 1833, and other parallel societies in Paris, Berlin, and New York), and culminated with emphasis during the present century on rapid and precise survey techniques.

Formal definitions of the field have been attempted at each stage of its growth. Richard Hartshorne, the leading geographical philosopher of this century, has explicitly stated its historical role as follows: 'Geography is concerned to provide accurate, orderly, and rational description and interpretation of the variable character of the earth's surface' (Hartshorne, 1959, p. 21). In order to perform this considerable task, Hartshorne argues that geographers are primarily concerned with region construction (see Chapter 14), or with what he terms the *areal differentiation* of the earth's surface. Other geographers have laid greater stress on the interrelations of man and environment. For example, Ackerman (1963, p. 435) described the discipline's goal as '. . . nothing less than an understanding of the vast, interacting system comprising all humanity and its natural environment on the surface of the earth.' Against this catholic, wide-sweeping view stand those scholars who see the emphasis on a more limited range of problems concerning location and spatial arrangement. Thus Taaffe (1970, p. 1), while noting the historical role of the subject in giving man an orderly description of his world, sees the contemporary stress as more 'on geography as the study of spatial organization expressed as pattern and processes.' Amadeo and Golledge, in their *Scientific reasoning in geography* (1975), go further when they conclude that the basic purpose of the vast majority of research problems in geography is simply 'to account for spatial variation'.

None of the definitions given above will satisfy all geographers, but most will recognize some common ground. Following Haggett (1975a, p. 582), we may identify at least three themes running through the various attempts at definition. First, geography shares with the earth sciences a concern with a common arena, the earth's surface, rather than abstract space, but it looks at that arena from the viewpoint of the social sciences. Geography is concerned with the earth as the environment of man, an environment that influences how he lives and organizes himself, but which is at the same time an environment that man himself has helped to modify and to build. Second, geography focusses on man's spatial organization and his ecological relationship to his environment. It seeks means of improving the ways in which space and resources are used, and it emphasizes the role of appropriate regional organization in reaching this end. Third, geography is sensitive to the richness and variety of the earth. It does not lead to blanket solutions to development problems; instead, geographers feel that policy should be carefully tuned to the spatial variety concealed by terms like 'tropics', 'Appalachia', and 'ghetto'. At each geographical scale, geographers seek always to disaggregate and to dissect the uniform space of the legislator so that it will have greater congruence with the complex space of the real world.

Although there is thus a broadly defined working tradition, there still remains a strong emphasis on different approaches. We look here at three of what Pattison (1964) sees as the four main such approaches in the field—spatial, ecological, and regional—and see how each contributes to the structure of the remaining chapters in this book.

### 1.2.2 *Locational traditions and spatial concepts*

The view that geography is essentially a distributional science is a theme recurrent throughout this book. Bunge (1962) has emphasized the strong dependence of geography on the concepts of geometry and topological mathematics, a good example being provided by the analysis of transport networks using graph theory (see Section 9.7); and nearly a century ago Marthe (1878) described the field of geography as the study of 'the where of things'. Certainly a central concern for location and distribution is a hallmark of geographical writing remarked upon in methodological reviews. Thus

Harvey, in *Explanation in geography* (1969, p. 228) recognized that notions about space were, in part, heavily culture-bound but that . . .

> in part the geographic concept of space is special to geography. It has developed and evolved out of the especial experience which geographers have of working with actual spatial problems. In this respect the especial interpretation of the notions of 'space and distance' forms one of the key identifiers of the discipliniary sub-culture that forms geography itself.

Harvey goes on to differentiate between an absolute view of space using Euclidian geometry, and relational space, in which distance is measured in whatever terms (cost, time, convenience, psychic returns, social contact, etc.) that the particular process or activity makes relevant.

The strongest spur to the early development of locational 'theory' has come from one of the social sciences, economics, rather than from within human geography. Both the early classics of locational theory, von Thünen (1875) on agricultural location (see Section 6.3.2), and Weber (1909) on industrial location (Section 5.6.1), were concerned essentially with economic location; and the object of both contemporary and subsequent workers (Launhardt, Predöhl, Ohlin, Palander, Hoover, Lösch, and Isard) has been largely '. . . to improve the spatial and regional frameworks of the social sciences, especially economics' (Isard, 1956, p. viii). Modern locational theory by geographers (e.g. Webber, 1972) draws heavily on these economic foundations.

To acknowledge this fundamental role of locational concepts within human geography is not to dismiss its importance for every systematic science. Works like the *Atlas of the British flora* (Perring and Walters, 1962) or the *National atlas of disease mortality in the United Kingdom* (Howe, 1963) show the importance of distributional studies to two systematic studies, botany and medicine. Hettner saw clearly the dangers in over-emphasizing location as a purely geographical concept: 'Distribution by place forms a characteristic of the objects . . . and must therefore necessarily be included in the compass of their research and presentation' (Hettner, 1905; cited by Hartshorne, 1939, p. 127). The simple and plausible links between history as a study of 'when' and geography as a study of 'where' does less than justice to both fields. Similar doubts underly the thinking of modern workers. King (1969a) suggests that spatial structure does not seem to emerge as the logical output of theorizing, but rather it has to be specified in advance, as in central place theory (Chapter 5), by means of some very heavy behavioural assumptions. The whole question of the independent existence of laws in the spatial dimension has been discussed by Sack (1972, 1974) whose conclusion is that

> all laws explain (and therefore predict) aspects of the geometric properties of events. Some laws are more useful to geographers than others, but the usefulness of a law as an explanation of geographic questions cannot be foretold merely by counting the number of geometric or spatial terms in it. Laws without geometric terms may explain geographic questions as well as, or better than, laws that do have these terms . . . geometric laws alone cannot answer geographic questions (Sack, 1972, p. 78).

It seems unlikely that process can be inferred with certainty from geometric properties alone. Point pattern analysis (Chapter 13; especially Section 13.4.2) is the classic example of this fact. In practice, as Langton (1972) and Chappell (1975) argue, two-dimensional spatial information is supplemented by non-spatial 'ecological' information establishing the interrelations between the spatial objectives and the processes which activate and produce them. It is to this missing dimension that we now turn.

### 1.2.3 *Ecological traditions and systems concepts*

A second approach to geography is through ecological analysis, which interrelates human and environmental variables and interprets their links. In this type of analysis, geographers shift their emphasis from spatial variation between areas to the relationships within a single, bounded, geographical area. The origins of the idea of geography as the study of the relationships between man and the earth lie in a country where it subsequently played a paradoxically small part in the development of geographical thinking, i.e. Germany. Friedrich Ratzel's views on 'anthropogeography' appear to have had an indirect but important impact on Vidal de la Blache in France, and more particularly upon Ellen Churchill Semple in the United States. Her *Influences of geographical environment* (1911) had a decisive effect in spreading the idea of the study of 'geographical influences' (physical determinism) as a major goal in geographical study throughout the English-speaking world.

A separate and less extreme branch of this environmental school evolved around H. H. Barrows at the University of Chicago. His view of geography was as 'human ecology' (Barrows, 1923); a study in which physical geography is largely eliminated from the field and in which geography becomes a social science concerned with the relationships between human society and its physical environment. Hartshorne (1939, p. 123) suggests that, under this view, geography stands in relation to the social sciences in an exactly similar location as does plant ecology to the biological sciences. Certainly the dividing line between this view of human geography and the work of sociologists like McKenzie (1933) and Hawley (1950) is very finely drawn. The convergence of sociological and geographical lines of thought in Britain has been considered by Pahl (in Chorley and Haggett, 1965, Chapter 5).

It is perhaps in France, however, that the ecological view of human geography has had the most important influence. Two of the most decisive studies of human geography yet produced, the *Géographie humaine* of Jean Brunhes (1925) and the *Principes de géographie humaine* of Vidal de la Blache (1922) show a strongly environmental approach to the 'essential facts' of man's occupation of the earth's surface; and Max Sorre in his *Fondements de la géographie humaine* (1947–52, 1961) has followed this trend. For their detailed treatment of an abundance of regional examples and for their broad philosophy of man as part of a closely knit environmental syndrome, these three scholars—Brunhes, Vidal de la Blache, Sorre—may be regarded as corner-stones upon which much of the discipline of human geography has been built.

The most important contribution of the ecological approach in modern, as opposed to traditional, work in human geography comes through the *ecosystem concept*, which is an attempt, via systems theory, to integrate the environment and man in a mixed system. Definitions of systems (Hall and Fagan, 1956) lay emphasis on the way in which the interrelated units or objects of a system form a 'set' with common properties. The set displays organization resulting from the causal, functional or normative relationships between its constituent units. In everyday plumbing parlance we speak of a 'hotwater system', in which the set of objects (stove, pipes, cylinders, etc.) are related through circulating water, with inputs of energy in the form of heat. In geomorphology, we may speak of an 'erosional system', in which the set of objects (watershed, slopes, streams) are related through the circulation of water and sediment, with inputs of energy in the form of rainstorms. This set of objects, or system, is often part of a larger set or system within which it has a functional role, and it may also in turn be composed of several subsystems. Although we do not use the terminology of systems analysis in this book, it will be self-evident throughout the text that we are seeking to understand the functional interrelationships between spatially and temporally located observation units. Indeed, the precise identification of these relationships forms the basis of the forecasting models described in Chapter 16.

### 1.2.4 *Regional traditions and scale concepts*

The third approach to geography is by way of regional analysis, in which the results of spatial and ecological analysis are combined. Appropriate regional units are identified through areal differentiation, and then the flows and links between pairs of regions are established. We discuss some of the problems of delimiting regions in Section 14.2.

Historically, the study of regional geography has been obscured by its overlap with the notion of the earth's surface as 'landscape'. This idea is inherent in the double meaning attached in the extensive German literature to the apparently synonymous term, *Landschaft*. Confusion has apparently arisen from the meaning of *Landschaft* as either (a) the landscape, in the sense of the general appearance of a section of the earth's visible surface or (b) a restricted region of the earth's surface. In the first meaning, the terms *Landschaft* and landscape are synonyms; in the second, the appropriate English synonym must be 'region'. Hartshorne (1939, pp. 149–58) has expertly exposed the confusion in the original German literature—for example the different use of the same term by Passarge and Schlüter—and the inevitable take-over of some of this confusion into American literature, particularly through the important essay by Carl Sauer on the morphology of landscape (Sauer, 1925). Sauer argued that it was possible to break down the landscape of an area into two separate components: the 'natural landscape' (*Urlandschaft*) and the 'cultural landscape' (*Kulturlandschaft*). He conceived as natural landscape the original landscape of the area before the entry of man; as cultural landscape, that landscape transformed by man. The most important effect of Sauer's essay was in urging that the same morphological methods, so fruitful in the analysis of the physical landscape, could be transferred to the study of the cultural landscape. Before Sauer's 1925 essay, the role of man as a morphological agent had been recognized, notably by George Perkins Marsh (1864), but it was in the Berkeley school (described by Clark, in James, Jones, and Wright, 1954, p. 86) that Sauer gathered together a group of scholars who like Broek (*The Santa Clara Valley*, 1932) organized their work around the theme of landscape change. *Man's role in changing the earth* (Thomas, 1956), an international symposium in which Sauer played a leading part, gives the clearest picture of the strength and vitality of this important theme in the development of human geography.

In the contemporary context, a central working problem is to identify a regional unit appropriate to the spatial analysis of the cultural landscape. Here we recognize the *nodal* region as our basic unit and use it as a basis for the arrangement of chapters in the first part of this book. By a nodal region we mean the area that surrounds a human settlement and which is tied to it in terms of its spatial organization. Figure 1.1 shows the essential elements in the

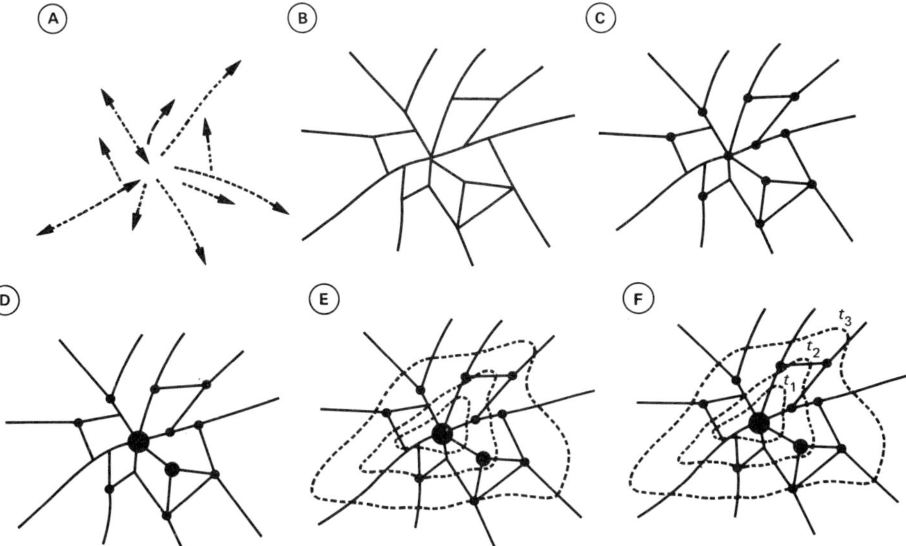


**Figure 1.1** Stages in the analysis of nodal regional systems. **A** Interaction (Chapter 2); **B** Networks (Chapter 3); **C** Nodes (Chapter 4); **D** Hierarchies (Chapter 5); **E** Surfaces (Chapter 6); **F** Diffusion (Chapter 7).

make-up of the nodal region, and relates it to the organization of chapters. Chapter 2 identifies the spatial *interaction* between a settlement and its surrounding area in terms of the movements of people, goods, finance, information, and influence. These flows are usually channelled into discrete *networks* (Chapter 3), linking together the individual settlements, the *nodes* (Chapter 4), located on the networks. Since the nodes are not uniform or undifferentiated, we consider in Chapter 5 how they are structured into finely articulated *hierarchies*. Integration of the individual elements—interaction, networks, nodes and hierarchies—is attempted in Chapter 6, which views the nodal regional structure in terms of continuous *surfaces* of variate values, each describing some aspect of the human geography of the region. Finally,

Chapter 7 introduces a time element into the static cultural landscape by considering spatial change over time in terms of diffusion processes.

The arguments for adopting the nodal region as the basic spatial unit are persuasive (Haggett, 1975a, p. 420). A growing proportion of the world's population is concentrated in cities, and consequently man's organization of the globe is increasingly centred about its major population nodes. Cities form easily identifiable and mappable nodal regional units for which a flood of reasonably uniform statistical data has been available for the last century and a half. Second, city regions stress the comparability of different parts of the world, and thus encourage the search for general theories of human spatial organization. Third, city regions are hierarchic. Like watersheds, they nest inside one another, and the city-region concept can be enlarged up to the world level or reduced down to the level of the smallest hamlet. Fourth, nodal regions may be viewed in system terms. Von Bertalanffy (1950) distinguishes two separate frameworks: the *closed system* and the *open system.* Closed systems have definable boundaries across which no exchange of energy occurs, but they are likely, by this definition, to be rather rare in geographical studies (except in the limiting case of a world-wide study). By contrast, an open system, which is very common, presents the following characteristics (Chorley, 1962, pp. 3–8): (i) the need for an energy supply for the system's maintenance and preservation, together with the capacity to (ii) attain a 'steady-state' in which the import and export of energy and material is met by form adjustments, (iii) regulate itself by homeostatic adjustments, (iv) maintain optimum magnitudes over periods of time, (v) maintain its organization and form over time rather than tending (as do closed systems) towards maximum entropy (defined in Section 2.5.2), and (vi) behave 'equifinally', in the sense that different initial conditions may lead to similar end results.

In nodal systems, we certainly find some of these six characteristics. Thus regional organization needs a constant movement of people, goods, money and information to maintain it; an excess of inward movements may be met by form changes (city expansion and urban sprawl), just as decreased movement may lead to contraction and ghost towns. The first two conditions are clearly met. Similarly, on the third condition, the nodal region follows Le Châtelier's Principle in that its hinterland may expand or contract to meet increased or decreased flows. The evidence about the fourth and fifth requirements is less clear. On the one hand, the fact that, say, urban rank-size relationships (see Section 4.3) tend to be relatively constant over both space and time suggests that (iv) and (v) *are* met. Conversely, Wilson's (1970) work shows that both interaction models (Section 2.5) and the rank-size rule (Section 4.3.3) are maximum entropy distributions. Finally, the growing convergence of the form of the major cities in different continents suggests that the urban open system is capable of behaving equifinally. The advantages of viewing the nodal region as an open system are that it directs our attention towards the links between process and form, and places human geography alongside other biological and social sciences that are organizing their thinking in this manner.

Throughout this book, we are concerned with nodal units that vary greatly in scale. A city like New York may show recognizable 'field' effects (see Section 2.6) some thousands of miles from the centre, while the market range of a small village may peter out within one or two miles. Haggett, Chorley and Stoddart (1965) showed that geography was characteristically concerned with only a narrow scale 'window' within a much larger zone of scientific inquiry. For example, astronomers study phenomena in galactic space up to a diameter of $10^{27}$ cm, while physicists measure sub-atomic phenomena with diameters down to $10^{-13}$ cm (Brillouin, 1964, and Figure 1.2). Within this size spread, the regional units with which geographers deal occupy a middle range, from $4.01 \times 10^9$ cm (the circumference of the earth) down to around $10^3$ cm. Table 1.1

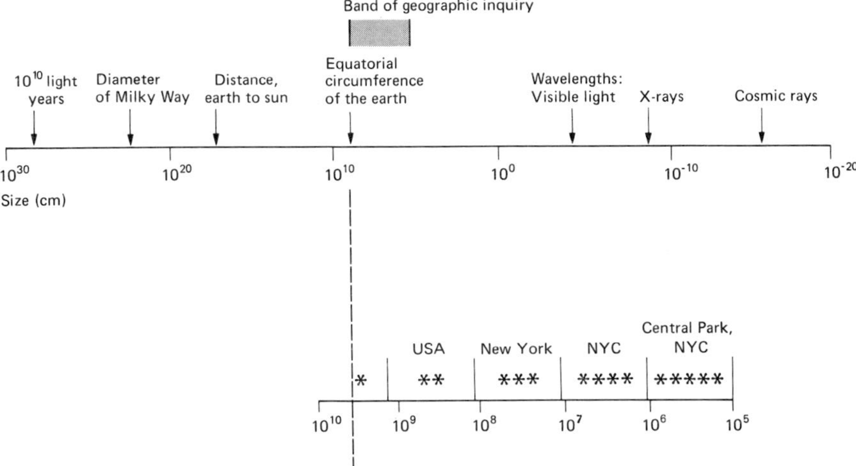


**Figure 1.2** Scales of geographical inquiry.

shows the convention followed in this book to indicate the size of the regional units considered as a five point (nominal) order of magnitude scale.[1] The advantage of this notation as a geographical reference system stems from three characteristics. First, it uses a natural standard, the surface of the earth, rather than several arbitrary standards. Second, through its logarithmic nature, it reduces a very wide range of values to a simple scale. Third, it allows ready comparison of the relative size of areas, in that regions which are different in area by a factor of ten have values *one* unit apart on the scale, regions which are different in area by a factor of one hundred are *two* units apart, and so on.

Whether these differences in regional magnitude have any deeper significance is a matter for debate, but it is perhaps worth noting that dimensional differences are of key importance in classical physics, where changes in one dimension (e.g. length) may be associated with disproportionate changes in area, mass, viscosity, and so on. These problems in 'similitude' also have crucial importance in biology. Thus, D'Arcy Thompson (1917) devoted a considerable part of his *On growth and form* to a consideration of magnitude in zoological and botanical design. Ray (1974) has shown that changes in the dimensions of cities may also follow allometric

[1] This scale is shown by a size-rating [*(largest), **, ***, ****, ***** (smallest)] on all maps in the volume. It replaces the G-scale (see Haggett, Chorley, and Stoddart, 1965) used throughout the first edition of this book.

principles. Where geographers draw on physical models or their biological derivatives, they need to be alive to the dangers of 'spatial or dimensional anachronisms' if we may call them such. Measurements of distance inputs (length), boundaries (perimeters), populations (masses) in the 'gravitational' models of economic geography (see Section 2.3) may need to be successively re-cast at different areal levels if we are to retain their principles of similitude.

Table 1.1 Orders of geographical magnitude

| Order | Size range (diameter), miles | Regional example |
|---|---|---|
| First,* | 24,860 *to* 7,770 | *World*† |
| Second,** | 7,770 *to* 777 | *Conterminous U.S.A.*‡ |
| Third,*** | 777 *to* 77.7 | *New York State*‡ |
| Fourth,**** | 77.7 *to* 7.77 | *New York City (NYC)*‡ |
| Fifth,***** | 7.77 *to* 0.777 | *Central Park, NYC*‡ |

The star convention for order is used on all maps in the book
†Upper limit of size range ‡Middle of size range
Source: Haggett, 1975a, p. 17.

Changes in regional scale bring two associated problems. First, inferences about spatial patterns are scale dependent. As we change the spatial resolution, say the relevant size of the collecting grid, so the results we obtain vary: findings at one level of analysis may be misleading at another. The discussion of Robinson's 'ecological fallacy' in Section 10.6.1 of this book shows the extent of this problem, while Chapter 12 suggests how scale components may be measured.

A second effect of change in regional scale is to limit sample size. The smaller the unit of regional study, the greater the population size from which samples may be drawn. Conversely, the larger the unit, the fewer the cases there are to compare. It may not be accidental that, while the study of central place systems has allowed replicated observation and hypothesis testing, leading to some reasonably well supported models, the study of very large population clusters (say, northwest Europe or northern India) is inevitably the study of once-off spatial patterns. Such hypotheses as have been developed tend to derive from speculative climatic or historical models, and are largely untestable.

## 1.3 Geography: External Relations

Geography has long been a thorn in the side of school and university administrators. It seems doubtful whether it has a natural home in either the VIth Science or VIth Arts side of English school organization. Similarly, at university level it has been classified both as an 'earth science' (at Cambridge it is part of the Faculty of Geography and Geology, which includes geophysics, mineralogy, and petrology), and as a 'social science' (as in most universities in the United States). Less commonly, it is seen as 'geometrical science', a position it held in Greek times.

Figure 1.3 attempts to show the 'location' of geography within the structure of other disciplines. The overlap and interlinking of various fields underlines

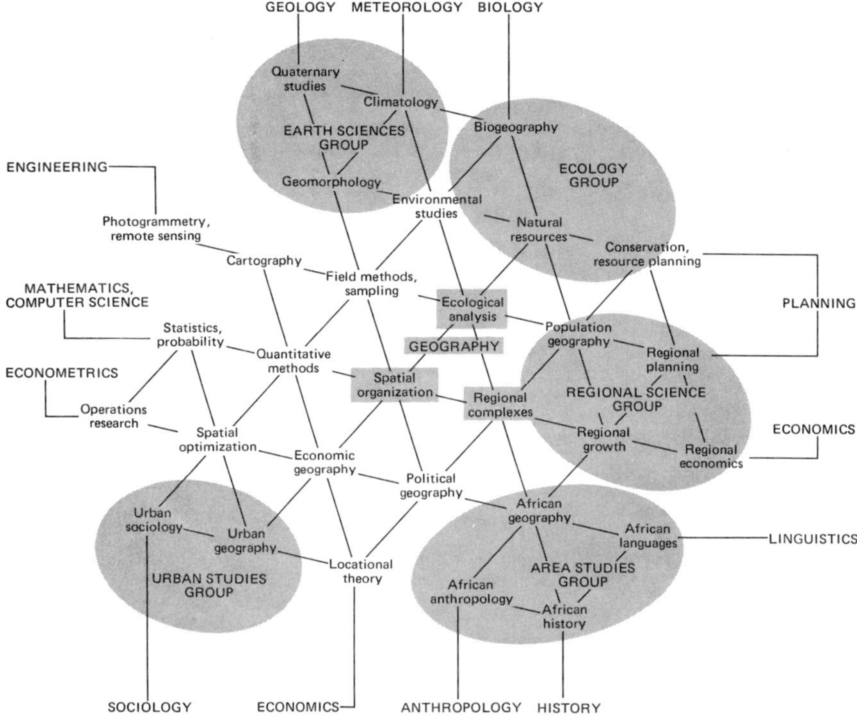


**Figure 1.3** Links between geography and supporting fields. Source: Haggett, 1975a, p. 587.

the somewhat arbitrary nature of most subject divisions. Although mathematics is shown on this figure, it may be thought to run vertically to the plane of the other subjects, providing a common language by which geographers can express their spatial, ecological, and regional concepts in a concise and comparable way.

From the viewpoint of human geography, one of the most important external contacts is with regional science. Regional science, to a remarkable degree the product of the pioneering work of one man, Walter Isard, brought to regional study a wide range of mainly econometric techniques and resulted in a major text, *Methods of regional analysis* (Isard, Bramhall, Carrothers, Cumberland, Moses, Price and Schooler, 1960). The emphasis was on the region as a laboratory for the testing of a variety of locational, diffusion (Chapter 7), optimising (Chapter 15) and accounting techniques (see for example Chapter 13), most of them concerned with economic status and growth. Since the early days of regional science, the range of techniques has widened considerably to cope with the difficult agglomeration, returns to scale and input substitution problems. In addition, the range of topics studied has been expanded to include welfare economics and less rational decision-making, and to pay more attention to the region *per se*. The needs of planning have ensured that regional science has not only become multidisciplinary, but also that it has been made to focus on problem-solving in specific areas (see Part Three of this book). The effect on geography has been catalytic, allowing analytical techniques not developed indigenously to be absorbed. Whether the present interests shown by economists in regions is a major departure, or whether in the future '. . . regional economics may increasingly be indistinguishable from the rest of economics', as argued by Meyer (1963, p. 48), remains to be seen.

## 1.4 Trends in Geography

Study of the size and growth of any discipline poses acute problems of measurement. 'Geography' has no mass or length, and to construct any agreed list of solved problems or breaks-through would be as difficult as it would be contentious. Stoddart (1967) has attempted to outflank this difficulty by measuring the output of geography in terms of its publications. As Figure 1.4 shows, the quantity of geographical research, as measured by the number of specialized geographical serials, has been doubling every 30 years since around

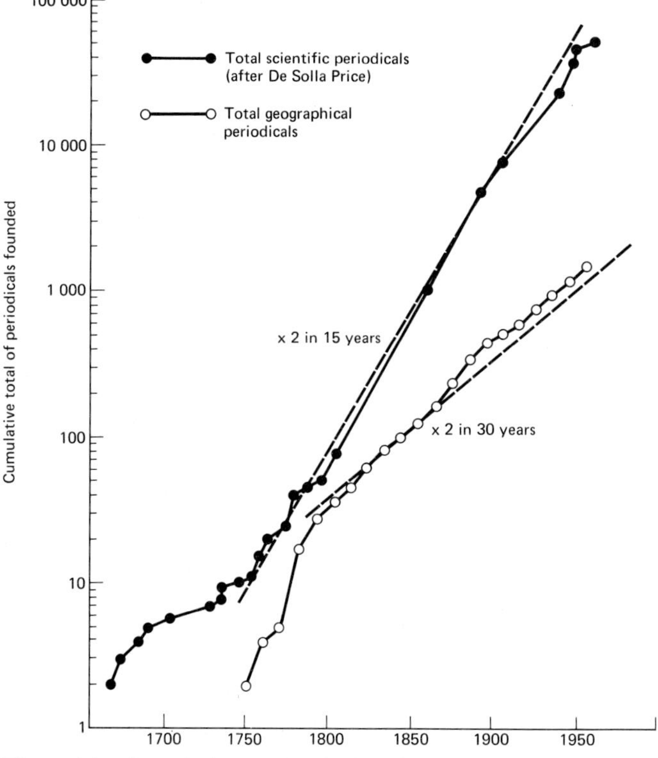


**Figure 1.4** Cumulative totals of scientific and geographical periodicals founded. The dashed lines represent doubling in 15 and 30 years, respectively. Source: Stoddart, 1967, p. 3.

1780. For the increase in more recent years, a variety of other measures is available, including memberships in professional societies, enrolments in classes, degrees granted, research published, and so on. These indicators all confirm the general exponential rate of past growth. Even though individual decades are likely to have spurts or slows-down above or below a long-term rate of increase in geographical research, it would be unreasonable not to expect further substantial increases. At the same time, we must note that the short term exponential trend must eventually be replaced by a longer run logistic one.

Accompanying the increase in growth has been a fission of geography into specialized sub-disciplines. Each individual scholar finds increasing economies of scale by specializing in a limited range of problems; his limited time and resources (books, equipment, maps, computing time, or whatever) can be concentrated on intensive study of a limited topic or region. As a result, an increasing number of geographers tend to think of themselves as South Asian geographers, or diffusion specialists, or arid-zone geomorphologists. This trend is not confined to geography. We may argue, however, that changes in numbers, or the hiving-off of sub-disciplines, are less important than are the qualitative changes in how geographers 'see' their subject; changes in our interpretation of information may be wholly independent of changes in data (see Figure 1.5). These qualitative changes form the substance of this section.

### 1.4.1 *Paradigm shifts within geography*

Paradigms may be regarded as stable patterns of scientific activity. Their relevance to changes within geography has been discussed by Chorley and Haggett (1967, Chapter 1), who argue that workers whose research is based on shared paradigms are committed to the same problems, rules and standards, i.e. they form a continuing community devoted to a particular research tradition. Thomas Kuhn, in his *Structure of Scientific Revolutions* (1962), has assigned to the origin, continuance, and obsolescence of paradigms a prime place in the history of the evolution of science. Although Kuhn's views have been strongly criticized (see Lakatos and Musgrave, 1970) in terms of detailed reconstructions of growth, most philosophers of science accept his broad interpretations of revolutionary, rather than evolutionary, growth for science (Jevons, 1973, Chapter 4). In Kuhn's view, progress in research requires the continual discarding of outdated models, and subsequent remodelling. The more internally consistent the original concepts, the more difficult it may be to remodel an existing structure in step with changing notions and increasing data. It is usual, therefore, for the most significant intellectual steps to be marked by the emergence of completely new models (Skilling, 1964, p. 389A). As Kuhn (1962, p. 17) has argued '. . . no natural history can be interpreted in the absence of at least some implicit body of intertwined theoretical and methodological belief that permits selection, evaluation, and criticism.' Without such paradigms, all the available facts may seem equally likely candidates for inclusion. As a direct consequence, there is (1) no case for the highly-defined fact-gathering so typical of the exact sciences; and (2) a tendency to restrict fact-gathering to the wealth of available data which comes

**Figure 1.5** Changes in interpretation of spatial form without changes in the data. A section from an Escher drawing showing fish and birds ('Lucht en water II'). Source: Escher, 1960, p. 14.

easily to hand. The fact that many of these data are a secondary by-product of administrative systems adds further to the massive data-handling problem. Certainly, most geographical accounts are strongly 'circumstantial', juxtaposing facts of theoretical interest with others so unrelated or so complex as to be outside the bounds of available explanatory models.

In Kuhn's thinking, the importance of the paradigm lies in providing rules that: (1) tell us what both the world—and our science—are like; and (2) allow us to concentrate on the problems that these rules, together with existing knowledge, define. Paradigms tend to be, by nature, highly restrictive. They focus attention upon a small range of problems, often enough somewhat esoteric problems, to allow the concentration of investigation on some part of the man–environment system in a detail and depth that might otherwise prove unlikely, if not inconceivable. This concentration appears to have been a necessary part of scientific advance, allowing the solution of puzzles outside the limits of pre-paradigm thinking.

The conventional structure of the geographical paradigm is summarized in Figure 1.6 by a data matrix. Information about the earth's surface is stored in

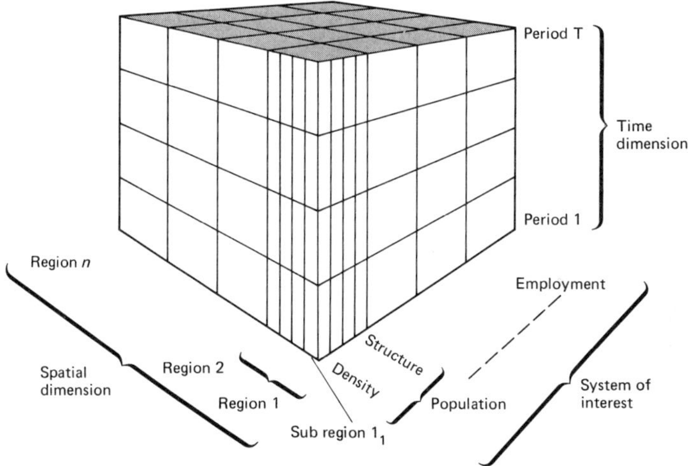


**Figure 1.6** Approaches to the geographical data matrix.

terms of its spatial and temporal dimensions, and in terms of the intrinsic characteristics of the system of interest. Analysis of the data matrix proceeds by focussing attention on one of the dimensions, thereby yielding the traditional fields of inquiry: regional geography (via the spatial dimension), systematic or topical geography (via the system dimension), and historical geography (via the time dimension). Berry (1964) has extended this idea further, identifying most geographical approaches by appropriate vector or matrix operations.

Chorley and Haggett (1967, Chapter 1) have suggested that the 'data matrix' paradigm is under increasing stress. The exponential increase in global data is inevitably leading to sub-division after sub-division within geography as individual researchers are forced to concentrate on ever narrower fields. The dangers in this situation may be caricatured by seeing geography as a 'doughnut' shaped discipline, with growth and high activity only at the outer periphery, leaving an empty core. From the viewpoint of the 1970s, it is not easy to see the shape of the new paradigm to replace the old. The direction taken in this book, one urged by Chorley and Haggett, is to modify the traditional data matrix by: (i) stressing relative space (whether measured in time, cost, perception, or another appropriate metric), rather than absolute location; (ii) emphasizing spatial form (e.g. surface or network) rather than the intrinsic characteristics of the phenomena; and (iii) by integrating the time dimension

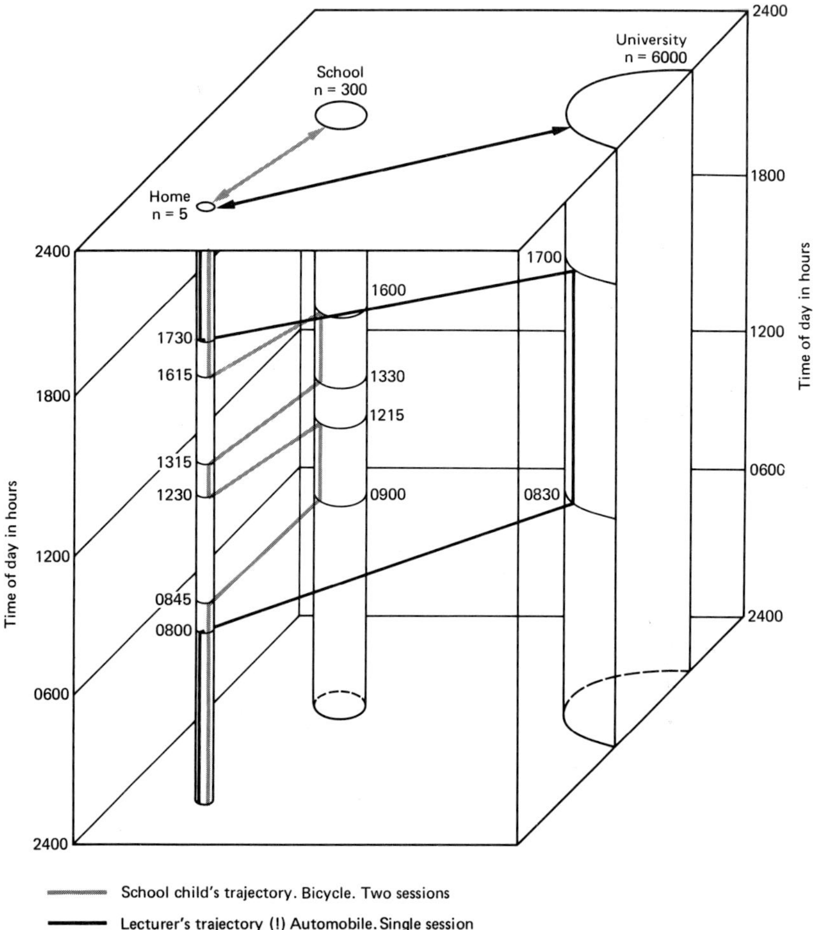


**Figure 1.7** Time constraints on the spatial mobility of individuals. The diagram shows 'time lines' for two individuals in a family during one working day. Detailed space-time budgets assembled by Swedish geographers allow a comprehensive picture of the space-time trajectories of urban settlements to be built up. *n* denotes the number of individuals at each spatial location.

into spatial models, with a special emphasis on spatial diffusion (Chapter 7) and forecasting (Chapter 16). Other solutions to the stress on the conventional paradigm are also being sought through a more behaviourally-oriented geography. The work of Hägerstrand's group at Lund on the time-space trajectories of individuals and groups seems an especially promising line of development (see Figure 1.7).

### 1.4.2 *Model building and quantification*

If we try to identify the major shift in emphasis within geography in the last two decades, it lies in method rather than in philosophy. This is the trend towards model building, or what Burton (1963a) called the 'quantitative revolution'. A model may be described as a simplified version of reality, built in order to demonstrate certain of the properties of reality. Conceptual models have a high degree of abstraction and are often called 'theoretical', while models based on empirical considerations have a low level of abstraction and are often termed 'operational'. The role of different kinds of models in geography has been extensively discussed elsewhere [see, for example, Chorley and Haggett's *Models in geography* (1967)] and we wish here only to establish the essential links between model building and quantification.

Let us assume that we wish to model the differences in the values of real world observations on a specific variate, say unemployment levels. The variate of interest is termed the dependent variable, $Y$. Through research, we find that values of $Y$ may be influenced in a supposedly 'causal' way by other variables, say occupational structure or remoteness from major urban centres. These supposedly 'causal' variables are termed the independent variables, $X_1, X_2, \ldots, X_k$. That is, we can express our relationship as

$$Y = f(X_1, X_2, \ldots, X_k). \tag{1.1}$$

or, in a graphic manner, as in Figure 1.8A.

If we now measure the values of the variables, both dependent and independent, on some appropriate scale (see Section 9.2) in each of a set of $i = 1, 2, \ldots, n$ areas, we can begin to estimate something of the nature of the functional relations ($f$) that appear to link the variables together. For example, we may postulate that the variables are linearly related, so that

$$Y_i = \beta_0 + \sum_{j=1}^{k} \beta_j X_{ij} + \varepsilon_i, \quad i = 1, 2, \ldots, n, \tag{1.2}$$

where the $\{\beta\}$ are unknown parameters and the $\{\varepsilon\}$ are independently normally distributed, mean zero, constant variance, stochastic error terms. This familiar form of the general linear regression model can be estimated by ordinary least squares. In this case, the estimated coefficient values, $\{\hat{\beta}\}$, allow us to measure the supposed direction and strength of the effect of independent variables on $Y$. (Note that for the moment we ignore the complex issues of multicollinearity, autocorrelation of residuals, etc.: these are developed further in Chapters 10 and 11 and in Johnston, 1972).

However, equation (1.2) represents only the beginning of the modelling process. For example, unemployment may be linked to the other variables in a time-lagged manner [e.g. $Y_t = f(X_{1,t-k})$ as in Figure 1.8B]; unemployment in one area ($i$) may be related to unemployment in another area ($j$) [e.g. $Y_{it} = f(Y_{j,t-1})$], and there may be significant intercorrelations between the independent variables themselves (Figure 1.8C). By selecting appropriate models and by *validly* estimating the parameters, the notions or hunches about geographical patterns can be formally built up and tested against observed data.

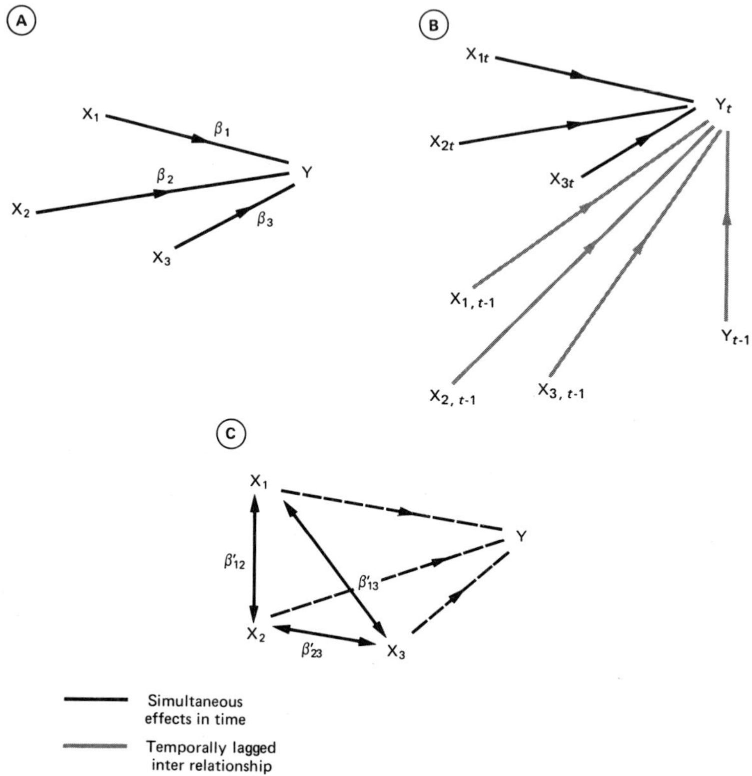


**Figure 1.8** Relations between independent ($X$) and dependent ($Y$) variables.

This iterative (cyclical) process of (a) imaginative hypothesis building and (b) sceptical hypothesis testing are the 'two successive and complementary episodes of thought that occur in every advance of scientific understanding' (Medawar, 1969). Thus we may see many of the models put forward in Part One of this book as what Francis Bacon would have termed 'anticipations, rash and premature', while Part Two of the book, with its concern for critical hypothesis testing and modelling, falls into the second of Medawar's two episodes of thought. We stress the role of models in human geography for three main reasons:

(i) Model building is inevitable because there is no fixed dividing line between facts and beliefs; in Skilling's terms '. . . belief in a universe of real things is merely a belief . . . a belief with high probability certainly, but a belief none the less' (1964, p. 394A). Models are theories, laws, equations, or hunches which state our beliefs about the universe we think we see.

(ii) Model building is economical because it allows us to pass on generalized information in a highly compressed form. Like rules for the plurals of French adjectives there may be exceptions, but the rule is none the less an important ladder in learning the language. This use of models as teaching aids is discussed by Chorley and Haggett (1965a, pp. 360–4).

(iii) Model building is stimulating in that, through its very over-generalizations, it makes clear those areas where improvement is necessary. The building and testing of models is as important to geography as to aeronautics; the test flight of a hypothesis is no less exciting, nor much less dangerous, than the test flight of a prototype Concorde. Each leads on to further research and modifications.

In short, the role of models in geography is to codify what has gone before and to excite fresh inquiry. To be sure, the present stock of models may be unprepossessing enough, but as Lösch asked, '. . . does not the path of science include many precarious emergency bridges over which we have all been willing to pass provided they would help us forward on our road?' Certainly his hope that his work on regions would open '. . . a path into a rich but almost unknown country' (Lösch, 1954, p. 100) has been fulfilled.

The fact that most model building is now mathematical to some degree is borne out by a comparison of research papers in the geographical journals of the 1970s with those of the 1950s. In the earlier period, the main mathematical applications were of spherical geometry in cartography and surveying, and of probability and statistics in climatology. Today, the range of mathematical models has significantly expanded, and the applications now affect most branches of the field. We find historical geographers fitting polynomial surfaces to the spread of early settlement, or industrial location analysts modelling siting decisions as Markov chains. During the 1960s, there was a skirmish between those geographers anxious to innovate with mathematical methods and those sceptical of their usefulness in solving orthodox problems. Today, the general acceptance of such techniques, the more complete mathematical training of a new generation, and the widespread availability of standard computers in the universities make the conflict of a decade ago seem unreal. The first few years of overenthusiastic pressing of quantitative methods on a reluctant profession have given way to the present phase in which mathematical methods are just one of many tools for approaching geographical problems. One of the most encouraging trends is a broadening interest in mathematical and statistical *modelling* as opposed to the initial concern in the early 1960s with simple statistical hypothesis testing. For Wilson (1972, p. 41) this 'collective ability to branch out and be more ambitious' is essential to future progress.

### 1.4.3 *Deterministic and probabilistic explanation*

In the spirit of optimism that seized science after Newton's triumphant demonstration of the laws of gravitation, there was much nonsense dreamed about scientific prediction. It was the French mathematician, Laplace, who suggested that it was *conceptually* possible to forecast the fate of every atom of the universe both forwards and backwards through time. Although all believed that the technical possibility lay remotely far in the future, it served as a goal towards which science might slowly progress. In geography, this optimism had its expression in the ideas of *environmental determinism*, in which human behaviour was seen to be predictable in terms of the physical environment. The excessive claims, the burnt fingers, the debate over 'possibilism' are a part of the history of geographical development (see Hartshorne 1939, pp. 56–60) which reflects little credit on our powers of observation, let alone discrimination.

Reactions to the period of excessive environmentalism in geography were both negative and positive. On the negative side, the retreat led to an almost complete rejection of any kind of theory, so that our literature became at once more accurate but infinitely less exciting. Description was substituted for hypothesis, repetition for debate. On the positive side, geographers approached the intricate regional systems wary of any simple cause-and-effect keys. Meinig's (1962) analysis of the railway network of the Columbia basin in the northwestern United States is a case in point. Figure 1.9B shows the railways built by the Northern Pacific Railroad in the second half of the nineteenth century. Viewed in relation to present conditions, they yield a satisfying logic in which terrain and cities served as either barriers or magnets to shape the twisting geometry of the network. However as Meinig stresses, such logic is largely illusory. Most of the cities were subsequent products of the railway, rather than its antecedent causes. As for the rigorous influence of terrain, the map of projected routes obtained from the files of the railway's consulting engineers (Figure 1.9A) shows a cordon of routes, *all* of which on purely technical grounds were serious contenders for the railway route. Meinig's

***

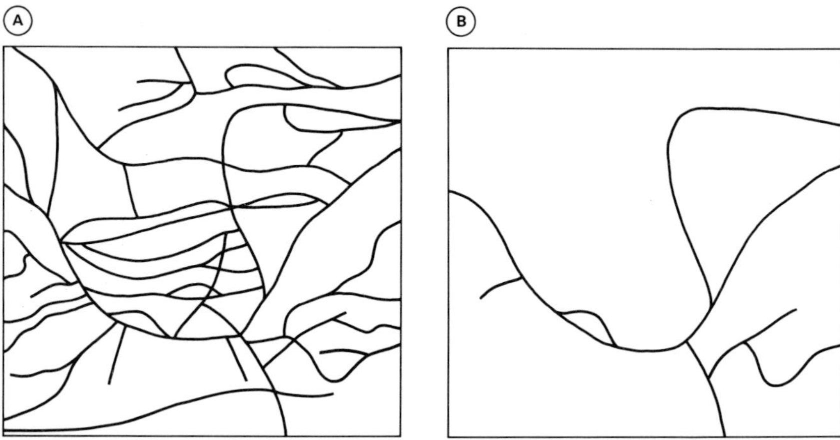


**Figure 1.9** Contrast between routes which were proposed (**A**) and actually built (**B**) by the Northern Pacific Railroad Company in a sector of the northwestern United States. Source: Meinig, 1962, p. 413.

point is that in order to 'explain' the reason why one route was chosen, another abandoned, would involve nothing short of a psychological analysis of board-room decisions. Indeed, the detailed examination of most aspects of human behaviour of interest to human geography (e.g. migration, industrial location, choice of land use) tends to '... leave one stranded in the thickets of the decision-making process' (Meinig, 1962, p. 413).

Meinig's view is reinforced by Morrill (1963), in a study of town location in central Sweden, where it is suggested that man is not always able to distinguish between equally good choices, nor can he always recognize optimum locations, should these exist. There are, Morrill contends, basic uncertainties in the pattern of human behaviour that we simply cannot wish away. These difficulties are compounded by two further sources of indeterminacy: first, the multiplicity of equal choices, and second, the inability to take into account the myriad of very small effects from many small sources. There are far more potential town sites than towns in central Sweden, so that no unique locational significance springs from site alone; there is, instead, a multiplicity of factors that enter into urban growth, each factor linking with the other in a labyrinth of small-scale causal links. If Newton was right in principle that an alighting butterfly shifts the earth, it is equally true that the net effect of such infinitesimal causes may be considered random. Unless we wish to follow Aquinas in the metaphysics of the 'First Cause' we can hope only to disentangle some of the main threads in any situation; the rest we can only regard as a sort of background noise, a Brownian motion.

One of the fundamental doubts cast on the possibility of extending cause-and-effect interpretations into the world of human behaviour came from the field of small scale or quantum physics. Once Max Planck had discovered in 1900 that energy, like matter, is not continuous, but appears in small groups or quanta, both the theoretical and empirical study of this branch of physics ran into increasing problems. It proved impossible to apply rigid mechanistic laws to these tiny particles, and it was a German physicist, Heisenberg, who in 1927 put this problem into a formal principle: the *uncertainty principle.* This stated, in effect, that all our observations of the natural world contain some final and essential uncertainty. If we try to measure location more accurately, we must sacrifice some aspect of its precise time; in estimating its speed more accurately, we are less sure of its position.

Despite later revision of Heisenberg's physical experiments, this principle, together with the spread of the concepts of Francis Galton and Karl Pearson on statistical probability, had a dramatic effect on the metaphysical battle over determinacy. The replacement of laws by the idea of probabilistic trends allowed a totally new view of human behaviour in which both 'free will' and 'determinacy' could be accommodated. Indeed, both extreme views may be based on a misunderstanding of scale, for Bronowski (1960, p. 93) would argue that '... a society moves under material pressure like a stream of gas; and on the average, its individuals obey the pressure; but at any instance, any individual may, like an atom of gas, be moving across or against the stream.'

It is tempting to see an analogy between the behaviour of the tiny sub-atomic particles of physics and individual humans, the empirical regularities of both behaviours obeying probabilistic laws whose criteria of acceptability are dictated by the laws of statistics. In the pages that follow, we illustrate the difficult problems that arise in attempting to achieve such statistical confirmation. The analogy between a common problem in physics and social science should not be pressed too far, however, for, as Nagel (1961, p. 316) has stated, 'the statistical content of quantum mechanics does not annul the deterministic and non-statistical structure of other physical laws.' Guelke (1971, p. 43) also reminds us that, although the movements of subatomic particles and gases are confined within strict limits, those of individual humans are much less constrained.

Incorporation of formal probability theory into human geography came late. Lukermann (1965) has traced the adoption of non-mathematical probability notions by the French-school geographers in the early 20th century, and the much later taking up of a mathematical calculus of probability in the 1950s by such geographers as Hägerstrand (see Chapter 7). This late adoption by geographers can partly be explained by their relative isolation, even within social science methodology. However, probability theory, with its implications about chance and uncertainty, does permit us to model more accurately than could be accomplished within a deterministic framework the world which, as individuals, we know: a world that is neither wholly rational nor wholly chaotic, but an amalgam of choice, calculation, and chance. Throughout this book, our use of probability and statistics is firmly grounded in the long-run relative frequency approach of Neyman and Pearson. Bayesian ideas of subjective probability are not employed, not because they are not important, but because their use within geography remains undemonstrated in terms of 'hard' models, except in a fairly superficial fashion.

### 1.4.4 *Positivism and phenomenology*

One difficulty for the non-geographer observing activities within our field is to decide whether geography is a science or a humanity. For the economist Kenneth Boulding (1966, p. 108), the answer seems to be the former: 'Of all the disciplines, geography is the one that has caught the vision of the study of the earth as a total system, and it has strong claims to be the queen of the human sciences.' To one philosopher of science, Mario Bunge, it is clear that geography is one of a group of disciplines which, since they are strictly descriptive and taxonomic, are not sciences but 'non-scientific disciplines however exact they may be' (cited by Amadeo and Golledge, 1975, p. 2). Bunge's view that geography is 'at most proto science' is based on the supposed absence of the statement and testing of hypotheses, perhaps true of regional geography but hardly of its systematic counterparts. Geographical facts, like Newton's apple (see page 1), are inert and do not dictate how one may interpret them. Journeys from farm to market around an English town may lead to one of Hardy's Wessex novels or to a theory of spatial interaction.

Within geography itself, the science/non-science question is now seen as less important than the question of what kind of a 'science' we want to build. Thus, the debates which Schaefer (1953) originated over whether geography is a 'normal' or 'exceptional' science have now been overtaken by concern over our mode of explanation. For example, human geographers have become increasingly uneasy about the 'positivist' nature of much geographical research. *Positivism* is a philosophical approach which holds that our sensory experiences are the exclusive source of valid information about the world. This attitude developed in the natural sciences (like physics) but has been borrowed by geographers working in social science areas. A positivistic approach leads to the discussion of human behaviour in terms of analogies drawn from the natural sciences. Thus in Section 2.3 we discuss human migration in terms of Newton's laws of gravity. Much geographical effort in the 1960s went into trying to explain patterns of human behaviour with neat, lawlike statements. Ultimate causes and the essential nature of phenomena like migration were put aside as being unknowable or inscrutable.

Given the discipline's historical pattern of evolution, it is understandable that positivism should have played a major part in geographical explanations of phenomena. Whatever its virtues in the more physical parts of the field, its effect on human geography was to lead to a stylized, sometimes overacademic kind of research. What then, should we replace it with? The current decade favours renewed interest in a phenomenological approach (Guelke, 1971). *Phenomenology* is an existential philosophical approach which admits that introspective or intuitive attempts to gain knowledge are valid. It accepts subjective categories (cf. Bayesian statistics) in the experience of the person behaving. The Great Plains are a 'desert' if the person or group settling them believes them to be one and acts accordingly! Phenomenologists look with scepticism at the attempts at lawlike statements so characteristic of the previous decade. This shift in philosophical position has also occurred in other fields like social anthropology and social psychology, and has reinforced the links between geography and other social sciences. Of course no geographer's work is ever 'purely' positivistic or 'purely' phenomenological. Most geographers adopt a position between these two extremes, with systematic approaches to the field (like that in this book) tending to stress the positivistic side and works with a regional emphasis adopting a more phenomenological viewpoint.

### 1.4.5 *Geography as critical science*

The decade of the 1970s has been a time of increasing debate about the role of science in relation to society and its problems. J. R. Ravetz, in his book *Scientific knowledge and its social problems* (1971), is typical of a group of scholars who have argued that a major part of science in the future should be 'critical science'. Ravetz means by this not critical in the conventional research sense of critical hypothesis testing, but socially critical—stressing the role of science in politics and public affairs. Here lie obvious problems, like those of pollution and poverty, nuclear warfare and biological engineering.

Within geography, a concern for environmental balance and a sensitivity to problems of regional deprivation have long been central to the field. As Stoddart (1975) has shown, the tradition of social relevance in geography can be traced back to the writings and actions of the two 'gentle anarchists', Elisée Reclus and Prince Kropotkin, a century ago. Reclus's *Nouvelle Géographie Universelle* written in exile in Switzerland, and Kropotkin's paper written from prison on 'What geography ought to be' are singled out by Stoddart as among the earliest deeply humane statements of geography as a socially significant study. By the early twentieth century these radical contributions had largely been forgotten and geographers' social contributions were beginning to be made through more institutional channels. Thus, in the inter-war years, scholars like Isiah Bowman, Griffith Taylor, and Dudley Stamp were prominent both as advisors and critics of both international organizations and national governments. In the years since World War II, geographers in countries like France, Sweden, and Britain have played a major role in regional planning. But the past decade has been marked by a new and more harshly critical view of the role of government, bureaucracy, and class divisions in the spatial structuring of society to achieve partisan ends. The work of Bunge (1971) in Detroit shows how spatial arrangements may be politically contrived in ways inimical to the interests of deprived groups. Clearly, many locational problems are far too deeply rooted to suppose that we need only to be freed from the yoke of a given political system to see them solved. The tensions between aggregating and dispersing forces, and the dilemma of scale economies versus regional equalization would remain in any state, real or hypothetical. One of the roles of locational analysis in human geography is to point out the constrained set of spatial options within which *any* form of political or social decision-making is set. The journal, *Antipode*, has provided a major new outlet for 'radical geography' (Folke, 1972) and the exploration of Marxist revolutionary and counter-revolutionary thought in a geographical context (Harvey, 1972).

## 1.5 Conclusions

We have looked in this chapter at certain assumptions upon which this book has been based. Among those of primary importance are its concern with only part of geography (human rather than environmental), its emphasis on quantitative (rather than qualitative) methods, and its dominantly positivist (rather than phenomenological) approach to model building. It is, too, concerned in the main only with aggregate populations in space (macrogeography, if you will) rather than with individuals. Doubtless there will be other sources of bias of which the authors were only dimly aware. For example, the Russian translation of the first edition of this book made clear how heavily the locational explanations were rooted in the classical economics of the capitalist world. Inevitably, the lopsidedness of the book will appeal to certain readers and condemn it to others. We present the chapters which follow as a view, albeit one among many, of the spatial order which may be discovered in human geography.

# Part One:

# Models of Locational Structure

*Bold ideas, unjustified anticipations, and speculative thoughts, are our only means of interpreting nature; our only organon, our only instrument for grasping her. And we must hazard to win our prize. Those among us who are unwilling to expose their ideas to the hazard of refutation do not take part in the scientific game.* (KARL POPPER, The Logic of Scientific Discovery, 1959, p. 280.)

# 2 Interaction

2.1 **Introduction.** 2.2 **Interaction and Spatial Form:** 1 Movement and morphology; 2 Regional studies of lapse rates. 2.3 **Elementary Interaction Models:** 1 Ravenstein model; 2 Reilly-Converse model; 3 Casey-Huff model; 4 Intervening opportunity model. 2.4 **Interpretation of Model Components:** 1 Mass component; 2 Distance component; 3 Relations between mass and distance; 4 Refinements of the basic gravity model; 5 Potential surfaces. 2.5. **Maximum Entropy Models:** 1 Concepts of entropy; 2 Application to spatial interaction models. 2.6 **Interaction Fields:** 1 Size of fields; 2 Shape of fields. 2.7 **Interaction Territories:** 1 Elementary packing theory; 2 Regional packing studies; 3 Modification of the hexagon model. 2.8 **Conclusions.**

## 2.1 Introduction

One of the difficulties we face in trying to analyse the integrated regional systems described in Chapter 1 is that there is no obvious or single point of entry. Indeed, the more integrated the system, the harder it is to crack. Thus in the case of nodal regions, it is just as logical to begin with the study of settlements as with the study of routes. As Isard comments: '. . . the maze of interdependencies in reality is indeed formidable, its tale unending, its circularity unquestionable. Yet its dissection is imperative . . . at some point we must cut into its circumference' (Isard *et al.*, 1960, p. 3). We choose to make that cut with spatial interactions or movements.

This chapter outlines the various types of movement that are important in the build-up of other parts of the regional system and reviews some of the models that have been evolved to describe their pattern. The idea of interaction leads on to a consideration of the natural fields that are created by them and to the difficulties that arise when overlapping fields need to be demarcated. Ideas of spatial diffusion—movement through time—are treated as a separate theme in Chapter 7.

## 2.2 Interaction and Spatial Form

### 2.2.1 *Movement and morphology*

Movement is an aspect of regional organization that has been only lightly stressed in human geography. Crowe (1938) took his geographical colleagues to task for their overweening concern with the static elements on the earth's surface. Is progressive geography, he asked, to be solely concerned with the distribution of *Homo dormiens*? To be sure, the generation since Crowe's strictures has seen a growing recognition of momentum and circulation patterns in geographical research, not least in migration studies where the Lund School have put population movements at the centre of their field (Hannerberg, Hägerstrand, and Odeving, 1957). In this more contemporary view, human population is regarded not as a static feature (the dot maps of conventional geographical analysis) but as a complex of oscillating particles, with short loops connecting places of sleep, work, and recreation, and longer loops connecting old hearths and new areas of migration. Other components in the regional system may be viewed in a similar manner—agricultural zones in terms of freight movements, or city growth in terms of commuting (Kain, 1962). Each of these types of movement leaves its special mark on the face of the earth. Bunge has suggested that both physical and social processes leave comparable trails: '. . . Davis's streams move the earth material to the sea and leave the earth etched with valleys; Thünen's agricultural products are moved to the market and leave their mark on the earth with rings of agriculture; . . . agricultural innovations creep across Europe, as do glacial fronts, to yield Hägerstrand's regions of agricultural progress and terminal moraines' (Bunge, 1962, p. 196).

This dualism between physical and human geography is part of a far wider parallelism between movement and geometry. In biology, the classic work in this field is D'Arcy Thompson's *On growth and form* (1917) in which he attempted to show how mathematical concepts (e.g. magnitude and transformation) and dynamic principles (e.g. available energy) help to explain biological forms. Like another biologist, Henri Fabre, Thompson was fascinated by the regularity and mathematical perfection of a bee's cell or a dragon-fly's wing and drew them together in a basic consideration of geometry and movement. A similar ability to recognize links between fields that are conventionally divided was shared by one of the greatest locational theorists, August Lösch, who saw fundamental parallels between biological and economic forms.

Lösch (1954, p. 184) drew attention to what he termed, grandiosely, the *lex parsimoniae* or 'law of minimum effort'. This concept suggests that natural events reach their goal by the shortest route. It appears first in physics in the eighteenth century with the work of Lagrange as the *principle of least action* and reappears in systems analysis as the concept of *minimum potential energy*, in operations research as *geodesics* (or optimal movement paths), and in the social sciences as the *principle of least effort* (Zipf, 1949).

We shall be resorting to 'least movement' as an explanatory model in many places in Part One of this book where the geometry of settlement arrangements (Chapter 4), or industrial patterns (Chapter 5) or agricultural zones (Chapter 6) conforms to regular and often symmetrical distributions. The symmetry discovered in these sections may well be critical, for in 1883 Mach (1942) argued that 'forms of equilibrium' are often symmetrical and regular, and that in mechanical terms they correspond to a maximum or minimum of work. Figure 2.1 shows a practical application of the minimum work concept (as modified by the probabilistic viewpoint outlined in Chapter 1). If we assume a uniform plane, then the least-effort path between points *i* and *j* is shown by the broken line in Figure 2.1A. However, we may argue (e.g. from Meinig's findings on railway routes in the northwestern United States discussed on page 20) that the actual paths are likely to diverge from the optimum paths (in distance terms) for a wide range of rational and irrational reasons. Examples of actual paths are shown by the bundle of lines connecting

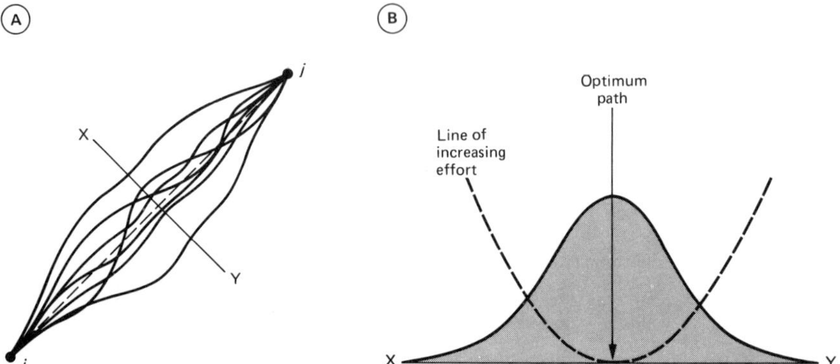


**Figure 2.1** Optimum paths between centres viewed in terms of probability theory.

*i* and *j*. If we draw a cross-section from *X* to *Y* across the shortest route we can show that as paths diverge further from the optimum path the amount of work they have to do, in distance travelled, goes up. This is plotted as the parabolic line in Figure 2.1B. We may suspect that the actual paths will tend to fluctuate about the optimum in a random way to give a Gaussian distribution about the least-effort path (the shaded normal curve in Figure 2.1B).

### 2.2.2 *Regional studies of lapse rates*

The attenuating effect of distance on movement has been recognized intuitively by societies at all levels of development; for at least ninety years, since the work of Ravenstein (1885–9) in England, and of Andersson (1897) in Sweden, this effect has been scientifically investigated. Ravenstein's observations on the relations between distance and the volume of migration proved so striking that a number of attempts were made to express this relationship in a general, often mathematical, form. Studies of spatial interactions over distance have ranged very widely in terms of both the movements studied and the range of distances involved. Figure 2.2 draws together three typical examples of freight movements over three different scales. At one scale (Figure 2.2C) the volume of freight moving between 25 areas in ocean-going shipping in 1925 is plotted against distance. Despite the limitations of the data, the steady fall-off of movement with distance up to 13,000 miles is clearly apparent. Over a more limited area, that of the continental United States, the fall-off of the tonnage of Class I railroad shipments in 1949 with distance up to 1,500 miles is also clearly shown (Figure 2.2B). For a still smaller area, the Chicago region, Helvig (1964) has shown that the number of truck trips is also associated with distance in a zone extending out to around 350 miles (Figure 2.2A).

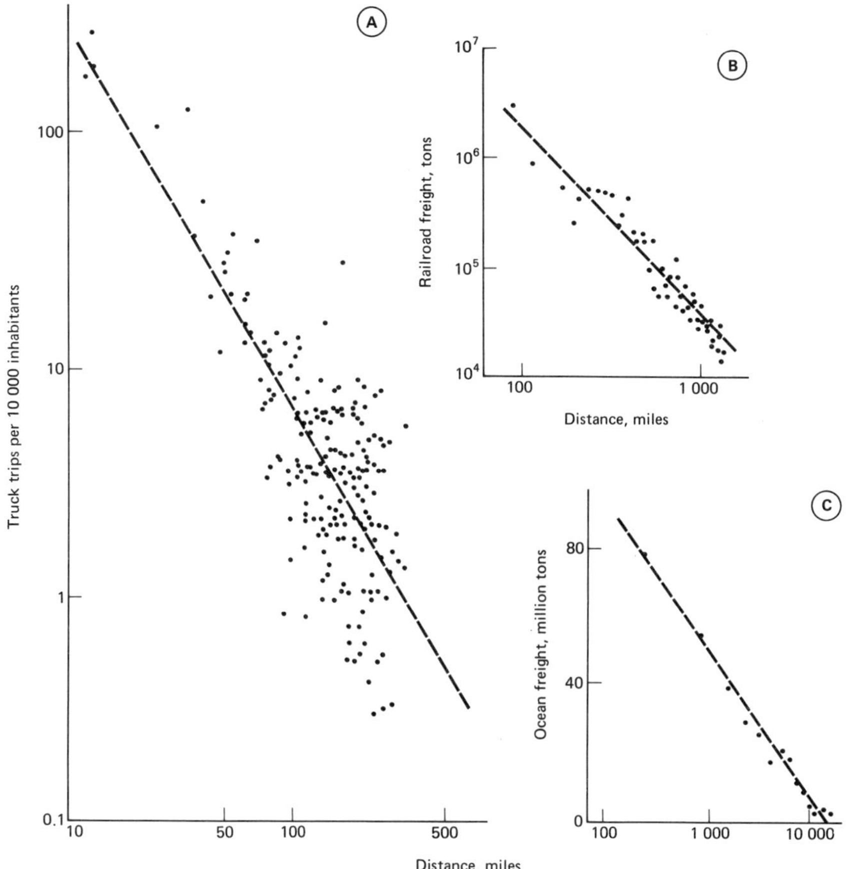


**Figure 2.2** Distance decay rates. **A** Truck trips around Chicago, United States. **B** Class I railway shipments, United States, 1949. **C** World ocean-going freight, 1925. Sources: Helvig, 1964, p. 78; Zipf, 1949.

Studies of freight movements are paralleled by a very large number of studies of other movements. Dåhl's (1957) study of the contacts between the town of Västerås, Sweden, with the rest of that country is typical. He mapped movements of population, passenger traffic, telephone traffic, newspaper subscriptions, business contacts, retail trade contacts, and goods traffic. Despite detailed variations, as between movements based on private and business contacts and from one time period to the next, Dåhl found the general fall-off of movement with distance was strikingly confirmed. Alongside such regional studies stand a few systematic studies. Zipf (1949), in an intriguing book *Human behaviour and the principle of least effort*, brought together dozens of varied examples of movements mostly for the United States. Isard (1956, pp. 55–76) prefaced his *Location and the space economy* with a review of similar distance-movement studies, while Olsson (1965) has reviewed more recent work in his *Distance and human interaction.*

## 2.3 Elementary Interaction Models

Most of the models used by geographers to analyze the movements described above draw on physical analogies, in particular on Newtonian gravitation theory. Sir Isaac Newton's Law of Universal Gravitation propounded in 1687 stated that two bodies attract each other in proportion to the product of their masses and inversely as the square of their distances apart. This gives the familiar formula,

$$F = \frac{GM_1 M_2}{d_{12}^2} \tag{2.1}$$

where $F$ is the force with which each mass pulls the other, $G$ is a universal constant, the pull of gravity, $M_1$ and $M_2$ are the sizes of the two masses concerned, and $d_{12}$ is the distance between them. In relating Newton's original terms to the geographical literature, 'force' is identified with movements or trips between locations, while 'mass' is some measure of the trip-generating or trip-attracting character of a location such as the population size. Distance may be measured not only in physical terms but also in terms of costs, time, or psychological perception of separation. The gravitational constant has no direct analogy in geography; in practice it is replaced by a regionally-variable multiplier.

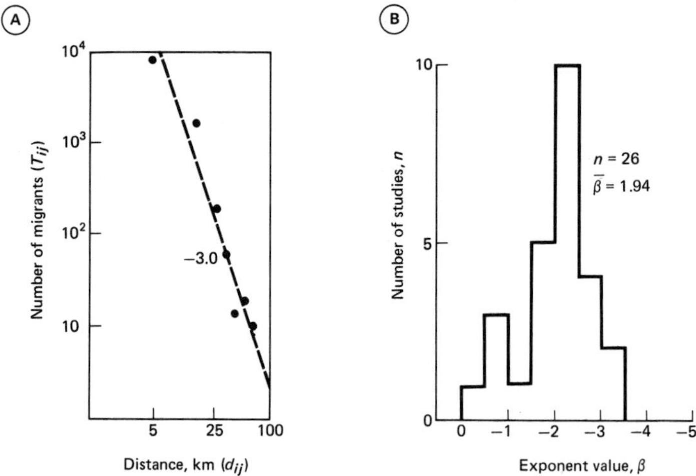


**Figure 2.3** **A** Outward migration from Asby, southern Sweden, 1860–1939. **B** Histogram of exponent values in Pareto-type formulae fitted to migration data for selected Swedish parishes. Source: Hägerstrand, 1957, pp. 114, 115.

Table 2.1. General typology of distance decay functions

| Name | Function | Linear regression transformation |
|---|---|---|
| *GENERAL MODEL:* | $T = ae^{-bf(d)}$ | |
| *SINGLE LOG MODELS:* | | |
| Normal | $T_{ij} = ae^{-bd_{ij}^2}$ | $\ln T_{ij} = \ln a - bd_{ij}^2$ |
| Exponential | $T_{ij} = ae^{-bd_{ij}}$ | $\ln T_{ij} = \ln a - bd_{ij}$ |
| Square root exponential | $T_{ij} = ae^{-bd_{ij}^{0.5}}$ | $\ln T_{ij} = \ln a - bd_{ij}^{0.5}$ |
| *DOUBLE LOG MODELS:* | | |
| Pareto model | $T_{ij} = ae^{-b \ln d_{ij}}$ | $\ln T_{ij} = \ln a - b \ln d_{ij}$ |
| Lognormal | $T_{ij} = ae^{-b(\ln d_{ij})^2}$ | $\ln T_{ij} = \ln a - b(\ln d_{ij})^2$ |

*Notation:* $T_{ij}$ = Interaction between locations $i$ and $j$. $d_{ij}$ = Distance between $i$ and $j$. $a,b$ = Constants. $e$ = Exponential constant (2.7183).

Source: Taylor, 1975, pp. 23–4.

### 2.3.1 *Ravenstein's model*

The first formal use of the Newtonian model in a social science context was by the English demographer, E. G. Ravenstein, in the 1880s. From empirical studies of migration in England and Wales, Ravenstein observed that migration of workers tended to be towards larger cities and that, as distance increased between the source and destination areas, so the volume of migration decreased.

In Newton's terms, this implied that migration ($T_{ij}$) between an origin or source area, $i$, and a destination area, $j$, was proportional to the product of their sizes, $O_i$ and $D_j$ respectively, and inversely proportional to the distance between them ($d_{ij}$), raised to some power. This gives the formula

$$T_{ij} = kO_i D_j d_{ij}^{-\beta} \tag{2.2}$$

where $k$ is a constant and $\beta$ is a distance exponent. Models of this form are readily fitted by ordinary least squares. What value should be given to the distance exponent is a source of debate. In the original gravity model [equation (2.1)], the value is $(-2)$, but experiments in curve fitting suggest considerable variability (Figure 2.3B). Figure 2.3A shows a Pareto-type curve fitted to out-migration from the parish of Asby (Sweden) during the period 1860–1939 with the values

$$\begin{aligned} T_{ij} &= 2.1 \times 10^6 (d_{ij}^{-3.0}) \\ &= D_j \times k(d_{ij}^{-\beta}) \end{aligned}$$

(Hägerstrand, 1957, p. 113). In this particular estimate, the high distance decay term $(-3.0)$ describes a steep fall off in migration with distance. We have summarized in Table 2.1 the most commonly used distance decay functions in gravity models, together with their linear regression transformations.

### 2.3.2 *Reilly-Converse model*

In the 1920s and 1930s, gravity models of spatial interaction were widely used in trade area studies. Study of the retail trade areas of 225 Texas cities led Reilly in 1929 to propound a 'Law of Retail Gravitation', viz: two cities, *i* and *j*, attract retail trade from any intermediate town or city, in the vicinity of the break point, approximately in direct proportion to the population of the two cities, and inversely proportional to the square of the distance from these two cities to the intermediate town.

This 'law' was re-stated by Converse (1930) in a succinct form as

$$B_i = \frac{d_{ij}}{1+\sqrt[2]{O_i/O_j}} \tag{2.3}$$

where $B_i$ is the location of the break point between cities *i* and *j* in terms of distance from the first city, *i*, which is of population size $O_i$. Clearly the square root, $\sqrt[2]{\ }$, could be replaced with any appropriate root from empirical evidence.

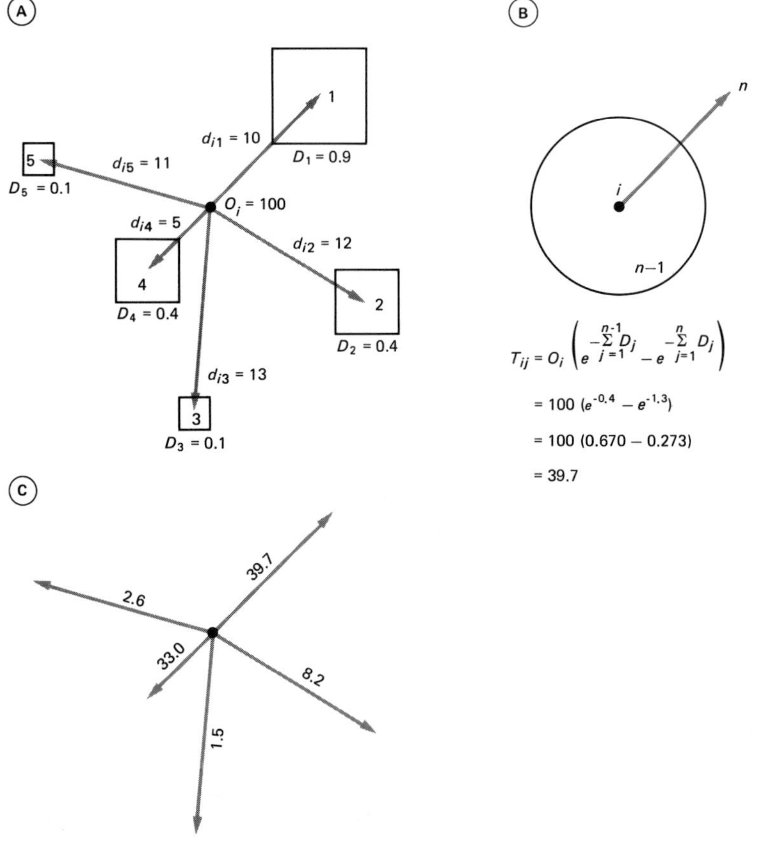


**Figure 2.4** Example of computing flows ($T_{ij}$) using the intervening opportunity model specified in equation (2.5).

Work by traffic engineers like Casey, and psychologists like Huff, extended the gravity model into a widening area of applied studies in the 1950s and 1960s. Both workers restated the gravity model in a more probabilistic form, *viz.*

$$T_{ij} = S_i \left( \frac{O_j d_{ij}^{-\beta}}{\sum_{j=1}^{n} O_j d_{ij}^{-\beta}} \right) \tag{2.4}$$

where $S_i$ is a measure of the significance attached to the $i$th location. Clearly the interaction between $i$ and $j$ is expressed as a proportion of $i$'s interaction with all the other $n$ places in the region under study.

### 2.3.4 *Intervening-opportunity model*

An interesting variant of the classic gravity model was proposed by Stouffer (1940). This introduces distance into the model indirectly in terms of 'nearer' or 'intervening' locations. Stouffer argued the simple proposition that the number of trips from an origin to a destination zone is directly proportional to the number of opportunities in the destination zone and inversely proportional to the number of intervening opportunities (that is, opportunities located between the origin and destination zones). The model was widely used in traffic-flow studies in the 1960s, notably in the Chicago Area Transportation Study (CATS, 1959) in the form:

$$T_{ij} = O_i\left(e^{-\sum_{j=1}^{n-1} D_j} - e^{-\sum_{j=1}^{n} D_j}\right). \tag{2.5}$$

The two terms within the brackets describe the $n$ destinations in the system up to and inclusive of location, $j$, and the $n-1$ 'intervening' destinations up to, *but exclusive of*, location, $j$. Figure 2.4 shows the ways in which the equation may be used to estimate flows in a simple five location region.

## 2.4 Interpretation of Model Components

The wide range of elementary models of spatial interaction proposed appears to offer simple and effective guides to estimating flows between areas. In practice, they run into a number of difficulties; it is not clear how the various components in the models should be defined, nor how they should be related to each other. Here we examine this problem for each component: for mass, for distance, and for the relations between mass and distance.

### 2.4.1 *Mass component*

*Mass* has conventionally been equated with population size in many gravity studies. Population has the prime advantage of convenience as data on the size of most population clusters in the world are readily available. On the other hand, population may conceal important differences between regions, and the use of some system of weighting has been urged. Even in terms of the original physical concepts, this weighting may be justified, for as Isard argues: 'Just as the weights of molecules of different elements are unequal, so should the weights of different kinds of people be different. The average Chinese peasant does not make the same contribution . . . as the United States urban dweller' (Isard *et al.*, 1960, p. 506). Empirical weights of 0.8 for population in the Deep South, 2.0 for population in the Far West, and 1.0 for population in other areas of the United States are given by Isard as a rough indication of the range such regional 'multipliers' might show. Alternatively, multiplication of the population of each cluster by its mean *per caput* income suggests itself as a useful improvement on Isard's weighting system, although it still does not yield a unique answer. In practice, interaction studies have used indices like commodity output (Warntz, 1959) or volume of retail sales (Dunn, 1954) as relevant measures of mass in gravity formulae.

### 2.4.2 *Distance component*

Distance can also be measured in a number of ways. The conventional measure is simply that of the straight line or cross country distance between the two points. Although Bunge (1962, p. 52) has illustrated that distance is a much more complex function, Yeates (1963) found that cross country distance may be a useful yardstick in rural areas with a good road network. In commuting studies, time rather than distance might be a more appropriate measure, with small distances in the urban areas being equivalent to longer distances in the rural areas. Where different transport media are introduced, the difficulty becomes more acute and costs might be used. Here Harris (1954) has suggested that 100 miles by truck (at, then, 4.0 cents per ton-mile), might be equivalent to 160 miles by rail (at 2.5 cents per ton-mile), or to 1,600 miles by ship (at 0.25 cents per ton-mile), though even these weightings are complicated by terminal costs and delivery charges at destination.

***

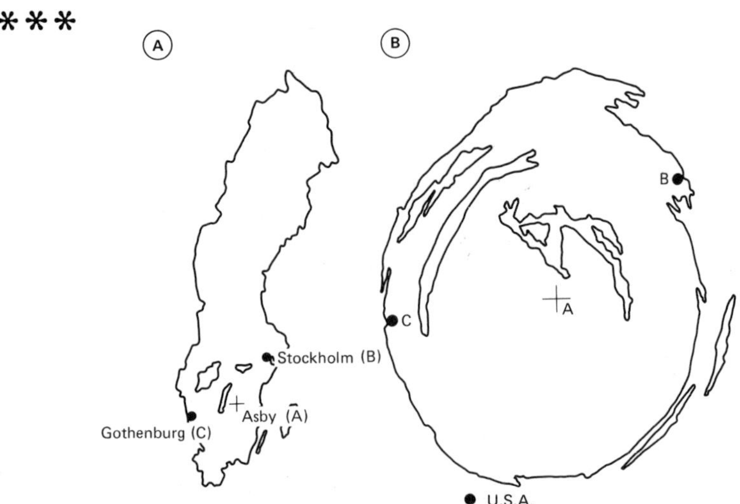


**Figure 2.5** **A** Conventional map of Sweden. **B** Transformed to an azimuth, logarithmic-distance map based on Asby. Source: Hägerstrand, 1957, p. 154.

Huff (1960) has stressed that the migrant's view of remoteness and distance may not be a simple geographical one; we may well regard nearby areas as strongly differentiated and remote areas as uniform, a view reinforced by the curvilinear relations of travelling costs to distance. Hägerstrand (1957) has suggested that we may generalize both the psychological and economic view of distance within a logarithmic transformation of distance. He uses an azimuthal logarithmic projection centred on the place of migration, Asby in central Sweden, to suggest the migrant's impression of distance. The contrast between the conventional map of Sweden (Figure 2.5A) with the transformed map on the azimuthal logarithmic projection (Figure 2.5B) shows the drastic change in spatial relationships: note the location of Stockholm and Gothenburg on both maps, and the approximate location of the United States on the second map! See also Gould and White (1974) for a detailed account of the way in which distance in mental maps differs very dramatically from Euclidean distance.

Even if we can measure distance in a satisfactory metric, there remains a debate about the interpretation of the estimated distance exponent, $\hat{\beta}$, in interaction models like equation (2.2). Curry (1972) and Curry, Griffith and Sheppard (1975) have argued that estimates of the distance exponent in interaction models confound two distinct distance components: (i) a *behavioural* component describing how human behaviour is modified by increasing separation, and (ii) a *map pattern* component describing the particular configuration of locations between which flows are occurring. More precisely, this map pattern effect is defined by Curry as *spatial autocorrelation* (see Chapter 11) among the mass terms of the model. In addition, Johnston (1973, 1975) has urged caution in the interpretation of place-to-place variations in regression coefficients for distance estimated from gravity models fitted *separately* to each origin in turn, as opposed to fitting over the system as a whole. His experiments with simulated flows between 25 locations used the following regression model,

$$\log_{10}(T_{ij}/O_i D_j) = \log_{10} a + b \log_{10} d_{ij} + \varepsilon, \tag{2.6}$$

which was fitted to each of the locations in turn. The results showed substantial variations in the $\{\hat{b}\}$ values obtained; the maximum values (e.g. $\hat{b} = -4.21$) were generated by the remoter locations on the edge of the map, and the minimum values (e.g. $\hat{b} = -1.64$) were yielded by locations nearer the geographical centre of the map. Consistent variations of more than $\times 2$ between the minimum and maximum $\hat{b}$ values suggest, on the face of it, that map structure may substantially affect the value of the distance decay coefficients and make between-area comparisons invalid. Even if this were true, however, comparison of the relative variations in the $\{\hat{b}\}$ values for the same spatial configurations, say over time or over different commodities, would remain valid if the map structure remained constant.

Cliff, Martin and Ord (1974, 1975a) take a different view from that advanced by Curry *et al.* and Johnston. It is evident that the parameters of models like (2.2) and (2.6) can be readily estimated by ordinary least squares, since the models assume a regression format upon taking logarithms of the terms in the equations. Cliff, Martin and Ord list three basic propositions regarding the linear regression model:

(i) provided the regressor variables are not perfectly collinear, all the parameters of the model are *estimable* and the ordinary least squares (OLS) estimates are *b*est *l*inear *u*nbiased *e*stimators (BLUE);

(ii) autocorrelation among the regressor variables, spatial or otherwise, may affect the *precision* of the OLS estimators, but they remain BLUE;

(iii) if the model is *mis-specified* (that is, the data really conform to one kind of gravity model, but mistakenly a different, wrong, model is fitted), the OLS or any other estimators will, in general, be biased and inconsistent.

Points (i)–(iii) carry the following implications for Curry's and Johnston's remarks:

(i) In the absence of mis-specification, a map pattern effect will affect only the sampling variances of the estimated coefficients. It does not prevent those coefficients from being estimated or the estimates from being the best available. They are unbiased.

(ii) the difficulties noted by Curry and Johnston appear to arise largely because, in their empirical work, they used mis-specified models. Thus, as noted, Johnston (1975) fitted model (2.6) to the interaction data he generated; however, he generated these data as a function of *ranked distances*, rather than the *actual* distances, between points. That is, a gravity model using ranked distances should have been fitted to the data, rather than model (2.6). Similar remarks hold for Curry *et al.*'s (1975) paper. In that paper, the results in their Table A were obtained by fitting a different model to the data from that actually used to generate the data. Details are provided in Cliff, Martin and Ord (1975a).

(iii) the spatial variability in the $\{\hat{b}\}$ noted by Johnston reflects the mis-specification problem and the fact that the coefficients are not scale free. Cliff, Martin and Ord (1975a) give a scale free version.

### 2.4.3 *Relations between mass and distance*

The relations between mass and distance pose the third difficult problem. The rather simple functions proposed in both the gravity models and the Pareto models describe a straight-line relationship on double-log graph paper. However, Isard has shown that it is equally possible to fit a quadratic rather than a linear function to a set of interaction data, and that this must modify our view of the attenuating effect of distance (Isard *et al.*, 1960, p. 510). Helvig (1964) has supported this view in a regional study of truck movements in the Chicago area. He adopted a quadratic form for the familiar mass-distance model, *viz.*,

$$T_{ij} = 0.42\{\sqrt{P_i P_j}/d_{ij}^2\}^2 + 4.9\{\sqrt{P_i P_j}/d_{ij}^2\} + 160, \tag{2.7}$$

where $P_i$ = the population of the *i*th origin and $P_j$ = the population of the *j*th destination. His justification for this more complex form was entirely empirical: it gave a better fit to the particular movement lapse rates he was studying. Clearly there are a number of ways in which the gravity type of model can be adapted to make it more valuable in empirical studies.

Haynes (1975) has criticized the structural relationships between mass and distance in the gravity model from the standpoint of dimensional analysis. The conventional form of the gravity model,

$$T_{ij} = k\frac{P_i P_j}{d_{ij}^b}, \tag{2.8}$$

can be rewritten in dimensional terms as

$$N^2 \stackrel{d}{=} k\frac{N^2}{L^b}. \tag{2.9}$$

In equation (2.9) $N$ refers to the dimension of population size and $L$ to length; the symbol, $\stackrel{d}{=}$, means 'is dimensionally equivalent to'. That spatial interaction is assigned the dimension $N^2$ stems from the fact that 'doubling a population causes the total number of pairings to be quadrupled, trebling a population multiplies the possible interactions by nine, and so on' (Haynes, 1975, p. 53). Typical values for $b$ from Swedish migration studies are 1.2 for 'workers' moving out of Lund in 1950, and 0.4 for 'intellectuals' (Hägerstrand, 1957). The appropriately balanced dimensional equations are therefore:

$$N^2 \stackrel{d}{=} L^{1\cdot 2}\frac{N^2}{L^{1\cdot 2}} \tag{2.10}$$

and

$$N^2 \stackrel{d}{=} L^{0\cdot 4}\frac{N^2}{L^{0\cdot 4}}. \tag{2.11}$$

It is clear that $k$ is not a 'constant' but must change its very units of measurement in order to balance. (Recall that since $L$ is length, and area is length times length, $L^2$, then a unit $L^{1\cdot 2}$ has a very curious dimensional property.) Changes in the distance exponent enforce inevitable changes not only in $k$'s numerical value (which is acceptable) but in the basic physical interpretation of the so-called constant (which is not). Haynes's analysis casts serious doubts on the theoretical acceptability of conventional gravity models, whatever their very considerable practical value in flow estimation.

Can any appropriate substitute be found? Haynes suggests that the negative exponential model (see Wilson's work discussed in Section 2.5) is dimensionally balanced. In this case, the equation:

$$T_{ij} = kP_i P_j e^{-md_{ij}} \tag{2.12}$$

reduces to

$$N^2 \stackrel{d}{=} 1.N.N.1^{L^{-1}L}. \tag{2.13}$$

In equation (2.12), $k$ is a dimensionless scaling constant which reduces to 1 in equation (2.13); $m$ is a constant measuring the proportion of interaction decrease per unit of distance increase, which reduces to dimension $L^{-1}$. Unlike the gravity formulation, the exponential decay statement of the relationship of mass and distance is dimensionally correct.

### 2.4.4 *Refinements of the basic gravity model*

We are familiar in economic theory with the 'push-pull' concept of supply and demand. Ullman (in Thomas 1956, pp. 862–80) mapped the tendency for material flows to move from areas of abundance to areas of scarcity, while Bunge (1962, pp. 121–2) suggests that we may recognize here a wider principle, that of 'self-repulsion', introduced from the mathematical theory of heat conduction by Hotelling (1921). Goodrich (1936) in a study of *Migration and economic opportunity* traced population movements within the United States from 'undesirable' to 'desirable' areas.

How important is such regional *complementarity* in modifying the gravity type of relationships? Kariel (1963) analysed by multivariate methods population growth due to net migration in the United States in the 1950–60 decade. As Table 2.2 shows, two hypotheses were tested by Kariel: (i) *desirability* as measured by the three factors, increase in manufacturing employment, median family income, and proportion of professional and technical workers in the population: (ii) *size* as measured by the factor, number in the employed labour force. The proportion of the variation 'explained' by the four factors was measured by the coefficient of determination. This showed striking confirmation of the importance of size in determining the volume of migration: it was nearly four times as important as any of the other three factors. Even with Kariel's reminder, that in the period of study there were local short-term slumps (e.g. in the Detroit area's motor industry) which might affect the findings, this result is important in showing surprisingly strong support for the gravity type of model.

Table 2.2 Complementarity models and migration movements*

| | *Variance reduction* |
|---|---|
| Complementarity hypothesis: | |
| Increase in manufacturing employment | 12% |
| Median family income | 12% |
| Professional and technical workers (per cent) | 10% |
| Size hypothesis: | |
| Size of employed labour force | 44% |
| Joint four-factor hypothesis: | 47% |
| Joint four-factor hypothesis with climatic adjustment | 55% |

Source: Kariel, 1963, p. 210.
*United States, 1950–60.

Isard has attempted to build this complementarity of areas into the simple inverse-distance gravity model. This may be written as,

$$T_{ij} = (P_j/d_{ij}).f(A_j), \tag{2.14}$$

where $T_{ij}$, $P_j$, and $d_{ij}$ are defined as before, and $f(A_j)$ is some function of $A_j$ where $A_j$ measures the attractive force of destination $j$ (Isard *et al.*, 1960, p. 68). 'Attractive force' remains to be defined in detail, and we can at this stage point only to its variability. For example, in migration studies it seems clear that

**

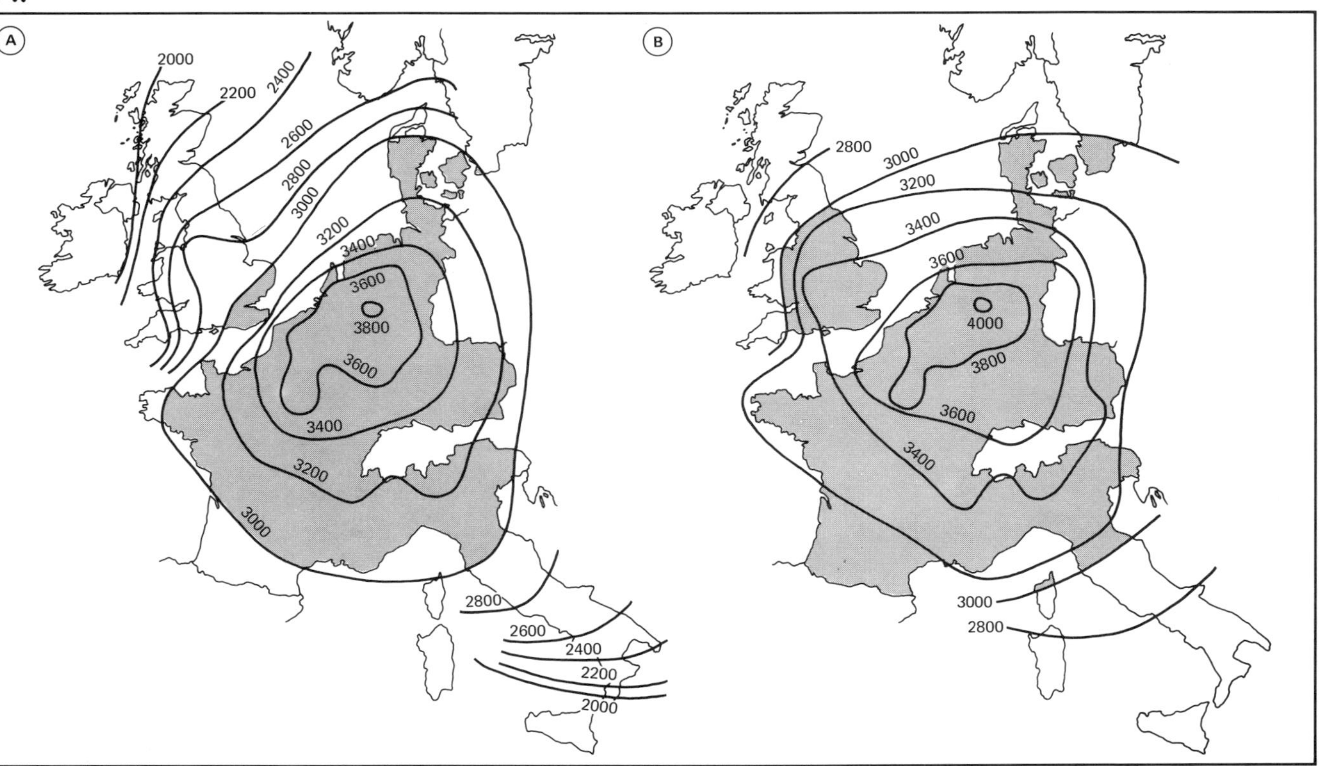


**Figure 2.6** Predicted economic potential of the countries of the European Economic Community in anticipation of the joining of the UK, Eire, Norway and Denmark (**A**), and anticipating the construction of the Channel Tunnel (**B**). Source: Clark, Wilson and Bradley, 1969, pp. 205–6.

amenities in general, and climate in particular, are playing an increasing part in migration within more developed countries. This gives point to Kariel's finding that his overall level of 'explanation' jumped by 8 per cent (Table 2.2) when results were adjusted for climatic desirability by contrasting areas to the north and south of the 45°F mean winter isotherm.

### 2.4.5 *Potential surfaces*

Work by Stewart and Warntz (1958) has been on extensions of the gravity model to give continuous potential surfaces. For example, the population potential of a series of points ($V_1$, $V_2$, $V_3$, ..., $V_n$) may be given as:

$$\begin{aligned}
V_1 &= kP_1(\tfrac{1}{2}d_{1*})^{-\beta} + kP_2(d_{12})^{-\beta} + kP_3(d_{13})^{-\beta} + \ldots + kP_n(d_{1n})^{-\beta} \\
V_2 &= kP_1(d_{21})^{-\beta} + kP_2(\tfrac{1}{2}d_{2*})^{-\beta} + kP_3(d_{23})^{-\beta} + \ldots + kP_n(d_{2n})^{-\beta} \\
V_3 &= kP_1(d_{31})^{-\beta} + kP_2(d_{32})^{-\beta} + kP_3(\tfrac{1}{2}d_{3*})^{-\beta} + \ldots + kP_n(d_{3n})^{-\beta} \qquad (2.15) \\
&\vdots \\
V_n &= kP_1(d_{n1})^{-\beta} + kP_2(d_{n2})^{-\beta} + kP_3(d_{n3})^{-\beta} + \ldots + kP_n(\tfrac{1}{2}d_{n*})^{-\beta}
\end{aligned}$$

where, as before, $P_i$ is the population of centre *i*. A continuous surface as in Figure 2.6 is produced by interpolating between the potential totals $\{V_i\}$ for the set of points. One problem in computing such surfaces is how to handle the contribution of a particular centre to its own potential. In the above equation, this is done by an arbitrary device, *viz.*, the population potential of the first centre, $V_1$, includes a term where its own population, $P_1$, is divided by half the distance, $d_{1*}$, between its own location and that of its first nearest neighbour. Similar self-potential terms are included for each of the other locations used in constructing a surface.

## 2.5 Maximum Entropy Models

One major innovation in the building of spatial interaction models came in the 1960s with the work of A. G. Wilson and his associates. Wilson's approach to spatial interaction was to return to physics in general and to statistical mechanics in particular. He argued that, although concepts transferred from physics to social physics had been based on unsound analogies, systematic application of statistical mechanical concepts could throw a powerful light on our understanding of complex spatial systems (Wilson, 1970).

### 2.5.1 *Concepts of entropy*

Entropy, 'the most likely state of a system', formed the cornerstone of Wilson's work. As a concept, it relates directly to ideas of probability and uncertainty, and forms a directly-measurable system property. Gould (1972) has provided a useful illustration of entropy (see Figure 2.7). Assume that there are twenty individuals within the population of an urban area who can reside at various distances from their workplaces (assumed located in the city centre), depending upon how much energy (i.e. funds for transport) is available. The distances away from the city centre that the individuals are able to live is assumed to be a function of their available funds for transport, and this acts as a constraint on the different spatial configurations of residences with respect to workplaces that the twenty individuals can adopt.

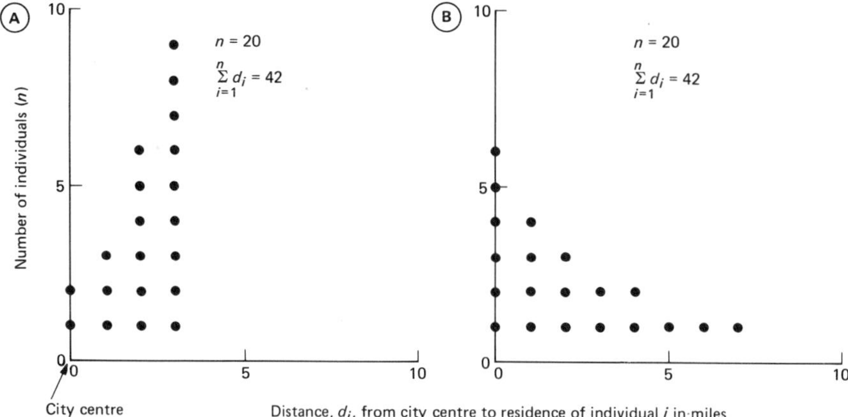


**Figure 2.7** Location of residences of $n = 20$ individuals with respect to a city centre so that the total distance moved to the city centre ($\Sigma d_i$) is 42 miles. The 'unlikely' ascending situation in (**A**) has a probability of occurrence which is only 1/7560 of that of the 'likely' descending situation shown in (**B**). Source: Gould, 1972, pp. 691–2.

Figure 2.7 shows an 'unlikely' configuration (A) and a 'likely' configuration (B), when exactly 42 units of energy are available. 'Likelihood' is measured by the expression:

$$W = \frac{n!}{\prod_i n_i!} \tag{2.16}$$

In equation (2.16), $n$ is the total number of individuals, and $n_i$ is the number of individuals who live at a given distance, $i$, from their workplace. $W$ then gives the total number of distinct ways that a *specified* allocation of individuals to distance bands can occur. Suppose, for example, that $n = 5$, and that our five individuals are assigned the identity numbers 1–5. Let us suppose that the energy constraints mean that, of these five individuals, three must live two miles from work, and the other two, seven miles from work. Then from equation (2.16), $W = 5!/(3!2!) = 10$. That is, there are ten ways that our five individuals could be arranged so that two live seven miles from work and the other three live two miles from work. The arrangements are:

| | Miles from work | |
|---|---|---|
| | Two | Seven |
| | 1, 2, 3 | 4, 5 |
| | 1, 2, 4 | 3, 5 |
| | 1, 2, 5 | 3, 4 |
| Individual | 1, 3, 5 | 2, 4 |
| identity | 1, 4, 5 | 2, 3 |
| numbers | 1, 3, 4 | 2, 5 |
| | 2, 3, 4 | 1, 5 |
| | 2, 4, 5 | 1, 3 |
| | 2, 3, 5 | 1, 4 |
| | 3, 4, 5 | 1, 2 |

Applying equation (2.16) to the sequence shown in Figure 2.7A, with twenty individuals, the value of $W$ is

$$\frac{20!}{2!\,3!\,6!\,9!} = 7.8 \times 10^8.$$

Although the number of different arrangements appears huge it is several orders of magnitude smaller than the 'likely state' shown in Figure 2.7B. In this case, the value of $W$ is

$$\frac{20!}{6!\,4!\,3!\,2!\,2!\,1!\,1!\,1!} = 5.9 \times 10^{12}.$$

Thus the descending order, with most individuals residing near their workplace, has a much greater chance of occurring, in a frequency sense, given the same energy constraints. For any reasonably large system, the most likely state will, under suitable constraints, form a descending series in which the distribution of individuals in a population at various distances from a centre (or at various levels of activity) can be described by:

$$P_j = P_0^{e^{-bj}}. \tag{2.17}$$

This equation states that the number of individuals living at distance $j$ from a focus will be a simple negative exponential function of the number of individuals, $P_0$, in the ground state (i.e. in the distance band nearest to the centre or workplace, or at the lowest level of activity), the distance, $j$, and some parameter $b$. Wilson (1970) and Gould (1972) point out that this expression is basically similar to Boltzmann's Law, describing such physical phenomena as the decay of radioactive materials. The parameter, $b$, is a function of the average energy available to each particle or individual in the system: as the energy level increases, $b$ decreases in value.

### 2.5.2 *Application to spatial interaction models*

Extension of the ideas of the most likely state to the spatial interaction within a system is illustrated by a simple example shown in Figure 2.8. In this case, we suppose that we have seven workers and seven jobs, but we do not know how many workers and jobs there are in each of the origins (homes, $i = 1, 2$) and destinations (workplaces, $j = 1, 2, 3$) respectively. Figure 2.8A gives just one of the many possible configurations of workers, jobs and journey-to-work patterns. Let $T_{ij}$ denote the number of individuals living in $i$ and working in $j$. The flow pattern of journey-to-work trips shown, $\{T_{ij}\}$, may be called the trip distribution pattern. This particular trip distribution pattern can occur in the following number of ways [equation (2.16)]:

$$W(\{T_{ij}\}) = \frac{T!}{\prod_{i,j} T_{ij}!} = \frac{7!}{2!\,2!\,1!\,1!\,1!\,0!} = 1260. \tag{2.18}$$

Here, $T = \sum_i \sum_j T_{ij}$. In other words, $W(\{T_{ij}\})$ is the number of distinct arrangements of individuals which give rise to the trip distribution pattern, $\{T_{ij}\}$, shown in Figure 2.8A

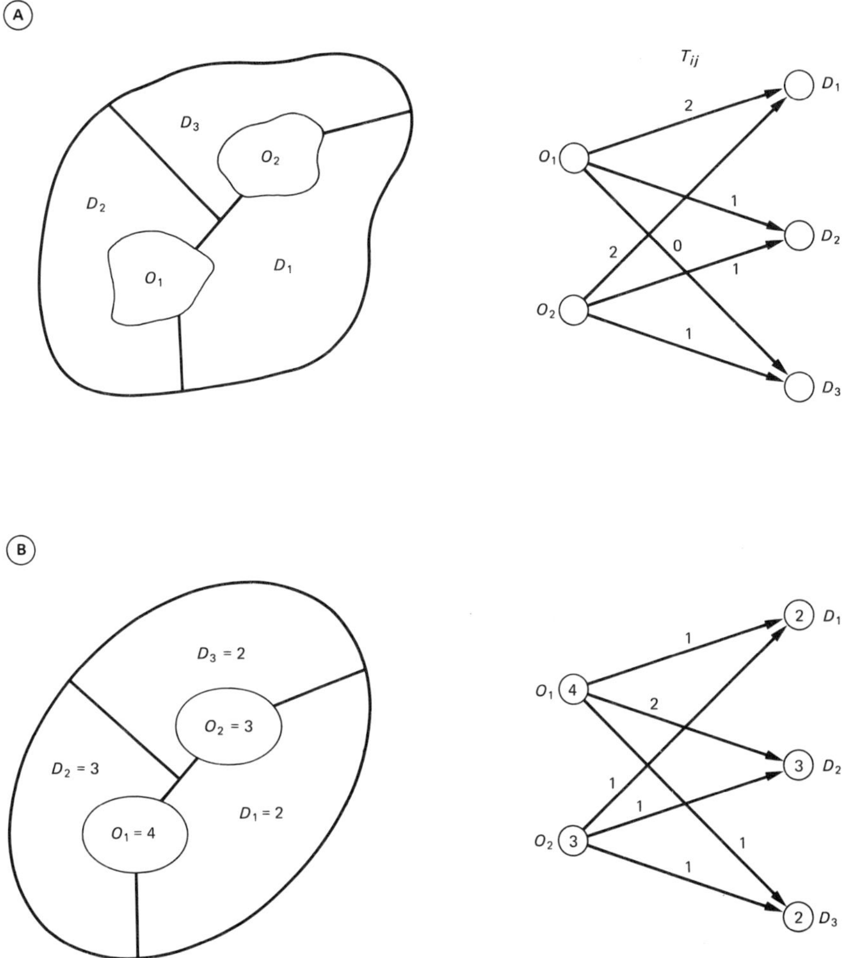


**Figure 2.8** Possible configurations of workers, jobs, and journey-to-work patterns. **A** Unconstrained case. **B** Most probable distribution subject to the constrains shown.

However, this analysis neglects one critical factor which has also been neglected in most earlier spatial interaction studies. $T_{ij}$ is, in practice, constrained by the total number of jobs, $D_j$, available in each $j$, and the total number of workers, $O_i$, who live in $i$. This information is usually given exogenously, so that we have

$$\sum_j T_{ij} = O_i \quad \text{and} \quad \sum_i T_{ij} = D_j. \tag{2.19}$$

Once we introduce these constraints, the number of possible different trip distribution patterns is greatly reduced. Suppose that $O_1 = 4$, $O_2 = 3$, $D_1 = 2$, $D_2 = 3$ and $D_3 = 2$. The pattern shown in Figure 2.8A is immediately ruled out since it breaks both parts of constraint (2.19). In fact, the only trip distribution patterns which satisfy the constraints appear in Table 2.3. The $\{T_{ij}\}$ appear in the body of each table, and the value of $W$ for each pattern is given underneath. Of these patterns, $G$ occurs in the greatest possible number of ways, and we refer to this as the most likely, or most probable, state of the system; that is, given all the available information, the trip distribution pattern, $G$, is combinatorially most likely to arise (see Figure 2.8B). Formally, what this trip distribution pattern does is to

$$\text{Maximize } W\{T_{ij}\} = \frac{T!}{\prod_{i,j} T_{ij}!} \tag{2.20}$$

subject to the constraints

$$\sum_j T_{ij} = O_i, \tag{2.21}$$

$$\sum_i T_{ij} = D_j. \tag{2.22}$$

We shall come across models of the form of equations (2.20)–(2.22) again in Section 4.3.3 in connection with the rank-size rule for city sizes, and also in Section 15.5.1, when we look at linear programming models and their relationship to maximum entropy models. Equation (2.20) is referred to as the *entropy function*, which we wish to maximize.

Commonly, $\{T_{ij}\}$ is limited further by a third constraint over and above those given in equation (2.19), namely the impedance or cost, $c_{ij}$, of travelling between $i$ and $j$. We can express this travel cost constraint as

$$\sum_i \sum_j T_{ij} = C, \tag{2.23}$$

where $C$ represents the fixed amount spent on travel within the region. Thus, in terms of our earlier illustration (Figure 2.7), $C$ is equivalent to the fixed total of energy, 42 units.

The example given in Figure 2.8 was deliberately chosen to be small so that it was possible to write down explicitly in Table 2.3 all the distinct trip distribution patterns that satisfied the constraints. In practice, however, actual problems will be far too large to permit this to be done. However, using the concept of entropy (defined below), Wilson has been able to show that for any problem of the form of equations (2.20)–(2.22), there is one trip distribution pattern, or state, $\{T_{ij}\}$, that satisfies the constraints and which dominates all other trip distribution patterns in terms of its frequency of occurrence. Computation of this most probable state proceeds via the method of Lagrangian multipliers. Lagrangian multipliers are simply a mathematical device for finding the maximum of any function [e.g. (2.20)], subject to a series of constraints [e.g. (2.21)–(2.22)]—see Gould (1972)—just as differentiation can be used to find the maximum of any function when there are no constraints.

To provide a definition of entropy, we need to make some intermediate definitions. Following Wilson (1970, Chapter 1), any trip distribution pattern, $\{T_{ij}\}$, is referred to as a *macrostate* description of a system, while the many individual arrangements of workers which produce a given macrostate are referred to as *microstates*. The constraints imposed fix what macrostates are possible; thus Table 2.3 gives eight macrostates and *G* has 2520 microstates. The idea of entropy is then to find some assignment of probabilities of occurrence to all the various microstates which make up the possible macrostates 'which avoids bias while agreeing with whatever information is given' (Jaynes, 1957). Since we have no further information available about the microstates, the only reasonable assignment is to assume that all microstates are equally likely to occur. 'The entropy-maximizing method . . . in effect assigns equal probability [of occurrence—cf. the definition of simple randomness] to any state which is not excluded by prior information.'

Table 2.3 Trip distribution patterns which satisfy the constraints shown in Figure 2.8B, and likelihood of occurrence, $W(\{T_{ij}\})$, of each pattern.

A

| | $D_1$ | $D_2$ | $D_3$ | Totals |
|---|---|---|---|---|
| $O_1$ | 1 | 3 | 0 | 4 |
| $O_2$ | 1 | 0 | 2 | 3 |
| Totals | 2 | 3 | 2 | |

$W(\{T_{ij}\}) = 420$

B

| | $D_1$ | $D_2$ | $D_3$ | Totals |
|---|---|---|---|---|
| $O_1$ | 2 | 2 | 0 | 4 |
| $O_2$ | 0 | 1 | 2 | 3 |
| Totals | 2 | 3 | 2 | |

$W(\{T_{ij}\}) = 630$

C

| | | |
|---|---|---|
| 0 | 3 | 1 |
| 2 | 0 | 1 |

$W(\{T_{ij}\}) = 420$

D

| | | |
|---|---|---|
| 2 | 0 | 2 |
| 0 | 3 | 0 |

$W(\{T_{ij}\}) = 210$

E

| | | |
|---|---|---|
| 2 | 1 | 1 |
| 0 | 2 | 1 |

$W(\{T_{ij}\}) = 1260$

F

| | | |
|---|---|---|
| 0 | 2 | 2 |
| 2 | 1 | 0 |

$W(\{T_{ij}\}) = 630$

G

| | | |
|---|---|---|
| 1 | 2 | 1 |
| 1 | 1 | 1 |

$W(\{T_{ij}\}) = 2520$

H

| | | |
|---|---|---|
| 1 | 1 | 2 |
| 1 | 2 | 0 |

$W(\{T_{ij}\}) = 1260$

(Wilson, 1970, p. 133.) It is only by making an assignment of equal probabilities that we can justify our choice on frequency grounds of the macrostate with the most microstates ($G$ in Table 2.3) as the most probable state of the system. The most probable state is referred to as the *maximum entropy* state because it 'corresponds to the position where we are most uncertain about the microstate of the system, as there are the largest possible number of such states in it and we have no grounds for choosing between them' (Wilson, 1970, p. 6).

Returning to equations (2.20)–(2.23), maximization of (2.20) subject to constraints (2.21)–(2.23) yields

$$T_{ij} = A_i B_j O_i D_j \exp(-\beta c_{ij}), \tag{2.24}$$

where $A_i$, $B_j$ and $\beta$ are functions of Lagrangian multipliers, which have the effect of balancing changes within the system, associated with constraints

***

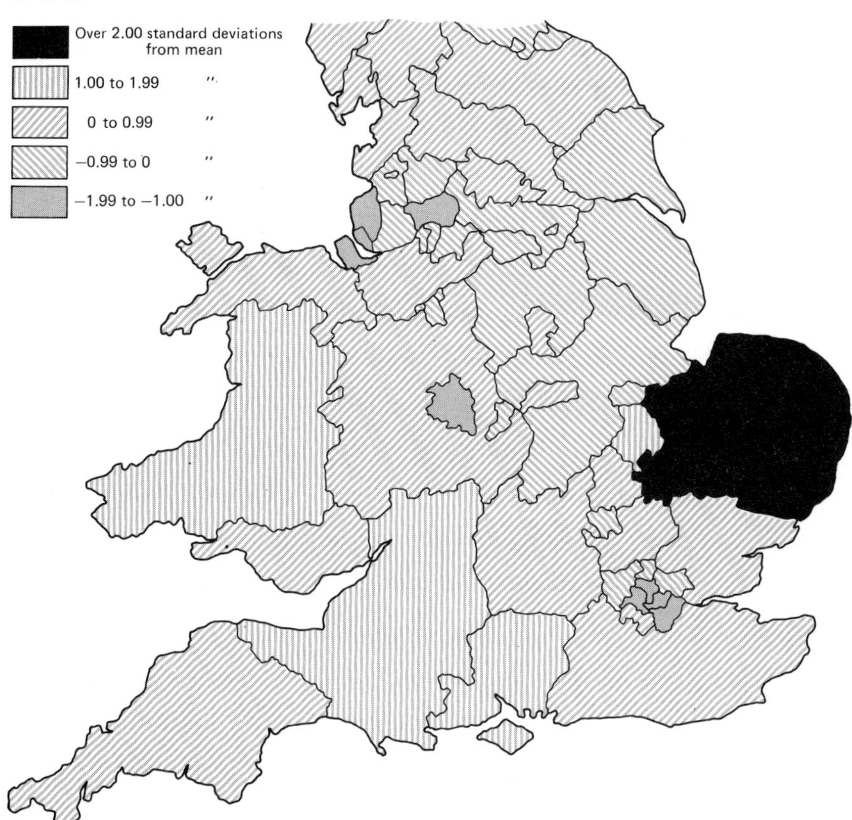


**Figure 2.9** Use of Wilson's gravity model to predict road traffic freight flows originating in different areas of Britain. The map shows distance exponents [$\beta$ in equation (2.24)] for each area in terms of standard deviations from the national mean value of $\hat{\beta} = -2.4$. Source: Chisholm and O'Sullivan, 1973, p. 71.

(2.21)–(2.23) respectively. All other terms are as defined earlier in this section. Comparison of (2.24) with the gravity models discussed earlier in this chapter [equations (2.1)–(2.5) and (2.8)] reveals the fundamentally similar structure of all the models. As Wilson (1967, p. 258) has said: 'This [maximum entropy] statistical theory is effectively saying that, given total numbers of trip origins and destinations for each zone for a homogenous person–trip category, given the costs of travelling between each zone, and given that there is some fixed total expenditure on transport in the region, then there is a most probable distribution of trips between zones, and this distribution is the same as that normally described as the gravity-model distribution.'

Wilson's work provided a firmer theoretical basis for many of the spatial interaction models based on loose physical analogy and 'raises the gravity model phoenix-like from the ashes' (Gould, 1972, p. 696). It ensures that flow patterns meet origin, destination and overall cost constraints, while linking the likelihood of individual trip behaviour to the aggregate pattern of flows. Some indication of its achievements are to be seen in its widening use in applied regional studies. Chisholm and O'Sullivan (1973) provide a good example of its use in predicting road traffic freight flows in Britain (Figure 2.9).

## 2.6 Interaction Fields

The view of interactions given in the preceding section is clearly an over-simplified one: movements do not in fact take place solely along one-dimensional lines linking pairs of points, but over a two-dimensional area. We are familiar with such areas in human geography in a number of guises—the 'sphere of influence' of a city, the 'hinterland' of a port, the 'migration field' of a parish. All hold in common the fact of interaction between a centre and its periphery: here we refer to them by the common term *field.*

### 2.6.1 *Size of fields*

One of the striking features of the relationships between movement and distance is that the graphs are frequently drawn on double-log paper, and thus in no case is a zero origin shown for movement. This fact underlines a fundamental characteristic of interaction fields—they are theoretically *continuous* distributions with a very rapid fall-off near their centre and a very slow, almost asymptotic, fall-off at their outer ranges. Because of their continuous nature we cannot always describe the size of fields by their absolute limits, but we can make a useful generalization about their size if we are prepared to substitute the concept of *mean field* for that of maximum field. Thus if we take any local English newspaper (e.g. the *Bridgwater Mercury*), we are likely to find that its maximum field is immense (i.e. a few copies are sent to expatriates in Argentina or New Zealand), but its mean field is very small, perhaps not more than ten miles across. For the San Francisco Bay area, Vance (1962, p. 509) has shown that while about 17 per cent of the customers of the regional shopping centres come from over ten miles away, one half the customers live within three miles of the centre. Similarly, although one per cent of the visitors to the Shenandoah National Park come from over 2,000 miles, its mean field is less than 300 miles in radius (Clawson, Held, and Stoddard, 1960, p. 171). This decay over space is analogous to the weakening over space in a magnetic field with distance from a magnet.

For mean fields, two generalizations appear valid: (i) The size of mean fields varies with the *transferability* of the item being moved. Ullman (in Thomas, 1956, pp. 862–80) has shown for the United States that different products move with unequal ease, and that this friction is reflected in relative freight costs. His atlas of commodity movements (Ullman, 1957) shows clearly the contrast between products. Duerr (1960, p. 167) has attempted to define Ullman's concept of transferability more rigorously, arguing that we may measure transferability as the *specific value* of a product—that is, its value per unit of weight or bulk. As Table 2.4 shows, low value products (e.g. mine props)

Table 2.4 Relative transportability of three products

| *Lumber product:* | *Type I (veneer logs)* | *Type II (pulpwood)* | *Type III (mine props)* |
|---|---|---|---|
| Specific value, dollars/ton | 150 | 20 | 5 |
| Maximum railroad haul, miles | 400 | 100 | 25 |

Source: Duerr, 1960, p. 167.

normally move short distances, while high value products (e.g. veneer logs) move relatively long distances. Christaller (1933) suggested the same basic idea in his concept of the 'range of a good' (Chapter 5), and in a reverse sense we may regard von Thünen's discussion of agricultural location (Chapter 6) in the same way. Products with low specific value (e.g. forest products) tend to cluster near the city in von Thünen's ideal landscape.

(ii) The size of mean fields varies over *time*. Rapidly increasing mobility is

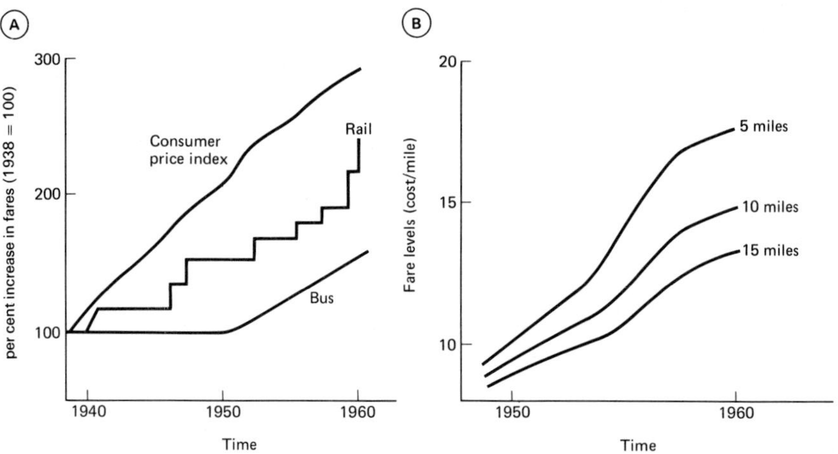


**Figure 2.10** Sample changes in movement costs over time. **A** British passenger transport. **B** Scottish omnibuses. Source: Ministry of Transport, 1961, pp. 66, 67.

one of the dominant features of movement this century. Mean fields for the movement of information, population, and goods have grown steadily larger as technical innovations have reduced the *relative* cost of distance. Chisholm (1962, pp. 171–97) has brought together a number of examples of this trend, showing for example that the real cost of ocean shipping fell by about three-fifths between 1876 and 1955, and that railway freight costs in New Zealand fell by about one-quarter between 1884 and 1956.

For the United Kingdom, the Jack Report (Ministry of Transport, 1961) has shown the relative fall in the cost of rural bus services. Figure 2.10A shows the increase in rail and bus fares over the period 1938 to 1960 in relation to the general index of consumer prices. Despite recent increases, the cost of both services has lagged well behind the general price index. A second important finding of the Jack Report is illustrated in Figure 2.10B. This shows the relative increase of bus fares over the same time period for three distances (five, ten and fifteen miles). It is interesting that the increase over the longer distances has been less than over the shorter, so that the relative cost of long distance travel has been specially reduced.

The result of lowering in relative movement costs is seen in the widening range of interactions of all kinds. For passenger traffic, the average distance travelled in the United States in the year 1906 was 631 miles (Table 2.5). Within

Table 2.5 Changing patterns of movement*

| *Period:* | 1906 | 1956 |
|---|---|---|
| Travel, miles *per caput* | 631 | 5,080 |
| Means of travel, proportion of total passenger miles: | | |
| Airlines | — | 2.6% |
| Automobiles | 0.6% | 87.0% |
| Inland waterways | 1.5% | 0.2% |
| Inter-city buses | — | 3.0% |
| Local public carriers | 51.0% | 3.9% |
| Railroads | 46.9% | 3.3% |

Source: Clawson, Held and Stoddard, 1960, pp. 534–6.
* United States.

half a century, this distance had increased eightfold to over 5,000 miles, although the main cause here was less the reduction in the costs of conventional media but the introduction of entirely new transport media, notably the automobile. Vance (1960) has mapped this growing zone of interaction for the Massachusetts town of Natick (Figure 2.11).

This growing range of interaction has made the complicated problem of field overlap and field definition still more acute. Traditionally, attempts to delimit fields have been based on a variety of measures. Theodorson (1961, pp. 511–94) brings together a collection of typical studies of field delimitation in which newspaper circulation, wholesale trade, commuting, telephone calls, banking, bus services, and the like have been tried with varying degrees of success. Little attempt has been made to test the comparative values of the various measures, and no general conclusions can be drawn on optimum indices. These are likely to vary considerably over time—local bus service areas have been widely used in field delimitation in England and Wales (e.g. Green, 1950)—but there is strong evidence that their importance is dwindling. The very rapid rise in importance of automobile travel (see Table 2.5) in the United States is well documented, and in post-war Britain the motor-car 'bulge' introduced a new and not fully understood element into the interaction

****

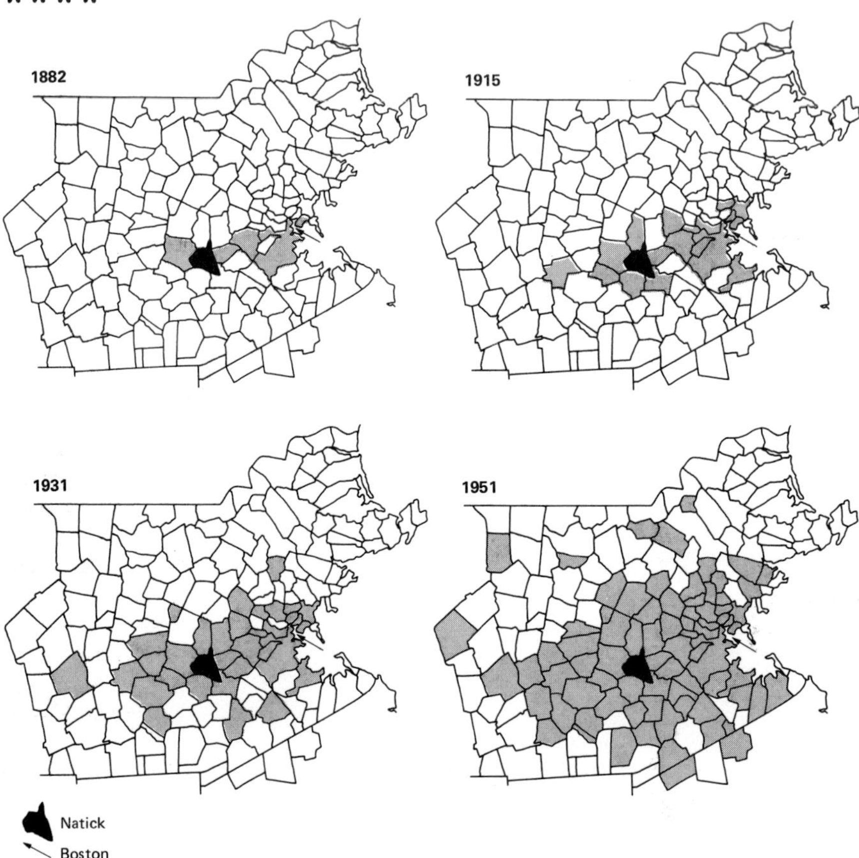


**Figure 2.11** Historical evolution of employment fields (shaded) for the town of Natick, Massachusetts. Source: Vance, 1960, p. 213.

patterns of this country. Certainly, when many indices are plotted for interaction about the same centre, the most likely outcome is a 'garland' of intertwining lines after the manner of Figure 2.12A. Exact coincidence of the boundaries, which are in any case arbitrary limits (as argued above), is very rare, and if a single synthetic boundary to a field is needed, some inexact compromise such as the median line may serve for those purposes where a firm line is required whatever its shortcomings. Other types of compromise are discussed in Chapter 9.

### 2.6.2 *Shape of fields*

If we allow that some line, however arbitrary and subject to changes over time, may be drawn around a centre to delimit its field, then we can make some observations on the shape of that field. We are, in fact, putting a section through our density distribution (parallel to the plane over which it is spread), and we should therefore expect our fields to be circular in shape only if our original notion of interaction fields as 'conic' forms is correct. In fact, truly circular fields are not found by empirical regional study; the most common form tends to be an irregular, amoeba-like, closed figure. Davis (1926, p. 106) described them as 'roughly circular in outline' and little work has been done since then to measure their shape with more precision, or to improve on Davis's verdict. Certainly most fields approximate the circle (Figure 2.12B) and

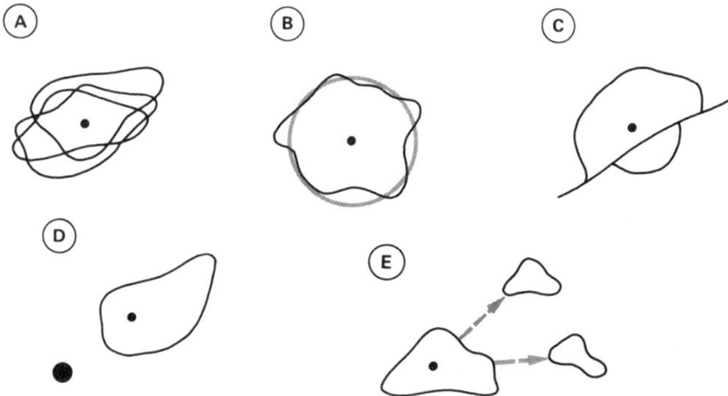


**Figure 2.12** Alternative types of movement fields. **C** *Truncated* field. **D** *Distorted* field. **E** *Fragmented* field.

we might well accommodate random variations (lobes, waves, and indentations) within a theory which allowed stochastic 'blurring' of the regular form. Beckmann (1958) has shown the value of a random element in reconciling Christaller's stepped hierarchy with the lognormal distribution (Section 5.2.4) and we might borrow his argument here and apply it to field shape.

There are, however, departures from the theoretical form which are more serious and more persistent. Some fields are severely truncated, others are systematically distorted, still others are fragmented. These non-symmetric forms demand a different type of explanation and are treated separately here:

(i) A typical form for the *truncated* field is shown in Figure 2.12C. Perhaps the most dramatic and well-known illustration of this type comes from a study of the location of El Paso bank accounts made by Lösch (1954, p. 448). He was able to show for an American bank on the United States–Mexican border that in 1914 the radius of its field on the Mexican side was only half that of the United States side.

A similar indication of the distorting effect of political boundaries has been given by Mackay (1958). He fitted to the observed interactions between Montreal and surrounding cities (as measured by long-distance telephone traffic) a gravity model whose basic form was similar to that given in equation (2.2); that is, in the notation of this chapter,

$$T_{ij} = k. \frac{P_i^a P_j^b}{d_{ij}^\beta} \tag{2.25}$$

where $a$, $b$ and $\beta$ are parameters to be estimated, and $k$ is a constant. $\beta$ represents, as before, the estimated average fall off in interaction with increasing distance. His results showed that the traffic between Montreal, which is in Quebec Province, and other cities in Quebec province (Figure 2.13A) was from five to ten times greater than traffic between Montreal and

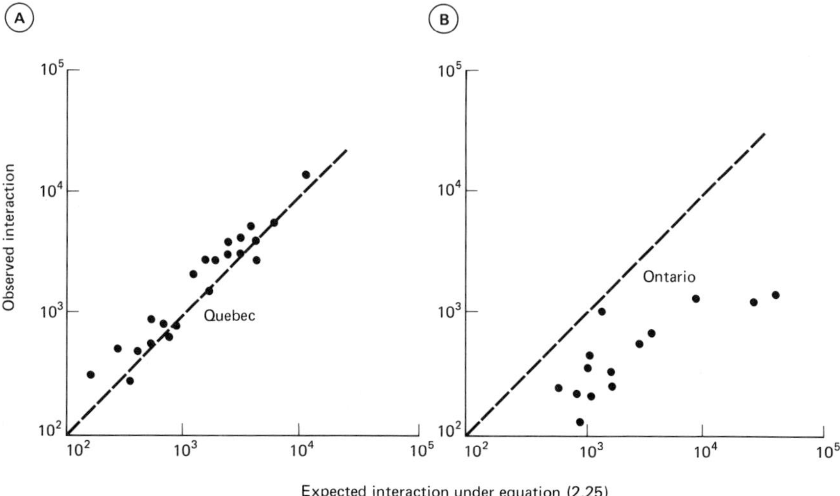


**Figure 2.13** Impact of the Quebec–Ontario border on interaction around the city of Montreal. The pecked lines represent equality between observed and expected levels of interaction. Note that calls to Ontario fall below this line, whereas those to Quebec are scattered around it. Source: Mackay, 1958, p. 5.

cities of comparable size and distance away in the neighbouring Ontario province (Figure 2.13B). The strength of the provincial barrier in blocking the extension of the Montreal field was itself overshadowed by the blocking effect of the international boundary to the south. Traffic with comparable cities in the United States was down to one-fiftieth of that of the Quebec traffic. Mackay's technique allows a rather clear measurement to be made of the effect of boundaries on shaping fields and it might usefully be extended to other areas. Truncation may not, however, be just a political effect. Vance (1962) has shown how the trade areas of eleven regional shopping centres in the San Francisco Bay area are modified by the north-south trend of the Coastal Ranges and more specifically by the relatively high toll costs in crossing the inlets of the Bay itself.

A general graphical model which relates the blocking action of both physical and political elements has been devised by Lösch (1954, p. 341). When the barrier is a political one, marked by tariff increases, the potential field of centre *i* is restricted by the distance, *d*, to the barrier, but the actual form of the truncated field may vary. Figure 2.14A shows the probable form if the political boundary can be crossed at all points along its length; Figure 2.14B the probable form if it can be crossed only at a customs point, *j*. If the boundary is not a political one, but a natural feature (e.g. a river) with a single crossing point at *j*, the field will probably conform to that of Figure 2.14C (cf. the effect of barriers on diffusion waves discussed in Section 7.5.1).

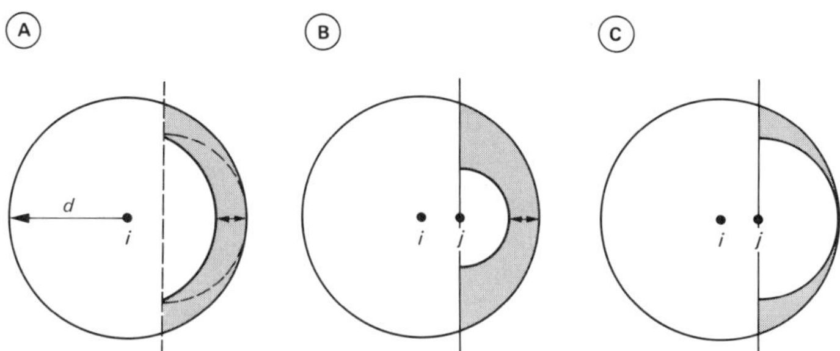


**Figure 2.14** Impact of boundaries on the size of field centred on *i*. Source: Lösch, 1954, p. 341.

(ii) *Distorted* fields vary more widely in shape. Applebaum and Cohen (1961, p. 81) describe the shape of the trading areas of outlying shopping centres as parabolically elongated away from the central business district. Similarly, Park (1929) was able to show that the circulation fields for daily newspapers in part of the central United States (South Dakota) were asymmetrically elongated away from the areas of intense competition. Figure 2.12D shows a general case for these types of distorted field.

There is a strong probability that some of this asymmetry can be accommodated within the ideas of Isard and Getis (reviewed in Section 2.7.3) who argue that fields may *appear* as distortions, merely because they are the transformations of fields which are regular in terms of non-geographic space. In the special case of migration fields, Stouffer (1940) has suggested that we should not in any case expect fields to be circular because there is no necessary deterministic relation between migration and geographical distance. His intervening opportunity model has been reviewed earlier in this chapter (see Section 2.3.4). The model has been used by Isbell (1944) and Folger (1953) in studies of internal migration in Sweden and the Tennessee Valley in the eastern United States. In both cases the intervening-opportunity model gave better prediction than the simple gravity-type model.

In terms of our distorted fields (Figure 2.12D) we may argue that Stouffer's model allows an adequate explanation both for the restriction of the field on the inner side (i.e. the intervening opportunities of the larger centre cut into its potential area) and the extension on the outer side (i.e. lack of intervening opportunity gives the centre a clear run to extend on this side). While more realistic models are clearly needed, some progress has been made towards accommodating our distorted fields within general interaction models.

(iii) *Fragmented* fields consist of a contiguous inner area with one or more 'outliers' of high interaction. Figure 2.12E suggests the general form of such a field. Hägerstrand (1957, pp. 126–54) has drawn together a number of regional examples of this type of field in migration movements. One of the most striking examples is that of Värmland, in central Sweden, which was the main source of migrants for nearby areas and for an area 400 kilometres away but *not* for intervening areas. Other cases of similar discontinuities come from migration into Paris and Budapest at the national level, and the remarkable concentrations of German migration within specific small areas of North America at the international level (Johnson, 1941).

Hägerstrand finds three common elements in all these cases: (i) the importance of the information chain represented by individual contacts, (ii) the division of migrants into *active* and *passive* elements, with the latter importance of the information chain represented by individual contacts, (ii) the division of migrants into *active* and *passive* elements, with the latter following the definite channels made by the former, and (iii) the random element in the initial choice of areas. While it was not possible to build a comprehensive *feedback* model to accommodate all three elements, Hägerstrand has suggested a short term model. This is given by the expression

$$M_{ij} = (V_j I_j)/P_j . k \qquad (2.26)$$

where $M_{ij}$ is the number of migrants moving from location $i$ to location $j$, $V_j$ is the number of vacancies at $j$, $I_j$ is the *information level* about these vacancies existing at the source $i$, $P_j$ is the population of the destination $j$, and $k$ is a constant. Thus, the volume of migration is related to the *vacancy density* of the destination and the level of information about it. Here distance is introduced indirectly through the information level since there is likely to be more information available about very near places than about very distant places.

Table 2.6 Comparison of intervening-opportunity and feedback models in predicting migration*

| *Distance zone (kilometres):* | 0–19 | 20–39 | 40–59 | 60–79 | 80–99 |
|---|---|---|---|---|---|
| Observed migration | 86 | 132 | 42 | 18 | 12 |
| Predicted migration using model: | | | | | |
| Intervening-opportunity | 105 | 89 | 39 | 29 | 29 |
| Feedback | 89† | 131† | 41† | 17† | 13† |

Source: Hägerstrand, 1957, pp. 125, 153.

* Dädesjö, Sweden, 1946–50.
† Estimates within ±10 per cent of observed migration.

Hägerstrand has tested his model on Swedish migration data, using Monte Carlo methods to simulate the random selection of areas and their rates of growth. Some indication of the considerable relative success of the feedback model is shown in Table 2.6 where its predictions are compared with a simple intervening-opportunity model.

## 2.7 Interaction Territories

While continuous fields which fluctuate over time are the dominant pattern in the organization of regional systems, they pose such severe administrative problems that human society establishes boundaries (where there are continuities) and discrete non-overlapping territories (where there are overlapping and indistinct fields). Political areas are the most readily recognizable reaction to this problem, but they are by no means unique, and we can argue that the clerical diocese in England, the state planning *oblast* in Soviet Russia, and the tribal area in Amerindian Brazil are all reactions to that common problem. To be sure, there are differences between parish and state but each involves the notion of property and here we refer to them by the general term territory. Parallel ideas of territory are common in biology (Howard, 1920; Wynne-Edwards, 1962).

### 2.7.1 *Elementary packing theory*

With discrete territories, the basic problem is simply that of the efficient partitioning of areas between competing centres. We may define efficiency in two ways: *efficiency of movement* as measured by the distance from the centre to outlying parts within the territory, and *efficiency of boundaries* as measured by the length of the territory's perimeter. This second criterion, important in practical terms as fencing costs on the farm or defence costs for the state, is not pertinent in continuous fields.

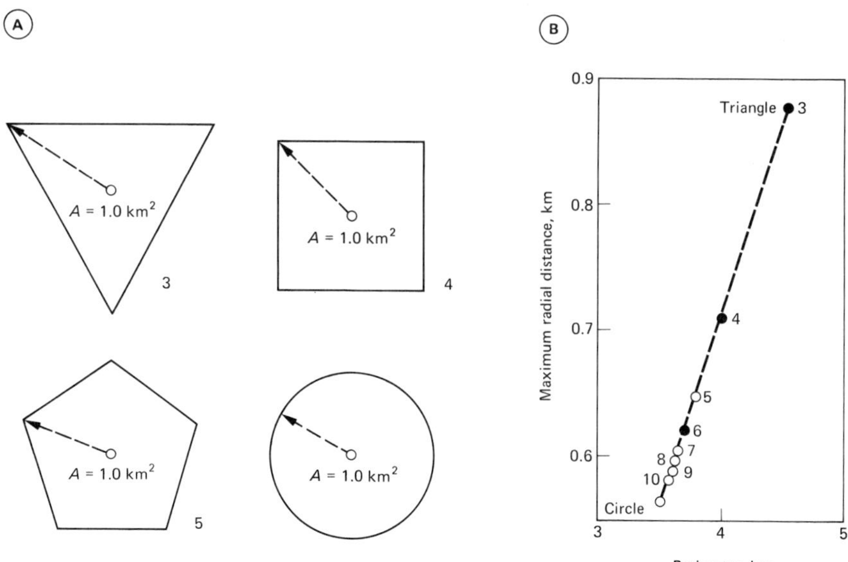


**Figure 2.15** Efficiency of alternative types of regular polygon in relation to distance from centres and perimeter length. The numbers indicate the number of sides to the figure, while the solid circles denote shapes which will form a regular tesselation. $A$ = area.

Three geometrical principles are important in applying these minimum energy criteria to the division of an area (Coxeter, 1961):

(i) Regular polygons are more economical shapes than irregular polygons. If we take the familiar four-sided polygon, we can illustrate that, for the regular square shape with an area of one square kilometre, the furthest movement (i.e. from the centre to the furthest point within the square) is 0.707 kilometres and the perimeter is four kilometres. If we convert the regular square form to a rectangle of similar area but with two of its sides twice as long as the others, the furthest movement goes up to 1.031 kilometres and the perimeter to five kilometres. Experimentation demonstrates how, the greater the contrast in the sides of the rectangle, the less economical it becomes in terms of both accessibility from the centre and length of perimeter.

(ii) Circles are the most economical of the regular polygons. If we imagine a continuum of regular polygons running from the triangle, square, pentagon and hexagon upwards, then at each stage we are increasing the number of sides and vertices by one. The limiting case is clearly the circle which we may regard as a regular polygon with an infinite number of sides and vertices. If we examine this sequence (Figure 2.15A) we see that, if the area remains constant, the accessibility from the centre as measured by the *maximum radial distance* improves and the perimeter becomes shorter. The relation of these two parameters is plotted in Figure 2.15B, and it is important to note that though the improvement in economy is consistent, the gains are not regular: the

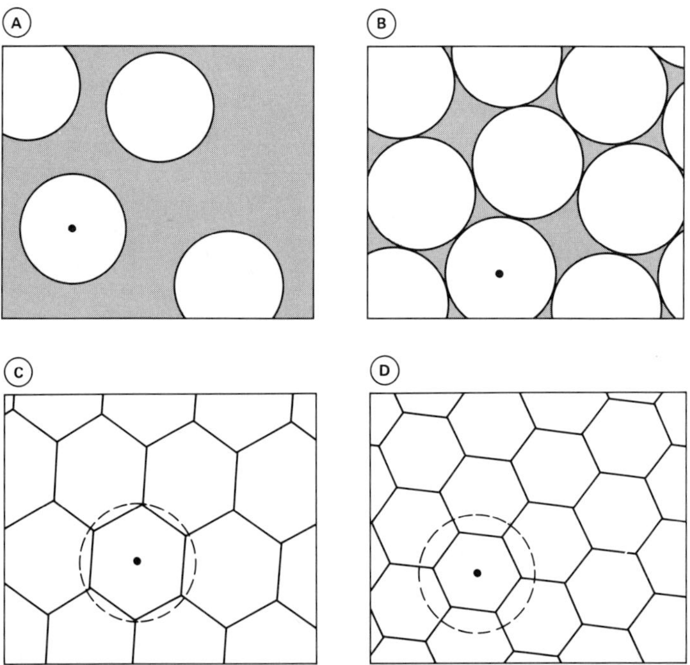


**Figure 2.16** Packing of centres in the colonization of a plain to give hexagonal territories. Source: Lösch, 1954, p. 110.

square is about half as efficient as the circle and the decagon about 90 per cent as efficient as the circle.

(iii) Hexagons are the regular polygons which allow the greatest amount of packing into an area, consistent with minimizing movement and boundary costs. The problem of packing circular fields into a hypothetical area is illustrated in Figure 2.16, which shows with shading its inefficiency as measured by the unused areas lying between the circles. The problem of filling a plane with equal area regular polygons was first investigated by Kepler in the early seventeenth century, who suggested there were three solutions: the regular triangle, the regular square, and the regular hexagon. Of these three regular tessellations (Coxeter, 1961, pp. 61–4), the hexagon retains most of the advantages of the circle. Indeed, as Figure 2.15B shows, the hexagon is about four-fifths as efficient as the circle in terms of maximum radial distance and perimeter.

Hexagons have held a fascination for natural scientists and mathematicians since the Greeks; concepts of hexagonal symmetry played a key role in the growth of crystallography, and Thompson (1961, pp. 102–25) has shown its importance throughout the biological sciences. It is not surprising, therefore, that the two main theoretical works on settlements and their support fields, Christaller's *Die zentralen Orte in Süddeutschland* (1933; trans. 1966) and Lösch's *Die raumliche Ordnung der Wirtschaft* (1940; 1954) should have used the hexagon as the modular unit in their models of settlement structure. These are discussed in Chapter 5.

### 2.6.2 *Regional packing studies*

In addition to the theoretical interest in the hexagon, some concern has been shown in trying to test whether hexagonal arrangements do in fact exist in reality. The dominant impression one receives on examining maps of territories such as counties, or parishes or states, is one of irregularity and complexity. To test whether this impression is a correct one, a simple random sample of 100 counties was drawn from one country (Brazil) and their packing characteristics examined. Since this country had, in 1960, some 2,800 counties (*municipios*) and since, unlike the United States with its 'township and range' system (see Section 4.1), it did not set out its administrative units on geometrical lines, Brazil represents a reasonably unbiased sample for such an examination.

A simple shape index, $S$, was used to measure the shape characteristics of the Brazilian sample. It was given as

$$S = 1.27A/l^2 \qquad (2.27)$$

where $A$ is the area of the county in square kilometres, and $l$ is the long axis of the county drawn as a straight line connecting the two most distant points on the perimeter. The multiplier (1.27) adjusted the index so that a circle would have an index of 1.00 with values ranging down towards zero. (Note that other and more elaborate measures of shape are reviewed in Sections 9.6 and 14.5.2; see also Massam, 1975, Chapter 2). The actual shape values recorded by this method are shown in Figure 2.17 and range from values as low as 0.06 for very elongated counties to values as high as 0.93 for compact near-circular counties.

In this measuring system, the values for the three regular lattices are 0.42 for triangular, 0.64 for square, and 0.83 for hexagonal, and boundary lines have been interpolated on Figure 2.17 to divide the sequence into three zones about these values. The results strongly suggest the generally elongated nature of the counties. However, the possible correspondence of the lattice boundaries with gaps in the frequency distribution may suggest that shapes tend to cluster about the three alternative tessellations proposed by Kepler.

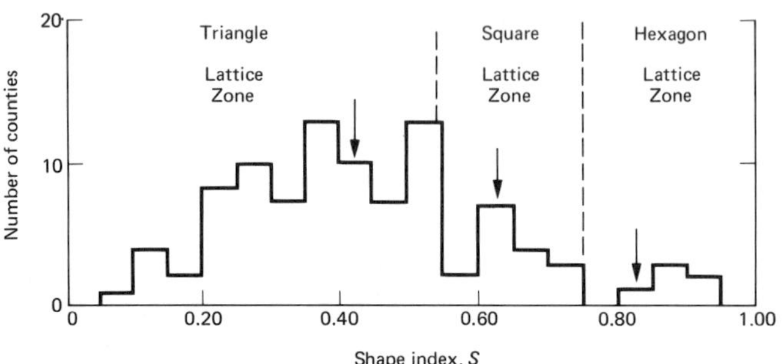


**Figure 2.17** Shape characteristics of a sample of 100 Brazilian counties in relation to lattice zones.

A second characteristic associated with the regular hexagonal tessellation is the number of contacts between any one territory and adjacent territories. In a regular hexagonal system, the *contact number* is clearly six, as one area is contiguous with its six neighbours, each of which has in turn six neighbours. To examine the contact number with the Brazilian data, coastal counties and those on the international frontier were eliminated from the sample since these had their fields truncated. The remaining 84 counties were examined and their contact numbers recorded. The frequency curve of the results is shown in Figure 2.18A. It shows that, although the number of contacts varied from two to thirteen, nearly one in three counties had exactly six neighbours. The mean contact number for the sample was 5.71. This rather striking approximation to the hexagonal number proposed by Christaller and Lösch may suggest that criticism of the hexagonal system as over-theoretical is too hasty. Preliminary counts by Haggett on administrative areas in France and China suggest that the Brazilian figure is not exceptional, but further investigation is necessary before we can be sure we have isolated a regularity in territorial organization.

Pedersen (1967) has made some move in this direction by making counts of contact numbers of the administrative communes in Scotland and of Fyn in Denmark. For the 553 communes studied, the average number of neighbours was found to be 5.83. It was shown, however, that this number should not be interpreted as indicative of the existence of a hexagonal net structure, for 'blurring' of basic triangular or square nets can give very similar averages. Comparison of the distribution of all communes, together with an analysis of their shape characteristics, led Pedersen to conclude that the administrative net in Denmark is basically triangular (about sixty per cent) with hexagonal elements largely absent.

Experimental evidence on contact numbers is available from work by

Dacey and Tung (1962), who constructed a series of synthetic point patterns in which points were randomly dislocated a mean distance, $\rho$, from the positions they would assume on a hexagonal lattice. The amount of random disturbance was measured by an index, $k$, where:

$$k = \rho/(1.075\lambda^{-1/2}) \tag{2.28}$$

and $\lambda$ is the expectation that a unit area contains a nucleus. Points were used as the nuclei for the construction of Dirichlet regions (see Section 13.5), so that sets of pseudo-random polygons were produced with the properties that (i) any two polygons have at most one edge in common; (ii) the tesselation of polygons is uniquely determined, and (iii) each vertex is connected to three or four other edges (Dacey, 1963, p. 3). Contact numbers were studied for patterns with slight disturbance ($k = 0.05$) to patterns in which the degree of random disturbance was so large that all trace of the underlying hexagonal lattice was lost ($k = 3.00$). For each of the patterns studied, the mean number of edges was found to be less than six, and for values of $k$ greater than 0.30 the mean number of contacts was between 5.7 and 5.8. Dacey (1963) has derived an expected value of 5.7888 for the number of contacts in a system of random polygons, rather than the value of six assumed in random crystal aggregates (Meijering, 1953; cf. the discussion on Thiessen polygons in Section 13.5).

One recognizable trend within the Brazilian sample was for counties with a high population density to be more closely packed, and therefore to have a higher contact number than lightly populated areas. Figure 2.18B shows the contact index (contact number/area of the county) plotted against the population density of each county to give a positive relationship. This relationship has been examined over a ninety-year period for one of the

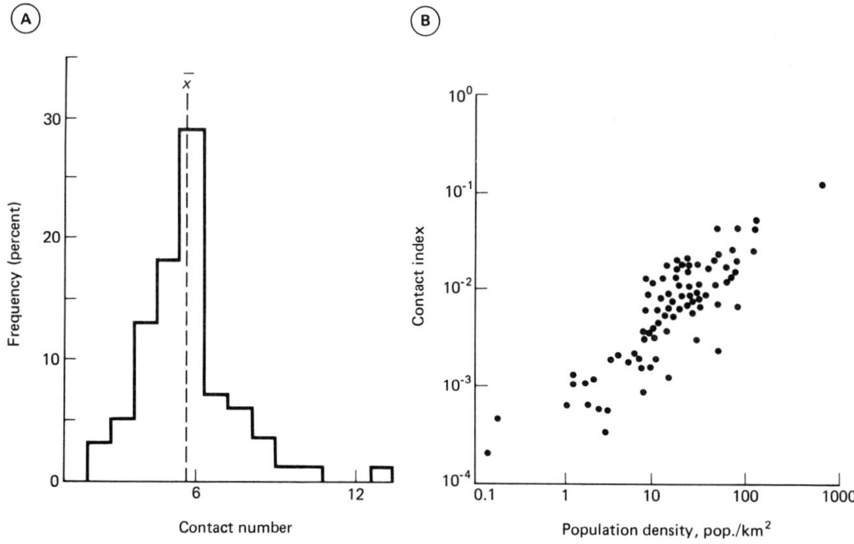


**Figure 2.18** Histogram of contact numbers of 100 Brazilian counties (**A**) and their relation to population density (**B**). The contact index = contact number/area of county.

Brazilian states (Santa Catarina) and shows that with the build-up of population density the counties have become smaller (Figure 2.19) while the contact numbers have increased from 3.50 in 1872 to 5.22 in 1960. The lower numbers in the latter period, compared to the rest of Brazil, are due to the nature of the sample: all counties (including those in coastal and state-line locations) were examined. How far the increasing congruence with 'minimum energy' solutions over time can be interpreted in rational terms remains to be seen.

### 2.7.3 *Modifications of the hexagon model*

Isard (1956) has shown that the *regular* (i.e. equal area) pattern of hexagons suggested by Christaller and Lösch is unlikely to occur in practice. Because of

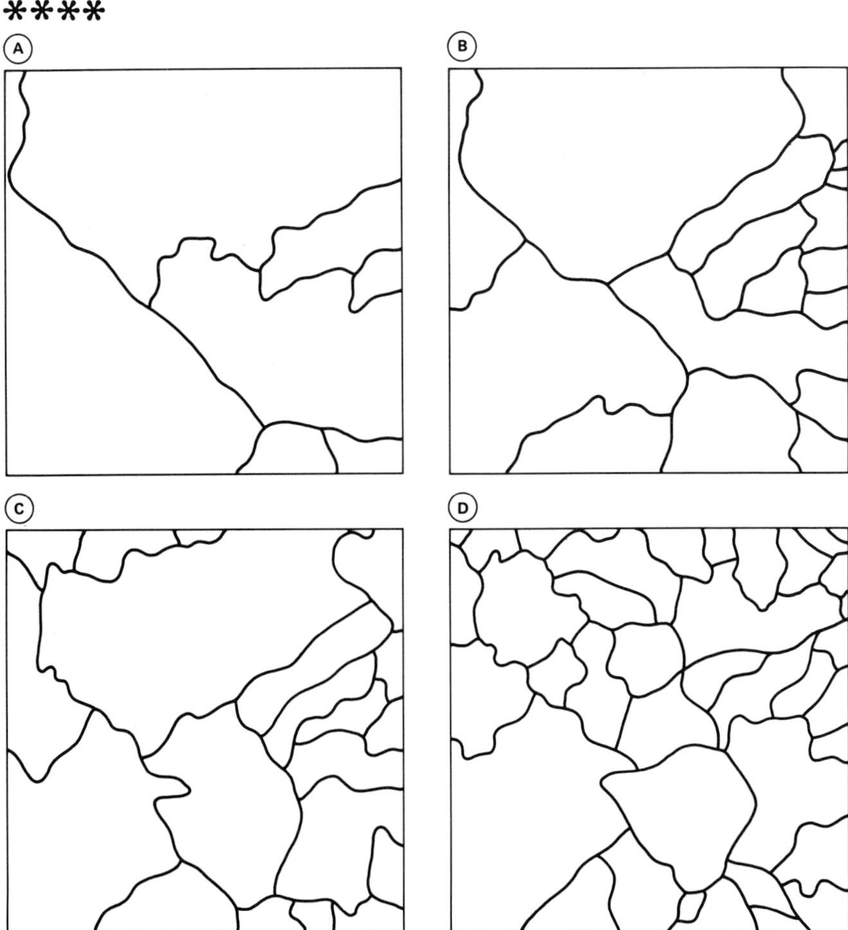


**Figure 2.19** Progressive territorial subdivision of sample quadrat in Santa Catarina state, Brazil. **A** 1872. **B** 1907. **C** 1930. **D** 1960. Source: Buchéle, 1958.

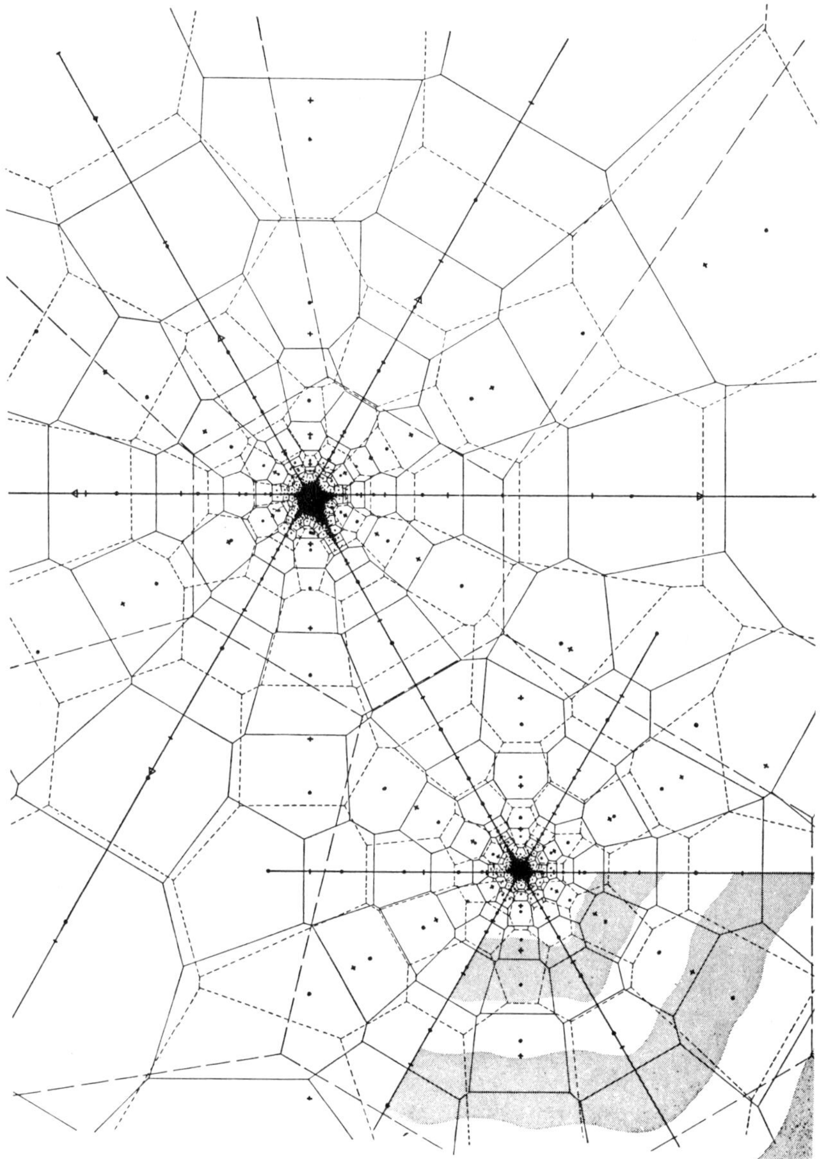

**Figure 2.20** Löschian system of hexagonal territories as modified by agglomeration. Source: Isard, 1956, p. 272.

the high density of population at the central core postulated by Lösch, the size of the market area here is likely to be smaller, while away from the market it is likely to be larger. Isard has produced a figure (Figure 2.20) which retains as many of the assumptions of the Löschian system as possible, but introduces this concept of more closely packed centres near the overall nodal point.

Extreme difficulty was found in working with the hexagonal form and, as the figure shows, it was impossible to retain both the hexagon and urbanization economies. As Isard points out, the hexagon is a pure concept much as perfect competition is a pure concept to the economist. It loses its significance as a spatial form once the inevitable agglomeration forces—which are themselves inherent in the Löschian system—are allowed to operate.

Confirmation of the changing size of territories away from the dense urban centres is available from Brazil. By using the same sample of 100 Brazilian counties described earlier, the size of territories in relation to population density was investigated. County areas were found to be approximately lognormal in distribution with a few very large areas (like Sena Madureira in the Acre Territory of the upper Amazon with an area of 46,000 square kilometres) extending down to areas as small as London boroughs in the Rio de Janeiro area. Size was rather strongly but inversely correlated with population density so that the large fields occurred in lightly populated areas whereas the small fields were characteristic of areas of dense population. Again, this phenomenon does not appear to be limited to Brazil: the county

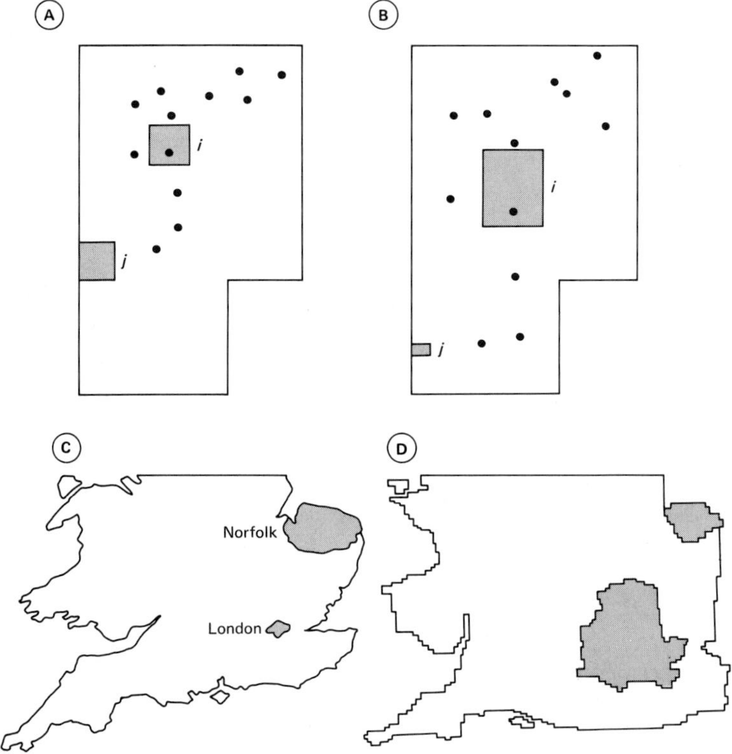


**Figure 2.21** Transformation of conventional maps into income and population space. **A, B** Transformation of sample sector of Tacoma city, United States, into income-space map. **C, D** Transformation of southern England into population-space map. Sources: Getis, 1963, pp. 18, 20; *The Times*, London, October 19, 1964, p. 18.

maps of the United States or the parish maps of Britain show a generally similar trend.

A second source of confirmation for Isard's modification has come from a study by Getis (1963) of the southeastern part of the city of Tacoma in the United States. Getis investigated the distribution of stores within this urban area in relation to locational theory. He found that the 'normal' geographical pattern shown by the regular divisions of township-and-range on Figure 2.21A showed little suggestion of any regularities in store distribution (shown by black dots) throughout the area. Income values were computed for each of the 48 cells within this and a map drawn (Figure 2.21B) to show the size of each cell proportional to its income value; thus cell $i$ with a high income has a large area, and cell $j$ with a low income has a small area. In this map, the distribution of stores appears far more regular.

It will be clear from both maps that the overall size and shape of the maps is the same and that only the internal divisions, the cells, have been changed. What Getis has achieved is a transformation of normal or geographical space into income space. As Tobler (1963) has urged, there are a number of such projections or transformations that might prove useful in testing locational theory. One example of a *population-space* map is shown for southern Britain. Figure 2.21C shows the familiar geographical shape, and Figure 2.21D a transformation of this shape on the basis of the voting population of electoral districts in 1964. The relative change in size of the counties of Norfolk and London show the extent of the distortion. In this case contiguity between electoral districts has been preserved but otherwise distortion in the outline of the area has been allowed.

We may argue from the work of both Isard and Getis that we should not expect regular hexagonal territories to be generally visible on the earth's surface, because they are related not to geographical space but to population or income space. Hexagons may therefore be thought to be latent in most human organization but only through appropriate transformations of geographical space is their form likely to be made visible.

## 2.8 Conclusions

In this chapter, we have begun our study of the interconnected web of regional structure with consideration of spatial interaction. These interactions, or flows across geographical space, are the major force shaping the locational form of the networks, nodes and surfaces that we next examine. Using Newtonian analogies, early locational models of spatial flow had begun to be developed in the last century. In the last two decades, work on these so-called gravity models has intensified and Wilson's reformulation in the terms of statistical mechanics has provided a more secure theoretical base for further work.

Study of interaction leads inevitably to a consideration of the dual concept, the boundary or edge at which flows cease or fall below some relevant threshold. The fields and territories which are created by these boundaries are picked up again later in the book—notably in considering settlement systems (Chapter 5) and regional aggregation (Chapter 14).

# 3 Networks

3.1 **Introduction.** 3.2 **Location of Routes:** 1 Positive deviations; 2 Negative deviations; 3 Other distortions. 3.3 **Network Location:** 1 Floating-point location problems; 2 Optimum network designs. 3.4 **Routes Through Networks:** 1 Combinatorial aspects of network structure; 2 Travelling salesman problem; 3 Spanning tree problems; 4 Other shortest-path problems. 3.5 **Empirical Studies of Network Structure:** 1 Regional variations in network geometry; 2 Density patterns of route networks; 3 Route development models. 3.6 **Conclusions.**

## 3.1 Introduction

Although many of the interactions considered in Chapter 2 were unrestricted in the sense that they could flow freely in any direction, most movements are constricted in some sort of channel. Even air-routes are, as Warntz (1961) has shown for the North Atlantic, confined to corridors; most movements flow along fixed channels—roads, pipelines, telephone wires. These features themselves pose distinct locational problems which are regarded here as part of a general class of network problems. Network location has a literature which includes some classic early studies (e.g. Lalanne, 1863) but it is a topic which has been strangely neglected in standard treatments of locational theory. It represents an area of common interest for both human geography and physical geography (Haggett and Chorley, 1969).

Here we develop some of the more elementary spatial models of network structure relating to location, density, and change over time. Readers are referred to Chapter 9 (see especially Section 9.7) for a description of measures of network structure.

## 3.2 Location of Routes

Route location is one of the least developed parts of locational theory and, in treating it here, an attempt is made to piece together some of the fragments rather than to illustrate a complete structure. We begin by considering the location of the simplest component, the single route, and then move on to the form of the route network. If we assume the need to build a route between two settlements, $i$ and $j$, then the intuitive answer to the locational problem of where to build the route is simply to join them by a straight line (Figure 3.1A). However, when we observe the actual location of routes we find that, with very few exceptions, all routes between centres follow a more or less complex path which deviates at least slightly from the geometrical straight-line solution. Two types of deviation have received special mention in locational theory.

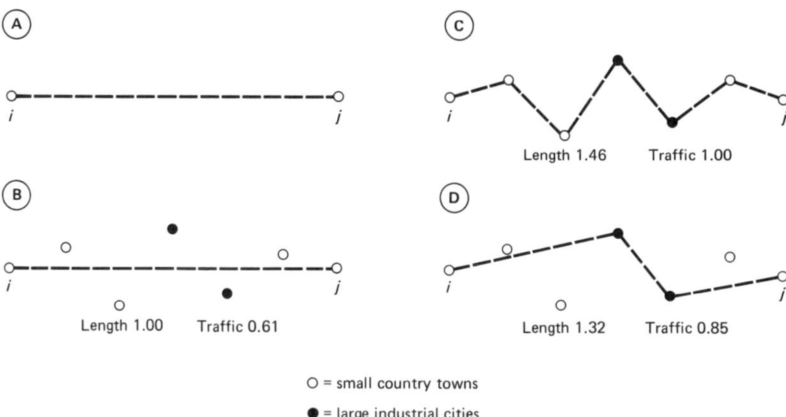


**Figure 3.1** Alternative paths between two points which ignore intermediate centres (**A**), minimize length (**B**), maximize traffic (**C**), and optimize length and traffic (**D**).

### 3.2.1 *Positive deviations*

One type of deviation, in which the route is lengthened in order to collect more freight, here termed *positive* deviation, has been considered in an early work by Wellington (1887). Wellington, a mining engineer, worked for some time in the third quarter of the nineteenth century on the planning of the railway system in Mexico, and was particularly concerned with alternative routes between the capital, Mexico City, and the gulf port, Vera Cruz (Wellington, 1886). His major difficulty was to estimate the effect of connecting or ignoring smaller centres lying between Mexico City and Vera Cruz along the general line of the route. His dilemma is shown in Figure 3.1. It consists essentially of a problem in optimizing the relationship between length of railroad (the shorter the better) and the amount of traffic (the greater the better). From the data he was able to assemble, Wellington put forward three basic propositions: (i) that if all intermediate points were of equal generating capacity and if they were equally spaced, then traffic varied as the square of the number of points served; (ii) that if the intermediate points were 'small country towns' without a competing alternative railway, then the effect of placing the station away from the town (Figure 3.1B) was to reduce gross revenue by 10 per cent for every mile that the station was removed from the town centre; (iii) that if the intermediate points were 'large industrial cities' with competing railway facilities, then the loss would be still more abrupt: a reduction of 25 per cent for every mile that the station was removed from the town centre.

Extreme solutions to a hypothetical problem are to minimize length of line

(Figure 3.1B) or to maximize traffic (Figure 3.1C). If we assume that the direct distance from $i$ to $j$ is 1.0, and that the maximum traffic generated *in toto* from the intermediate towns (open circles) and industrial cities (closed circles) is 1.0, then the first solution reduces traffic to 0.61 and the second solution increases the rail-length to 1.46. An intermediate compromise (Figure 3.1D) linking only the industrial centres keeps the traffic to 0.85 and increases rail-length to only 1.32.

The value of this early analysis lies not in its absolute findings so much as in its illustration of the kind of locational problems faced in route construction. The actual values used by Wellington were of doubtful accuracy even for nineteenth-century Mexico, and like von Thünen's ring distances (Chapter 6), their use is largely illustrative. Railway location was largely a problem for the middle and late nineteenth century rather than today, and we should perhaps view the rationale of railroad location over most of the world's railroad systems in this historical context.

### 3.2.2 *Negative deviations*

The second type of deviation, here termed a *negative* deviation, comes from the need to avoid certain barriers or to minimize the distance travelled through high-cost areas. Lösch (1954, p. 184) has commented on the application of the 'laws of refraction' to the study of route location. Figure 3.2 shows two

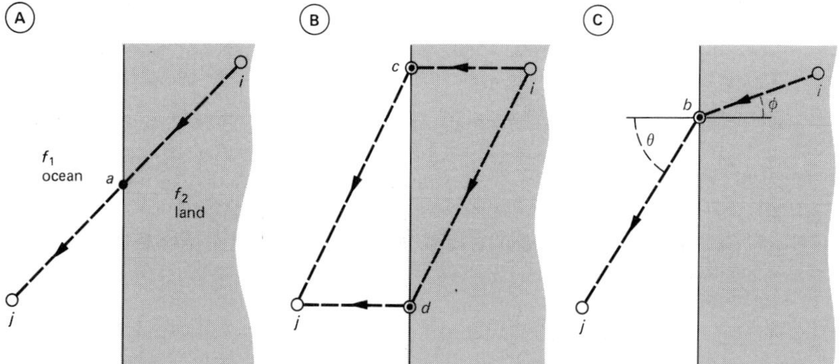


**Figure 3.2** Laws of refraction applied to route location. Source: Lösch, 1954, p. 184.

standard applications of Snell's law (Sears and Zemansky, 1964, p. 842) in a simplified context. The problem is to find a sea–land route by which a product can be shipped as cheaply as possible from $i$ to $j$, and to locate a new port along the coastline at the trans-shipment point. We assume that the coastline is everywhere favourable and equally costly for port construction. The direct route between $i$ and $j$ crosses the coastline at $a$ (Figure 3.2A). If we introduce a practical element of transport cost, we know that the cost of overland hauls is not the same as for ocean hauls. We assume a cheap ocean freight rate, $f_1$, and a more costly land freight rate, $f_2$. Lösch has shown that the least-cost location of the port will be where

$$f_1 \sin\theta - f_2 \sin\phi = 0 \qquad (3.1)$$

where $\theta$ and $\phi$ are the angles that the two transport routes make to the coastline. This gives the least transport cost port site, *b* (Figure 3.2C). The greater the cost of rail freight in relation to ocean freight the nearer will the location of the port approach to *c*; conversely as ocean freight rates rise, the optimum trans-shipment point moves towards *d* (Figure 3.2B).

Figure 3.3 shows a more complex case of the same refraction principle. Here,

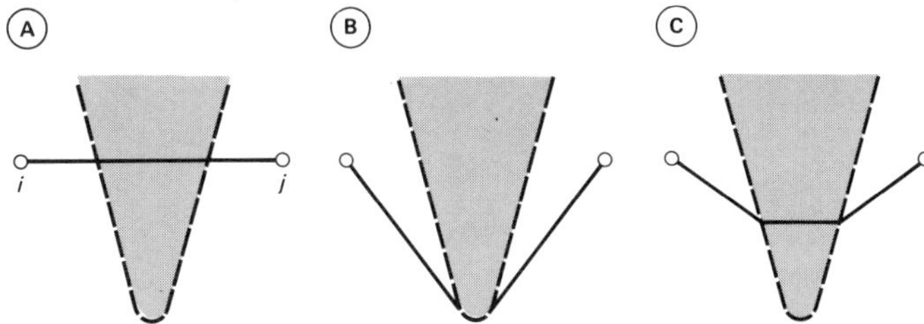


**Figure 3.3** Alternative cases of route refraction. Source: Lösch, 1954, p. 186.

the route between *i* and *j* has to cross a mountain range (stippled). The cost per mile of the route across the plains is much smaller than the cost through the mountains, so that the direct route is not the cheapest. The higher the cost of traversing the mountain area (or the greater the refractive index in Lösch's analogy) the more the least effort route will be deflected southwards (Figure 3.3B). The final compromise location (Figure 3.3C) will depend on the construction and running costs over the two media of plain and mountain.

Lest this example seems too highly theoretical, Lösch reminds us of the 'deflection' of a great deal of nineteenth-century trade between the east coast of the United States and California via the Cape Horn route, a diversion which added some 9,200 miles to the direct distance overland across the United States. An equally direct parallel occurs in this century with the planning of a trans-isthmian canal across central America. Of the two major routes considered (the Nicaraguan cut and the Panama cut), the sea distance between the eastern and western United States would have been most strikingly reduced by the northern route (the Nicaraguan cut) but this saving was insignificant compared to the saving in construction costs on the shorter Panama cut. Again, it is the ratio of the costs that is important. Had the cost of ocean transport been much higher, the advantages of a more northerly route might have been decisive. Since other than United States shipping used the canal, the decision was far less simple in reality, but the basis of Lösch's idea remains valid. Specht (1959) has drawn attention to ferry costs and resultant route 'bending' around Lake Michigan, while a small-scale example from the English countryside that makes the point as well is the orientation of bridges across railway lines. Unless a road is of major importance the bridge spans the railway at or near a right angle, deviating from the general direction of the road on either side of the bridge. Lösch would describe this as a result of the very strong refractive or bending power of the bridge-construction costs on the alignment of the route. Similar effects occurred with the construction of Brindley's contour canals in the eighteenth century, such as the Trent and Mersey, and may be contrasted with Telford's straight cuts such as the

Shropshire Union; Telford's canals were much dearer to build but produced increased revenue by drastically reducing travel times.

The law of refraction has been extended by Werner (1968) to allow the identification of a transport route that minimizes total construction cost when an area is partitioned into a number of cost regions. The refraction analogue can be supplemented by network selection methods in which an optimum set of links may be chosen from a large range of possible connection patterns. Developments in more advanced route location models are discussed in Haggett and Chorley (1969, Chapter 4).

### 3.2.3 *Other distortions*

Empirical studies of individual routes, like those of Vance (1961) on the contrasting course of the Oregon Trail and the Union Pacific Railroad across the Rocky Mountains, or of Monbeig (1952) on the routes across the Serra do Mar in southeastern Brazil, show that in no case was the location ever as simple as Lösch's geometry suggests. Equally, in no case does its influence appear to be lacking. One major factor causing variation from the *lex parsimoniae*, Lösch's law of least effort, is the political aspect of a transport route. This was considered by C. H. Cooley in one of the earliest studies of transport theory (Cooley, 1894, p. 53) and also by Wolfe in *Transportation and politics* (1963). Certainly in railroad building, the association between the Canadian Pacific Railroad and the unification of Canada, and similarly between the Trans-Siberian railroad and Russia, is symbolic, even though the impact of the railroads may have been less decisive than was once thought. Even the detailed pattern of route networks may reflect major and minor political differences. In Figure 3.4 the 'aligning' effect of the major boundary between the United States and Canada (stippled) on railroads (Figure 3.4A) is

***

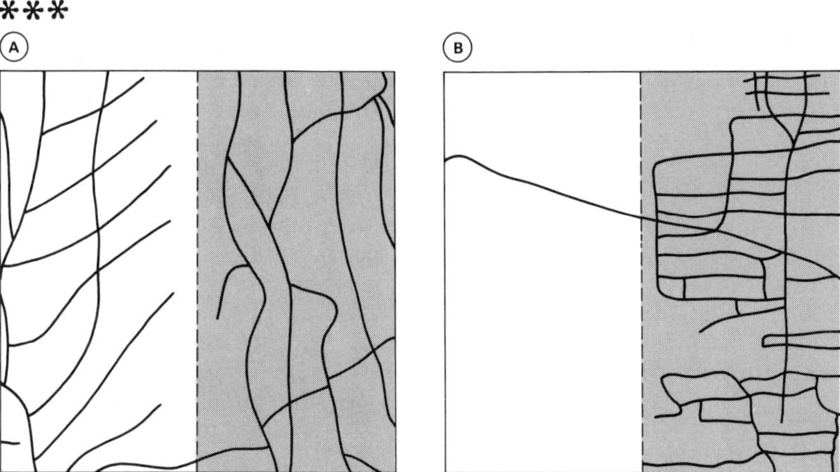


**Figure 3.4** Truncation of networks by territorial boundaries. **A** Rail network in a sample quadrat on the Canada–United States border. **B** Road network in a sample quadrat on the Ontario–Quebec border, Canada. Source: Wolfe, 1962, pp. 184, 185.

paralleled by the 'blocking' effect of the minor boundary between Ontario and Quebec (stippled) on road patterns (Figure 3.4B).

Meinig (1962) has examined the historical geography of two railnets: (i) a wholly state-directed enterprise in South Australia and (ii) one built and operated by several private companies in the Columbia Basin of the northwestern United States. They were chosen for comparative study since they were built and developed at roughly the same time, were both in wheat-growing regions, and were both designed largely to move export grain from the farming districts to tidewater ports. Meinig found a number of common features in the railway net developed in the two areas. Both extended at about the same pace, the one (i) in response to political pressure and concepts of public service, and the other (ii) in response to profit possibilities. Both were complicated by changes in the general orientation of trade to different ports and both were affected by the influence of local communities on routing. In both, too, the number of possible routes from an engineering standpoint always outweighed the routes that were financially feasible (see Figure 1.9). Differences between the state and private networks were found, however, to be the more striking, Meinig placing first the level of duplication of lines and services. In the Columbia basin, the links between inland exporting centres and tidewater ports were commonly duplicated and the exporter was faced with a choice of competitive services to different tidewater ports. There is a complete absence of such alternatives in South Australia. Moreover, the hinterlands of individual lines in South Australia remained stable in contrast to the constant piracy and 'invasion' of territories in the Columbia basin. Such fluidity in the privately owned network is suggested by Meinig as a cause of the rapid conversion and subsequent development of the Columbia basin system to a uniform gauge, while the South Australian system retained its relatively watertight hinterlands, each served by its own gauge. With the growth of government regulation in the United States, the original contrasts in the patterns are now fading slightly. The behavioural aspect of route construction at both the company and national government level is stressed by Hurst (1974) and readers are referred to this collection of readings for studies on this theme.

## 3.3 Network Location

In the case of the single route between two main centres, the solution to the location problem is basically trivial, subject to the empirical complications discussed in Section 3.2. However, once we extend the network to three or more centres, then route location rapidly becomes more complex, and we have a set of separate network location problems. Two main classes are examined here: (a) 'floating point' problems, where junctions in the network are allowed to occur at any location in the plane and (b) 'fixed point' problems, where junctions are confined to a finite set of locations (e.g. cities).

### 3.3.1 *Floating point location problems*

Let us assume a simple case where we wish to design a shortest-path network to connect three centres, each of similar population size. In this case, the problem becomes that of minimizing the sum ($H$) of the radial distances from a single junction to each city. This is equal to

$$\text{minimize } H = \sum_{i=1}^{3} \sum_{j=1}^{3} d_{ij} \tag{3.2}$$

where $d_{ij}$ is the network distance between any pair of centres, $i$ and $j$. Figure 3.5 shows two possible outcomes. If the triangle formed by three centres has no angle greater than or equal to 120°, then the optimum location for the junction is that point where the radial routes to each centre form three angles of 120° (Figure 3.5A). If the triangle contains an angle greater than 120° the optimal location for the junction is at that vertex (Figure 3.5B).

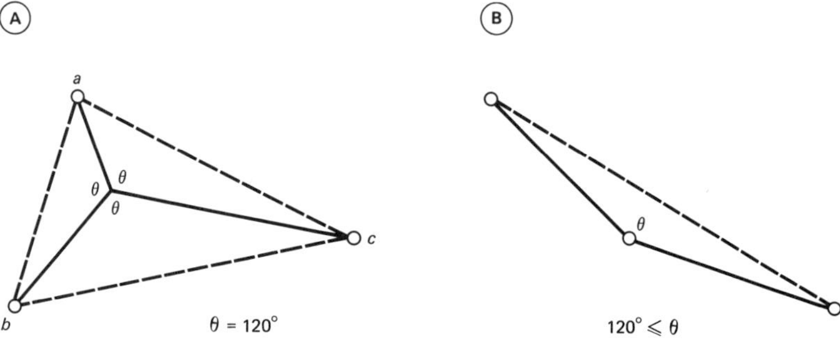


**Figure 3.5** Location of routes within a three city system.

From this simple base, the floating point problem can be extended in two main ways: (i) by considering networks connecting more than three centres, and (ii) by relaxing the assumption of 'uniform' size of centre.

(*a*) *Networks connecting four or more centres.* Miehle (1958) has shown that, for an $N$ point network, the *maximum* number of floating point junctions needed to construct a network which minimizes $H$ in (3.2) is $N-2$, where $N$ is the number of cities to be connected. For the example shown in Figure 3.6, the *maximum* number of three point junctions will therefore be 60. Note, however, that the *actual* number of junctions appears to be considerably less than this (only 23 in the case shown). The difference between the observed and expected numbers of junctions is due to the floating point being pulled into a location coincident with one of the fixed points or centres. The rule about 120° junctions shown in Figure 3.5A and B still holds in more complex figures, but the problem of which true floating point junctions to retain becomes the critical one.

Although no simple analytical solutions to this problem have been proposed, various iterative procedures have been used. For example, early 'hardware' analogue models were developed in an attempt to give direct solutions. Two of these methods, the *mechanical link-length minimizer* and the *soap-film method*, have been described at length by Morgan in Chorley and Haggett (1967, pp. 768–71). The soap-film method creates the necessary junctions and their locations by forming shapes which automatically reduce their area to a minimum. However, constraints on junction spacing and weighting of links are not possible and solutions for large numbers of points are not unique. In practice, therefore, the mechanical method has proved more workable as, despite its bulky appearance and inconvenient operation, large systems of points can be treated with integral weights assigned to individual links, and very rapid solutions of reasonable accuracy can be obtained. Silk (1965) made extensive use of a 33-point model in a study of optimal road designs for the county of Monmouth. Here, fixed pegs located on a 1/63,360 base board were used to represent settlements within the county, and a system of pulleys and string was employed to structure the network.

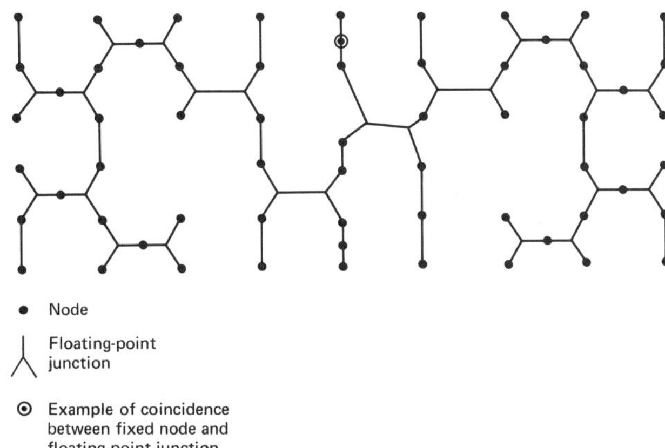


**Figure 3.6** Shortest-distance paths for 62 nodes. Each node is assumed to have equal weight. Source: Miehle, 1958.

The numerical version of the Silk model demands the solution of non-linear equations of the form (for the representative floating point junction, *A*)

$$\frac{\partial D}{\partial x_A} = w_{A1}\frac{(x_A - x_1)}{d_{A1}} + w_{A2}\frac{(x_A - x_2)}{d_{A2}} \dots + w_{AN}\frac{(x_A - x_N)}{d_{AN}} + \dots = 0$$
$$\frac{\partial D}{\partial y_A} = w_{A1}\frac{(y_A - y_1)}{d_{A1}} + w_{A2}\frac{(y_A - y_2)}{d_{A2}} \dots + w_{AN}\frac{(y_A - y_N)}{d_{AN}} + \dots = 0 \qquad (3.3)$$

(Miehle, 1958, p. 237). Here the *N* cities are designated by numbers (1, 2, 3, ... *N*) and the $N-2$ floating point junctions by the letters (*A*, *B*, *C*, ... $N-2$). Their spatial co-ordinates on an *xy* cartesian grid are given by the appropriate subscripts (e.g. $x_A$, $x_1$, so that the total distance to be minimized, *D*, is measured in terms of $d_{ij}$, where

$$d_{ij} = \sqrt[2]{(x_i - x_j)^2 + (y_i - y_j)^2}. \qquad (3.4)$$

In addition, $w_{ij}$ is a weighting factor applied to the link connecting floating point junction *i* to city *j*. Since the equations are non-linear, an iterative method is used where the positions of the movable junctions (*A*, *B*, ...) converge on the minimum solution. Clearly the numerical analysis of the shortest path problem is complex and becomes increasingly so when constraints (e.g. minimum separation distances) are placed on the junction locations: the solution proceeds using Lagrangian multipliers (cf. Section 2.5).

(*b*) *Centres of unequal size.* Once we relax our simplifying assumption of centres of equal size, then we return to the locational situation that intrigued Wellington (see Section 3.2.1). If we glance back at Figure 3.5A it will be clear that the junction location shown there is only optimal if all the centres are of equal size. If centre *a* was very large in relation to centres *b* and *c*, then we would expect the junction to shift towards *a*, as shown in Figure 3.7.

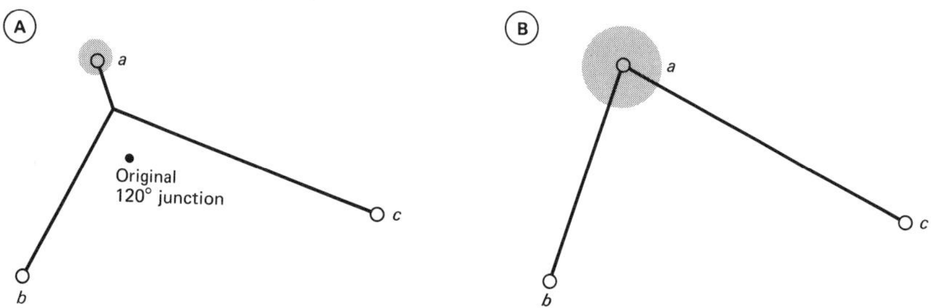


**Figure 3.7** Modification of the 120° junction position with increasing pull of node *a*.

In this case, the problem is that of minimizing the sum of the *weighted* distances from the junction point to each centre. We can express this formally by modifying equation (3.2) to give, for the three-centre case,

$$\text{minimize } H = \sum_{i=1}^{3} \sum_{j=1}^{3} w_j d_{ij}, \tag{3.5}$$

where $w_j$ is the weight (say, population or traffic generation capacity) assigned to the *j*th city. Solution of the location problem for single or multiple junctions then becomes a special example of the plant location problem, which may be approached by the Kuhn-Kuenne numerical approximation method described in Section 5.6.1. Note that solution for large networks demands multiple iterations based on alternative 'trial' locations for the junctions, and that the best of these is used to approximate the optimal configuration.

(*c*) *Alternative definitions of distance.* The shift in location shown in Figure 3.7A assumes that the only relevant item in determining the network configuration is that of movement costs [i.e. weighted distance in equation (3.5)], and building costs are ignored. If the network were very expensive to build, then we would expect equation (3.2) to remain the relevant criterion to keep mileage, and therefore construction costs, as low as possible.

This dilemma in defining exactly what we mean by 'minimum distance' is illustrated by Figure 3.8. In this diagram, six line networks have been drawn, each of which provides a different answer to the problem of building a route network linking five cities. The first network (Figure 3.8A) shows the minimum distance network for starting at a particular point, *i*, and travelling to all the others in the shortest mileage, a solution described by Bunge as a 'Paul Revere' type of network. Figure 3.8B shows a similar distance problem, that of the shortest distance around the five points (the 'travelling salesman' problem; see Section 3.4.2). The next two definitions, shown in Figure 3.8C and Figure 3.8D. are for more complete networks; the first is for a hierarchy connecting one point, *i*, to all the others, and the second is for a complete network connecting any point to all the others. If we examine this last solution, it appears to be the complete answer to our network problem in that it contains all the possible lines for the three solutions that precede it. Quandt (1960) and others certainly make that assumption when they regard the optimal transport network as containing links from a completely connected network.

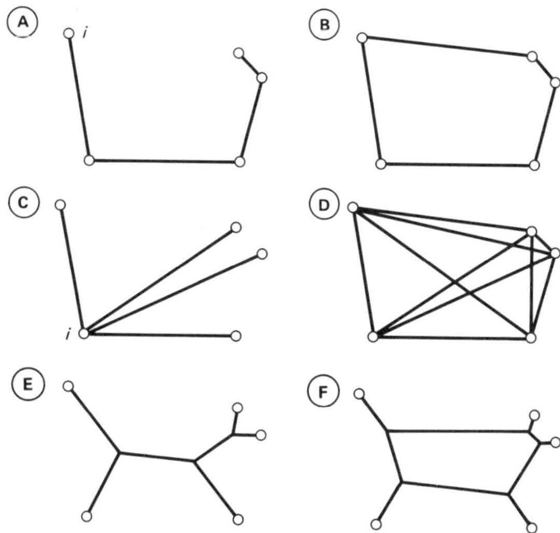


**Figure 3.8** Alternative definitions of minimum-distance networks. Source: Bunge, 1962, pp. 183–9.

As Bunge points out, however, the *shortest* set of lines connecting all five points does not in fact contain any of the elements shown in the previous diagrams. This shortest set solution is given in Figure 3.8E. Note, as we would expect from the discussion earlier in this section, that this solution consists of seven line segments meeting at three junctions so located that all segments meet at 120° angles. Finally, Figure 3.8F shows the general topological case for a network of lines connecting five points as presented by Beckmann (Bunge, 1962, p. 189). Examination of this final diagram shows that the two preceding cases—the completely linked network (D) and the shortest link network (E)—are but special cases of Beckmann's general network.

### 3.3.2 *Optimum network designs*

The Bunge-Beckmann problem shown in Figure 3.8 illustrates the considerable practical application of optimum network designs. If we replace the abstract topological symbols of points and lines by the empirical one of cities and railroads, this relevance becomes clear. Basically, solution D in Figure 3.8 represents the railroad pattern which is the least cost from the point of view of the *user* (i.e. it is the shortest and most convenient to and from any of the five cities). Solution E on the other hand is least cost from the point of view of the *builder*, i.e. it is the shortest railway length linking all five cities.

Bunge (1962, p. 187) suggests that the actual pattern of railway building depends on the ratio between these two costs: user costs and builder costs. Where large cities are clustered, he suggests that the great flow of traffic generated between them will favour the least cost to user pattern; a pattern which may be visible in the railroad network of the northeastern United States (Ullman, 1949). Away from this area, where cities are sparse and traffic is lighter, the building costs become dominant and the least cost to builder patterns dominate. Again the railway pattern of the western United States (admittedly strongly influenced by terrain) may be held to show this type of pattern, although detailed analyses (like those of F. H. Thomas, 1960, on the Denver and Rio Grande Railroad) suggest this is somewhat blanketed by other factors.

A further practical application of the kind of minimization problem posed by Bunge is seen in the planning of road networks in rural areas. Where new farm settlements are being planned, as in the reclaimed Dutch polders, there are at least two distances to be minimized (Chisholm, 1962, pp. 136–8): (i) internal distance from farmstead to fields, and (ii) external distance from farm to public services (roads, water supply, electricity). If we assume that for cadastral and operating reasons the farm must be organized within rectangular boundaries, then Figure 3.9 illustrates four possible arrange-

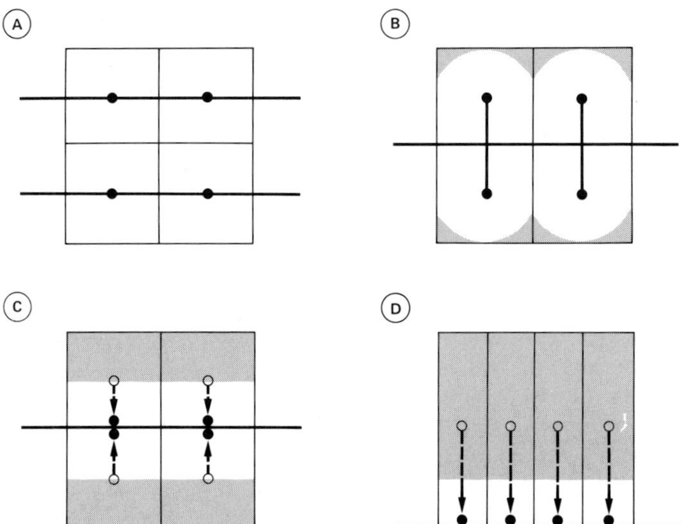


**Figure 3.9** Alternative locations of farmsteads (solid circles) and access roads (heavy lines). Areas more than $\frac{1}{4}$ mile from roads are stippled. Source: Chisholm, 1962, p. 156.

ments of farmstead, roads, and farm boundaries. In the first two cases (Figure 3.9A and Figure 3.9B), the farm units are square, and the farmsteads are optimally sited (from the operator's viewpoint) in the centre of the square; but this solution has the disadvantage that it takes 2.0 miles of service road to connect all four farmsteads in the square mile block. The second case has a marginal advantage over the first in that the farm area is less interrupted by the public road, but this is partly offset by the fact that parts of the 160-acre farms are further than a quarter mile from the nearest public service road. These less accessible areas are stippled on the diagrams. In the third case (Figure 3.9C), the square farm shape is retained but farmsteads are moved from their optimum central location. Service road length is halved to one mile, but overland hauls from the farmstead to the fields are increased. This trend is continued in the fourth case (Figure 3.9D), where the farm unit is changed to a less convenient rectangular strip, the farmsteads are eccentrically located (on the road), but the total length of service road is halved again to only half a mile (assuming similar farmsteads are located on the southern flank of the road).

More complex combinations of alternative boundaries, roads, and farmsteads are possible if we introduce another factor to be maximized, size of farmstead cluster. In the first two cases, single farmsteads form the settlement module, but in the third and fourth cases two farmsteads cluster together. If these are moved to corner locations on their properties, this unit goes up to four. This 'social contact' principle gives modified alternatives of Figure 3.9C and Figure 3.9D which appear to be ones adopted in practice. Empirical evidence from the Dutch polders, from West German land consolidation schemes, from *rang* settlement in Canada (Mead and Brown, 1962), and from strip settlement in Japan (Inouye, in International Geographical Union, 1964, p. 308) and southern Brazil (Monbeig, 1952), appears to conform to this modified pattern.

Ways of laying out optimal systems of roads in newly developed areas have attracted special attention from plantation and forestry developers. Tanner (1967) explored how road systems could be laid out in large plantations to minimize transport costs. Assuming that straight harvesting roads are parallel and equally spaced, a system of optimal 'arterial' roads can be designed as in Figure 3.10. The distance, $d$, between harvesting roads is given as

$$d = \sqrt{\frac{2v}{wn}\left(\frac{C}{kn} + \frac{x}{n}\right)} \qquad (3.6)$$

where $v$ is the walking speed of labourers (distance per hour), $w$ represents the wages per hour of labour for carrying, $n$ is the number of loads carried from each unit area at each cropping, $k$ is the number of croppings per year, $C$ is the cost per year of unit length of road and $x$ is the cost per unit distance of operating collecting vehicles. It is suggested that systems based on three or four arterials will give appreciably shorter distances to the centre than two, but that systems using more than four radial arterials are not likely to be required. It was found usually to be preferable for harvesting roads to meet arterial roads obliquely, the junction angle varying with costs of operating on and off the arterials (Tanner, 1967, p. 11). Further extensions of these ideas of optimal road designs in urban areas are discussed in Haggett and Chorley (1969, pp. 118–30).

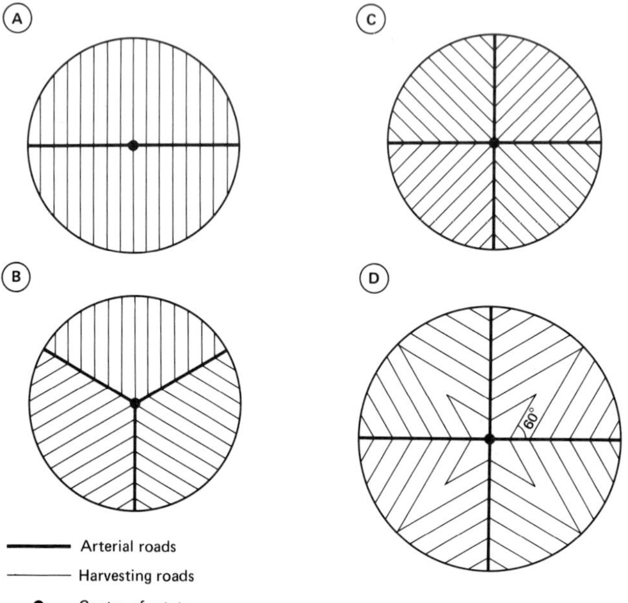


**Figure 3.10** Alternative arrangements for harvesting roads on a circular plantation. Source: Tanner, 1967, pp. 13–14.

## 3.4 Routes Through Networks

The second set of network location problems are 'fixed point' in the sense that all junctions are confined to the nodes or cities to be connected. We describe them here under the title of routes through networks since designing the network may be more simply regarded as selecting one particular configuration from the very large (but finite) range of possible networks.

Before proceeding with our discussion, we define the following terms which are used to describe networks made up of $n$ points or *nodes* joined by $r$ *links*. A link is simply a line connecting two points, and a *Hamiltonian circuit* is a sequence of links which forms an unbroken chain passing through all the $n$ points, and in which the first and last points coincide. The *travelling salesman tour* is the shortest Hamiltonian circuit. A *spanning tree* is a collection of $n-1$ links joining the $n$ points, such that any point can be reached from any other point. The *minimal spanning tree* is the shortest of all such spanning trees.

### 3.4.1 *Combinatorial aspects of network structure*

Many problems in network theory are well known because they are easy to state, can be solved by trivial methods for small blackboard examples, but which are virtually intractable in large scale, realistic situations. Most of the difficulties arise from the explosive, combinatorial nature of the mathematics. Consider, for example, the building of a network to link the three towns shown in Figure 3.11. Given the cost of constructing each link, we can easily specify the total costs of the eight alternatives open to us. These range from 75 cost units for building a complete network, down to zero for inaction, and a choice can be made depending on the budget and objectives available.

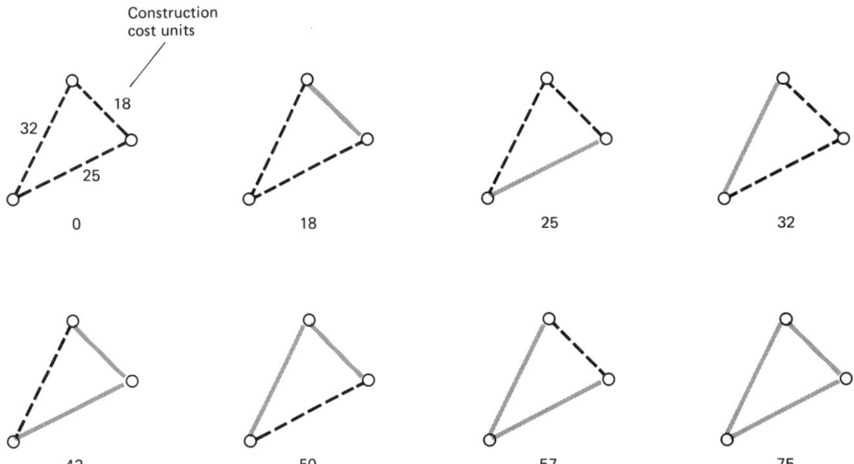


**Figure 3.11** Network configurations for a three-city problem, with the associated construction costs. Pecked lines denote links not built.

However, the situation remains tractable only where $n$, the number of cities is very small. If we add only one more city, so that $n = 4$, then the total number of alternatives is squared from eight to 64 (Figure 3.12). Again, complete enumeration of all alternative building strategies is possible, though now more tedious. But with $n = 5$, the alternatives leap to 1,024, and for $n = 6$ to 32,768. A general expression for the number of alternatives is given by the formula,

$$2^{\{\frac{1}{2}n(n-1)\}}. \tag{3.7}$$

This means that for a modest-sized problem of only 32 cities, the number of different fixed point networks is an astronomical $2^{496}$.

In situations of this kind, the direct enumeration methods become irrelevant. If we look at the kinds of networks which are generated by a link-addition process, it will be apparent that many are inefficient. For example, only four of the 64 networks for our four-city problem shown in Figure 3.12 join all cities in an efficient way (i.e., such that each city can be reached from any other city, and the total network length is simultaneously kept to a minimum. These cases are starred in Figure 3.12. Note that diagonal links are clearly longer than other links, which eliminates solutions such as the 'N' and 'Z' configurations). We are anxious therefore to try to reduce the vast number of possible solutions to a feasible sub-set of real interest.

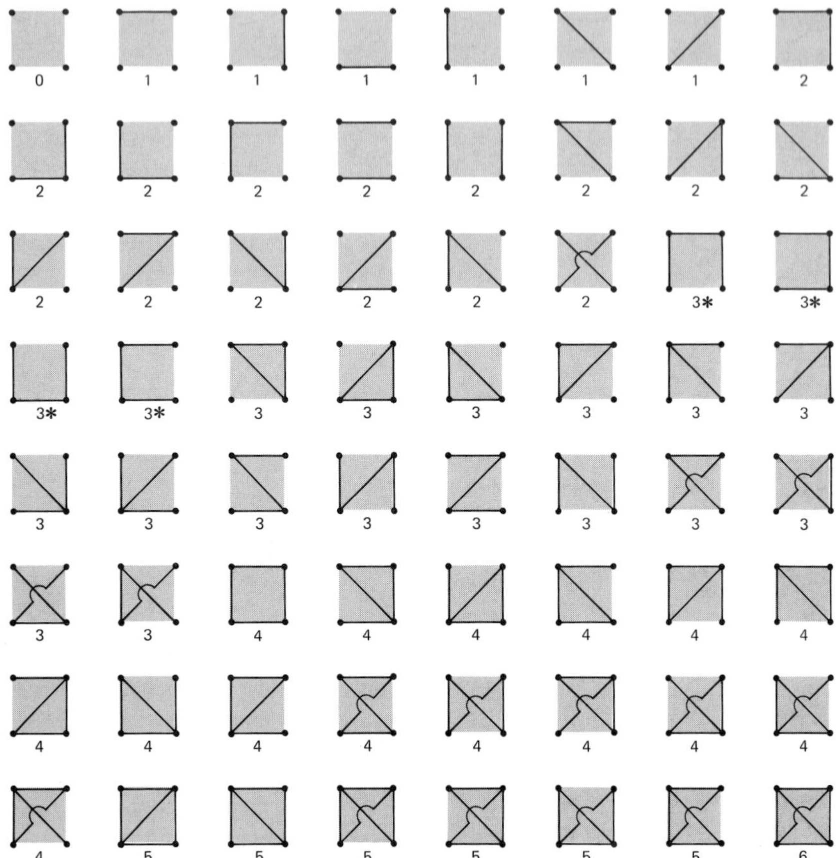


**Figure 3.12** Sixty-four network configurations within a three-city system. The digit below each diagram indicates the number of links.

### 3.4.2 *Travelling salesman problems*

The travelling salesman problem is to design an optimal route through $n$ cities, so as to start at city 1, to visit each of the other $n-1$ cities only once, and then return to city 1. Let us assume a symmetrical cost matrix where $c_{ij} = c_{ji}$, expressing the cost in terms of Euclidean distance. Then the cost of the typical tour, $i$, is

$$H = \sum_{j=1}^{n-1} c_{i_j i_{j+1}} + c_{i_n i_1}, \tag{3.8}$$

where $(i_1, i_2, \ldots i_n)$ is a permutation of the integers from 1 to $n$ giving the order in which the cities $(i_1, i_2, \ldots i_n, i_1)$ are visited on the $i$th tour.

The total possible number of tours or Hamiltonian circuits with a symmetrical cost matrix is

$$\tfrac{1}{2}(n-1)! \tag{3.9}$$

Thus the solution shown in Figure 3.13A is only one of 2520 ways of connecting eight cities. Given that the map distances in Figure 3.13 are the appropriate units to be minimized, then we can reduce the range of alternative solutions very substantially by using two theorems:

(1) The optimal tour does not intersect itself, since any two intersecting links can always be replaced by two non-intersecting links of a shorter total distance (compare Figures 3.13A and B).

(2) If we form a convex polygon or hull bounding the points to be connected (Figure 3.13C), then the points which form its vertices occur in the same order on the optimal tour as they do on the convex hull.

The effect of these two theorems is greatly to reduce the number of shortest-path tours which are worth considering. Instead of (3.9), the number of tours is reduced to

$$(n-1)!/(m-1)! \qquad (3.10)$$

where $m$ is the number of cities out of the total of $n$ that lie on the convex hull. Thus, in Figure 3.13C, the number of tours is reduced from 2520 to $(8-1)!/(5-1)!$, or 210. Several algorithms have been developed to find the minimum length circuit (shown in Figure 3.13D) in this reduced set. When the cost matrices are asymmetric ($c_{ij} \neq c_{ji}$), and non-Euclidean elements (e.g. time or cost) are used, finding the minimum length circuit is considerably more difficult than in the simple case shown here. Pollack and Wiebenson (1960), in a review of the solutions put forward to this general travelling salesman

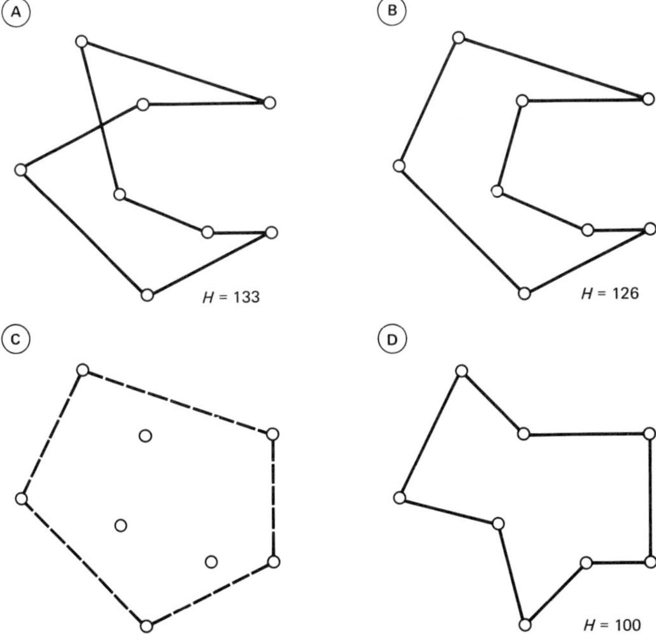


**Figure 3.13** Hamiltonian circuits linking eight cities. $H$ is the length of the circuit measured in arbitrary distance units.

problem, draw a distinction between computational/mathematical solutions (such as the work by Moore, 1959, at Harvard on the shortest paths through a maze) and analogue solutions (such as Rapoport and Abramson's, 1959, model, in which electric and electron 'timers' are substituted for distance, and the shortest route is shown by a set of illuminated links). The basic aim of both approaches is to reduce the long and expensive computations needed. Continuing research is producing still more efficient algorithms (e.g. the 'Cascade' algorithm of Farbey, Land and Murchland, and the Shen Lin algorithm developed at the Bell Telephone Laboratories). Scott (1971b, pp. 68–117) and Eilon, *et al.* (1971, pp. 113–30) provide an extensive review of these algorithms, together with examples of their use.

### 3.4.3 *Spanning tree problems*

In network terminology, a 'tree' is simply a network of links and nodes such that there is exactly one path connecting any two nodes. Thus for $n$ cities, the tree connecting them will consist of $n-1$ links. Figure 3.14 shows the way in which a set of points may be linked by a minimum spanning tree (MST) when the $n$ points are distributed in a Euclidean space. First, each point is joined to its nearest neighbour (Figure 3.14B). Second, each subgraph so formed is linked its nearest neighbour (Figure 3.14C). Third, this second step is repeated until all subgraphs form part of one single graph connecting all points (Figure 3.14D).

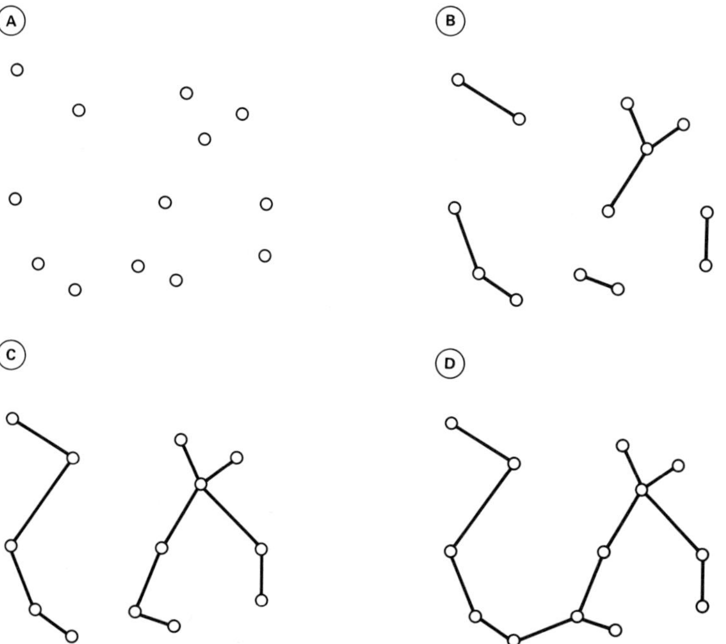


**Figure 3.14** Steps in the construction of a minimum spanning tree (MST).

***

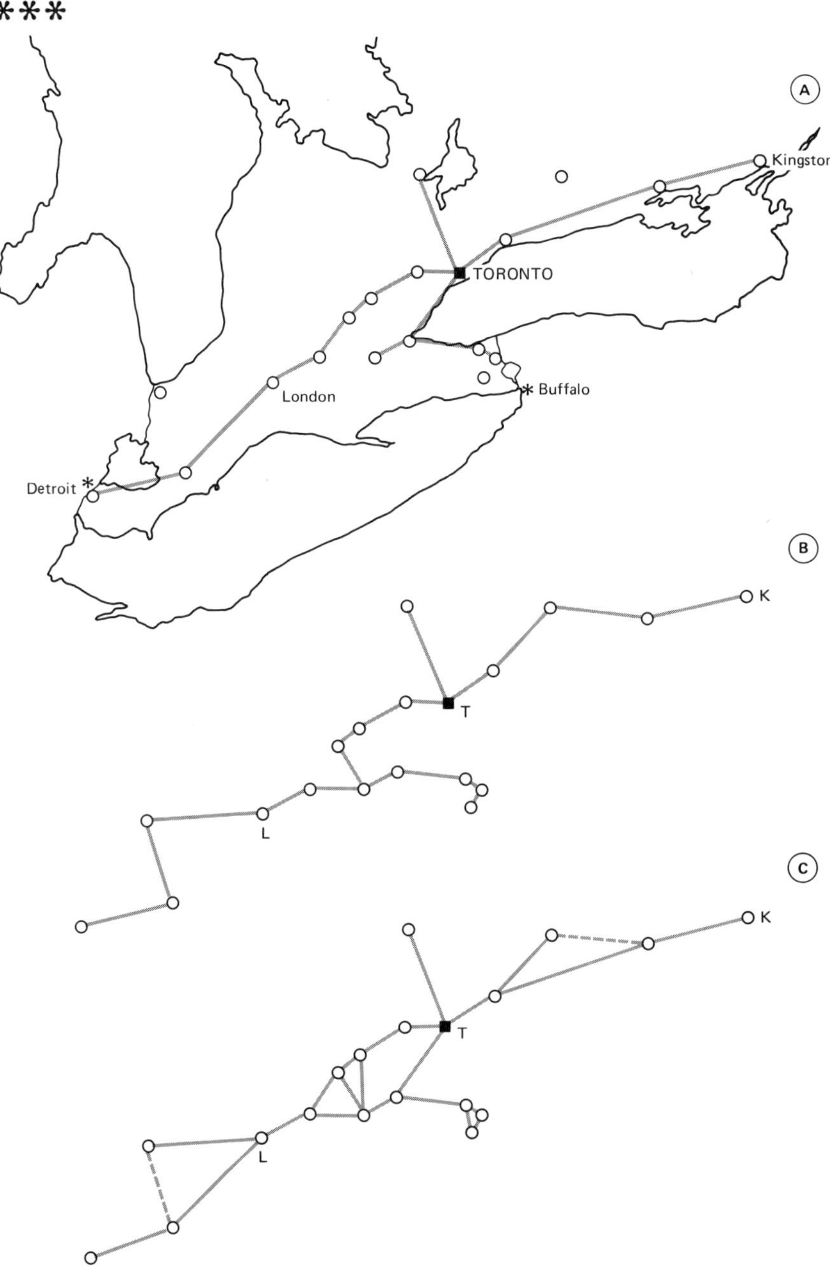


**Figure 3.15** Network generation using minimum-spanning tree and gravity models in Southern Ontario. **A** Existing multilane highway network, simplified; **B** Minimum-spanning tree (MST); **C** Minimum-spanning tree augmented by gravity model and with two MST links (pecked) eliminated. Source: MacKinnon and Hodgson, 1969, pp. 4, 10, 33.

Stated more formally, we wish to find the values of the binary variables, $\lambda_{ij}$, such that

$$H = \sum_{i=1}^{n} \sum_{j=1}^{n} \lambda_{ij} d_{ij} \tag{3.11}$$

is minimized, where $d_{ij}$ is the length of link *ij*, and $\lambda_{ij}$ takes on the value of 1 if a link directly connecting *i* and *j* exists but is otherwise zero. Very simple algorithms have been developed for generating the MST of a set of points in both Euclidean and non-Euclidean space, and we consider their use again in Section 14.3.

The importance of the MST is that (i) it is the simplest network configuration such that all nodes are linked and (ii) it provides a lower bound on total network length (i.e. all other connecting networks must have a length greater than that of the MST). Figure 3.15 shows the MST joining a system of cities in southern Ontario and Quebec. This was used by MacKinnon and Hodgson (1969) in a study of the relative efficiency of the multi-lane highway system connecting the 32 largest urban centres in that region. Their models successively added links to the MST, so as to maximize the total flow ($T$) in the network (estimated by gravity models) within the constraints of the existing highway mileage ($L$). The model

$$\text{maximizes } T = \sum_{i=1}^{n} \sum_{j=1}^{n} P_i P_j d_{ij}^{-b}, \tag{3.12}$$

subject to

$$\sum_{i=1}^{n} \sum_{j=1}^{n} \lambda_{ij} \mathrm{d}_{ij} \leqslant L, \tag{3.13}$$

where $P_i$ and $P_j$ are the populations (or other appropriate estimates of urban size) of cities *i* and *j*, and *b* is a parameter specified exogenously. The gravity formulation follows that given in Section 2.3. As Figure 3.15 shows, the effect of the gravity model is to supplement the number of links within the general length constraint of *L*. Less heavily used links within the MST are eliminated. The general limitations of the model, including the boundary effect of Detroit and Buffalo (which, although they lie across the U.S.A./Canada border, affect Ontario's highway network requirements) are discussed at length by MacKinnon and Hodgson (1969).

Shortest-path trees have also been used as a basis for simulating the growth of past transport networks. Kansky's (1963) study of development of the 1908 railway network of Sicily is typical (Figure 3.16). The aim of the model was to predict the probable local density of railway routes from the geographical characteristics of the area. The lengths, number and rate of extension of the routes were either obtained directly from the historical evidence or predicted from comparative studies of railway parameters [such as the number of vertices, (towns, junctions) in the network, and the average length of rail link between vertices] in terms of an area's general level of economic development. The operation of the model may be generalized into four stages: (i) list and weight all major settlements in the area in terms of a 'population income' score; (ii) select probable vertices to be linked from this list of settlements by a randomization process; (iii) connect the two largest vertices by a rail link; (iv) add the other edges in sequence such that '. . . the next largest centre joins the largest and closest centre which is already located on the network' (Kansky, 1963, p. 138). If, after all the vertices have been connected to the railroad system, un-allocated links remain, then, (v) add the links in such a way that the circuit between the first, second, and third largest centres is completed, and continue to complete the circuits bringing in the fourth, fifth and lower order centres in turn. The map of routes may be finally adjusted by (vi) the adoption of delta-wye ($\Delta \rightarrow Y$) transformations (Akers, 1960) to simplify the links between triangles of three points, and (vii) local adjustment of the routes to physical variations in the relief.

Kolars and Malin (1970) have developed the Kansky model by using the

***

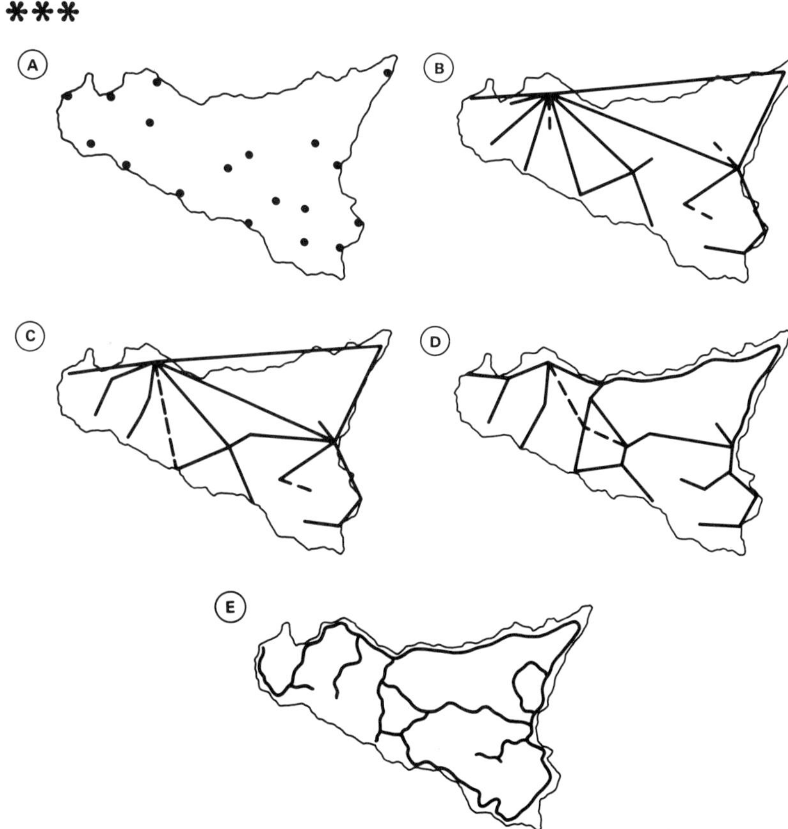


**Figure 3.16** Stages in link allocation for simulating the Sicilian 1908 railroad network. **A** Selected vertices, **B–C** Stages in link allocation, **D** Postdicted 1908 network, **E** Actual 1908 network. The pecked lines indicate routes which should have been constructed according to the algorithm; they were not added because they would have resulted in the construction of circuits which followed very closely the general direction of other circuits. Source: Kansky, 1963, pp. 139–46.

population within twenty miles of selected points to identify 'ridges' of high population potentials; such ridges were then incorporated into the model as generators of route links on the railway system.

### 3.4.4 *Other shortest-path problems*

Further sets of problems concern the maximum flow that can be passed between two points in a network. Clearly the capacity of individual links may be constrained (see Figure 3.17), and the problem is to identify the path (or

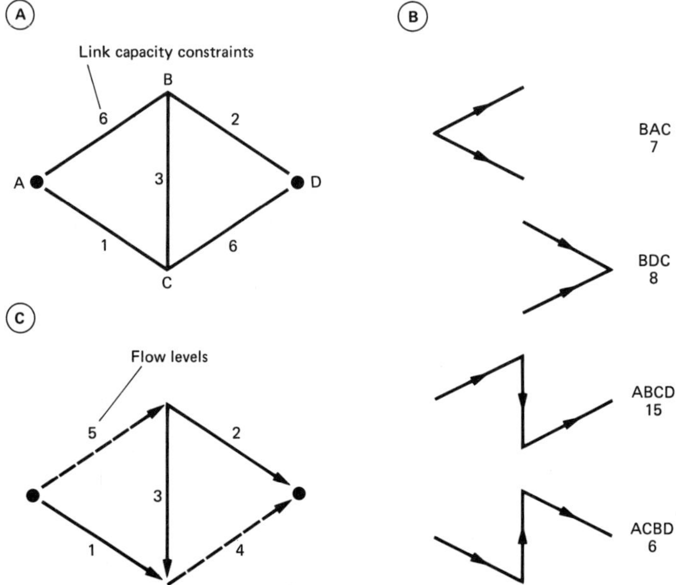


**Figure 3.17** Derivation of the max flow–min cut flow graph from **A** to **D** for a simple network. In **C**, the pecked lines denote links with flow levels less than their capacity constraints. Source: Akers, 1960, p. 312.

paths) that the maximum flow must follow. The problem of defining maximum 'flow' was solved in 1955 by Dantzig and Fulkerson through their 'max flow–min cut' theorem which showed that the maximum flow through a network was equal to the sum of the capacity of the branches of the minimum cut. A 'cut' is any collection of branches which, when removed, separates two terminals in the network. Thus, in Figure 3.17, we can see that there are four possible cuts which separate A from D (these are plotted in Figure 3.17B). The minimum cut is the line ACBD with a total capacity of 6 units. This is also the maximum flow through this simple network (Figure 3.17C).

Locational selection of the paths which the maximum flow must follow posed few problems in this simple case. All links were employed, although two of them (shown by pecked lines) were carrying less than their total capacity. A number of algorithms for finding maximum flow paths through very complex networks have been evolved (Ford and Fulkerson, 1962), but these are largely concerned with steady-state flow. Kleinrock's (1964) work has been concerned, on the other hand, with paths through networks where the flow is not steady but fluctuating and rather unpredictable (e.g. messages through telephone networks): here stochastic simulation models for alternative arrangements of the network have proved valuable. Work on paths of this kind have direct analogies with flood routing problems on large river control networks.

The most complex of the path finding problems is that of finding a least cost flow path through a network. Ford and Fulkerson (1962, Chapter 3) suggest that something like half the time spent on industrial and military applications of linear programming (see Chapter 15) is concerned with this topic. Here we do little more than point out the nature of the problem and the kind of path solutions that may be obtained.

Figure 3.18 illustrates a simple example in determining minimal cost paths through a network while obtaining maximum flow (Ford and Fulkerson, 1962, pp. 123–127). The network consists of a set of 21 links (edges) joining the two terminal points $(i, j)$. Figure 3.18A shows the maximum flow capacity of each link and Figure 3.18B the unit shipping costs. If we assume our problem is to ship goods from $i$ to $j$, then it is possible to compute that a positive *minimum-cost* flow will get through the network to $j$ by utilizing the paths shown by the arrows in Figure 3.18C. However, for the *maximum* flow through the network (given the cost and capacity constraints), almost all the links are utilized (Figure 3.18D). Two points worth noting are that (i) not all the links along the paths operate at their full capacity (the links which are not fully 'saturated' with traffic are shown by broken lines) and (ii) the direction of flow along some of the links may change as total flow through the network increases.

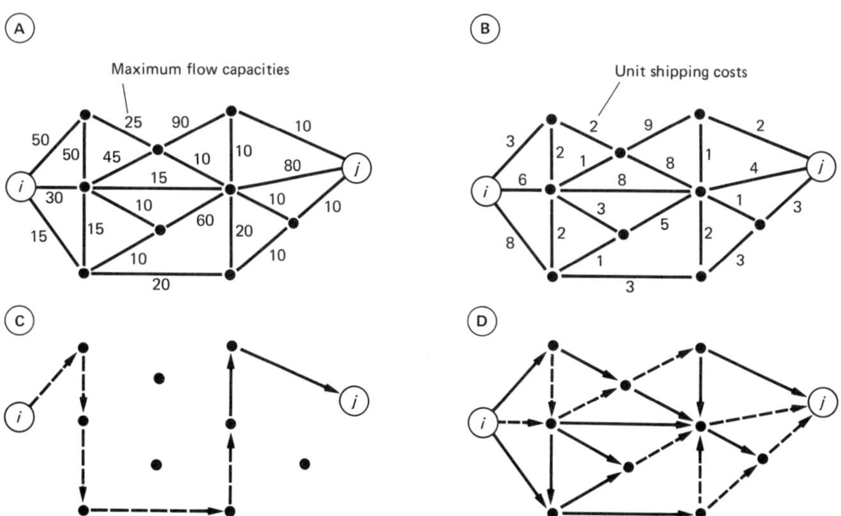


**Figure 3.18** Minimal-cost flow through a complex network: **A** maximum flow capacity of each link; **B** unit shipping costs along each link; **C** initial positive minimum-cost flow pattern; **D** maximum flow pattern. Links not fully 'saturated' with flow shown by broken lines. Source: Ford and Fulkerson, 1962, pp. 123–7.

## 3.5 Empirical Studies of Network Structure

Geographers have tended to study transport networks within a regional–empirical context, rather than in terms of formal locational models. We review here some examples from the large literature that has accrued in this field. Hurst (1974) gives a full account of the major contributions.

### 3.5.1 *Regional variations in network geometry*

Study of the particular structure of regional networks has been greatly helped by the development of a set of measures based on graph theory. These measures are described at length in Section 9.7, and readers are referred to that section for formal definitions of terms used in the following discussion.

Two illustrations of Kansky's (1963) findings are given in Figure 3.19, where the railway networks of selected countries are related to their general level of economic development. In the first graph (Figure 3.19A), energy consumption

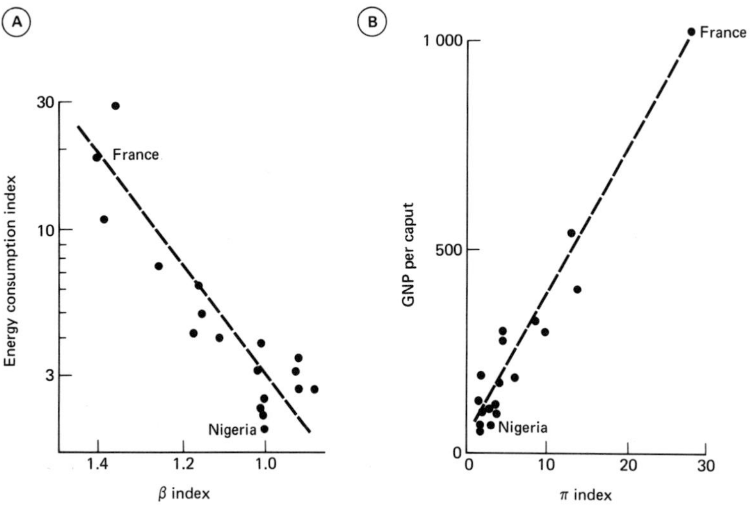


**Figure 3.19** Relation of topological measures of the connectivity (**A**) and shape (**B**) of railway networks to indices of economic development. Source: Kansky, 1963, p. 42.

($y$-axis) is plotted against a measure of connectivity, the Beta ($\beta$) index ($x$-axis); as connectivity increases, so does the Beta index. Highly developed countries like France have large connectivity indices for their railway system, while underdeveloped countries like Nigeria have low connectivity indices. In the second graph (Figure 3.19B) another measure of development, gross national product *per caput* ($y$-axis), is plotted against a measure of network shape, the $\pi$ index ($x$-axis). Again, France with its high shape values (approximating to a circle) stands in sharp contrast to Nigeria with its elongated system. In both graphs there is a consistent relationship which is statistically significant and strongly suggests that the geometry of some route networks may be very closely allied to the general development of regional resources. Should this be so, we must slightly modify Cooley's views on the importance of purely political factors; we suggest that while such factors may have a dramatic effect on individual routes, the major pattern suggests the importance of more purely economic considerations.

Network analysis using graph theory has also proved useful for the analysis of the position of particular places on a route system. Using one measure of accessibility, Garrison (1960, pp. 131–5) was able to analyse the relative accessibility of 45 places in the southeastern part of the United States which were linked together by the Interstate Highway System (Figure 3.20A). The

**Figure 3.20** **A** Interstate highway network in the southeastern United States. **B**, **C** Graphic simplification of the railway network of Sardinia. Sources: Garrison, 1960, p. 132; Kansky, 1963, p. 8.

places were defined partly on urban size criteria and partly on their topological position (e.g. at the end of a route). Atlanta (a) turned out to be the most accessible point on the network, and may be compared with St Petersburg (b), which is among the least accessible of places. Part of the reason for this contrast lies in the fact that graph theory concentrates on the topological property of the network, its connectivity, rather than on its dimensions. Kansky (1963) has reminded us that, from the topological point of view, the railways of Sardinia do not look like Figure 3.20B, but more like Figure 3.20C. The advantages that this more abstract model confers from the viewpoint of analysis must, of course, be weighed against the loss of other significant detail.

### 3.5.2 *Density patterns of route networks*

If we stand back from the route network, its individual characteristics blur. We observe a simple density pattern in which some areas have a very dense route network, while in others the network is very sparse. In approaching this problem, we proceed from the local scale of the city street and subdivision network, up through regional differences within a state, to the world scale. Scale problems are considered more formally in Section 10.6 and in Chapter 12.

(*a*) *Local and regional levels.* Examination of the large scale maps or plans for any urban or rural areas usually reveals rather strong differences in route density. Villages stand out with their denser pattern from the surrounding countryside; downtown urban areas (even in geometrically planned American cities) stand out by their denser street pattern from the more open network of the suburbs. The strongly concentric pattern of the road network density zones about the two city centres in the twin-cities area of Minneapolis/St Paul is an example (Figure 3.21; Borchert, 1961). At the regional level, a very thorough investigation of the distribution of road densities in Ghana and

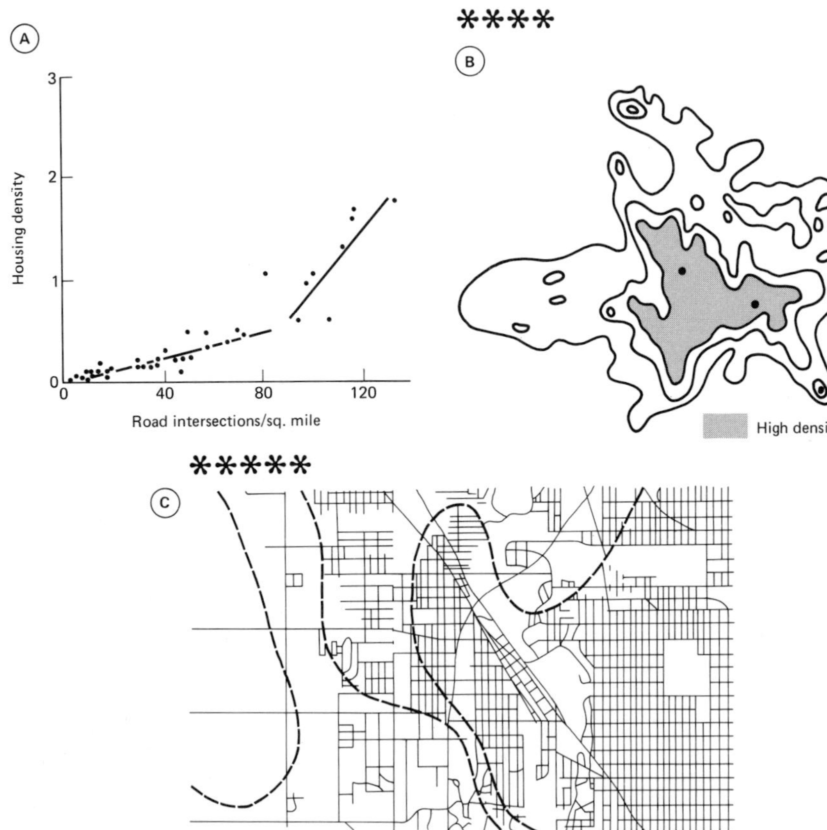


**Figure 3.21** Density of road networks in and around Minneapolis–St Paul, United States. **A** Relationship of network to housing density. **B** Concentric zones of network density. The city centres of Minneapolis and St Paul are shown by the heavy dots. **C** Sample quadrat of network with density contours. Source: Borchert, 1961, pp. 50–6.

Nigeria has been made by Taaffe, Morrill and Gould (1963). The route density of each of Ghana's 30, and Nigeria's 50, sub-regions was measured for first and second class roads, and was related in the first instance to the population and the area of each unit. Using a simple regression, population was found to explain about 50 per cent of the variation in road density in both Ghana and Nigeria. When area was included with population in a multiple regression, the levels of explanation rose to 75 and 81 per cent respectively. Taaffe, Morrill and Gould went on to suggest four other less important variables that might help to account for the residual differences between the actual densities and the expected densities from the regression analysis. These four variables were identified as: (i) hostile environment; (ii) rail/road competition; (iii) intermediate location; and (iv) commercialization and relation to the development sequence.

Hostile environment, a familiar and basic geographical theme, was illustrated in Ghana by the very low route densities in the swampy lands of the Volta river district and where the Mampong escarpment sharply restricts the development of feeder routes. Railroad competition was found to be a more complex factor, in that one could argue either that railroads would curtail the need for roads by providing an alternative form of transport, or that railroads would stimulate road building by their gingering effects on production for inter-regional trade. The second argument appeared the stronger in Ghana and Nigeria.

Units with an intermediate location between two important high-population areas were found to have densities well above those expected on the basis of population and area alone. Road density was positively associated with the degree of commercial activity; the more productive areas had a heavier road pattern than more backward areas. An anomaly noted from this pattern was the mining areas; these rely largely on rail movements and did not follow the resource development/road density relationship.

(*b*) *International level.* The comparison of network densities between countries raises acute problems of differences in the operational definition of routes. Not only are definitional problems multiplied (for example, differences between single and multiple track railways, or farm roads and eight lane freeways), but similar information is recorded and classified in very different ways. Ginsburg has attempted to standardize these conflicting figures in his *Atlas of economic development* (1961) and his findings will be used here as a basis for argument.

Two critical maps in the Ginsburg atlas are of railway density (Map XXIV) and road density (Map XXIX) on a world scale. Both maps show density as length of route per 100 km$^2$, although there are a number of other and equally valid ways of showing density (for example, in relation to population, or population and distance). For our purposes, the density per unit area provides the more basic variable in that it describes the actual existence on the ground of specialized routes whether those routes be intensively or lightly used.

The basic characteristics of the world distribution pattern are shown in summary form in Table 3.1. Road density, an index compiled from a variety of sources and with rather unstandardized figures, gives a world average of around 10 kilometres/100 square kilometres or about ten times as great a density as that for railways. The gap between the maximum values and the means is, however, considerably greater for roads; Belgium, reported with the highest road density, had about thirty times as dense a network as the world mean, while Luxembourg with the highest railway network was only about twenty times as dense as the world mean. At the other end of the distribution, one country (Greenland) is reported with zero road density, and 27 countries have no railways. The distribution is then a very skewed one (cf. Section 10.5) with a few countries with very dense networks and many countries with very sparse networks. Nearly two-thirds of the countries have densities below the world mean.

Table 3.1 Distribution of route density*

| *Route media:* | *Roads* | *Railways* |
|---|---|---|
| Number of countries compared | 126 | 134 |
| World mean density, km/100 km$^2$ | 10.3 | 0.95 |
| Maximum density, km/100 km$^2$ | 302.0 | 17.90 |
| Minimum density, km/100 km$^2$ | 0.0 | 0.00 |
| Countries below world mean, per cent | 64% | 67% |

Source: Ginsburg, 1961, pp. 60, 70.
* World data, 1956–7.

Transport networks are demonstrably part of the development infrastructure, and the distribution of countries with high and low densities may be reasonably linked to their general level of economic development. This hypothesis can be explored by adopting the economic-demographic development scale developed by Berry (1960) from the values in the Ginsburg atlas (Ginsburg, 1961, pp. 110–19). The scale is derived from 43 separate indices of economic development, and is a plot of countries on a demographic measure (the $x$-axis) against a measure of technology on the $y$-axis. Some 95 countries are distributed along this scale (Figure 3.22A) with highly developed countries on the upper left and poorer countries on the lower right.

On this continuum, countries with high and low road and rail densities have been superimposed: the first ten countries with high densities are shown with large solid circles and the last ten countries with the lowest densities are shown by large open circles. The location of the United States on this continuum has been marked with an asterisk (*) for reference. The road density pattern (Figure 3.22A) shows a cluster of high ranking countries at the developed end of the spectrum. Nine of these ten are European countries; United Kingdom (1), West Germany (2), Belgium (3), France (4), Switzerland (5), Netherlands (6), Denmark (7), Poland (8), and Ireland (10). Only one other country, Hong Kong (11), lies outside this. Indeed the only highly developed countries in the study with relatively modest road densities are the United States, Canada, and Sweden. Railway density (Figure 3.22B) follows, in general, the same pattern with European countries in leading positions. Seven of the countries recur, with two eastern European countries, Czechoslovakia (21) and Hungary (22),

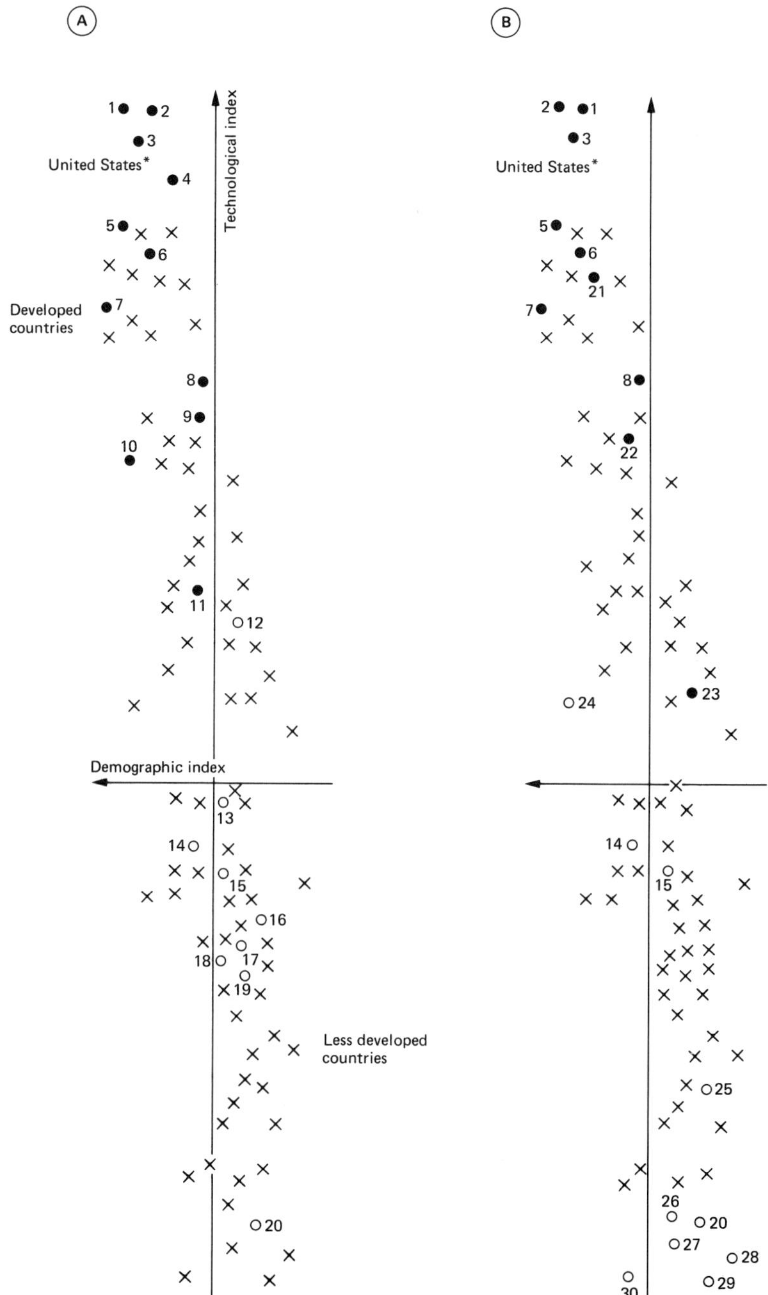


**Figure 3.22** Relationship of countries with high and low road (**A**) and railway (**B**) density to Berry's development spectrum. Source: Berry, 1960, p. 91.

and the far eastern state of Taiwan (23), coming into the picture. The apparently anomalous positions of some far eastern states reflect (i) the relatively high ranking status that the railway density map of a number of southeast Asian countries like India and Burma developed under the railroad-building British colonial administration and (ii) situations like that in Japan and Taiwan (a former Japanese colony) where transport was deliberately developed about the railroad net.

At the other end of the spectrum, the position of low ranking countries is complicated by the absence from Berry's economic-demographic development scale of most of the very underdeveloped countries. Not enough data were available to place them accurately on the scale, and the 'ten lowest density countries' are drawn only from the 95 countries on the continuum. Nevertheless, the pattern shown is an interesting one. In terms of railway density (Figure 3.22B), the low ranking countries cluster strikingly at the bottom of the development ladder. Six of the seven countries at this base are African states [Sudan (25), Ethiopia (28), Libya (30), Liberia (20), Gambia (27), and French Equatorial Africa (26)], together with Afghanistan (29). More developed colonial countries with low-density railroad nets are Surinam (14) and British Guiana (15), both with excellent river transport. The only major anomaly is Iceland (24). For road density (Figure 3.22A) the pattern of the low ranking countries is not so clear. Relatively developed countries with very large land areas [U.S.S.R. (9) and Brazil (12)], stand out as major anomalies. At the lower extreme, only Liberia represents the African cluster noted on the railway density map. Surinam and British Guiana here form the centre for a cluster of non-African tropical states in the lower/middle range of development, with Costa Rica (13), Ecuador (16), Bolivia (18) from the Americas, and Iran (19) and British Borneo (17) from Asia. In general, the road density pattern is less easy to interpret and reflects in part the wide range in the definition of 'roads'. The lack of correspondence between the lows on the two media suggests that railways have served as substitutes for roads; in other cases, like British Guiana, river and coastal shipping has served as a substitute for both.

### 3.5.3 *Route development models*

The growth of roads, railways, canals, and the like is inextricably woven into the whole process of economic growth and regional development. One of the few attempts to bring together the broad regularities in the growth of internal transport lines has been by Taaffe, Morrill and Gould (1963) in the paper considered in Section 3.5.2. On the basis of specific study of the growth of transport in Ghana and Nigeria, with less intensive study of Brazil, British East Africa, and Malaya they proposed a four phase sequence of development (Figure 3.23).

*Phase One* consists of a scatter of small ports and trading posts along the coast of the hypothetical region being developed (Figure 3.23A). Each small port has a small inland trading field but there is little contact along the coast except through occasional fishing boats and irregular traders. This phase they identify in Nigeria and Ghana as running from the fifteenth century to the end of the nineteenth century with groups of indigenous peoples around a European trading station.

*Phase Two* consists of the emergence of a few major lines of penetration, the growth of inland trading centres at the terminals, and the differential growth of coastal ports with inland connections (Figure 3.23B). With the growth of the coastal ports, the local hinterland also expands and diagonal routes begin to focus on the growing ports. Again the phase is identified in Ghana and Nigeria with the growth of inland trunk routes. These appear to have been built inland for three major reasons: (i) to connect a coastal administrative centre politically and militarily with its sphere of authority up-country, e.g. in Ghana the desire to reach Kumasi, capital of the rebellious Ashanti; (ii) to tap exploitable mineral resources, such as the Enugu coalfields in Nigeria; and (iii) to tap areas of potential agricultural export production, such as the cocoa areas north of Accra. Although each motive has played its part, the role of mineral exploitation has been a critical one in African railway building and examples from Uganda (Kasese copper line), the Cameroons (Garoua manganese line), and Mauritania (Fort Gourard iron-ore line) suggest that this phase has not yet ended.

*Phase Three* consists of the growth of feeder routes and the beginnings of

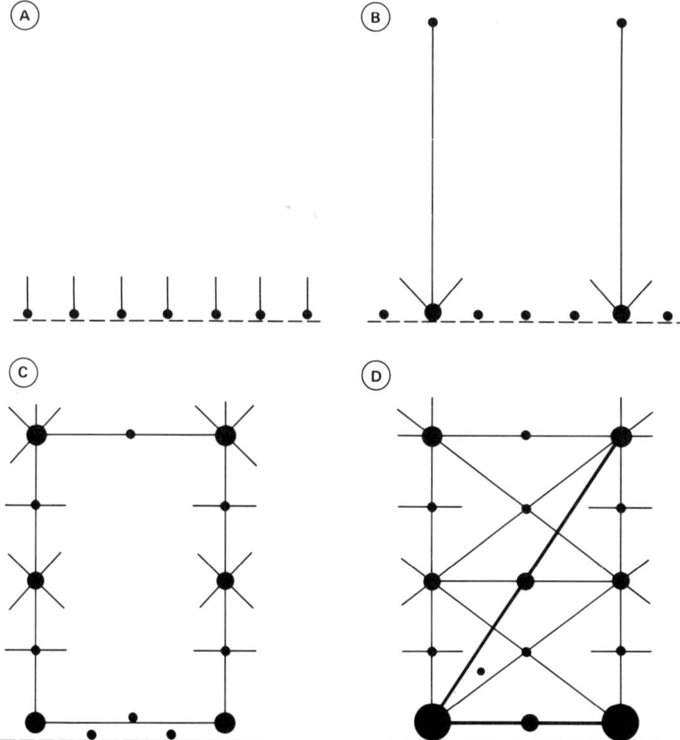


**Figure 3.23** Four-stage diachronic model of network development in an underdeveloped country. Source: Taaffe, Morrill, and Gould, 1963, p. 504.

lateral interconnection (Figure 3.23C). The development of feeder routes is accompanied by continued growth of the main seacoast terminals in a spiral of trade capture and expansion. Intermediate centres grow up between the coastal and interior terminals. Taaffe, Morrill and Gould (1963, pp. 511–14) show a series of maps of road development in Ghana and Nigeria in the period since 1920 to suggest the lateral connections of earlier disconnected lines of penetration and exploitation.

*Phase Four* repeats the process of linkage and concentration and shows the emergence of high priority linkages between the most important centres (indicated by a broader line in Figure 3.23D). The best paved roads, the heaviest rail schedules and airline connections will follow these 'main street' links between the three major centres. The heavy traffic in the 'triangle' of southern Ghana suggests such a development here.

There is little doubt that the model provides a very useful summary of certain regularities in the growth of internal route systems in colonial seaboard areas. The fact that Gould's careful historical analysis of the development of transportation in Ghana (Gould, 1960) was used as an empirical basis for the model ensured a strong realistic basis.

Two questions we must bear in mind in using the model are (i) how far is it applicable outside West Africa in particular and in colonial areas in general, and (ii) how far is the division into separate stages justified? Comparison with the growth of selected routes in southeastern Brazil (Figure 3.24), like the

***

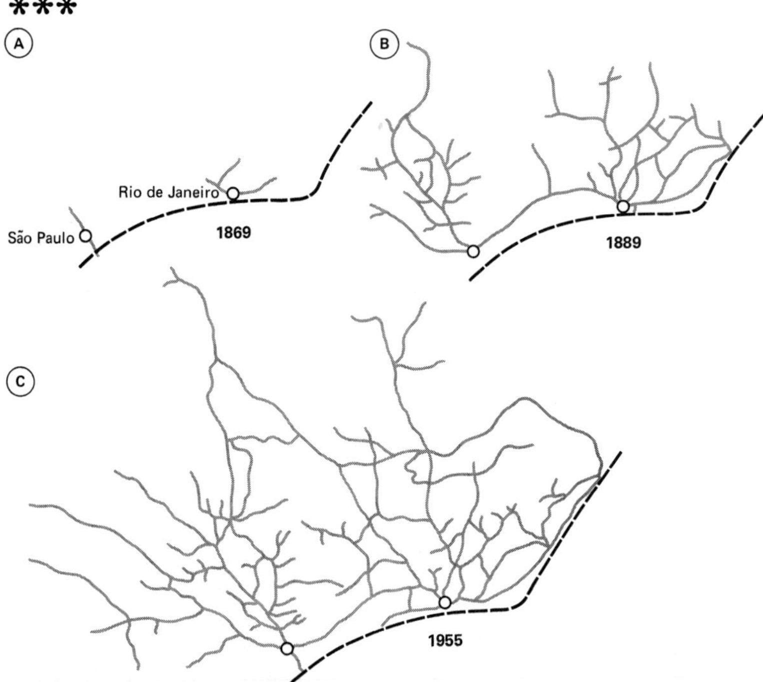


**Figure 3.24** Stages in the growth of the railway network in southeastern Brazil.

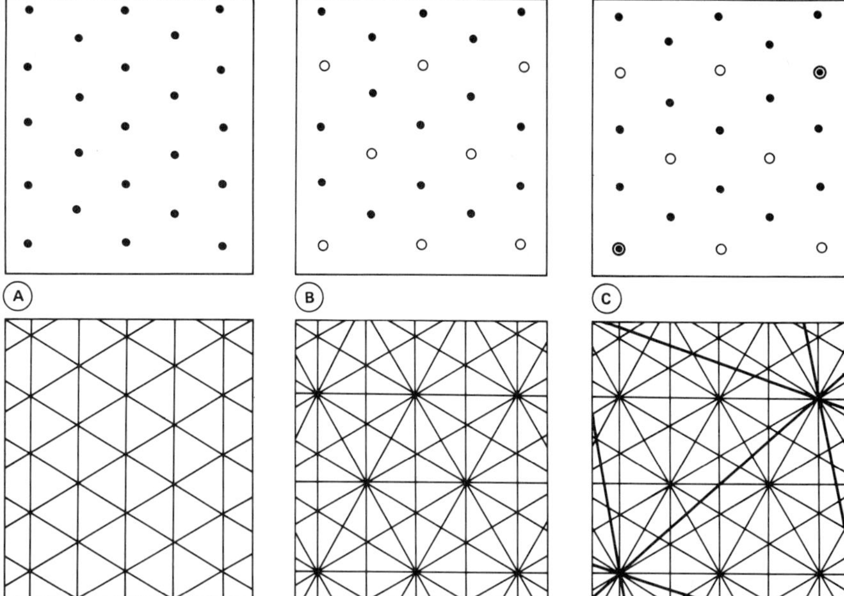


**Figure 3.25** Network development by route substitution between successively higher-order centres in a Löschian landscape.

railway route system focused on the cities of São Paulo and Rio de Janeiro are suggestive. The maps show the state of the rail system in 1869 (Figure 3.24A), in 1889 (Figure 3.24B), and in 1955 (Figure 3.24C), and one can readily see the characteristics of extension and branching mentioned in the Taaffe, Morrill and Gould model. Maps from other ex-colonial areas like the western United States show a rather similar pattern.

Since Taaffe, Morrill and Gould's original study, scholars in other parts of the world have looked in detail at the network growth process. Rimmer (1967) found a generally similar pattern of port competition and elimination in New Zealand and Australia, but Burghardt (1969) has argued that the evolution of the road system in the Niagara peninsula shows a different sequence. Like Rostow's *Stages of economic growth* (Rostow, 1960), the four stage sequence gains its greatest value in stimulating the study of growth and there is likely to be a good deal of academic discussion over how many stages we should recognize and where the significant breaks, if any, occur.

While these foregoing models may have wider application than was originally intended, there remains to be specified a comprehensive model of route development in developed areas. Here, we may assume, an existing route system already functions and we are concerned with the way in which networks are adjusted to technical changes in transport and the widening circles of interaction which accompany rising economic-social levels.

Some of the changing needs of road traffic were raised in the Buchanan Report (Ministry of Transport, 1963, pp. 71–136), which stresses that 'desire lines' (i.e. lines linking the origin and destination of movements) are lengthening and that they are being strongly constricted by routes developed to meet earlier shorter range desire lines. Slowly the old pattern is changing as new roads, motorways, freeways and by-passes are built around settlements. An attempt to fuse this sequence with a theoretical Löschian landscape (Lösch, 1954, p. 127) is shown in Figure 3.25. We begin with an idealized Löschian landscape, in which desire lines connect each settlement with the next in a network of intersecting pathways; this type of pattern is still discernible on maps of rural areas in tropical Africa. In the second stage (Figure 3.25B), the economic level has been raised to give a longer interaction distance, and to halve the number of major centres and to leave a series of by-passed smaller centres connected by smaller routes. In thc third stage (Figure 3.25C), the interaction has been raised still further with a new set of optimum routes, a new and smaller set of major centres, and a larger set of by-passed centres.

The Löschian model, unlike that of Buchanan, assumes that new routes will be built simultaneously to the demand generated by increasing traffic volumes between emerging centres. Buchanan, certainly more realistically for Britain, emphasizes the significant lags between the manifestation of demand and the creation of a supply, so that longer distance traffic is forever being forced along pre-existing smaller scale and capacity arteries with resulting slow movement, confused desire lines, high accident rates and grinding congestion. Relief comes in several ways: by the upgrading of these segments to the standards of longer distance routeways; the building of completely new routeways like motorways along paths that run generally between major cities but yet avoid their immediate urban sprawl; or by re-scheduling services on existing networks to allow rapid inter-city transit at the expense of rural provision.

## 3.6 Conclusions

Locational models of route structure are among the most poorly developed areas of locational analysis. Despite their evident importance in determining the configuration of many aspects of human settlement, the study of transport networks stands somewhat apart from the other topics covered in Part One of this book. Much of the little theory available comes from the mathematical models developed for network optimization. While these are formal and rigorous in structure, they tend to break down in two situations of special interest to the geographer: (a) where the network itself has a complex spatial structure, and (b) where there are multivariate forces at work on shaping its locational pattern. Later in the book, we shall encounter avenues along which networks are currently being explored, e.g. via diffusion models (see Section 7.5), via improvements in spatial definition (see Section 9.7) and via linear programming (see Section 15.4.2).

# 4 Nodes

4.1 **Introduction.** 4.2 **Settlement Patterns:** 1 Settlements as regular lattices; 2 Lattice distortion over space; 3 Lattice distortion over time. 4.3 **Size Distribution of Settlements:** 1 Rank-size regularities: large cities; 2 'Lower limb' relationships; 3 Settlement size as a lognormal distribution; 4 Regional evidence on lognormal city-size distribution. 4.4 **Changes Over Time:** 1 Historical changes in city-size distributions; 2 Changes in the role of individual cities. 4.5 **Relationship between Size and Spacing of Settlements:** 1 Spacing of discrete size groups; 2 Spacing as a continuous function of size. 4.6 **Impulse Transmission between Urban Areas:** 1 Transmission of discrete shocks; 2 Transmission of continuous waves; 3 Models of impulse transmission. 4.7 **Conclusions.**

## 4.1 Introduction

In the same way that a study of spatial interaction leads on to a consideration of networks, so the study of networks leads to a consideration of the nodes on those networks. 'Node' is used here to describe the junctions or vertices on the network, and as such it serves as a collective term which includes others—cities, central places, hamlets, population clusters—all of which names are heavily loaded with other and wider implications. Nodes can be identified at all levels of regional organization, from the macro-region, with its nodal metropolitan area, to the micro-region with its nodal farmstead.

In this chapter, we look at the distribution of settlements in terms of their size and spacing characteristics; in the next chapter, which is closely linked to this, we examine their organization into hierarchial structures. We begin our analysis with settlement patterns, and then consider the size and spacing of nodes. Finally we look at the way impulses move through a set of nodes, a theme taken up again in Chapters 7 and 16.

## 4.2 Settlement Patterns

Looking at the distribution of human population over the earth's surface is like looking up at the night sky. We can at once distinguish great galaxies and constellations, made up of clusters of population of vastly different sizes (see Section 4.3). The few great centres of metropolitan population stand out clearly, while at the other extreme the myriad of small rural communities lies at the extreme limit of our powers of statistical discrimination.

In discussing the basic arrangement of nodal clusters, it is convenient to use as a substitute their morphological expression, the settlement pattern (Table 4.1). In this approach, we are treating settlements as point-like objects and are ignoring their size characteristics which we consider later in the chapter. Despite the fact that such treatment represents, as Hägerstrand (1957, p. 27) has argued, only the 'centroid' or centre of gravity of continuous population movements, settlements are a concrete expression of human occupation of the earth's surface. As such, they form an essential element of landscape and have had a central part in the syllabus of human geography. In both early statements, like that of Jean Brunhes (1925), and more recent reviews, like that of Emrys Jones (1964), settlement patterns hold a dominant place.

Table 4.1 Alternative types of settlement classification

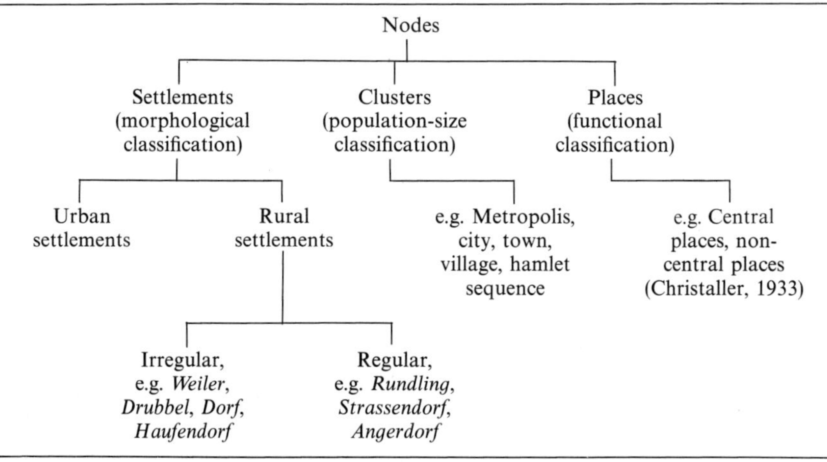


### 4.2.1 *Settlements as regular lattices*

In an earlier discussion of movements (Section 2.7.1), it was argued that the hexagon provides the most economical geometrical form for the equal division of an area between a number of points. By the same argument, we can show that the centres of these hexagons, the nodal points, must form a regular triangular lattice to conform with the same minimum energy requirements (Figure 4.1A).

The notion of settlements arranged in this regular triangular fashion was used by Christaller (1933) in his original development of central place theory, and by Lösch (1954) in his subsequent development of the Christaller model (see Section 5.2). We might therefore expect, on theoretical grounds, that settlements would be found to be arranged in the form of a triangular lattice. However, Lösch (1954, p. 133) has pointed out practical difficulties in adopting this arrangement, and has suggested that the square lattice might be adopted where new areas of settlement are being planned. Squares are (as Figure 2.15B shows) only moderately less efficient than hexagons and form a very useful substitute.

(*a*) *Observed regularities: qualitative evidence.* Inspection of settlement patterns described by European geographers shows little immediate indication of a regular lattice. Indeed attention has been focused on the shape of individual settlements rather than their general pattern. Thus, while a complex typology of village forms has been evolved (e.g. Meitzen, 1895; summarized by Pfeifer, in Thomas, 1956, pp. 240–77), particularly in the German literature (Table 4.1), the description of pattern has not moved much beyond a simple dispersed-nucleated dichotomy. There are, of course, certain regular geometric forms which are clearly recognizable. The Roman *centuriation* pattern or the arrangement of new villages on the reclaimed virgin land of the Dutch polders are small examples of regular lattices in Europe, but the major examples lie overseas in areas of European colonization.

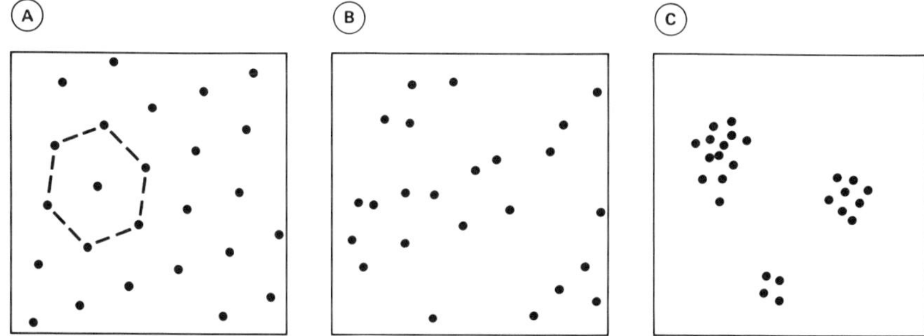


**Figure 4.1** Typical regular (**A**), random (**B**), and clustered (**C**) distributions.

In the most spectacular case, the 'township and range' system of the United States, a regular system of square subdivisions was laid out over an area of some two million square miles—the greater part of the central and western sections of the country. Pattison (1957) has traced the various solutions that were put forward from 1785 onwards to the problem of dividing the unoccupied lands of the Western Territories. The difficulty of meridional convergence created surveying problems and it was not until the nineteenth century that a relatively uniform scheme was adopted. The rectilinear system, with its nested divisions into square townships (36 square miles in area), sections (one square mile in area), and quarter-sections (160 acres in area) provided the common mould into which the complex society that settled the West was poured. Through the Homestead Act of 1862, the quarter-section became the module of farm organization at a critical time in land occupation, and despite subsequent revisions, its pattern has been firmly struck on landscapes as unlike as Oklahoma and Alaska. Mead and Brown (1962) give some excellent examples of the relation of the township and range system to roads, settlement, and land use in various parts of the United States.

In the century since its imposition, the rigid geometrical lines of the township and range system have been somewhat blurred. Johnson (1957) in a study of Whitewater basin, Minnesota state, has shown how the original quarter-section claims of 1853–4 were themselves made up of contiguous but irregular combinations of forty-acre units in an attempt to align the farm

boundaries with the basic soil and terrain characteristics of the area. Since then, the forces of abandonment, re-sale, and combination have further adjusted the pattern. As was shown in Section 3.3.2, access to highways plays a major part in the location of the farmstead within the quarter-section (Figure 3.9A), and a linear settlement pattern along the roads has developed over large areas. Kollmorgen and Jenks (1951) have confirmed this trend for another quarter-section area in western Kansas. Here farm size was found to have increased fivefold since 1890 with the new farms being arranged along the east-west highways (the main direction of the traffic movement) in a linear manner.
(*b*) *Observed regularities: quantitative evidence.* Dacey (1962) has analysed the distribution of hamlets, villages, and towns in an area of the United States settled under the township and range system. He selected an area of southwestern Wisconsin, previously studied by Brush (1953), which contained some 235 settlements divided into three strata: hamlets (61 per cent of the total settlements), villages (31 per cent), and towns (8 per cent). Dacey used the technique of nearest neighbour analysis to compare the observed pattern with three expected distributions: (i) a hexagonal distribution, (ii) a random (Poisson) distribution, and (iii) a clustered distribution (Figure 4.1). A full discussion of nearest neighbour and other methods of point pattern analysis is undertaken in Chapter 13. Table 4.2 shows the relationship between the observed and expected patterns by means of *D*-values which measure the difference between the two: high *D*-values indicate strong differences, and vice versa. Comparison of the three columns shows clearly that the pattern of settlements in this area approximates a random (rather than a regular or clustered) distribution. However, there is some variation between the three levels of the settlement strata—hamlets show the greatest degree of correspondence with the regular (hexagonal) grid. Dacey's work suggests, therefore, that even in an area of planned land division the dominant pattern of settlement appears to be random, but that the smallest settlements (the hamlets) show more vestiges of regular arrangement than do the higher-order settlements.

Table 4.2 Actual and theoretical settlement arrangements*

| *Class of settlement:* | *Hamlets* | *Villages* | *Towns* |
|---|---|---|---|
| Difference between observed and expected distribution (*D*-values): | | | |
| Regular (hexagonal) distribution | 5.41 | 6.31 | 5.81 |
| Random distribution | 1.79 | 1.57 | 2.73 |
| Clustered distribution | 13.39 | 15.21 | 15.52 |

Source: Dacey, 1962, p. 71.
* *Southwestern Wisconsin, United States.*

Nearest neighbour techniques have also been used by King (1962) in a comparative analysis of twenty sample areas within the United States (Figure 4.2A). Within each area, all urban places were plotted and a series of straight line measurements was taken between each place and its nearest neighbour (regardless of size). The number of towns analysed varied from 177 in the

Pennsylvania sample area down to 23 towns in the New Mexico sample area. By comparing the observed spacing with the expected spacing in a random distribution the nearest neighbour statistic, $D_1$ [defined in equation (13.9)], was calculated. Values for $D_1$ range from zero when all points are clustered in one location, through 1.00 which represents a random distribution, up to 2.15 for a uniform triangular lattice (see Section 13.6.1). Values for $D_1$ are plotted for the twenty sample areas in Figure 4.2B. They show a small range from 0.70 in the case of the Utah sample area with its relatively clustered distribution, to 1.38 for the Missouri sample area with its rather regular pattern. The actual distribution for these two areas is shown in Figure 4.2C. Thus the main conclusion from King's work is to support the view that the settlement pattern of the United States is not purely regular, but varies towards a random distribution.

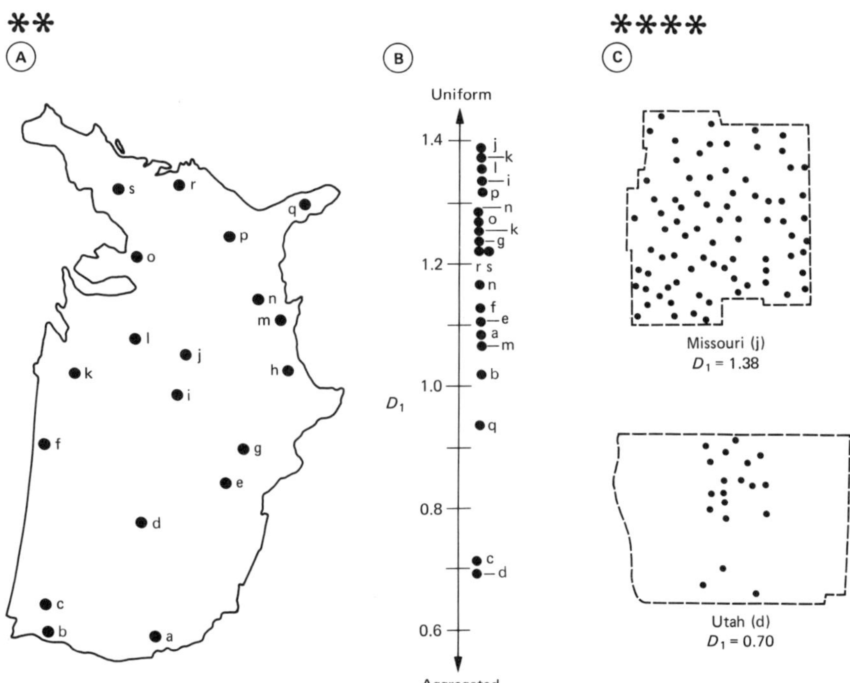


**Figure 4.2** **A** Sample study areas within the United States. **B** Scale of $D_1$ values. **C** Clustered settlements in the Utah sample area contrasted to regular settlements in the Missouri sample area. Source: King, 1962, pp. 3–4.

Other, more recent evidence, for a random component in U.S. settlement patterns appears in Rayner and Gollege (1972, 1973). Their work, which used *spectral analysis*, is considered in detail in Section 12.4.2, but we note here that they concluded that the spacing of settlements in Oregon and along U.S. highway 40 from Baltimore to San Francisco is random. In addition, Dacey (1964, 1965, 1966a, b, 1968, 1969a) developed a whole series of models based upon Poisson (random) processes in the plane to describe the spacing of towns in the American Mid-West, Puerto Rico and Japan. Dacey's models were all *quadrat count methods*, which we consider in Chapter 13. Cliff and Ord (1973, Chapter 3) have also used quadrat count approaches to confirm the presence of an important random element in settlement patterns in the Tonami Plain, Japan (see Section 13.4).

The results presented suggest, therefore, that while settlements are not purely randomly spaced, there is a significant random component involved. An attempt to provide a theoretical justification for this feature appears in Curry (1964, 1967). In these papers on the *random spatial economy*, Curry has used entropy arguments (cf. Sections 2.5 and 4.3.3) to indicate that, at the macro- (aggregate) level, random process models may form a convenient framework within which the overall effect may be examined of many individual decisions which cannot be separately studied.

### 4.2.2 *Lattice distortion over space*

The failure of the regular lattice as a model for actual settlement arrangements is hardly surprising. The triangular lattice, like the hexagon, is a pure theoretical concept, and in practice we would expect it to be distorted by other relevant considerations.

(*a*) *Distortion by agglomeration.* One of the most serious defects in the Löschian system of regular hexagons is its failure to allow for inevitable variations in hexagon size. Lösch postulated a high density of population around the core of his market area, but failed to adjust his hexagonal network (Figure 5.9) to accommodate it. Although a detailed formulation still waits to be made, a graphical modification has been attempted by Isard (1956, p. 272) in which hexagons get steadily smaller in size, the nearer their location to the central core (Figure 2.20). The implications for the settlement pattern are clear. We should expect settlements to be more closely packed around major urban centres than in the remoter parts of a region.

One of the most interesting confirmations of this trend comes from a study by Bogue (1950), in which he analysed the distribution of population around 67 of the major cities of the United States. Bogue has drawn up his results in the form of generalized cross-sections running from the city out to the rural peripheries, up to 300 miles away from the cities. These cross-sections suggest four general conclusions:

(i) Urban population declines with distance from the central city in a logarithmic fashion. In all the graphs in Figure 4.3 urban population density, averaged over the 67 cities, is plotted as a broken line on the $y$-axis against distance from the nearest metropolis on the $x$-axis, and both axes are transformed to logarithmic scales. At 25 miles from the city, the density is over 200 people per square mile; at 250 miles out it has fallen to about four per square mile. This result may be compared with those in Section 6.2, where urban population density gradients are considered in detail.

(ii) Density and rate of decline vary with the size of the central city. For the fourteen metropolitan communities with populations of over 500,000 inhabitants, the urban population density was found to be about eight times higher than for the 53 cities below this level at 25 miles out from the centre, but the difference diminishes at greater distances from the metropolis.

(iii) Density and rate of decline vary with the region of the United States. The contrast between the Northeast (Figure 4.3A), the South (Figure 4.3B), and the West (Figure 4.3C) comes out very strongly: the Northeast with its high overall density and steep lapse rate, the South with its lower density and irregular lapse rate, and the West with its precipitous lapse rate, stand in marked regional contrast.

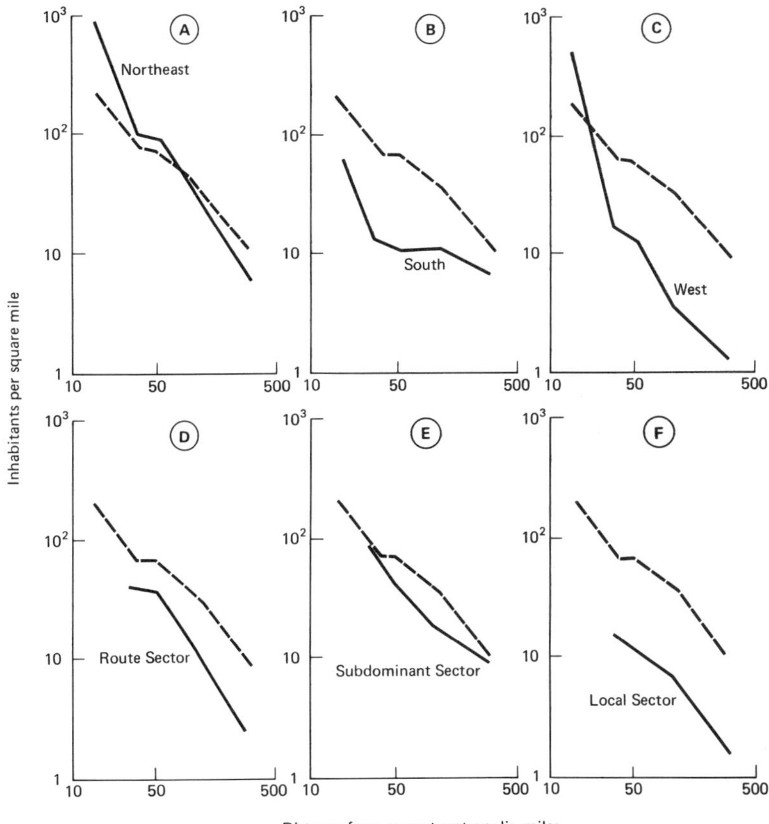


**Figure 4.3** Variations in urban population densities by region (**A**, **B**, **C**) and by sector (**D**, **E**, **F**) in the United States. The broken lines show the average density for all 67 cities in the sample. Source: Bogue, 1950, pp. 47, 58.

(iv) Density and rate of decline vary with direction from the city. Bogue divided the hinterlands around his 67 cities into three types of sector: the *route* sector, the *subdominant* sector, and the *local* sector. Twelve 30° sectors were demarcated on a transparent mask which was rotated about the city centre until the sector centres made the 'best fit' with the main highways leading from the city to other major metropolitan areas (Figure 4.4B). Sectors which contained a major highway were classed as route sectors, those that contained at least one city of 25,000 or more inhabitants were termed the subdominant sectors, and the remaining sectors were termed the local sectors. In each case, urban population was measured for counties and these were assigned to one or more of the sectors. Convergence of sector boundaries eliminated this process near the city and sector differences were only recorded for areas more than 25 miles out from the centre. Figure 4.4 shows the stages in sector delimination for one of the cities, Memphis (Tennessee): route sectors are unshaded, subdominant sectors are in black, and local sectors are stippled.

Examination of the trends in density for the three sectors (Figures 4.3D, E, F) shows that urban population is most dense in the subdominant sector. The effect of route sectors spilling urban settlement out along the major intermetropolitan highways is less strong than might be expected: local sectors are well below the levels of the other two.

(*b*) *Distortion by resource localization.* It is implicit in the assumptions of a triangular lattice of settlements, that the resources needed by each settlement are everywhere available—the assumption of an isotropic plane. If, however, we take a fairly simple settlement unit, the village, and list its traditional requirements—agricultural land, water, building materials, fuel, etc.—it is clear that in reality these resources are localized. The full analysis of the minimum energy location when resources are localized must wait until the next chapter (see Section 5.6.1) but it is clear that (i) the different requirements

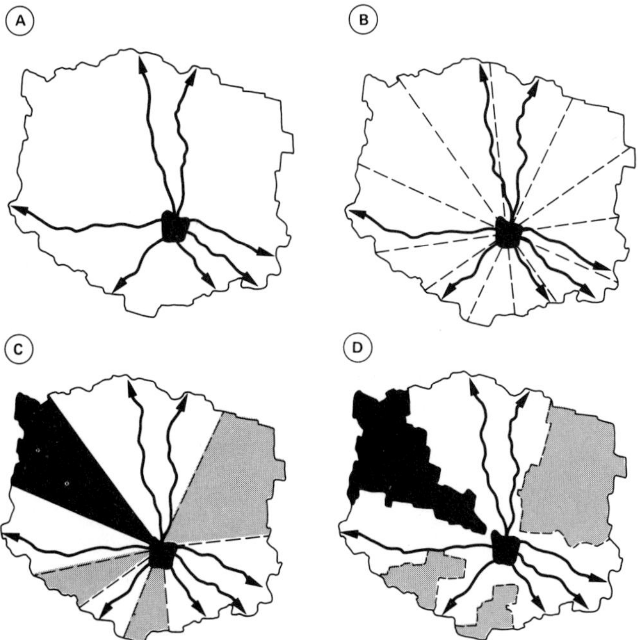


**Figure 4.4** Stages in the classification of urban hinterlands into sector types. **A** Routes. **B** Sectors. **C** Classification of sectors. **D** Alignment with local statistical units. Source: Bogue, 1950, p. 25.

will exert varying 'pulls' on the location of the settlement, and (ii) the regular lattice will be correspondingly distorted. Some indication of this distortion is given in Figure 4.5. In the first case, seven settlements are distributed regularly over areas of *uniform* resources (Figure 4.5A). In the second, a *zonal* resource (stippled) is introduced (Figure 4.5B). On the assumption that all settlements must have access to this resource, but that they will move as short a distance as possible from their lattice positions, a set of new locations is determined (with appropriate changes in their territories determined by Thiessen polygon techniques as described in Section 13.5). In the third, a *linear* resource (e.g. a stream or routeway) is assumed and an appropriate change in the location of the settlements calculated (Figure 4.5C). In the final case, a *point* resource is assumed (e.g. single well or defensive site), and the appropriate moves made (Figure 4.5D).

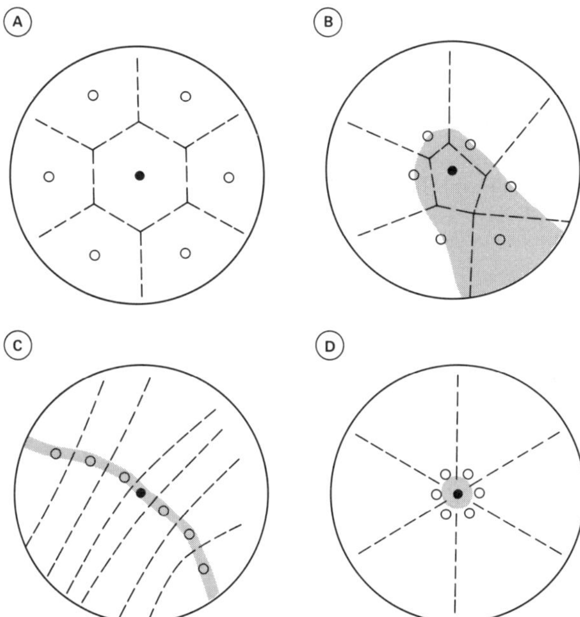


**Figure 4.5** Sequence of settlement patterns associated with an increasingly localized resource.

Clearly the four cases described are hypothetical and we should not expect such clear cut distortions to occur in practice. Nevertheless, if we compare them with the scheme of settlement types recognized by European scholars (Jones, 1964, pp. 123–7) there are a number of apparent similarities. We may see in Figure 4.5A some characteristics of the scattered farmsteads, the *Einzelhof*; in Figure 4.5C, traces of the *Waldhufendorf*, the *Strassendorf*, or the *Marschhufendorf*, all string-like villages of differing degrees of organization and environment; in Figure 4.5D, the *Rundling* with its radial fields, or the *Haufendorf* with its irregular, open field pattern. Clearly, the actual development of regional settlement patterns is a multivariate product in which social conventions play as big a part as environment. Nevertheless, basic geometrical considerations, even though severely modified, still play a part in that syndrome.

### 4.2.3 *Lattice distortion over time*

(*a*) *Models of settlement evolution over time.* One of the problems of the Christaller and Lösch models of settlement is that they are essentially static, whereas we know in reality that the central place hierarchy is complicated by time. Thus in an area like the eastern United States or eastern Brazil, the settlement hierarchy is heavily weighted towards the areas of earliest settlement: in the later areas, the hierarchy is still in a very active phase of evolution. Two major lines of theory are examined here in which the time element is made explicit: (i) deterministic models, and (ii) probabilistic models.

(i) One of the few attempts to place settlement expansion within a deterministic framework has come from Bylund (1960). An historical study of colonization in the central Lappland area of Sweden before 1867 led him to consider the way in which 'waves' of settlements moved within this area, and he produced four simple models (Figure 4.6) of development. In each of them the basic assumptions are first that the physical conditions of the land are equal in all areas (settled or unsettled) and second that further areas will not be settled until those close to the 'mother settlements' have been occupied. The only major difference between the four models is in the number and the location of the mother settlements; clearly the first and last cases assume

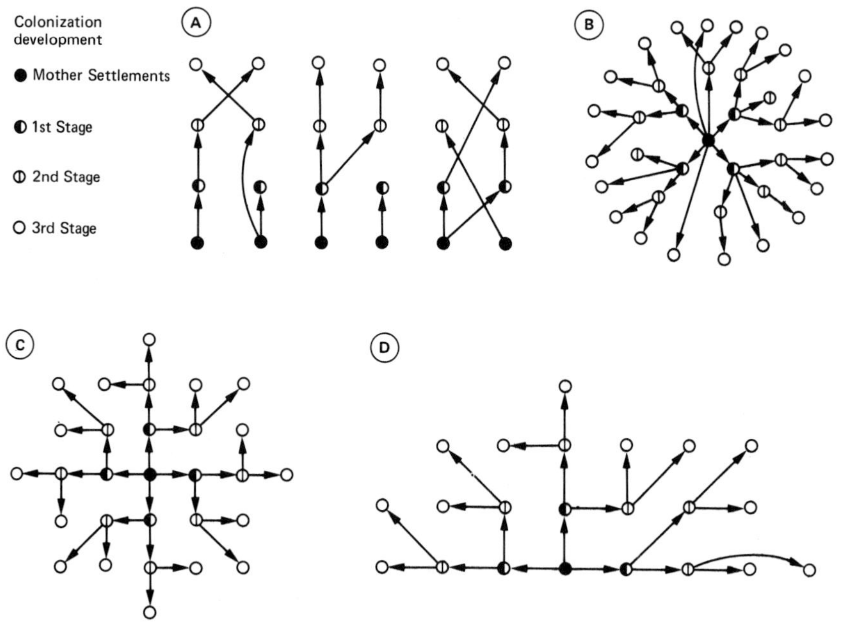


**Figure 4.6** Hypothetical models of settlement diffusion. Source: Bylund, 1960, p. 226.

spread from coastal locations. The models are similar in form to the probabilistic *perimeter models* described in Section 7.7.7.

Like von Thünen (Section 6.2), Bylund attempted to reintroduce reality into his model by varying the physical conditions of the land, access to roads, and variations in the number of migrant farmers moving out in each generation to found new farmsteads. Comparisons between a much more refined model and the historical records for Arvidsjaur parish between 1775 and 1867 show sufficient agreement to suggest that further research on the application of this von Thünen-like growth model to settlements might be rewarding.

(ii) An alternative approach to the evolution of settlement patterns is through the framework of Monte Carlo techniques (discussed in detail in Section 7.2). In this stochastic formulation, growth is simulated by random processes which are restricted by the operation of certain 'rules' based on empirical observations of settlement behaviour. A typical example of this simulation approach to settlement evolution is provided by Morrill (1962). He begins with an initial settlement, the founding settlement, and observes the build-up of a settlement hierarchy around it as governed by a sequence of random numbers (see Appendix, Table A6). The three basic rules followed by Morrill are: first, in each time period or generation ($t_0$, $t_1$, ..., $t_T$), every place generates at least one migrant in the order of its origin, with the total number of migrants from each place proportional to its size; second, any place may be settled more than once and enlarged in size, provided it does not clash with the 'distance–compatibility rule' which restricts the size of a place according to its distance from the larger places (e.g. a settlement five cells from the origin, may increase to five and then remain stagnant); third, the distance and direction of each migrant's move is governed by the numbers in the probability matrix shown in Figure 4.7A, a matrix based on empirical studies of local population movements in Scandinavia by Kulldorff (1955) and Hägerstrand (1957). The rules of this model are similar in some respects to those of the *centre–satellite* model considered in Section 13.4.4.

Figure 4.7B shows a simple example from Morrill of the growth of a six-settlement hierarchy (A, B, ... F). The sequence begins with the single settlement A, in a seaboard location and the probability matrix is centred over A. The grid shown in Figure 4.7B is assumed to be surrounded on all sides by sea. The numbers in brackets refer to random numbers. *First generation*: (10)—impossible (in the ocean), (22)—locate new settlement, B; A grows to size 'two'. *Second generation*: (24)— impossible (B cannot grow beyond size 'one' as it is only one cell from A), (42)—locate new settlement, C; A grows to size 'three'. *Third generation*: (37)—locate new settlement, D; A grows to size 'four', but B and C are too close for it to grow further. *Fourth generation*: (96)—locate new settlement, E, (77)—locate new settlement, F (n.b. matrix is centred on D, the parent centre for this operation); A grows to size 'five', D grows to size 'two'. At the end of this sequence, using seven random numbers (10, 22, 24, 42, 37, 96 and 77) and the probability matrix in Figure 4.7A, a hierarchy of six settlements has been formed with one large settlement (A at size 'five'), one medium settlement (D at size 'two'), and four smaller settlements (B, C, E, and F, each at size 'one').

By following these rules and re-centring the matrix over the settlement from which migrants are originating, a hierarchy can be slowly built up which simulates a general pattern of settlement (though not its exact location) (Figure 4.7c). Hierarchies and rank-size rules are built up even though they are (as in reality), imperfect and asymmetric. Robson (1973, Chapter 6) provides a good example of this approach to a settlement system.

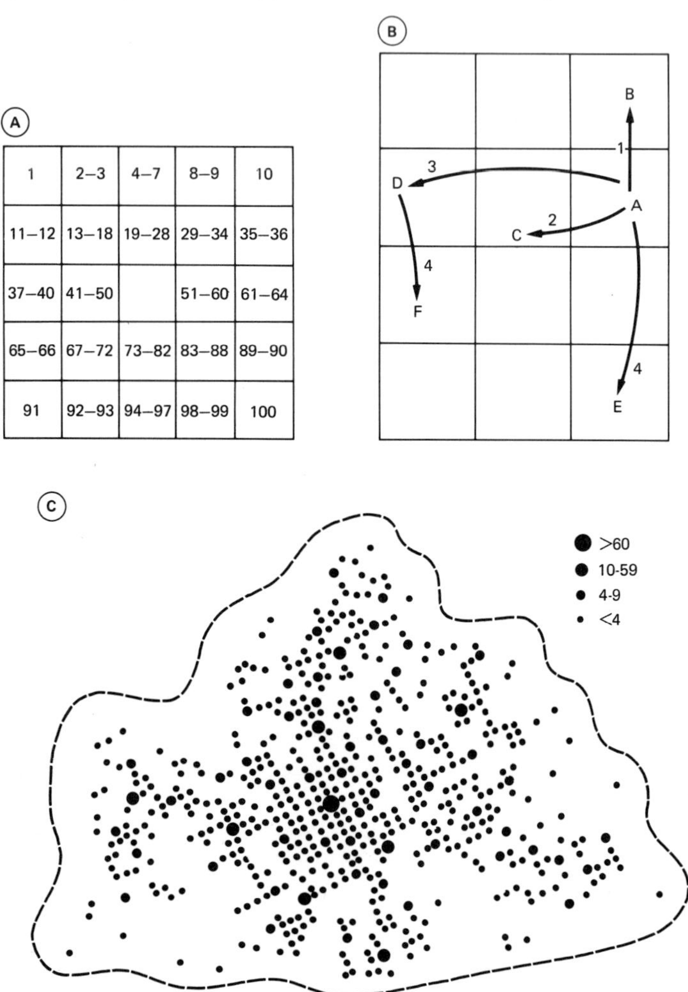


**Figure 4.7** Simulation of settlement hierarchies. **A** Distance and direction probability matrix. **B** Sample simulation sequence using Monte Carlo methods. In **B**, the numbers refer to generations, not size. **C** Simulated settlement pattern generated by Monte Carlo methods. Source: Morrill, 1962, p. 112, 119.

(*b*) *Observed evolution patterns.* The tracing of the complex patterns of actual settlement processes is a problem in historical detection which demands a wide range of evidence. Mitchell (1954), in her reconstruction of the evolution of settlement in East Anglia, has pieced together fragments of information as unlike as place-names, church architecture, and aerial photographs. Sandner (1961), in a survey of the spread of Spanish colonization in Costa Rica, relied more heavily on archival documents and, for the more recent phases, census records. Both studies, and others like them, have tended to recognize distinct phases in the settlement process, e.g. Mitchell distinguishes *primary* settlement in the river valleys from *secondary* settlement on the till-covered interfluves, and Sandner describes the process in which 'mother settlements' serve as bases for later offsprings.

Chisholm (1962) has suggested that the diffusion of new and smaller settlements around older and larger settlements may be linked to four major changes: (i) socio-economic changes in the land holding system, (ii) removal of the need for defensive agglomeration, (iii) elimination of such factors as disease, which inhibited earlier land settlement, and (iv) technical improvements in water supply. Of these, perhaps the most important in industrialized areas have been the changes in systems of land holding. Hoskins (1955, p. 157) in his *Makings of the English landscape* has discussed the impact of the Parliamentary enclosure of great tracts of land in England between 1750 and 1850. Isolated farmsteads with consolidated holdings were substituted for nucleated villages with communal strip-holdings, i.e. in terms of Figure 4.5, the fourth type reverted to the first type. For Japan, Inouye has traced the slow breakdown of linear villages (the third type in Figure 4.5) into a more dispersed form. For one village, Kamitome near Tokyo, a continuous record of farmsteads and holdings enabled the evolution to be traced in detail from the late seventeenth century: with successive population increases the width of the strip farms was progressively narrowed as new farms crowded along the roadside in the traditional manner until a point was reached when the roadside location was saturated. Further narrowing of the strips was then impractical and new farmsteads were set up away from the road.

New patterns of farm distribution in southern Italy, and the new colonization schemes in the Dry Zone of Ceylon (Farmer, 1957), suggest examples for Chisholm's second and third dispersal factors. Technical change, the fourth dispersal factor, has of course worked in both directions. For while barbed-wire and steel windmills may have allowed the dispersion of farm settlement over the Great Plains (Webb, 1927), further technical changes, notably the automobile and the combine harvester allowed the growth of absentee farming—the 'sidewalk' and 'suitcase' farming described in Section 6.1.3.

Hudson (1969b) has proposed a location theory for rural settlement assuming spatial processes similar to those found in plant ecology. The three components identified are (i) *colonization*, associated with the dispersal of settlement into new territory; (ii) *spread*, associated with increasing population density *in situ* and a general tendency to short-distance infilling of gaps; and (iii) *competition*, in which 'owing to limitations of the environment weak individuals are forced out by their stronger neighbours, density tends to decrease, and pattern stabilizes' (Hudson, 1969, p. 367). Figure 4.8 shows the relationship between the first two components in a one-dimensional situation: first, with colonization alone (Figure 4.8A), second with spread alone (Figure 4.8B), and third with the two components combined (Figure

4.8C). In all three diagrams, the number of settlements varies inversely with distance from an optimal location in the environment (*O* in Figure 4.8). Under colonization alone, the area available for occupation (the 'biotope' in ecological terms) will increase without changing the number of settlements, thereby lowering density in order to expand the frontier. Under a pure spread process, the magnitude function is shifted upwards but not outwards, producing an overall increase in density. Quadrat analysis (see Chapter 13) is used to measure the relative importance of the components for the changing pattern of rural settlement. Empirical evidence for farmstead evolution over a ninety-year period (1870–1960) in six Iowa counties shows that the expected increases in regularity implied by components (i)–(iii) does occur.

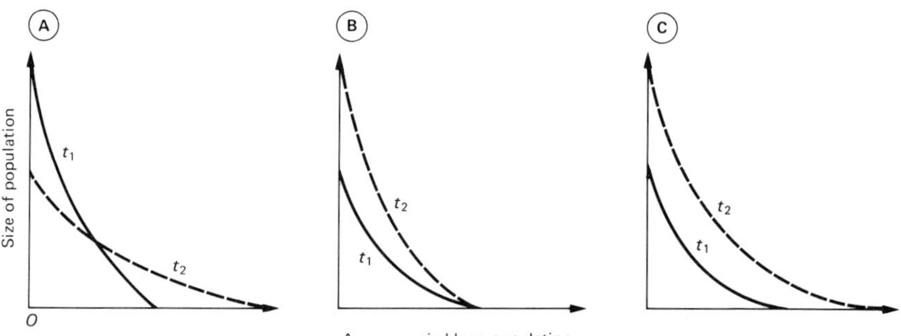


**Figure 4.8** Relationships between colonization and spread process in the Hudson model. **A** Colonization alone; **B** Infilling alone; **C** Colonization with infilling. Source: Hudson, 1969, p. 369.

## 4.3 Size Distribution of Settlements

Although it is very convenient to regard the world's population as distributed in a series of discrete and isolated *clusters*, we must recognize at the outset that this is a somewhat artificial concept. Our definition of a cluster depends largely upon how we draw our boundaries and how we define the term 'isolated'. Thus Inouye (International Geographical Union, 1964) defines an isolated unit of settlement as one which is at least 150 metres away from the next unit. Clearly we have to adopt some such artificial standard, but we must be prepared to modify this with larger settlements. The problem of the operational definition of 'cities' is a complex one and is discussed in detail in Section 8.2.3. In this chapter, we make extensive use of the survey by the International Urban Research Unit of the University of California at Berkeley, which has attempted to standardize the definition of metropolitan areas throughout the world (International Urban Research, 1959).

Examination of the available information on the larger, city-size clusters suggests a remarkable regularity. Like the regular branching of a drainage network (Leopold, Wolman and Miller, 1964), each cluster appears to occupy some definite place in the urban hierarchy, the whole system appearing as '. . . a chain, almost a feudal chain of vassalage, wherein one city may stand tributary to a bigger centre and yet be a metropolis of a sizeable region of its own' (Careless, 1954, p. 17). As Table 4.3 shows, there are relatively few large cities, many medium sized cities, and a host of smaller cities, whether we take our measurements at the world scale, for a single nation (e.g. United States), or for a single region within that nation (e.g. Texas): the number of clusters is clearly directly proportional to size at all three scales. Evidence of this kind, pointing to rather regular relationships, has led to a number of attempts to define the number-size ratio in precise terms. In this chapter, we look first at the size distribution of cities, and then move on to look at that for the smallest settlements—hamlets and villages.

Table 4.3 Distribution of cities by size*

| *Region:* | *Texas* | *United States* | *World†* |
|---|---|---|---|
| Size group by number of inhabitants: | | | |
| 100,000– 250,000 | 6 | 65 | 565 |
| 250,000– 500,000 | 3 | 23 | 163 |
| 500,000–1,000,000 | 1 | 13 | 86 |
| Over 1,000,000 | 1 | 5 | 53 |

Source: International Urban Research, 1959, and Berry, 1961a, p. 588.
* Data for early 1950s. † 40 countries.

### 4.3.1 *Rank-size regularities: large cities*

Regular relationships between the size of towns and their rank were noted over half a century ago by Auerbach (1913). We may state this relationship formally as the *rank-size rule*, given by the formula

$$p_i = p_1/i \tag{4.1}$$

where $p_i$ is the population of the $i$th town in the series 1, 2, 3, ... $n$ in which all towns in a region are arranged in descending order by population, and $p_1$ is the population of the largest town (the *primate* town) (Figure 4.9). We should therefore expect the fifth largest town to have a population exactly one-fifth that of the largest town, if the rank-size rule were an accurate description of the relationship. In the United States in 1940, Isard (1956, p. 58) has shown that with a $p_1$ of 11,690,000 (New York), the value of $p_5$ should be 2,338,000. In fact, Boston, the fifth ranking city, had a population of 2,351,000.

The rank-size rule may be rewritten as a general Pareto distribution, namely

$$p_i = a(i)^{-b}. \tag{4.2}$$

In equation (4.2), the population of the $i$th ranking city ($p_i$) is a function of that rank ($i$), and $a$ and $b$ are constants. For computational purposes, the relationship may be rewritten as

$$\log p_i = \log a - b(\log i), \tag{4.3}$$

and values of $a$ and $b$ estimated as in a simple linear regression by ordinary least squares.

As Stewart (1958) has argued, the rank-size rule may be viewed as a special case of the Pareto distribution in which $b = -1$. The rule may therefore be regarded as an empirical finding rather than a theoretical or logical necessity. We should thus gauge the usefulness of the rank-size rule by the degree to which it helps us to generalize observations on actual settlement distributions. Studies by Allen (1954) and Clark (1967) show considerable variations about the values of $\hat{b} = -1.00$. Egypt ($\hat{b} = -1.77$) or Portugal ($\hat{b} = -1.43$) show steeply-sloping curves in which city size falls off very rapidly with rank. Conversely, New Zealand ($\hat{b} = -0.74$) and Norway ($\hat{b} = -0.85$) have much flatter curves than expected. Table 4.4 shows the size distribution of cities with different $b$ values for comparison. The distributions are graphed in Figure 4.9.

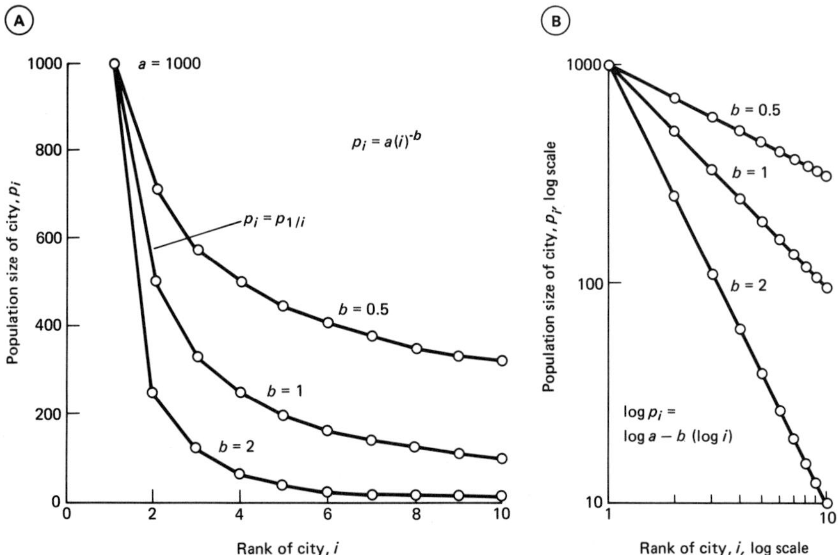


**Figure 4.9** Rank-size diagrams for the three distributions in Table 4.4.

Special interest has been shown in the size of the first-ranking or primate city, compared with other cities, in a nation. Stewart (1958) has examined the relationship between the primate city ($p_1$) and the second largest city ($p_2$) in a cross-section of 72 countries. He found that the ratios did not cluster around 0.50 as expected under the rank-size rule, but that for the whole sample the median relationship was 0.31 (i.e. the second city was characteristically one-third the size of the first). Ratios ranged from countries like Canada with values as high as 0.65 to Uruguay with only 0.06. Stewart found few regularities in the distribution of these ratios, other than the fact that the larger countries tended to have high ratios. For six of these countries (Australia, Brazil, Canada, India, United States, and U.S.S.R.) the ratios were also calculated for the cities in their various internal subdivisions (states, provinces, etc.). These ranged from median ratios of 0.43 for the United States to the remarkably low ratio of 0.07 for Australia, where five of its six states are strongly dominated by large urban centres (Holmes, 1973). Again, the results suggest that ratios at the provincial level are lower than the rank-size rule would predict. Linsky (1965) carried out a systematic comparison of primate city distributions on an international scale which suggested some links between high primacy and a generally low level of economic development, but the pattern was not a uniform or clear one (see also Section 4.3.3).

Table 4.4 Expected size distribution of cities with different $b$ values.

| | $p_i = a(i)^{-1}$ | | | $p_i = a(i)^{-0.5}$ | $p = a(i)^{-2}$ |
|---|---|---|---|---|---|
| *Settlement rank* | *Population size* | *Cumulative population* | *Cumulative population as % share of total population* | *Population size* | *Population size* |
| 1 | 1000 | 1000 | 34 | 1000 | 1000 |
| 2 | 500 | 1500 | 51 | 707 | 250 |
| 3 | 333 | 1833 | 63 | 577 | 111 |
| 4 | 250 | 2083 | 71 | 500 | 63 |
| 5 | 200 | 2283 | 78 | 447 | 40 |
| 6 | 167 | 2450 | 84 | 408 | 28 |
| 7 | 143 | 2593 | 89 | 378 | 20 |
| 8 | 125 | 2718 | 93 | 354 | 16 |
| 9 | 111 | 2829 | 97 | 333 | 12 |
| 10 | 100 | 2929 | 100 | 316 | 10 |
| Sum | 2929 | — | — | 5020 | 1550 |

Results based on the two leading cities might be expected to be highly variable because of the small size of the sample. A number of writers (Zipf, 1949; Stewart, 1958; Gibbs, 1961, pp. 438–51) have followed these relationships further down the urban spectrum. Figure 4.10A shows the ratios for the five largest cities in a number of contrasting countries. The United States shows a reasonably close correspondence with the expected sequence (i.e. 1, 0.50, 0.33, 0.25 and 0.20), while Australia shows strong divergence. When the rank-size relationship is extended over the full range of towns for which data are available, curves like those in Figure 4.10B are generated. The curves show two contrasting cases: the United States (unbroken line) in which the lines are relatively straight and in which the general form of the rank-size rule is confirmed, and Sweden (broken lines) which forms a much wavier curve. Comparison of the two curves shows an increasing linearity over time with the United States, but continuing irregularity over time with Sweden. Again, both cases suggest some range in the behaviour of the city-size distribution over time as well as space. We take up the theme of changes over time and urban growth in Section 4.4.

### 4.3.2 *'Lower limb' relationships*

Not surprisingly, most attention has been devoted to the largest cities and towns at the upper end of the settlement size distribution. The rank-size relationships of villages and hamlets have been rather neglected and represent an unsolved problem. Under the rank-size rule, the number of settlements of a given type should continue to increase as size decreases, so that we should not only expect more villages than towns, but more hamlets than villages, more isolated farms than hamlets. The same assumptions are made in the Christaller–Lösch ideas of the functional hierarchy (Section 5.2). But we know that this relationship may not hold universally: isolated farmsteads may not be more numerous than hamlets.

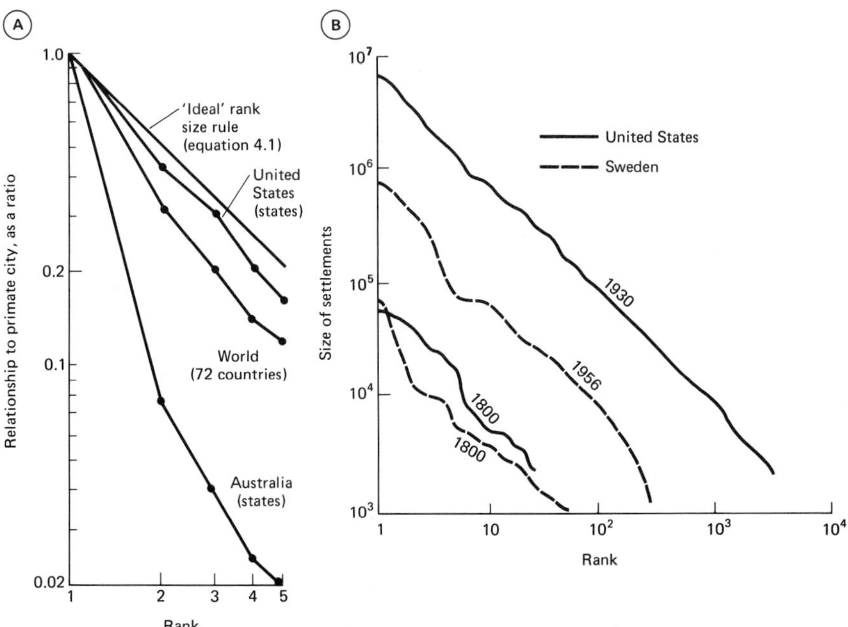


**Figure 4.10** **A** Size of cities as a fraction of the largest city. **B** Changes in the size distribution of cities in Sweden and the United States. Source: Stewart, 1958, pp. 228, 231; Zipf, 1949.

Gunawardena (1964) studied the settlement pattern in southern Ceylon and, from detailed headmen's lists, was able to break down settlements into discrete population clusters at the sub-village level. The size distribution of settlements, when plotted on double-log paper (Figure 4.11), shows a characteristic curve for both the Wet Zone and Dry Zone, suggesting that we may regard this as approximately a lognormal distribution. These results imply that the studies so far conducted on larger population clusters have, in fact, been describing only one limb (the upper or urban limb) of the population continuum. Indeed, when the data from Table 4.3 are plotted on Gunawardena's graph they roughly parallel the upper limb of the Dry and Wet Zone continua. Baker (1969) found a similar 'reversal' of the rank-size rule in his study of French rural settlement in the Loire area in 1846. In his study, the reversal point was at a population size value of seven, while Gülöksüz's (1975) study of settlements in Turkey found the reversals at populations of about 100 and 1,000.

There may therefore be a need to examine the lower part of the limb, the 'sub-village' limb, to see at what population threshold the rank-size rule may become reversed. Data difficulties at this level pose special problems and it seems probable that field survey, rather than secondary census records, are needed to clarify the intriguing relations between number and size of clusters in this rather unexplored topic.

### 4.3.3 *Settlement size as a lognormal distribution*

One way to reconcile the different results from the two preceding sections is to regard the frequency distribution of city sizes as lognormally distributed. The lognormal distribution would thus represent the whole range of settlements—from hamlet through to megalopolis—and may be written as (Richardson, 1973, p. 140)

$$N_{cum} = \log p \tag{4.4}$$

where $N_{cum}$ is the cumulative percentage of cities up to a given population size, $p$.

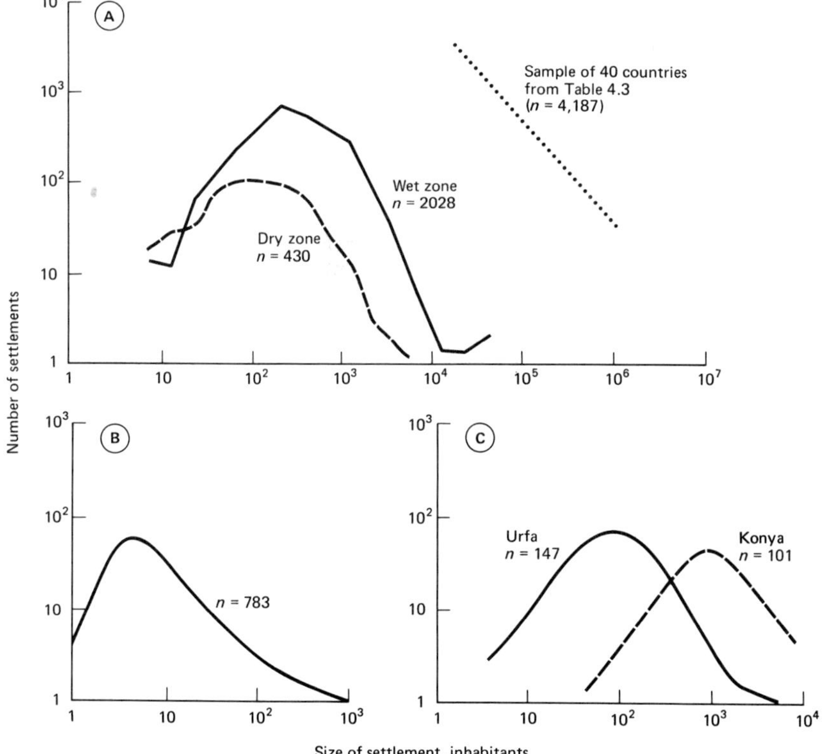


**Figure 4.11** Frequency distribution of settlement sizes in rural areas. **A** Wet Zone and Dry Zone of southern Ceylon. Source: Gunawardena, 1964, p. 167. **B** Plateau between the Loire and Loiv, central France, in 1846. Source: Baker, 1969, p. 390. **C** Two sample areas in southern Turkey. Source: Gülöksüz, 1975, p. 148.

Most frequently the lognormal distribution is truncated by arbitrarily imposing a size threshold (say, a population of 250,000) and confining attentions to settlements above this cut-off level. In this form, the truncated lognormal can be translated into a Pareto distribution (Aitchison and Brown, 1957).

A theoretical rationale for the truncated lognormal distribution has been attempted using the maximum entropy methods discussed in Section 2.5. For example, Berry (1967, p. 587; cited in Richardson, 1973, p. 142) has argued that 'when many forces act in many ways with none predominant a lognormal size distribution is found'; similar arguments were advanced by Curry (1964) as an aspect of the random spatial economy mentioned in Section 4.2.1. Suppose that the total population in a country is $P$ individuals (people). Then the total number of distinct ways in which $n$ cities may be allocated among $k$ city size classes (for example, the classes might be cities over 1 million people, 500,000–1 million people, and under 500,000 people) such that there are $f_1$ cities in size class 1, $f_2$ in size class 2, and so on, is given by

$$W = \frac{n!}{\prod_{i=0}^{k} f_i!}, \tag{4.5}$$

[cf. equation (2.16)]. Following Curry's (1964) argument, which is repeated in Fano (1969) and Richardson (1973, p. 148), in a large system, the entropy function $W$ given in equation (4.5), which we wish to maximize, may be rewritten as

$$E = \log W = n \log n - \sum f_i \log f_i. \tag{4.6}$$

(On taking $\log W$, Stirling's approximation is used to handle the factorial terms.) Chapman (1970) has shown that if (4.6) is maximized subject to the cost constraint,

$$\sum_{i=0}^{k} c_i f_i = K,$$

we obtain

$$f_i = (n \div P/n)\, e^{-(i \div P/n)}. \tag{4.7}$$

In the cost constraint, $c_i$ is the 'cost' of building and running a city in a given size class, and $K$ is the total national budget available for urbanization. These costs may be expected to increase more than linearly with city size (e.g. the present case of New York). Equation (4.7) may be rewritten as

$$f_i = f_1\{1 - e^{-(i \div P/n)}\}. \tag{4.8}$$

Let us suppose that city size class 1 is defined so that it contains only the primate city (i.e. $f_1$ can denote the size of the largest city as in the rank-size rule).Then clearly (4.8) is of the same form as the rank-size rule given in equation (4.1), and may be compared with equation (2.17) in form. Thus a city-size distribution following the rank-size rule may be regarded as the most probable distribution, the state in which entropy has been maximized—'a random arrangement of a given number of people in a given number of cities' (Richardson, 1973, p. 148). In addition, Richardson (1973, pp. 147–8) has commented 'entropy (derived from the second law of thermodynamics) is a measure of the degree of equalization reached within a system, and is maximized when the system reaches equilibrium. The steady-state equilibrium is the most probable state.'

A parallel approach formulated in a slightly different fashion has been put forward by Cliff, Haggett, Ord, Bassett and Davies (1975, Chapter 3). Suppose we define $p_i'$ as the population of the $i$th of $n$ cities in a nation when these cities are plotted from the largest or primate, rank $n$, to the smallest, rank 1. This is in the *reverse* order to the ranking in other equations of rank–size relations in this chapter. Put

$$g_{(i)} = p_i' / \sum_{i=1}^{n} p_i' \tag{4.9}$$

so that $g_{(i)}$ is the proportion of the total urban population of a nation in the $i$th smallest city, $i = 1, \ldots, n$. Then Zipf's rank–size rule is suggestive of the expressions

$$\begin{aligned} &E\{g_{(n)}\} = k, && E\{g_{(i)}\} = \frac{k}{n-i+1} \\ &E\{g_{(n-1)}\} = \frac{k}{2}, && \vdots \\ &\vdots && \\ &E\{g_{(n-i)}\} = \frac{k}{i+1}, && E\{g_{(1)}\} = \frac{k}{n}, \end{aligned} \tag{4.10}$$

where $k = 1/\Sigma_{i=1}^{n} i^{-1}$, and $g_{(n)}$ is the share of the largest city. From equation (4.10)

$$E\{g_{(i)} - g_{(i-1)}\} = \frac{k}{(n-i+1)(n-i+2)}, \quad i \geqslant 2. \tag{4.11}$$

If, however, Curry's suggestion of a random (maximum entropy) population share-size distribution holds, a suitable model may be obtained from Whitworth's (1934) work; see also Kendall and Moran (1963, pp. 28–31). Whitworth took a line of unit length cut at $(n-1)$ points located at random along it. That is, a line of unit length was broken at random into $n$ segments. If the segments are ranked from the smallest (1) to largest ($n$), and the $i$th segment is taken as $g_{(i)}$ given by equation (4.9), then the difference between the population shares of the $i$th and $(i-1)$th smallest cities, according to the Whitworth model, is

$$E\{g_{(i)} - g_{(i-1)}\} = \frac{1}{n(n-i+1)}, \quad i = 2, 3, \ldots, n. \tag{4.12}$$

Alternatively, Cohen (1966) has argued that there is a threshold minimum share size, $\Delta$ say, for the smallest city; that is $g_{(1)} \geqslant \Delta$. If there is a threshold then, under Whitworth's random splitting process,

$$E\{g_{(i)}\} = \left\{\left(\frac{1}{n} - \Delta\right) \sum_{r=1}^{i} \frac{1}{n+1-r}\right\} + \Delta, \quad i = 1, 2, \ldots, n. \tag{4.13}$$

The $g_{(i)}$ defined above are referred to as 'spacings' in the statistics literature (Pyke, 1965). Cliff *et al.* (1975), using Pyke's paper and Durbin's comments thereon, have developed test procedures which enable the goodness-of-fit of each of the models (Zipf, Whitworth and Cohen) to data sets to be evaluated. The three models were applied to nine sets of urban and county population data taken from the 1969 *Redcliffe–Maud Report*. In seven out of nine cases, the best fit was obtained with the Cohen model, and the observed population shares did not depart significantly from the expected values under the Cohen model. The only exceptions were provided by data sets containing a mixture of different units (such as cities and rural counties). This result again confirms the importance of Curry's idea that random component models may be very valuable in examining aggregate human behaviour.

### 4.3.4 *Regional evidence on lognormal city-size distributions*

On the basis of the discussion in the preceding section (4.3.3), we might expect to find the lognormal distribution of city sizes as the most widely occurring type of city-size distribution. Are these expectations fulfilled? Berry (1961a) studied the city-size distributions in 38 countries drawn with fair representation from all parts of the world, except Africa (which was under-represented). The sample countries ranged in size from Soviet Russia to El Salvador, and population data for the early 1950s were used. The data set consisted of 4,187 cities of over 20,000 inhabitants, although for some countries, notably France, data for the lower size classes were not available.

Berry plotted for each country the number of cities as a cumulative percentage on the $y$-axis, and the size of cities on the $x$-axis. By transforming the first axis to a normal probability scale and the second to a logarithmic scale, the lognormal distribution should appear simply as a straight line. Using this type of graph, two main types of size distribution with an intermediate class were recognized. Thirteen of the 38 countries were classed as lognormal in distribution (Figure 4.12A): this included both highly developed countries like the United States (a) and underdeveloped countries like Korea (b), both large countries like China (c) and small countries like El Salvador (d). Fifteen countries were classed as *primate* distributions with a marked gap between the leading city (or cities) and the smaller city distribution (Figure 4.12B). All the countries in this group are small, but the characteristic of their curves vary considerably: Thailand (a) lacks any signs of the lognormal curve, whereas Denmark (b) has signs of the lognormal distribution reasserting itself in the lower size range, while Japan (c) shows only a small break or step in the lognormal pattern.

Between these two classes, Berry recognized an *intermediate* distribution with nine countries (Figure 4.12C). This included countries like England and

Wales (a), which has primate cities grafted on top of the roughly lower lognormal distribution shown (Berry, 1961a, p. 576), Australia (b) and New Zealand (c), in which smaller cities are missing from the lognormal curve. Superimposition of all the curves for the 38 countries (Figure 4.12D) shows the general nature of the curves with a marked tendency towards a lognormal pattern for the world as a whole.

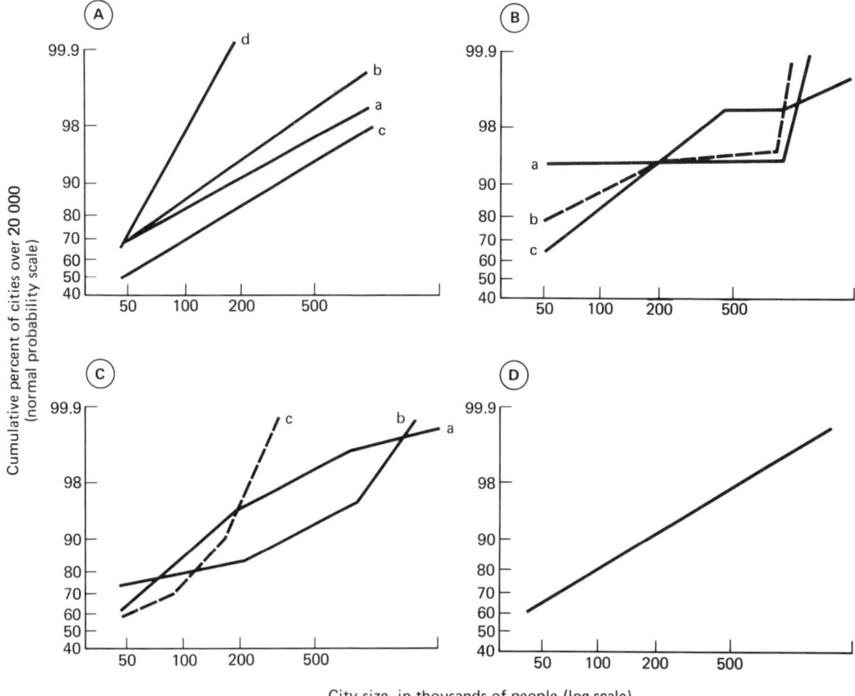


**Figure 4.12** Alternative forms of city-size distributions. **A** Log-normal (rank-size) distributions; **B** Primate distributions; **C** Intermediate distributions; **D** World distribution. Source: Berry, 1961a, pp. 575–8.

What do the variations between the various forms of the city-size distribution mean? Two groups of hypotheses are suggested by Berry:

(i) The first group of hypotheses contain ideas which seemed logical in the abstract, but were not confirmed by empirical observation. We might suggest for example an *urbanization hypothesis* in which the city-size type is related to the degree of urbanization. When, however, degree of urbanization as measured by the proportion of a country's total population in cities of 20,000 or more people, was plotted against the city-size distribution, no cross-relationship was found. The primate pattern, for example, was found for both highly urbanized countries (like the Netherlands and Japan) and for largely rural areas (like Mexico and Thailand). For lognormal patterns, the same was true.

A second hypothesis, the *economic development hypothesis*, was also tested and found to be ineffective. Here pattern was related to the degree of economic development as measured on a scale derived by Berry (1960) from 43 proposed indices of economic development. The scale has been used in an earlier discussion (Section 3.5.2). If economic development and city-size pattern are related, we would expect to find all the primate countries at one end of the spectrum and all the lognormal at the other. In fact, as Figure 4.13 shows, the pattern is essentially random. The primate countries (shown by open circles) and the lognormal countries (shown by closed circles) are irregularly arranged with no preferential grouping at any point in the development spectrum. We conclude therefore that the economic development hypothesis cannot be maintained.

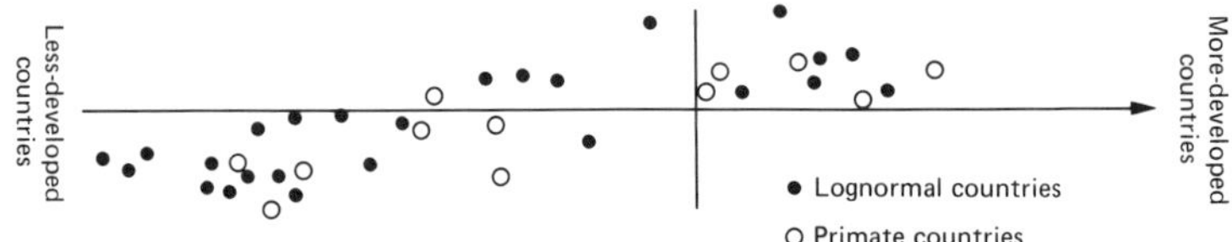


**Figure 4.13** Distribution of countries with *lognormal* and *primate* city-size distributions on Berry's development spectrum. Source: Berry, 1961a, p. 586.

(ii) The second group of hypotheses contain ideas which, though they seem less obvious, are supported by the evidence available. A general *stochastic hypothesis* has been suggested by Simon (1955), and its implications for the lognormal and primate distributions are important. Simon approached the city-size distribution from the broad viewpoint of general systems theory (see Section 1.4), arguing in the manner of Section 4.3.3, that the stability of the rank-size relationship over space and time suggested it might be viewed as steady-state phenomenon, i.e. a condition of entropy in which the distribution is affected by a myriad of small random forces. Simon approximated the rank-size rule with a probability formulation used by Yule in 1924 to explain the distribution of biological genera, in which the lognormal distribution is produced as a limiting case of stochastic growth processes. Berry and Garrison (1958a) have tested the Simon model for the distribution of city sizes in the state of Washington, United States, and as Table 4.5 shows, the approximation obtained was reasonably good.

Table 4.5 Expected and observed distribution of city sizes on Simon model*

| *Size of cities, inhabitants* ($\times 10^4$): | 0.5 | 1.5 | 2.5 | 3.5 |
|---|---|---|---|---|
| Number of cities: | | | | |
| Observed | 36 | 12 | 7 | 5 |
| Expected (on Simon model) | 36 | 14 | 9 | 6 |

Source: Berry and Garrison, 1958a, p. 89.
* Washington, United States, 1950.

In terms of the two country patterns, lognormal and primate, Berry (1961a) has argued that the Simon model implies two sets of sub-hypotheses. First, that lognormal patterns are the product of urbanization in countries which are (a) larger than average, (b) have a long history of urbanization, and (c) are economically and politically complex. Of the 13 countries in this group, the United States and Brazil qualify on the first sub-hypothesis, India and China and the six European countries on the second, and possibly, South Africa on the third. Clearly some qualify on all three grounds, while two in the lognormal group (Korea and El Salvador) appear to qualify on none.

Second, we may argue that primate patterns are the product of city development in countries which are (a) smaller than average, (b) have a short history of urbanization, and (c) are economically or politically simple. Certainly the 15 countries in this group are small to medium in size, and in some, the impact of a few strong forces is clearly seen. Thus Portugal, Spain, Austria, and the Netherlands have capital cities which were developed to serve empires rather than the local city hierarchy: e.g. Vienna's size is logical in terms of the Austro-Hungarian empire rather than contemporary Austria. Other countries have either a commercial export sector superimposed on a peasant agricultural system (e.g. the 'dual economy' of Ceylon), or a strong primary export system (e.g. Uruguay) or a single 'Westernized' city (e.g. Thailand).

## 4.4 Changes over Time

### 4.4.1 *Historical changes in city-size distributions*

In the preceding section, the argument has been largely confined to a static situation, with the empirical evidence drawn from a cross-section of settlements at a given point in time. Where evidence is available for long periods, historical changes in city-size distributions may be examined.

Figure 4.14 shows some different ways in which changes in a city-size distribution may be depicted. First, we may relate the logarithm of population size to rank order, as in the case of cities in the United States over the period 1790–1950 (Figure 4.14A). The rough parallelism of the 17 lines suggest a relatively constant Pareto function [equation (4.2)] which has been sometimes regarded as evidence of allometric growth; that is, maintenance of a stable equilibrium between city sizes over time. Allometric relations were first recognized in the growth of biological organisms and their extension to population phenomena is more debatable.

Second, we may plot the cumulative percentage of cities over a given size threshold against city size as in the truncated lognormal equation (Section 4.3.3). For Israel over the period 1922 to 1959 the size distribution has become increasingly linear as the country has developed economically (Figure 4.14B). The change from primacy to lognormality has been placed by Berry (1961a) within a general developmental model, in which a multi-stage progression from primate to rank-size distributions is envisaged as a country develops economically.

Third, we may plot the value of the *b* coefficient in the Pareto equation (4.2) against time. Figure 4.14C shows the change in the slope values for Australia

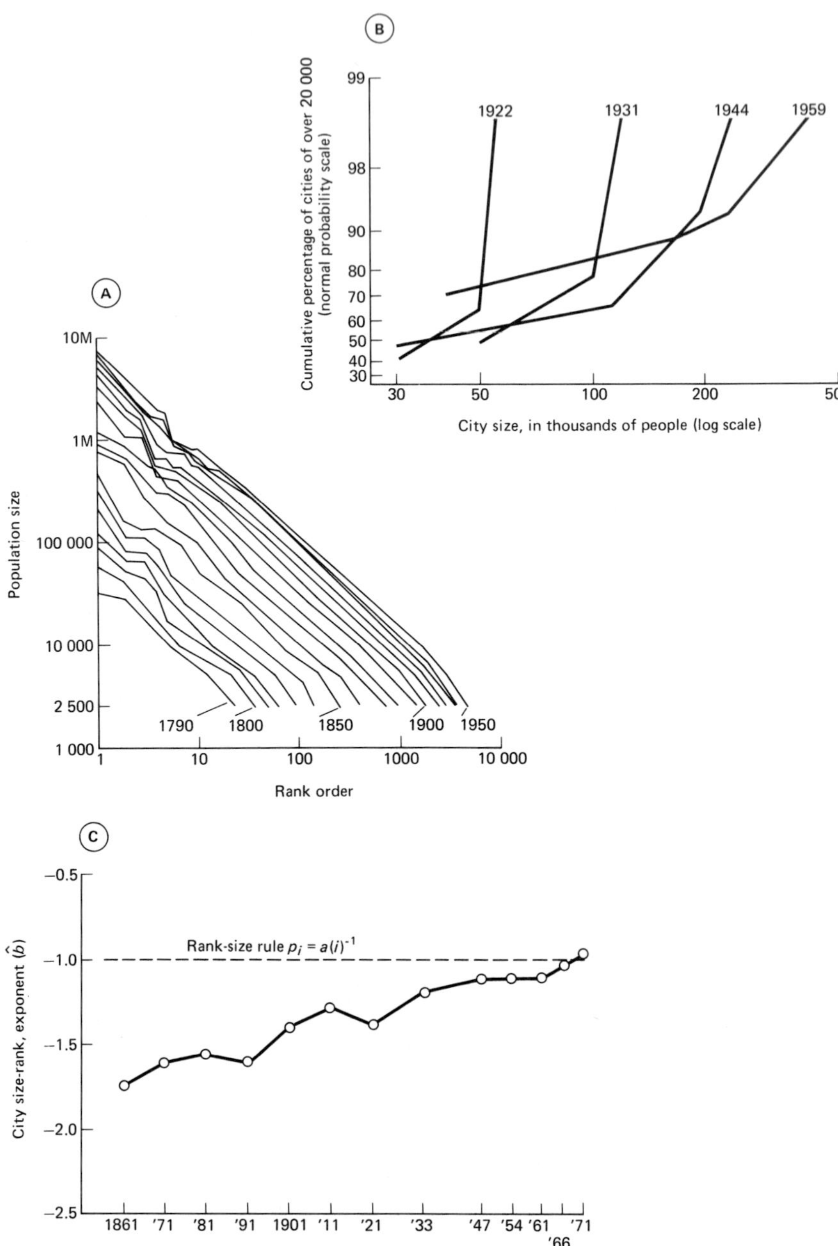


**Figure 4.14** Alternative ways of showing changes in city-size distributions over time. **A** Successive rank-size distributions for the United States, 1790–1950. Source: Robson, 1973, p. 30. **B** Cumulative share of population in different city sizes in Israel, 1922–59. Source: Bell, 1962, p. 103. **C** Slope coefficients ($\hat{b}$) for the rank-size relationships for the five largest Australian cities, 1861–1971. Source: Haggett, 1976.

over the period 1861 to 1971 for the five top ranking cities. This particular case conforms broadly to the Berry model (Figure 4.15) in so far as a rather primate pattern progressively drifts towards the rank-size position of $b = -1.0$. The case of Australia is, however, a complex one; Rose (1966) has argued convincingly for Australia that the primate pattern is the 'normal' case, so far as the relationships between the capital cities within each state and other cities in the state are concerned.

Cliff and Robson (1976) have tried to relate long term changes in city-size distributions to the maximum entropy notion discussed in Section 4.3.3. They have taken the rank–size distribution for all urban centres in England and Wales with a population in excess of 2,000 for each census from 1801–1911, and have fitted the Whitworth–Cohen models to these data. Some interesting points emerged. First, the observed population share-size distribution was markedly non-random throughout the nineteenth century, with an increasing concentration of the population into the larger cities. The fit of the models became consistently worse with the passage of each census throughout the century. The 1901 census represented a turning point in that the fit of the models to the data improved for the first time, and 1911 registered yet another improvement. We know from the results reported in Section 4.3.3 that by the time of Redcliffe–Maud, 1969, the rank-size distribution for administrative regions was largely random. These findings together suggest that, although the Industrial Revolution administered a severe shock to the system, there may be a general tendency for the urban system to move towards a dynamic equilibrium, maximum entropy, distribution. Certainly Robson (1973) has argued that city sizes throughout the nineteenth century were in disequilibrium. The Industrial Revolution made entirely new cities, while

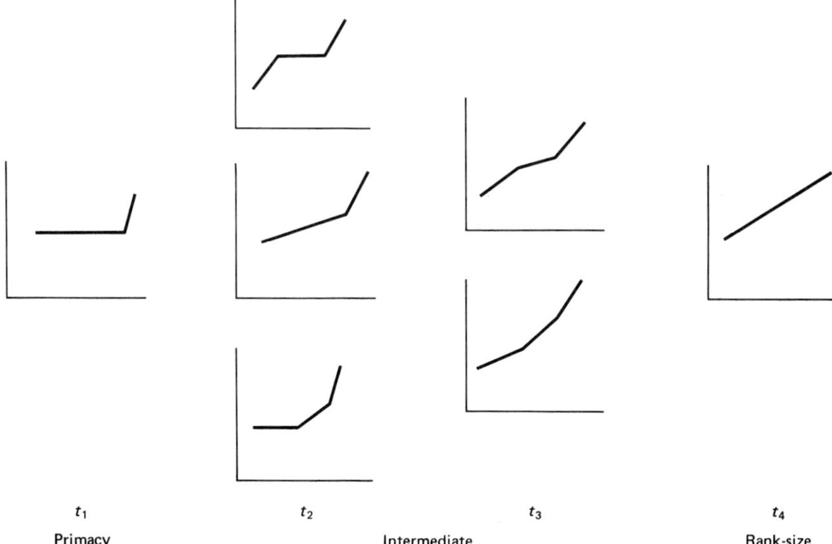


**Figure 4.15** Berry's development model for city-size distributions. Axes are as in Figure 4.12.

others failed. Robson goes on to argue that the forces of the Industrial Revolution in this context were largely worked out by about 1900. Conversely, the twentieth century has been dominated by shifts between existing urban centres and centre/suburb relationships, rather than by the birth and death of towns. That is, the system has been in dynamic equilibrium.

### 4.4.2 *Changes in the role of individual cities*

An alternative approach to the study of complete city systems over time is to study the growth of individual cities. Robson's (1973) findings on the change in rank order for towns in England and Wales, 1801–1911, are shown in Figure 4.16. Note how London retained its rank throughout the period while Leicester rose and Exeter fell. Still more dramatic shifts in the fortunes of individual cities have been shown by Madden (1958) and Lukermann (1966) in studies of the United States' urban system.

Clearly the crossing of the trajectory lines in plots like that of Figure 4.16 indicates the degree of instability within the growth process: a completely stable system in which each city held exactly the same rank position over time would consist of a series of parallel vertical lines in Figure 4.16. Carter (1969)

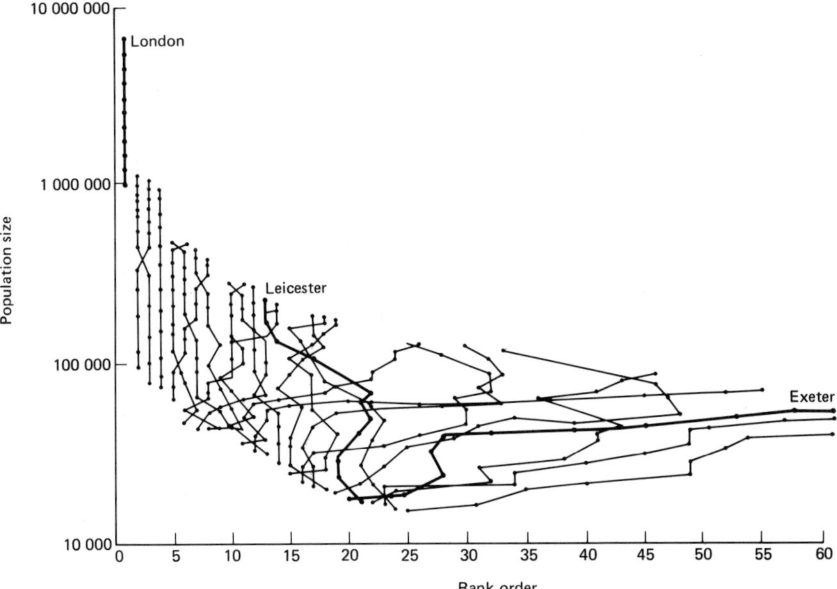


**Figure 4.16** Changes in rank order, 1801–1911. Successive ranks of the 25 largest towns in England and Wales in 1801. Each line represents one town; the lowest dot shows its rank and size in 1801 and successive dots show its rank and size at each decade up to 1911. The towns (ranked in their 1801 order) are as follows: London; Manchester/Salford; Liverpool; Birmingham; Bristol; Leeds; Portsmouth; Newcastle/Gateshead; Sheffield; Norwich; Bath; Nottingham; Hull; Sunderland; Medway Towns; Stockport; Bolton; Coventry; Exeter; Leicester; York; Plymouth; Oldham; Chester; Oxford. Source: Robson, 1973, p. 39.

used rank correlation methods to relate the position of cities from one period to the next. For Welsh towns in the nineteenth century, Carter found lower than average correlation between the rank positions for 1861/71 and 1871/81, decades linked to the emergence of new, rapidly growing coal mining towns in the southern part of Wales.

Biproportionate matrices (Bacharach, 1970) form another way of disentangling the relations between the growth of individual cities and the growth of the whole urban system of which they form a part. In biproportionate matrices, the values $\{x_{ij}\}$ in an $m \times n$ matrix are scaled so that each row sum is equal to $n$. Then the columns are scaled so that each column sum is equal to $m$. This process of column and row adjustment is successively repeated until adequate convergence to an equilibrium solution is obtained. We can express this process more formally as

$$\begin{bmatrix} x_{11} & x_{12} & \dots x_{1j} & \dots x_{1n} \\ x_{21} & x_{22} & \dots x_{2j} & \dots x_{2n} \\ \vdots & \vdots & \vdots & \vdots \\ x_{i1} & x_{i2} & \dots x_{ij} & \dots x_{in} \\ \vdots & \vdots & \vdots & \vdots \\ x_{m1} & x_{m2} & \dots x_{mj} & \dots x_{mn} \end{bmatrix} = \begin{bmatrix} \mathrm{n+e} \\ \mathrm{n+e} \\ \vdots \\ n+e \\ \vdots \\ n+e \end{bmatrix} \tag{4.14}$$

$$= \begin{bmatrix} m+e & m+e \dots m+e \dots m+e \end{bmatrix}$$

where $e$ is an allowable tolerance term. The procedure produces a standardization of the matrix values over the rows and columns of the matrix.

Table 4.6 shows a typical biproportionate matrix for the six Australian provincial capitals, excluding Port Darwin (Haggett, 1976). In Table 4.6, the non-boldface figures give the population of each capital in thousands. Working with these figures and reading down the columns we note the contrasts in growth between a slow-growing city, Hobart, which increased its size by × 5 over the 110 years, and fast-growing Brisbane which increased by over one hundredfold over the same period. A different picture emerges if we examine the boldface figures, which give the performance of each city at each time period as a standardized biproportionate score. Reading down the columns shows the *relative* change in each city over time: the precipitous decline of Hobart, the rapid rise of Perth, the *relative* stability of Sydney and Adelaide. Reading along the rows shows the situation in each time period: the strong contrasts between cities in 1861 decreasing during the remainder of the century to a minimum in 1901 (row standard deviation of 7) and gently increasing again thereafter.

Biproportionate matrices throw light on second order changes in growth within an urban system by relating $x_{ij}$ to a city's performance (i) over all cities in the system at a given time, and (ii) to its own performance over all time periods. If a system is arranged in a rank-ordered fashion and grows in an exponential manner, then all cell entries in the biproportional transformation will have unit values. The overall variance of the biproportional matrix is therefore a useful measure of the departure of the urban system from a model growth path.

Table 4.6 Biproportionate matrix of urban growth.*

| *Census dates* | *Sydney* | *Melbourne* | *Adelaide* | *Brisbane* | *Perth* | *Hobart* | *Standard deviation* |
|---|---|---|---|---|---|---|---|
| 1861 | 96 | 125 | 35 | 6 | 5 | 25 | |
| | **81** | **109** | **101** | **24** | **31** | **254** | **171** |
| 1871 | 138 | 191 | 51 | 15 | 7 | 26 | |
| | **88** | **125** | **111** | **45** | **33** | **199** | **106** |
| 1881 | 225 | 268 | 92 | 31 | 9 | 27 | |
| | **100** | **123** | **139** | **64** | **30** | **144** | **103** |
| 1891 | 400 | 473 | 117 | 87 | 16 | 33 | |
| | **109** | **132** | **108** | **111** | **32** | **108** | **87** |
| 1901 | 496 | 478 | 141 | 92 | 61 | 35 | |
| | **107** | **107** | **104** | **93** | **98** | **91** | **7** |
| 1911 | 648 | 593 | 169 | 117 | 107 | 40 | |
| | **106** | **100** | **94** | **90** | **130** | **79** | **18** |
| 1921 | 1030 | 783 | 249 | 210 | 115 | 52 | |
| | **120** | **94** | **99** | **115** | **99** | **73** | **19** |
| 1933 | 1235 | 992 | 313 | 300 | 207 | 60 | |
| | **106** | **88** | **92** | **121** | **132** | **62** | **30** |
| 1947 | 1484 | 1226 | 382 | 402 | 273 | 77 | |
| | **100** | **85** | **88** | **127** | **137** | **62** | **32** |
| 1954 | 1863 | 1532 | 484 | 502 | 349 | 95 | |
| | **100** | **85** | **89** | **126** | **139** | **61** | **33** |
| 1961 | 2183 | 1912 | 588 | 621 | 420 | 116 | |
| | **97** | **87** | **89** | **129** | **138** | **62** | **33** |
| 1966 | 2477 | 2108 | 728 | 716 | 500 | 119 | |
| | **94** | **84** | **95** | **129** | **143** | **55** | **40** |
| 1971 | 2717 | 2389 | 809 | 817 | 640 | 130 | |
| | **90** | **82** | **92** | **127** | **158** | **52** | **47** |
| Standard deviation | **11** | **18** | **14** | **98** | **124** | **72** | |

Source: Haggett, 1976.
*Australian state capitals, 1861–1971. Non-bold-face figures are populations in thousands; bold-face figures are biproportional indices ( × 100).

## 4.5 Relationship between Size and Spacing of Settlements

### 4.5.1 *Spacing of discrete size groups*

If the rank-size rule, uncomplicated by Gunawardena's findings (Section 4.3.2), were to operate, then we should expect the spacing of settlements to be governed mainly by their size. Large settlements would be widely spaced, small settlements closely spaced. Both Christaller (1933) and Lösch (1954) put forward evidence for discrete types of settlements to show that this proposition may be valid, at least for specified areas. For southern Germany, Christaller examined in detail the hierarchy of small towns and villages around the five great regional capitals (Frankfurt, Munich, Nüremburg, Strasbourg, and Stuttgart) and showed that, while these were 178 kilometres apart, the smaller provincial capitals were only 108 kilometres apart, the county seats 21 kilometres apart, and the villages seven kilometres apart. Lösch's evidence for Iowa, in the mid-western United States, is shown in Figure 4.17. It suggests both the close connection between size and spacing for three classes of settlement, namely cities with 300–1,000 inhabitants (Figure 4.17A), cities with 1,000–4,000 inhabitants (Figure 4.17B), and cities with 4,000–20,000 inhabitants (Figure 4.17C), and also the greater variability in spacing with increasing size.

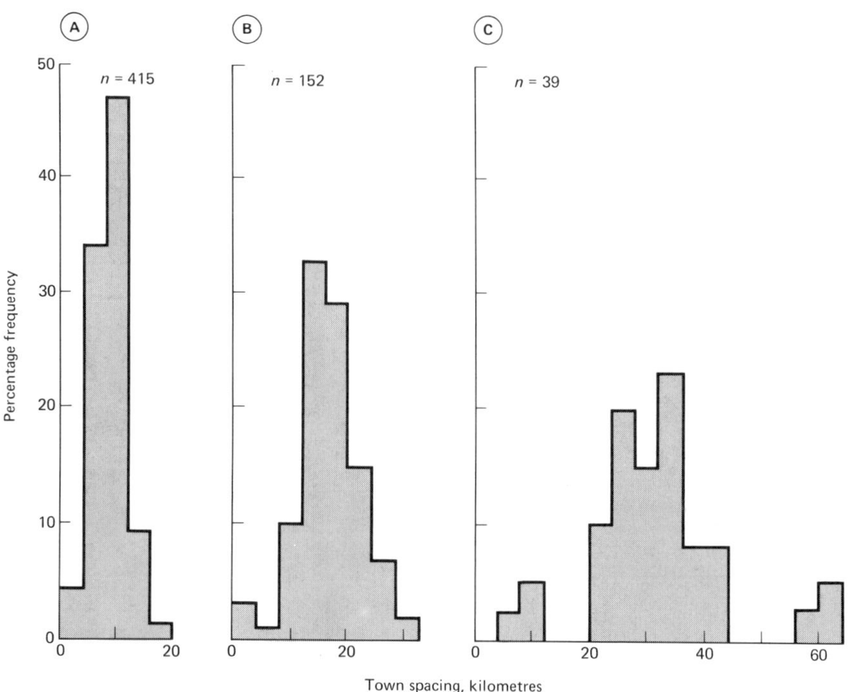


**Figure 4.17** Histograms of overland distances separating small towns (**A**), intermediate towns (**B**), and large towns (**C**) in Iowa, 1930. Source: Lösch, 1954, p. 391.

Since the 1930s, these findings have been supplemented by work like that of Brush and Bracey (1955) who compared rural central places in southwestern Wisconsin (United States) and southern England. They found that, despite the strong differences in population density, economic functions, and social and political history between the two areas, *both* showed two distinct tiers of central places: a tier of higher order centres spaced at 21 mile distances and a tier of lower order centres spaced at eight to ten mile intervals.

Somewhat different relations have been discovered by House (1953) in a study of medium sized towns in these same two industrial societies. House defined a medium sized town as one with a population of between 20,000 and

100,000, and studied their distribution in England and Wales and in the western part of the United States manufacturing belt (the five states of Illinois, Indiana, Michigan, Ohio, and Pennsylvania). As Table 4.7 shows, both areas had roughly comparable populations, but the American area was only half as densely populated and had only about one third as many medium sized towns as England and Wales. In both cases there is a general increase in the distance separating towns with increase in town size, but these distances are far less than Christaller's values. For south Germany, Christaller suggested that towns of 30,000 population would be spaced at intervals of about 38 miles; in England and Wales the corresponding figure is about seven miles and in the United States about 25 miles. Much of the difference in these findings springs from the industrial character of the latter areas. Although exact definitions are made difficult by contrasts in census classifications, House's figures suggest that about half of the British towns are mining and manufacturing towns, many of which are still clustered in characteristic huddles around their original coalfield locations. In the United States, towns are both less specialized and, developing at a later phase, are less tied to early coalfield concentrations. Both the degree and the timing of industrialization appear to distort the spacing characteristics in a fundamental way.

Table 4.7 Town spacing in two industrial regions

| *Region:* | *England and Wales* (1951) | *United States* (1950) |
|---|---|---|
| Population, millions of inhabitants | 43.8 | 37.5 |
| Density, inhabitants/sq. mile | 134 | 63 |
| Number of medium sized towns | 316 | 123 |
| Mean spacing of medium sized towns, miles: | | |
| 20,000– 30,000 inhabitants | 6.1 | 14.6 |
| 40,000– 50,000 inhabitants | 7.9 | 28.3 |
| 75,000–100,000 inhabitants | 10.0 | 38.0 |

Source: House, 1953, p. 63.

### 4.5.2 *Spacing as a continuous function of size*

(a) *Definition of spacing.* Alongside studies which have examined the spacing between settlements considered as point-like objects (that is, ignoring their size as in Section 4.2.1) may be ranged those studies in which spacing has been regarded as a continuous function and which take settlement sizes into account. With these, the method of study hinges on the definition of spacing adopted, in most cases measured as the overland distance between a sample settlement and its 'nearest neighbours of the same size'. However, as Thomas (1961) points out, this does not necessarily mean that the population of the sample city and the neighbour city are *exactly* the same size: rather that they are *approximately* the same size. Thomas introduces a probability concept which greatly sharpens the choice of what is meant by 'approximately the same size'. He shows, from a sample of city sizes approximating a log lognormal curve, that by adopting a given confidence level (e.g. 95 per cent) we can define the range that we expect a nearest-neighbour town of the 'same population' to have. The general form may be written as

$$p_i - xe_i < p_j < p_i + xe_i \tag{4.15}$$

where $p_i$ is the population of the sample town, $p_j$ is the population of the nearest neighbour, $e_i$ is the standard error of the distribution of city sizes, and $x$ is the abscissa of the standard normal curve associated with the desired confidence level (Thomas, 1961, p. 405). See Appendix Table A1. To translate this into practical terms: If the sample town has a population of 105 persons, we can define the 'same population' for the nearest neighbour as lying between 72 and 159 inhabitants. Any difference in population within these limits may be regarded as due to chance and disregarded. The fact that the limits are asymmetric about 105 is due to the characteristic log-log curve of the population of Iowan towns.

(b) *Spacing and cluster size.* Using this definition, Thomas (1961) investigated the relationships between population and spacing between settlements 'of the same size' for 89 sample towns in Iowa (Figure 4.18). Statistical investigation showed, as expected, a positive association between the logarithms of distance and population size, although the proportion of distance variation 'explained' by size was only about one third ($R^2 = 0.35$). In a follow-up study, Thomas (1962) was able to test his findings on the 1950 population against the five earlier census records for this century. He found a surprising degree of stability in the distance-size relationship. Only for the 1900 census did the degree of

***

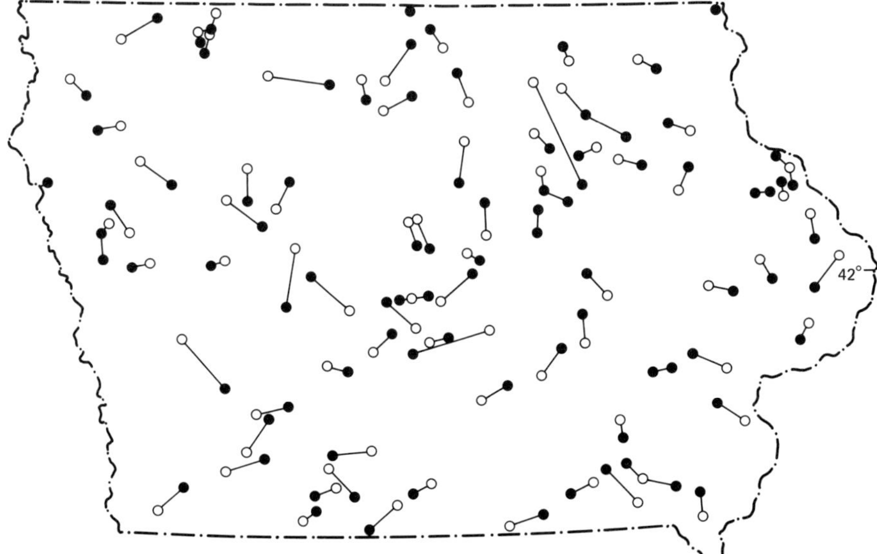


**Figure 4.18** Nearest neighbours of sample settlements in Iowa. Links to settlements outside the state are not shown. Source: Thomas, 1961, p. 408.

correlation differ markedly from that found in the 1950 survey, and even here the relationship showed up as statistically significant at the $\alpha = 0.05$ significance level. Distance separating the sample cities from their neighbours of the 'same size' (*Hypothesis I*) was also compared with distances separating sample cities from their neighbours of the 'same or greater size' (*Hypothesis II*).

Figure 4.19A shows the correlation values obtained on the first test against those obtained on the second. While for both sets of values the coefficients are statistically significant ($\alpha = 0.05$ significance level), the closer relationship is always obtained for the second test. It is clear for Iowa that town size is associated with spacing, and that this relationship holds in a hierarchical sense, since the sample towns are more closely associated with their larger neighbours. Whether the closing gap shown by the two sets of relationships represents a trend to a more highly integrated relationship between the settlements remains to be seen.

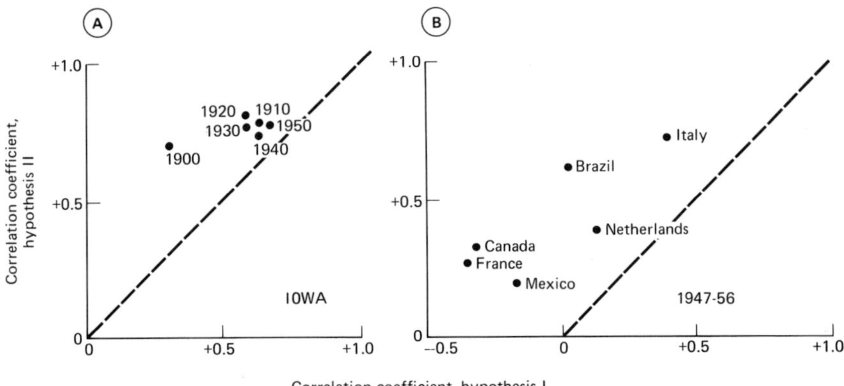


**Figure 4.19** Correlations between alternative hypotheses linking city size with spacing. The pecked line denotes equal correlation values for the two hypotheses. Sources: Thomas, 1962, p. 27; Gibbs, 1961, p. 458.

Gibbs (1961, pp. 451–9) has confirmed Thomas's hypothesis for the spacing of the major cities in six countries (Brazil, Canada, France, Italy, Mexico, and the Netherlands). As Figure 4.19B indicates, a higher correlation coefficient was found between the size of metropolitan area and the distance to the nearest larger metropolitan area, than between size and the distance to the nearest metropolitan area of the same type. Despite variations in the values of the coefficient, the consistently higher values for the second relationship are striking.

(c) *Spacing as a multivariate function.* In one of the few studies in which spacing has been treated in a wider context, King (1961) carried out a multiple regression analysis of several alternative hypotheses. Spacing was seen as a function of the size of a town, its occupational structure, and the characteristics of the zone in which it was located. A sample of 200 towns was drawn at random from the 1950 United States census giving a range in town size from five inhabitants (Slaughter Beach, Delaware) up to Seattle, Washington, with nearly half a million inhabitants. The 'nearest neighbour' was defined for each of the sample towns using Thomas's probability definition, equation (4.15), and first, a correlation analysis of spacing as a function only of size was carried out. Table 4.8 shows that the association discovered, though statistically significant, explained only about 2 per cent of the variations in spacing. Divisions of the sample into central places (162 towns) and non-central places showed that the spacing of the first group was marginally more predictable than that of the second. A breakdown of the towns into five major farming zones brought out important variations between the regions of the United States. In the Great Plains and the Far West the level of explanation rose sharply to over 40 per cent and in the Corn Belt to over 20 per cent, suggesting that the regularities described by Lösch (1954, pp. 389–93) might be less typical of the whole United States than often supposed.

Table 4.8 Relationship between settlement spacing and other variables*

| *Hypotheses:* | *Single hypothesis (Size of settlement)* | *Multiple hypothesis (Six factors)* |
|---|---|---|
| Coefficients of determination ($R^2$): | | |
| National results | 0.02† | 0.25† |
| Centre classification: | | |
| Central places | 0.09† | 0.26† |
| Non-central places | 0.01 | 0.42† |
| Regional agricultural classification: | | |
| Grazing and wheat zone | 0.42† | 0.67† |
| Specialized farming zone | 0.01 | 0.20† |
| General farming zone | 0.07 | 0.67† |
| Feed grain and livestock zone | 0.22† | 0.34† |
| Dairying zone | 0.04† | 0.36† |

Source: King, 1961, pp. 227–31.
*United States, 1950. †Significant at the $\alpha = 0.05$ significance.

With the exception of specific regions, the predictive performance of population size as a guide to spacing was poor, and King went on to test five other hypotheses related to the characteristics of the region in which the town was located and to its occupational structure. He argued that towns of a given size were likely to be more widely spaced where (i) rural population density is low, (ii) farming is extensive, (iii) agricultural production is low, (iv) where the overall population density is low, and (v) where the town itself has a low proportion of workers in manufacturing. Regression analysis showed that while all five were slightly more valuable than town size in predicting spacing, only one, overall population density, could explain more than 10 per cent of the variation. Indeed, all six hypotheses working together could only explain one quarter of the variation in spacing, though here again performance improved with certain agricultural zones (shown in the final column in Table 4.8). Clearly there is a very considerable problem in building accurate predictive models (cf. Chapter 16) for spacing for an area as large as the United States where differences in the historical development of settlements in the various regions are so marked. Future research using multivariate techniques but building historical factors into the model may uncover consistent explanations for the wide variation in the spacing characteristics of urban settlements.

## 4.6 Impulse Transmission between Urban Areas

So far in this chapter we have been concerned either with static settlement structures (e.g. size distributions of cities) or with slow temporal changes in these structures. Recently, increasing interest has been shown in the ways in which these relatively stable population nodes respond to short run changes. We may conceive of these changes as impulses: either a discrete 'shock' or a series of continuous 'waves' which travel through the urban system.

### 4.6.1 *Transmission of discrete shocks*

Typical of the work on discrete shocks is that by Pyle (1969) on the spread of cholera in the United States. By plotting the date of the first recorded outbreak of cholera in each affected city of the United States for the three great epidemics of 1832, 1849 and 1866, Pyle was able to reconstruct ways in which the waves were transmitted through the urban system. Figure 4.20 shows the relationships to city size of the time cholera first appeared. In the 1832 epidemic (Figure 4.20A), there is little association between time and size; distance from two separate foci in Canada and New York, and the mode of travel—by inland waterways and/or the eastern seaboard—appear more important. Seventeen years later (Figure 4.20B) the situation is still affected by the two corridors of movement, but the relationship to the urban hierarchy is greatly increased. By 1866 (Figure 4.20C) city size appears to be the prime factor in the spread of cholera. Similar studies to those of Pyle by Haggett (1972) and Cliff *et al.* (1975, Chapter 6) on measles, and by Hunt (1975) on heroin, reinforce the evidence for the importance of urban structure in the transmission of epidemics through a population. We return to this subject again in considering hierarchic forms of diffusion models and barriers to diffusion waves (Sections 7.4, 7.5, and 11.5).

### 4.6.2 *Transmission of continuous waves*

Although it may be convenient to consider the effect of an isolated incident being transmitted through an urban system, most short run changes (including many epidemics) can be more usefully visualized as continuous, wave-like phenomena. Thus Lösch (1954, Chapter 27), in looking at economic indicators of prosperity and depression (for example, interest-levels, and unemployment rates), noted the way in which the business crisis of 1857 'raced unchecked from the Ohio' (p. 496) and how that of the early 1930s reached its trough in North America's automobile cities in late 1933, but was nearly a year and a half delayed in some seaport cities (e.g. Seattle and Vancouver).

One attempt to relate a general wave impulse (say, a world-wide depression)

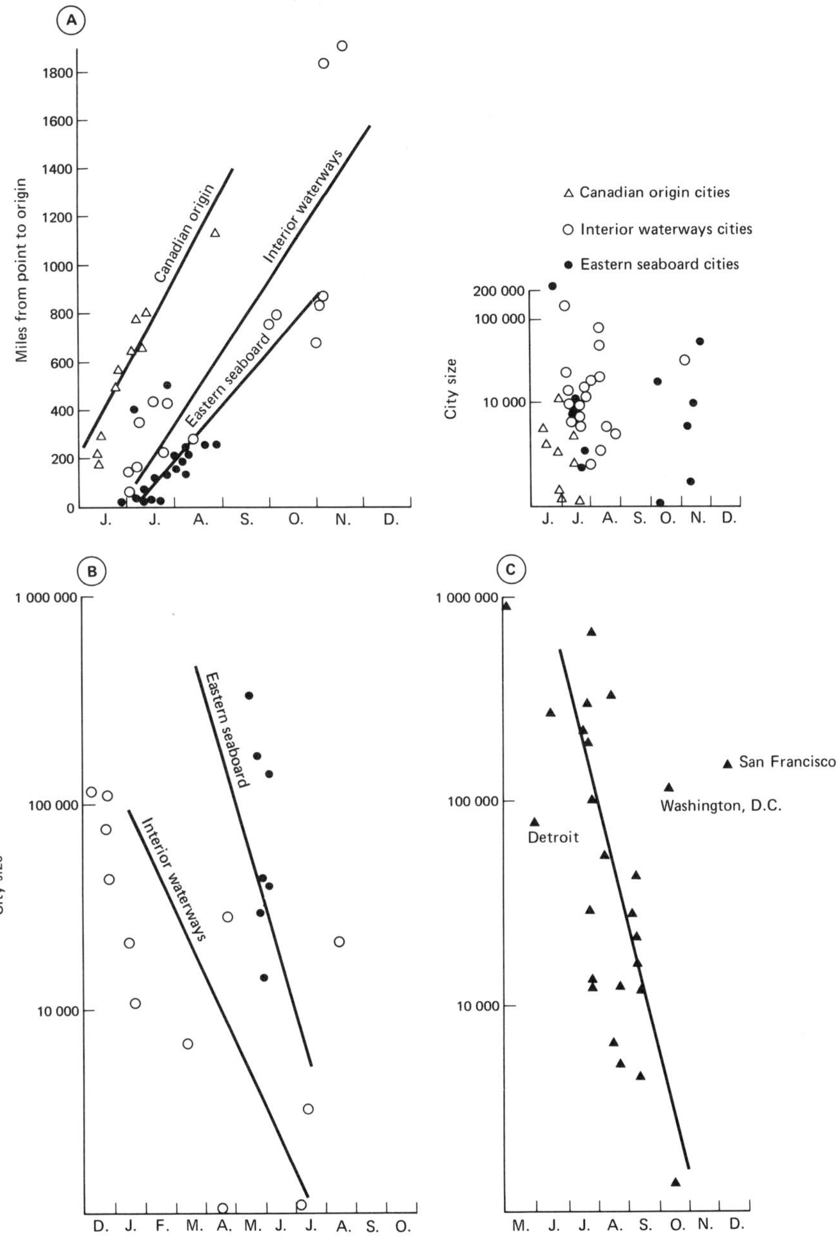


**Figure 4.20** Impact of the increasing hierarchic organization of the American urban system in the mid-nineteenth century in disease diffusion. Movement of cholera in the three major epidemics. **A** 1832; **B** 1848/9; and **C** 1866. Note that city size indicates population at the nearest census (i.e. 1830, 1850, and 1870 respectively). Source: Pyle, 1969.

to the response of individual towns in a region is given in Figure 4.21. Note how different towns respond in various ways: some amplifying the wave,

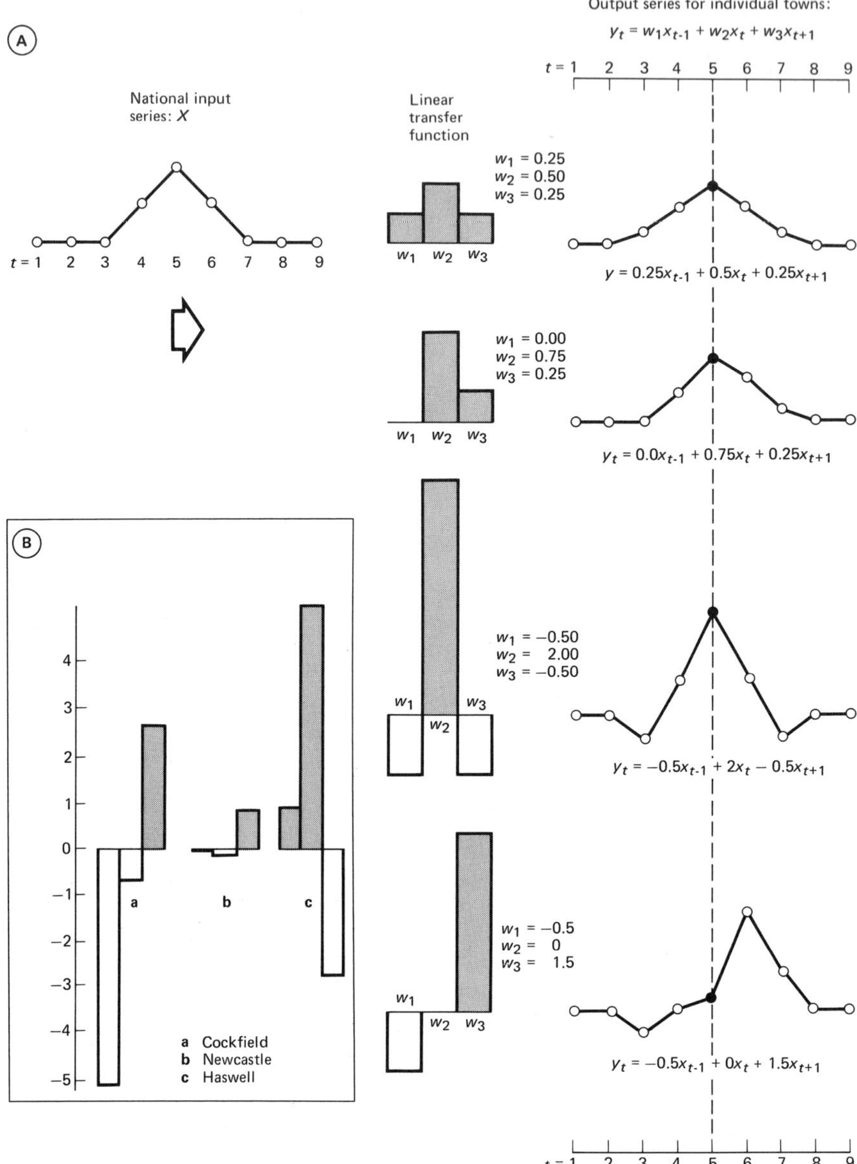


**Figure 4.21** Historical reconstruction of impulse transmissions in an urban system. **A** Response of individual towns as a linear transfer function of national variations over time. **B** Estimated response functions for three sample towns in northern England based on a study of monthly employment changes between 1927 and 1936. Source: Spooner, 1975, pp. 29–35.

others dampening it. The position of the response wave may also be shifted to the left or to the right to give a leading or lagging series. In this case, the external or input wave is designated by the series, $x_t$ and the response or output wave is designated by the series, $y_t$. The relationship between the two waves may be described by a *linear transfer function* with a set of weights, $\{w_i\}$. For example,

$$y_t = w_1 x_{t-1} + w_2 x_t + w_3 x_{t+1} + e_t, \tag{4.16}$$

in the simple case shown in Figure 4.21 (Spooner, 1975, p. 35). Note that equation (4.16) is simply a historical reconstruction of the relationships between two series, i.e. national unemployment, the input wave ($x$), and local unemployment, the output wave ($y$). Since information about $t+1$ appears on the right hand side of the model, it cannot be used for forecasting (see Chapter 16).

### 4.6.3 *Models of impulse transmission*

A formal model of impulse transmission has been proposed and tested by King, Casetti, and Jeffrey (1969). If cities form a closed system, then it can be postulated that each city's activity level is governed by only two forces: first, corresponding activity levels in other cities in the system, and second, exogenous 'national' factors, or their delayed consequences, which affect the whole city system. Figure 4.22 attempts to describe such a system.

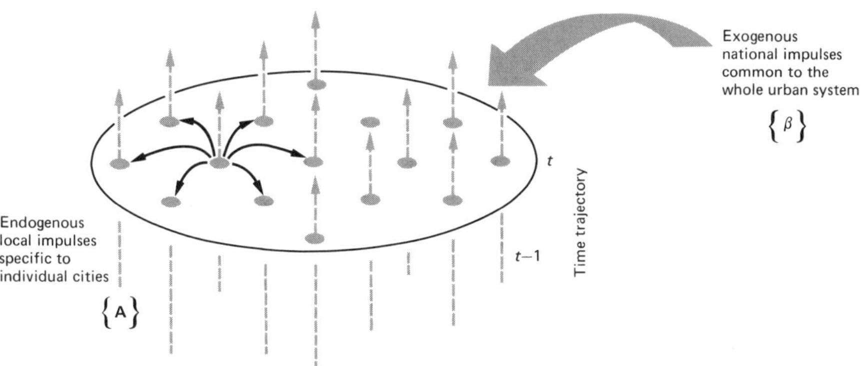


**Figure 4.22** Exogenous and endogenous components in modelling impulse transmissions in an urban system.

The relationships can be specified by a set of difference equations:

$$\underset{(n\times 1)}{\mathbf{y}_t} = \underset{(n\times n)}{\mathbf{A}_1} \cdot \underset{(n\times 1)}{\mathbf{y}_t} + \underset{(n\times n)}{\mathbf{A}_2} \cdot \underset{(n\times 1)}{\mathbf{y}_{t-1}} + \ldots + \underset{(n\times n)}{\mathbf{A}_k} \cdot \underset{(n\times 1)}{\mathbf{y}_{t-k}}$$

$$+ \underset{(n\times r)}{\boldsymbol{\beta}_1} \cdot \underset{(r\times 1)}{\mathbf{x}_t} + \ldots + \underset{(n\times r)}{\boldsymbol{\beta}_l} \cdot \underset{(r\times 1)}{\mathbf{x}_{t-l}}, \quad t = 1, 2, \ldots, T, \tag{4.17}$$

where $y$ is an $(n \times 1)$ column vector of the economic activity levels in each of $n$ cities at the times specified, and $\mathbf{x}$ is an $(r \times 1)$ column vector giving the level of each of the $r$ exogenous national factors which affect all the cities in the economic system at the times specified. We assume that there are $T$ time periods in all. The influence upon the $i$th city at time $t$ of activity levels in other cities, $j$, in the same and earlier time periods is specified by the $\{\mathbf{A}\}$ matrices; the influence on the $i$th city at time $t$ of exogenous factors in the same or in earlier times is specified by the $\{\boldsymbol{\beta}\}$ matrices.Thus 'the . . . coefficients identify patterns of interaction in the system, and determine (i) which cities affect which other cities, to what extent, and after which time lag, and (ii) to what extent and after which time lag, each city is affected by exogenous national factors' (King *et al.*, 1969, p. 214).

No extensive empirical testing of the impulse transmission models (4.16) and (4.17) has been carried out. There are, however, some partial tests which allow some idea of the utility of the models to be gained. Thus King *et al.* (1969) have used model (4.17) in a study of bimonthly unemployment data for 33 metropolitan areas in the American Midwest over the period, April 1960 to September 1964. The area chosen is one of traditionally high cyclical fluctuations in unemployment levels. The time period selected was one when unemployment rates were generally low, and the structural component in unemployment (that is, unemployment due to a mismatch between labour skills available in the economy and those required by industry) was relatively unimportant.

Table 4.9 Correlation between national employment cycles and those of individual cities.*

| $0.90 \leqslant r$ | $0.85 \leqslant r < 0.90$ | $0.80 \leqslant r < 0.85$ | $0 \leqslant r < 0.80$ |
|---|---|---|---|
| Akron (P) | Canton (P) | Detroit (D) | Davenport (I) |
| Chicago | Cincinnati | Terre Haute (I) | Evansville (I) |
| Madison | Cleveland (P) | Toledo (D) | Flint (D) |
| | Indianapolis (I) | Wheeling (P) | Gary (P) |
| | Lansing (D) | | Fort Wayne (P) |
| | Milwaukee | | Lorain (P) |
| | Peoria (I) | | Louisville (I) |
| | Saginaw (D) | | Pittsburgh (P) |
| | | | South Bend |
| | | | Steubenville (P) |
| | | | Youngstown (P) |

(P) Pittsburgh–Youngstown group (D) = Detroit group
(I) = Indianapolis group.
*Employment series for 26 Midwest American cities, 1960–64.
Source: King *et al.*, 1969, Table 1, p. 215.

The impact of the $\beta$ coefficients, the exogenous or national effects, was measured by correlating the unemployment series for each city with the national series. As Table 4.9 shows, there was a high degree of correlation for regional centres like Chicago, which tended to reflect the national pattern rather closely. Conversely, specialist steel towns like Gary and Youngstown showed higher independence from the national pattern. Regression of the city series on the national series yielded a set of residuals for each city, i.e. a set of observations from which the exogenous effect had been partly removed. For

***

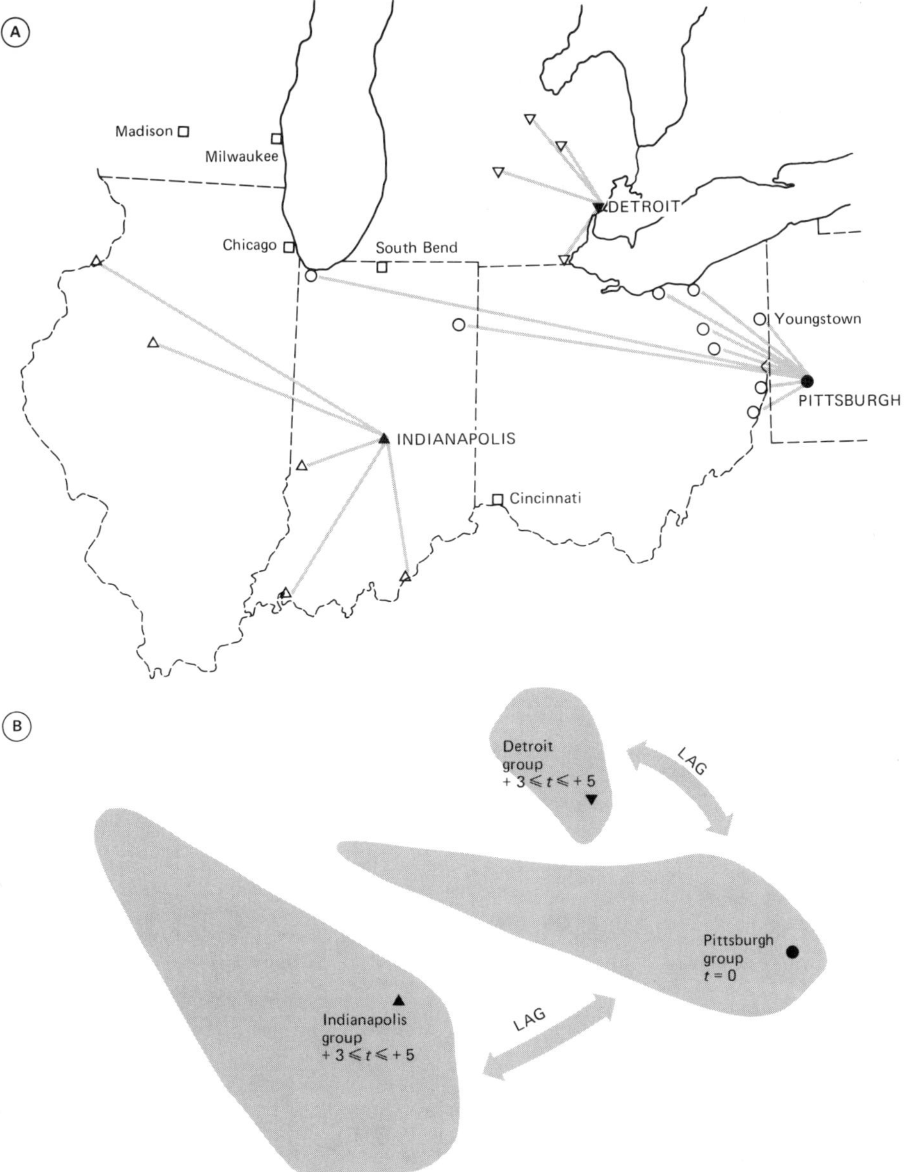


**Figure 4.23** Economic impulses between 25 cities in the American midwest showing (**A**) strong 'within-group' links with no time lags to form regional clusters and (**B**) weaker 'between-group' links with time lags indicated. Based on data from King, *et al.*, 1969, Table 2. Eight smaller cities with unclear group affiliations are not plotted. The five cities without bonds are linked closely to national trends rather than to the regional sub-systems.

each pair of cities, lagged correlations were computed between the residual series to give estimates of the inter-city effects (via the $\{\mathbf{A}\}$ matrices). Study of this correlation matrix suggested three main conclusions:

(1) Three regional clusters of cities were recognized on the evidence of strong, simultaneous interactions. The three clusters were focussed on the Pittsburgh–Youngstown area (ten cities), the Indianapolis area (six cities), and the Detroit area (five cities). See Figure 4.23. Unemployment impulses 'hit' each group at about the same time.

(2) Two of the clusters recognized above (Indianapolis and Detroit), lagged about three to five months *behind* the Pittsburgh–Youngstown group, i.e. the correlations were highest when one city series was lagged behind the others. Unemployment impulses 'hit' the steel-making group before the other two groups, which have different, but related, occupational structures.

(3) Some cities had low levels of interaction with other cities in the Midwest. For example, Chicago, Madison, and Cincinnati were rather independent of the cyclic behaviour of their neighbours. These same cities were, as Table 4.9 shows, closely connected to the national pattern.

Since the initial work of King and his associates in 1969, research upon the development of formal models of impulse transmission has grown considerably. Models (4.16) and (4.17) are particular examples of a general class of regression and auto-regression models. Several people, for example, Curry (1971), Cliff *et al.* (1975), Bennett (1975), Hepple (1975) and Bannister (1975) have begun to extend the basic methods considered here into more general space–time forecasting methods using mixed autoregressive–moving average equations. The structure of these more advanced models is taken up in Chapter 16. This kind of approach seems largely to have superseded the descriptive studies using cross-spectral methods (see Section 12.5), like those of Bassett and Haggett (1971), in tackling this class of problems.

## 4.7 Conclusions

Nodal models attempt to describe the macrostructure of human populations as it is arranged in sets of settlements. It will be evident from this chapter that our understanding of human settlements—even in the broad terms of size and spacing—is still superficial and incomplete. Despite the extensive research on size distributions of cities, there is no acceptable theory that meets all the counter cases that individual settlement patterns in different parts of the world may display. Some promising work on the growth of cities and the ways in which impulses are transmitted between them has been reported and the prospects for significant advances in our understanding in these areas remain good. In view of the significance of changing settlement patterns in a rapidly urbanizing world, and its relationship to national and regional planning policy, the need for continuing research on the locational structure of human settlements is likely to accelerate.

# 5 Hierarchies

5.1 **Introduction.** 5.2 **Functional Hierarchies of Settlements:** 1 Cluster size and cluster function; 2 Lattices and *k* functions; 3 Central place hierarchies: fixed *k* models; 4 Central place hierarchies: variable *k* models; 5 Empirical evidence on *k* values. 5.3 **Periodic and Evolving Settlement Hierarchies:** 1 Periodic cycles and rings; 2 Evolution of settlement systems; 3 City evolution and economic base theory. 5.4 **Specialized Centres within the Hierarchy:** 1 Concepts of specialization; 2 Evidence of accordance; 3 Distortion as a theoretical problem; 4 Distortion as a measurement problem. 5.5 **Hierarchic Distortion due to Agglomeration:** 1 Agglomeration within individual plants; 2 Agglomeration of groups of plants: regional 'swarming'; 3 Random nuclei: the problem of 'nonconformist' centres. 5.6 **Hierarchic Distortion due to Resource Localization:** 1 Movement minimization: Weberian analysis; 2 Variations in the locational surface; 3 Local substitution between inputs. 5.7 **Conclusions.**

## 5.1 Introduction

One of the most important questions about the nodal distribution of population was not answered in the last chapter. This is the question of the hierarchical organization of settlement. Some of the most prolific and significant of locational theorists—the Germans, Christaller and Lösch—were intrigued with this problem and evolved formal models to explain and illustrate their own concepts of locational hierarchies. These models are examined here, together with the empirical evidence for and against this type of structure. The second half of the chapter is concerned with the difficult, and apparently aberrant cases of industrial centres which 'distort' the regular hierarchy. In suggesting that this distortion is less fundamental than is sometimes urged, an attempt is made to place the industrial location models, notably that of Weber, within the general framework of settlement location.

## 5.2 Functional Hierarchies of Settlements

### 5.2.1 *Cluster size and cluster function*

When a recent paper reported that a small general store near Zürich stocked only one kind of champagne, while the Bahnhofstrasse in the city centre displayed over 20 kinds, it was confirming for centres within the urban area what has been well established in the central place literature for decades, and in everyday experience since time was, i.e. the fact that large centres of population have a much wider range of goods, services, and functions than smaller centres. Despite this general observation, the precise form of function/population relationships has remained elusive.

(a) *Continuous relationships between size and function.* A number of studies have tried to trace the precise form of the relationship between the population size of a settlement and its functional range. Figure 5.1 illustrates two sets of findings from areas of Western and non-Western society. First, we report the work of Stafford (1963), who examined the functions of a small sample of towns in southern Illinois, and found a positive Pearson product moment correlation of $r = 0.89$ between population and functional range (Figure 5.1A). Rather similar findings, with high positive relationships, are reported in other Western areas: King (1962) found values of $r = 0.82$ in the Canterbury district of New Zealand, and Berry and Garrison (1958b) obtained slightly lower values ($r = 0.75$) for Snohomish county, Washington, in the northwestern United States.

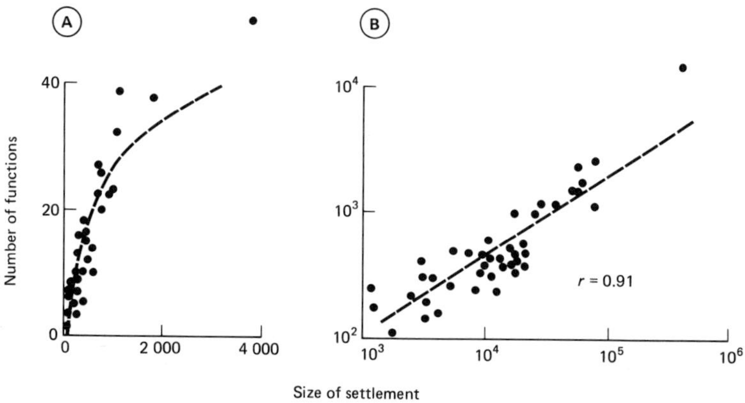


**Figure 5.1** Relationship of functional range to settlement size in southern Illinois, United States (**A**), and southern Ceylon (**B**). In the first graph the *y*-axis is arithmetic and in the second graph is logarithmic. Sources: Stafford, 1963, p. 170; Gunawardena, 1964.

For non-Western society, Gunawardena (1964) discovered a similar curvilinear and positive relationship for the southern part of Ceylon. Figure 5.1B shows the results obtained for the number of service establishments plotted against size of settlements ($r = 0.91$). Similar coefficients were obtained for the relationship with total shop numbers (0.89) and number of retail establishments (0.87). Although both sets of findings were drawn from mainly rural areas, Ullman and Dacey (1962) have suggested that they may be reasonably extended to larger towns and cities.

Higher positive correlations suggest that (i) larger centres have a far greater range of service functions than smaller centres, but that (ii) the relationship between size and functional range is curvilinear—as settlements become larger they add fewer new functions for each new increment in population size.

(b) *Definitions of population.* On theoretical grounds (see Sections 5.2.3 and 5.2.4), the relationship between settlement size and number of functions might be expected to be recognizably 'stepped' in character, rather than continuous. While the evidence available is not conclusive, a number of studies of both thresholds and discontinuities throw some light on this hypothesis. Haggett and Gunawardena (1964) suggest that we may view the *threshold* of any function as the middle point of its 'entry zone'. For a given function ($f_i$), there is a lower settlement population size below which no settlements will have $f_i$; conversely there is an upper settlement population size above which all settlements will have $f_i$. By modifying a standard bioassay technique, the Reed–Muench method, the middle point of this entry zone can be measured to give the *median population threshold*, ($T_{50}$). Figure 5.2 shows how $T_{50}$ may be

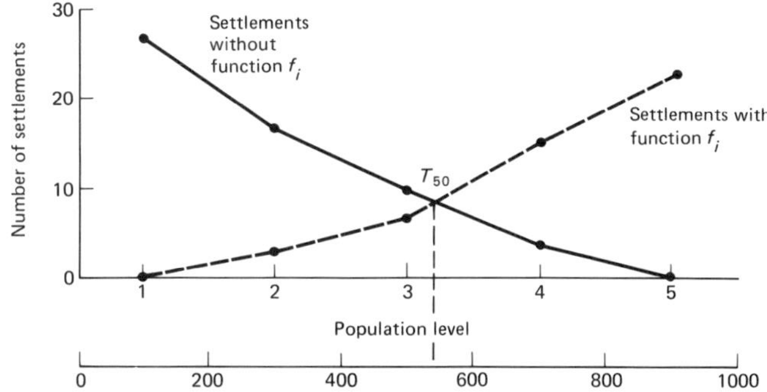


**Figure 5.2** Graphical determination of population thresholds ($T_{50}$) for settlement functions by the Reed–Muench method (1938). Source: Haggett and Gunawardena, 1964, p. 8.

determined in practice. The number of settlements with and without the function, $f_i$, is plotted on the $y$-axis, against the population size of the settlement transformed to a category scale on the $x$-axis. The point where the two curves cross gives the appropriate $T_{50}$ value in terms of the population scale. Using this technique, thresholds were determined by Gunawardena (1964) for a number of settlement functions in the southern part of Ceylon. Table 5.1 shows, for some sample functions, the range of $T_{50}$ values. Higher order functions (e.g. magistrates' courts' have median thresholds nearly twenty times as high as that for some lower order functions (e.g. primary schools), while the two main climatic zones of the island (Wet Zone and Dry Zone) are strongly contrasted.

Gunawardena's findings are important because they confirm for a non-Western area the type of threshold hierarchy which earlier work by Berry and Garrison (1958b) had established for the United States. Moreover, Bunge (1962, p. 146) had criticized American evidence of thresholds on the grounds that (i) it defined thresholds in terms of the population of the settlement rather than in terms of the population of the hinterland, and (ii) it ignored highway users who contributed to a large part of the true threshold population of settlements in the United States. For southern Ceylon, Gunawardena was able to show that the population of the central settlement was significantly correlated with the total hinterland population for all the functions studied. Also southern Ceylon is an area of such low mobility, at least relative to the United States, that the proportion of the threshold population that is contributed by 'through-traffic' is very small indeed.

Table 5.1 Median population thresholds for range of functions*

| *Environmental zone:* | *Wet zone* | *Dry zone* | *Ratio* |
|---|---|---|---|
| Service functions: | | | |
| Primary schools | 515 | 260 | 0.50 |
| Post offices | 1,590 | 565 | 0.36 |
| Markets and fairs | 2,870 | 1,300 | 0.45 |
| Secondary schools | 3,400 | 1,190 | 0.35 |
| Hospitals | 5,250 | 1,260 | 0.24 |
| Magistrates' courts | 9,200 | 2,370 | 0.26 |

Source: Gunawardena, 1964, p. 180.
*Southern Ceylon.

(c) *Discontinuities in size/function relationships.* It is of considerable theoretical interest as far as central place theory is concerned to know if size/function relationships are continuous, or if there are 'quantum jumps' (discontinuities) between the functions which are typical of one size band of settlements and the functions which are typical of another. This is clearly difficult to establish where the settlements form a regular size hierarchy of the kind described in the previous chapter. Thus Lösch (1954, p. 433) wrote of Iowa: 'I do not see how one could eliminate size-number effects to disclose

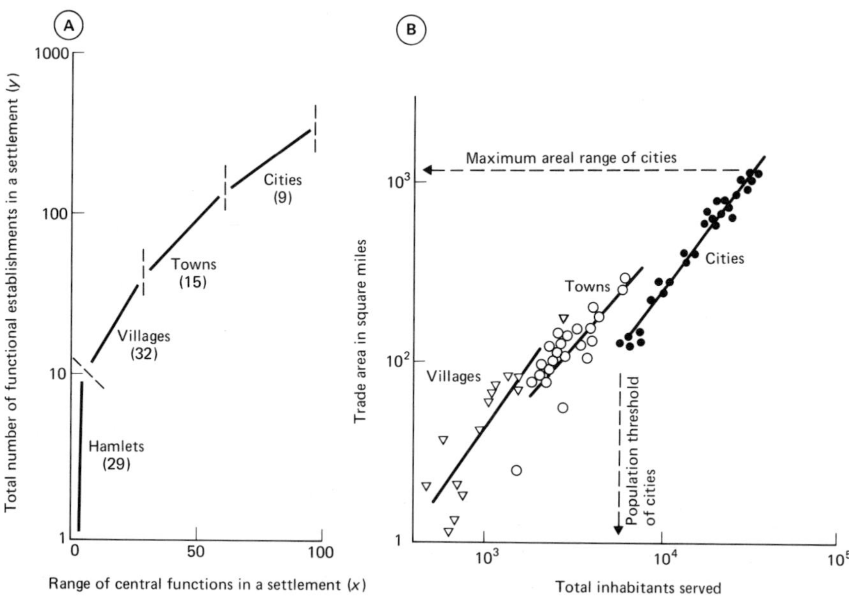


**Figure 5.3** Settlement hierarchy in southwestern Iowa, United States, for four classes of central places. Source: Berry, Barnum, and Tennant, 1962, pp. 79, 80.

possible hidden agglomerations'. Figure 5.3 shows some results of an attempt by Berry, Barnum and Tennant (1963) to solve Lösch's problem by the use of factor analysis to classify settlements in southwest Iowa. The discontinuities found suggest it is useful to think of settlements in this area as forming three rather discrete classes: *cities* with more than 55 functions, *towns* with from 28 to 50 functions, and *villages* with between ten and 25 functions. Although *hamlets* were not included in the factor analysis, Figure 5.3A shows that they occupied a distinct segment of the functional hierarchy. In this graph, the total number of functional establishments in each settlement (shops, garages, etc.) is plotted on the $y$-axis, against the range of functions on the $x$-axis. Thus, in a particular settlement, there might be 21 shops (functional establishments) spread among a range of three functions (butcher, baker, greengrocer), with, say, seven of each kind. For the three higher order settlements (Figure 5.3B), the distinctive locations of villages, towns and cities are shown in relation to the trade areas and the total populations served by each kind (both $x$- and $y$-axes are transformed to logarithmic scales). The advantage of this graph is that both the *threshold* and the *maximum range* can be readily determined for a specific order of the settlement hierarchy: the arrows on Figure 5.3B indicate these values for cities.

Subsequent research in other areas has tended to produce mixed results. In some, a rather continuous size/function relationship appears to dominate; in others a more stepped hierarchy is discernible. Clearly, any theory-building will need to accommodate the wide range of relationships observed.

### 5.2.2 *Lattices and k functions*

In an earlier discussion (Section 2.7.1), it was argued that settlements arranged in a triangular lattice, with a separate hexagonal field about each centre, represent the optimum spatial division of an undifferentiated landscape. If we now wish to introduce the notion of a hierarchy of settlements, in which some settlements provide specialized functions for others, we must disturb this simple pattern.

Figure 5.4 shows some of the ways in which hexagonal fields may be rearranged by the simple process of changing (i) the orientation of the hexagonal net and (ii) the size of each hexagonal cell. In these nine diagrams, the *central* places that are performing specialist functions are shown by a double circle, while the *dependent* places are shown by open circles if they lie within the field of a central place, and by closed circles if they lie on the perimeter of such a field. Note that central places are broadly synonymous with towns that serve as centres for the surrounding regional communities by providing them with *central goods* (such as farm machinery) and *central services* (like hospital treatment). Central places vary in importance. As we have seen in Figures 5.1 and 5.3A, higher order centres stock a wide range of goods and services; lower order centres stock a smaller range; that is, some limited part of the range offered by the higher centres. Dependent places are those lower order centres that consume the goods and services provided by central places.

In this system, the total number of settlements (including itself) served by

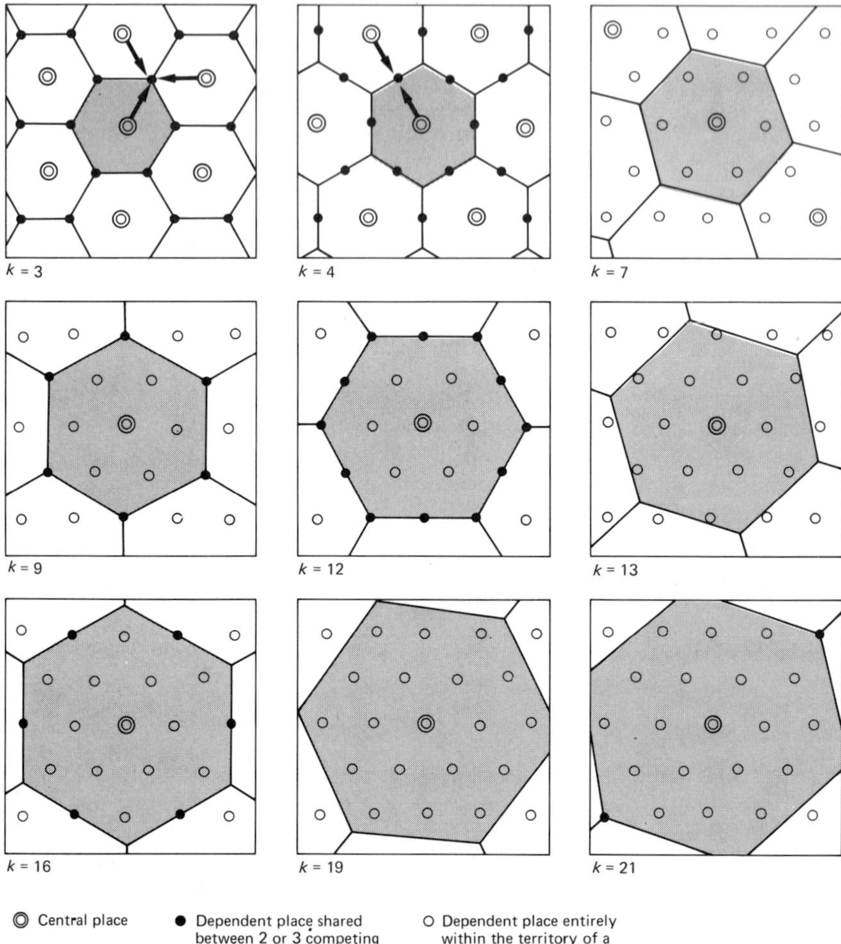


**Figure 5.4** Nine smallest hexagonal territories in a Löschian landscape. Source: Lösch, 1954, p. 118.

each central place is termed its *k* value (Christaller, 1933). In the first diagram of Figure 5.4 the *k* value of each central place is three. This is made up of the central place itself, plus a one third share in each of the six border settlements: this one third proportion arises because each dependent place is shared between three central places (see arrows). In the next diagram, the hexagonal net is turned through 90° so that border settlements are shared by only two central places; thus, the value of *k* rises to four. When this process of net orientation and enlargement is carried out over the size range covered by the nine smallest fields in a Löschian landscape, we obtain an irregular series of *k* values, i.e., three, four, seven, nine, twelve, thirteen, sixteen, nineteen, and twenty-one.

While there are a number of solutions to hexagonal hierarchies, each with its appropriate $k$ value, both Christaller and Lösch have argued that not all solutions are equally likely. When the number of settlements served by a central place is plotted on the $x$-axis of a graph against the distance from the central place to the furthest dependent place (on the $y$-axis), then irregularities are revealed (Figure 5.5). If we judge the efficiency (i.e. number of settlements served/distance travelled) of each solution by this graph, then clearly the solution, $k = 12$, is extremely inefficient, while the solutions, $k = 7$, $k = 13$, and $k = 19$ are very efficient. These three cases also have the advantage of consisting entirely of undivided dependent places (none of the satellite centres is shared with any other central place), which Lösch (1954, p. 120, footnote 16) suggests is both politically and economically stable and is therefore a solution likely to occur in practice. Using arguments of this kind, we can see that a regular lattice of settlements leads to (i) a discontinuous number of central place solutions, and (ii) irregularities in the relative efficiencies of these solutions. It is on these basic numbers, the $k$ values, of the hexagonal system that the central place hierarchies of Christaller and Lösch have been built.

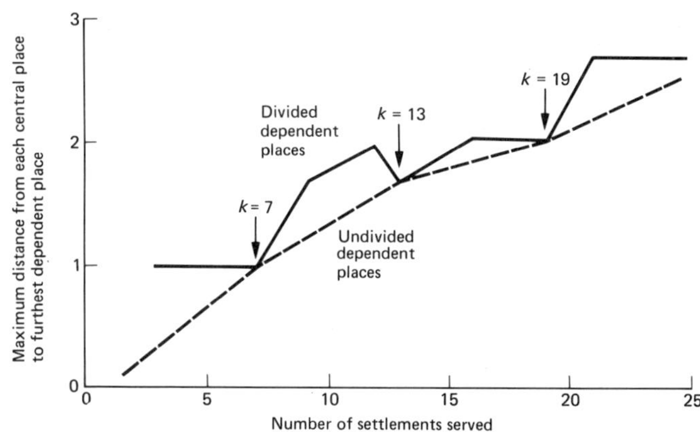


**Figure 5.5** Relative efficiency of the hexagonal territories mapped in Figure 5.4.

Critics of central-place theory might well point to the artificial regularity of the hexagonal grid. This grid is, however, much less restrictive than it appears. Small, random displacements of centres from the exact hexagonal lattice position have (a) little effect on the assumed trade area of each centre, but (b) make it difficult to recognize the map pattern as distinctively hexagonal in character. Consider the central place system shown in Figure 5.6. If the distance from a given centre to its nearest neighbour has a unit value of 1 km, say, then the size, $s_a$, of the trade area for centre $a$ is:

$$s_a = \sqrt{3/2} = 0.866 \text{ km}^2. \tag{5.1}$$

Goodchild (1972) has examined the effect of displacing the centre a distance, $d$, away from $a$ towards the location at $c$. The revised trade area around the displaced centre ($a'$) is shown in Figure 5.6. Its area is

$$s_{a'} = \frac{9\sqrt{3}(1-d^2)^2}{2(3-d^2)(3-4d^2)}, \tag{5.2}$$

so that a displacement of $d = 0.5$ km (that is, a distance half that of the hexagonal spacing) yields an area of $s_{a'} = 0.797$ km$^2$. Thus, the economic implications of distortion of the market area are clear: even with the major relocation of *a* in Figure 5.6, the market area is still 92 per cent of that expected

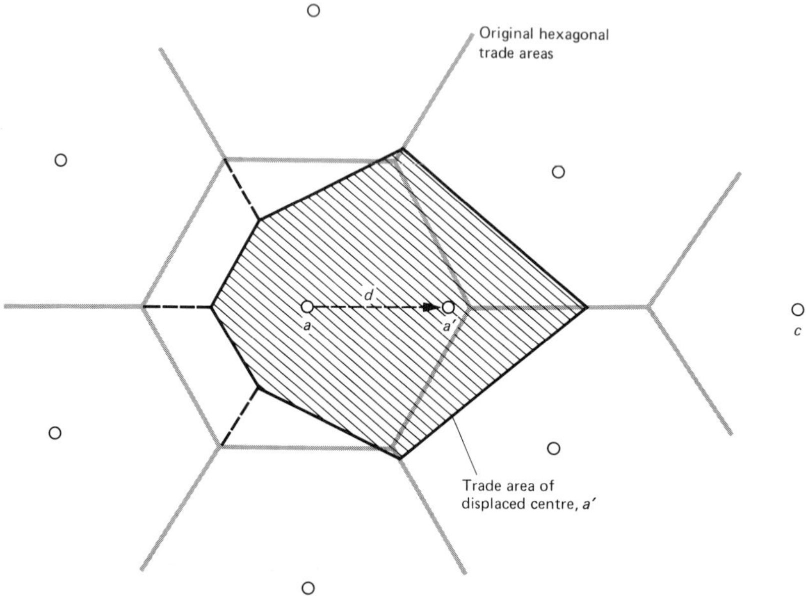


**Figure 5.6** Impact of displacement of central places from their symmetric lattice positions on their trade areas. Source: Goodchild, 1972, p. 106.

under the 'pure' hexagonal system. Note that equation (5.2) is valid for $d < 0.577$; above this figure, the displaced trade area shares a boundary with centre *b*. Up to $d = 0.17$, the displaced trade area is still 99 per cent or more of the full hexagonal value.

### 5.2.3 *Central place hierarchies: fixed k models*

Given a circular demand area for central goods, Christaller (1933) demonstrated that a group of similar central places will have hexagonal trade regions, with the central places arranged in a regular triangular lattice. We noted earlier (Section 4.2.3; see especially Figure 4.7) the stages by which such a pattern might emerge as population colonized a new area, and central places were established. The final hexagonal pattern follows directly from five simplified assumptions: (a) There must be an unbounded isotropic place with a homogeneous distribution of purchasing power; (b) Central goods must be purchased from the nearest central place; (c) All parts of the plane must be served by a central place, that is, the trade areas must completely fill the plane; (d) Consumer movement must be minimized; and (c) No excess profits may be earned by any central place (Haggett, 1975a, p. 364). Clearly, the hexagons result from our attempt to pack as many circular demand areas as possible on to the plane. If we require all parts of the plane to be served by a central place (assumption c), the circles will overlap. But because of our second assumption, that consumers will shop at the closest central place, the areas of overlap will be bisected. A perfect competitive situation will be achieved only when the plane is served by the maximal number of central places, offering identical central goods at identical prices to hexagonal trade regions of identical size. Only this arrangement ensures that consumers travel the least distance to central places. Since our major concern here is with the locational geometry of the models, and the implications the models hold for settlement structure, we shall not proceed further with the underlying economic assumptions and theory. Critical reviews of these aspects are provided by Berry and Pred (1961, pp. 3–18) and Webber (1972, Chapter 2).

Christaller (1933) developed a series of central place hierarchies on the assumption that the $k$ values in any region, once adopted, would be fixed; that is, he assumed that the $k$ value applied equally to the relationships between farms and villages, villages and towns, towns and cities, and so on, through all the *tiers* of the hierarchy. Figure 5.7A shows a very simple three-tier hierarchy based on the $k = 4$ assumption; it illustrates a lower stratum of dependent villages, on which is built a stratum of central towns, on which is built the higher stratum of central cities. The complete hierarchy for the $k = 4$ succession follows a regular geometrical progression (one, four, sixteen, sixty-four ...), while that for the next solution, $k = 7$, follows a similar progression (one, seven, forty-nine, three hundred and forty-three) (Figure 5.7B). The general expression giving the number of places dominated in each tier of the

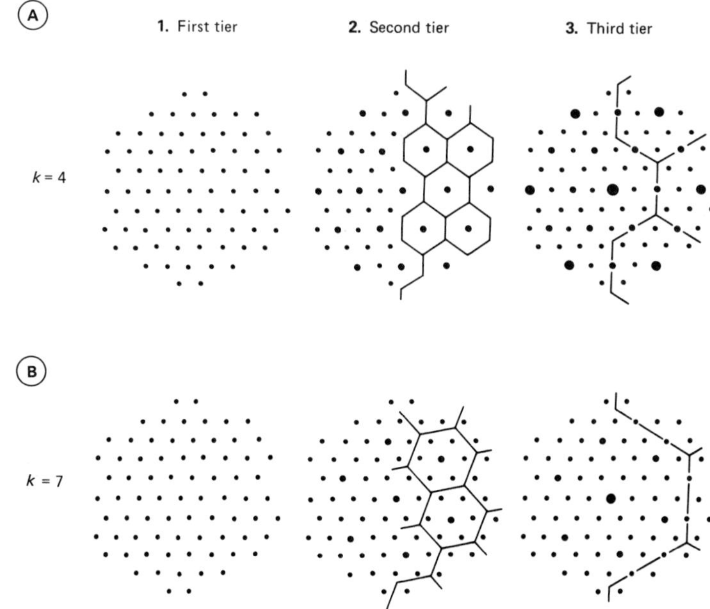


**Figure 5.7** Three-stage hierarchies in two regular fixed-$k$ systems.

fixed $k$ hierarchy is $n_i = k^i$, where $n$ is the number of dependent places and $i$ ($i \geqslant 0$) is the tier of the hierarchy. Using this formula, we would expect a central place in a $k = 7$ hierarchy to dominate 2,401 dependent places on the fourth tier of that hierarchy.

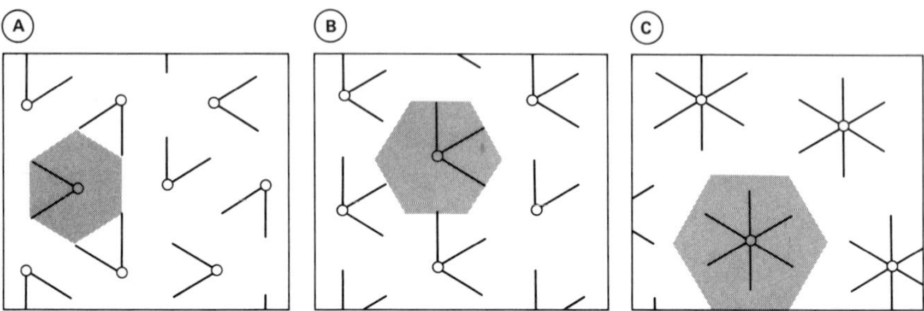


**Figure 5.8** Alternative nesting principles in the Christaller landscape. **A** Marketing principle, $k = 3$; **B** Traffic principle, $k = 4$; **C** Administrative principle, $k = 7$.

Although Christaller saw the advantages of undivided centres, he suggested that this might be achieved by 'nesting' of centres rather than by adopting optimum hexagonal boundaries of the sort shown in Figure 5.4. Three cases were envisaged: (i) Where the supply of goods from central places is to be as near as possible to the dependent places (Christaller's *marketing principle*) a $k = 3$ hierarchy is indicated, since this maximizes the number of central places. To overcome the difficulty of shared dependent places, Christaller suggested that connections will be made with only two of the six nearest dependent places (Figure 5.8A), and that this will give rise to a symmetrical nested hierarchy. (ii) Where the cost of transport is important (Christaller's *traffic principle*) a $k = 4$ hierarchy is indicated since '. . . as many important places as possible lie on one traffic route between larger towns, the route being established as cheaply as possible' (Berry and Pred, 1961, p. 16). Connections will be made with only three of the six nearest dependent places (Figure 5.8B) to give a different pattern of nesting. (iii) Where clear cut administrative control is important (Christaller's *administrative principle*) a $k = 7$ hierarchy is indicated, with connections between a central place and all six of the nearest dependent places (Figure 5.8C). Results from an Iowan study (Berry, Barnum, and Tennant, 1962, pp. 105–6) have suggested that, although nesting may occur in practice, it may be more irregular than Christaller's model suggests.

### 5.2.4 *Central place hierarchies: variable k models*

The major theoretical extension of the Christaller model was made by Lösch (1954). He clarified the ways in which spatial demand areas arise, and verified that the hexagonal shapes of trade regions are optimal where the population to be served is uniformly distributed in the plane. However, the major difference between the Lösch and Christaller approaches is that Lösch regarded the fixed $k$ assumption as a special case, and he used all the possible hexagonal solutions to construct hierarchies. After superimposing the various sizes of hexagons on

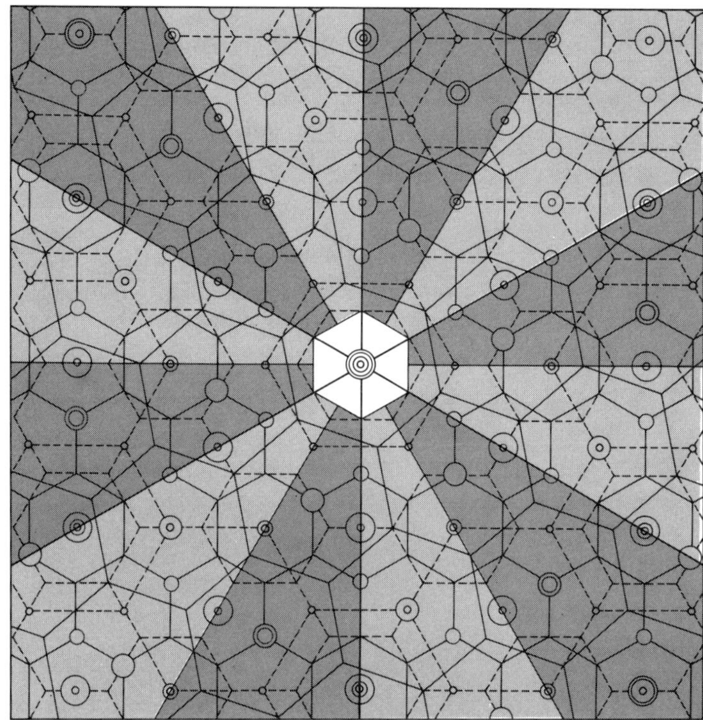

**Figure 5.9** Simplified Löschian landscape with systems of hexagonal nets. Source: Isard, 1956, p. 270.

a single point, he rotated the nets about that point to get six sectors with many, and six sectors with few, production sites (Figure 5.9). With this arrangement 'all nets have a centre in common . . . the greatest number of locations coincide . . . the sum of the minimum distances between industrial locations is least, and in consequence not only shipments but transport lines are reduced to a minimum' (Lösch, 1954, p. 124). As Figure 5.10 shows, the rotation produces a strong pattern of variation, both between sectors and with distance from the metropolis. Here, the metropolis is the centre of 150 separate fields. Those with centres of over four and over eight coincident fields are shown by the two larger classes of dots in Figure 5.10B. Tarrant (1973) has tabulated the 39 $k$ values to $k = 100$, and has devised a rapid and simple way for finding all possible $k$ networks within a Löschian central place landscape. His method uses the co-ordinates of the original settlement lattice to locate higher order centres directly, and avoids the ambiguities inherent in the rotational procedure described by Lösch.

Although Lösch used the same basic hexagonal unit and the same $k$ concept as Christaller, the hierarchy he evolved is markedly different. Christaller's hierarchy consists of a number of definite steps or tiers in which (i) all places in a particular tier are the same size and have the same functions, and (ii) all higher order places contain all the functions of the smaller central places. In contrast to this, the Löschian hierarchy is far less rigid. It consists of a nearly continuous sequence of centres, rather than distinct tiers, so that (i) settlements of the same size need not have the same functions (e.g. a centre serving seven settlements may be either a $k = 7$ central place or merely the coincident centre for both the $k = 3$ and the $k = 4$ networks). and (ii) larger places need not necessarily have all the functions of the smaller central places.

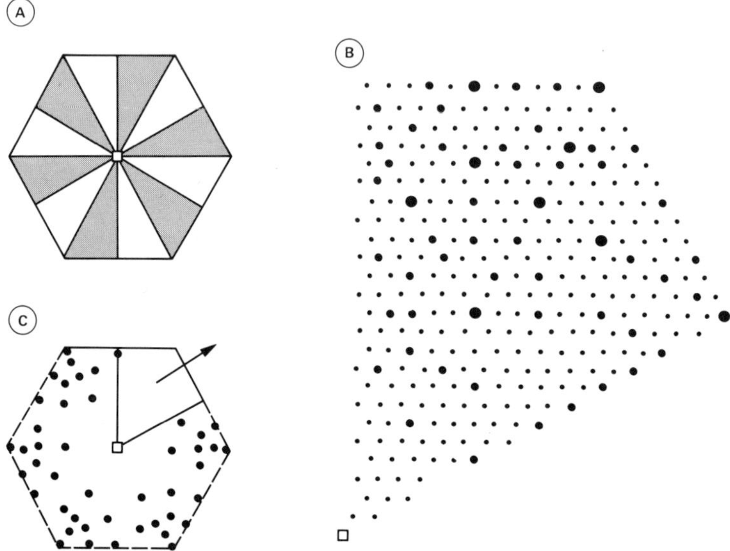


**Figure 5.10** Löschian landscape with alternating city-rich (shaded) and city-poor sectors (**A**); distribution of all centres within one sector (**B**); and distribution of large cities (**C**). Source: Lösch, 1954, p. 127.

In many ways, the Löschian system—at least when it is adjusted for concentration and resource irregularities (see Sections 2.7.3 and 4.2.2)—yields a pattern more in accord with reality than that of Christaller. Lösch's variable $k$ model produces a more continuous city rank-size distribution with rather small deviations from the logarithmic model considered in Section 4.3. Vining (1955) has attacked the Christaller fixed $k$ concept on the grounds that it leads to a 'stepped' size distribution of cities, while Beckmann (1958) has defended the Christaller model being both simpler and theoretically more satisfying. He argues that it may not be inconsistent with observed city size distributions if we allow the addition of a random element. This element be sufficient to blur the rigid steps of the hierarchy into the continuous rank-size sequence of reality.

Assume that there exists an overall hierarchy of urban functions, with the levels $i = 1, , \ldots, n$. In this notation, $i = 1$ is the lowest level functional order (appropriate to, say, the hamlet level) and $i = n$ is that appropriate to the largest metropolis in the system. A number of models have been advanced to link the population of a city, $p_i$, to a given hierarchic level, $i$, of urban functions. Thus, Lösch demonstrated that the following relationship holds where the hierarchic distribution of functions can be summarized by a Pareto curve with a slope of unity (see Parr, 1970, p. 223):

$$p_i = \frac{s_1 r_1}{1-s_1} c^{(i-1)}. \tag{5.3}$$

In equation (5.3), $r_1$ is the rural population required to support a first order urban function at the lowest level of the hierarchy; $s_1$ is a proportionality constant relating the population of a central place (at level 1) to the total population it serves, and $c$ is a nesting factor indicating the number of market areas at the $(i-1)$st level included in a market area at the $i$th level. Since $c$ is raised to a power, city-size increases exponentially in relation to the level of urban function. For example, if $r_1 = 1800$, $s_1 = 0.1$, and $c = 4$, then the population of a city with first order functions ($p_1$) is 200; repeated application of equation (5.3) yields $p_2 = 800$, $p_3 = 3200$, $p_4 = 12{,}800$ and so on. Beckmann (1958) has proposed a modification of the rule for cases in which the constant of proportionality, $s$, does not vary with order. In his formation,

$$p_i = \frac{sr_1}{1-s}\left(\frac{c-1}{1-s}\right)^{i-1} \tag{5.4}$$

Again, the increase in population with functional order is exponential ($p_1 = 200$, $p_2 = 866$, $p_3 = 3750$, $p_4 = 16{,}238$), but the progression component is greater than in the Lösch model.

Dacey (1966C) has adopted a more realistic and sophisticated approach in his attempt to relate urban functional order and urban size, by integrating a Keynesian multiplier concept into his model (see Section 5.3.3). He does this by introducing a second proportionality factor, $u_i$, which measures that section of the population in an $i$th level city which is directly dependent upon exporting goods not offered at the $(i-1)$th level, expressed as a proportion of the population of that market area. The total population of a city at the $i$th functional level is then

$$p_i = \frac{\sum_{j=1}^{i} u_j r_j}{1-\sum_{j=1}^{i} u_j}, \quad \sum_{j=1}^{i} u_j < 1. \tag{5.5}$$

If we adopt a fixed value for $u$, say 0.1, then the population progression with increasing hierarchic functional level is 200, 1200, 6343, 33,770, ..., where $r$ has the same value as in the Lösch and Beckmann calculations. Simple parameter values have been chosen in the three cases described above to illustrate equations (5.3) to (5.5). Realistic models would demand that the values for $s$ and $u$ were varied with different levels in the hierarchy.

### 5.2.5 *Empirical evidence on k values*

One of the by-products of empirical work on thresholds (see Section 5.2.1) has been to examine the concept of (i) *tiers* in the hierarchy, and (ii) the relations between them as shown by $k$ values. There has certainly been no lack of studies in which tiers were identified. Indeed, since Christaller (1933) recognized his seven tier heirarchy, ranging from the hamlet to the world-city, there have been perhaps as many tiers recognized in human geography as erosion surfaces in physical geography. The basic difficulty which such studies face is in defining 'breaks' in the sequence, whether of function or of terrain. In practice, more or less arbitrary divisions have to be made. Thus Bracey (1962), in a study of central place villages in Somerset, England, recognized first order, second order, and third order villages (Figure 5.11), but based this classification on a continuum (number of shops) with breaks at five, ten, and twenty shops. Improved techniques for recognizing significant breaks (e.g. the use of factor analysis by Berry, Barnum, and Tennant, 1962), may help to overcome this problem by providing objective tests for their recognition.

Where uniform methods of classification are used (see Sections 14.4 and 14.5) regional variations in the relationships between the various tiers can be picked out. Thus Gunawardena (1964), who recognized four functional tiers in the settlement hierarchy of southern Ceylon, was able to show that $k$ values ranged from 1.6 to 11.0 between the various provinces. This variation may be more important and characteristic than her other finding, i.e., that the modal class was $k = 3$, exactly accordant with Christaller's 'marketing principle'. Studies have also been conducted on the regional variability of the multipliers used in the Lösch, Beckmann and Dacey models. Table 5.2 shows the sample values for the two parameters, $s$ and $u$, yielded by empirical data from six regional hierarchies. Note the general tendency for both $s$ and $u$ to fall at

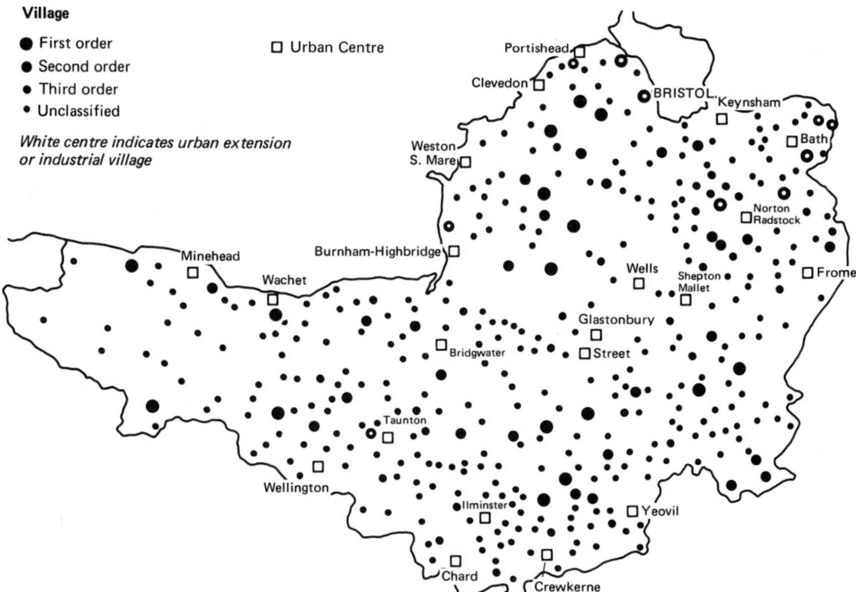


**Figure 5.11** Hierarchy of central villages in Somerset, southwestern England. Source: Bracey, 1962, p. 176.

higher levels of the hierarchy, but also the substantial region-to-region variation. We should expect such variations in behaviour to be related in part to the effects of non-nodal industry in increasing the size of city populations in the areas studied (see Section 5.4).

Table 5.2 Regional examples of model parameters in settlement hierarchies

| | | *Level of the hierarchy* | | | | |
|---|---|---|---|---|---|---|
| | | 1 | 2 | 3 | 4 | 5 |
| S. Germany (1930) | *s* | .29 | .18 | .11 | .10 | .09 |
| | *u* | .29 | .07 | .04 | .04 | .03 |
| Iowa (1930) | *s* | .47 | .37 | .28 | .26 | .16 |
| | *u* | .47 | .15 | .08 | .06 | .02 |
| Würtemberg (1960) | *s* | .67 | .51 | .33 | .25 | .20 |
| | *u* | .67 | .10 | .05 | .03 | .03 |
| S.W. Iowa (1960) | *s* | .44 | .33 | .24 | — | — |
| | *u* | .44 | .12 | .09 | — | — |
| Upper Midwest (1960) | *s* | .17 | .21 | .18 | .17 | .22 |
| | *u* | .17 | .14 | .06 | .04 | .10 |
| Quebec (1960) | *s* | .26 | .33 | .27 | .25 | .35 |
| | *u* | .26 | .17 | .13 | .07 | .11 |

Source: Parr, 1970, p. 233.

## 5.3 Periodic and Evolving Settlement Hierarchies

### 5.3.1 *Periodic cycles and rings*

Recent developments in central place theory have stressed the role of time in both the study of rural periodic markets, and in research into the historical bases of central place systems. The periodicity of rural markets has long attracted attention in cross-cultural, as well as historical, studies. Market periodicity is that phenomenon by which a market is held at centres on certain days, fixed in advance; such markets stand in contrast to permanent markets, where urban functions are continuously available. Periodic markets characterize rural settlements in which the purchasing power of the population is insufficient to maintain a continuous urban function. It will be clear (Figure 5.12) that a periodic function may form a 'market cycle' in time and a 'market ring' in space. In the simple example shown, the six smaller settlements in a $k = 7$ system form a regular, once a week cycle, with a seventh vacant day for rest or restocking: arrows indicate the ring in space formed by the presumed movement of an individual trader. Empirical regional studies show a wide variety of cycles which are unrelated, or only loosely related, to the conventional seven day week. Two day and four day systems have been described in East and West Africa (Hodder, 1966), and ten day cycles in China (Skinner, 1964–5).

Tinkler (1973) has approached the periodic market as a map colouring problem, in which no county (market town) in spatially adjacent (contiguous) counties can have the same colour (market day). Obviously, direct competition would be self-defeating for the markets in such a situation (akin to running

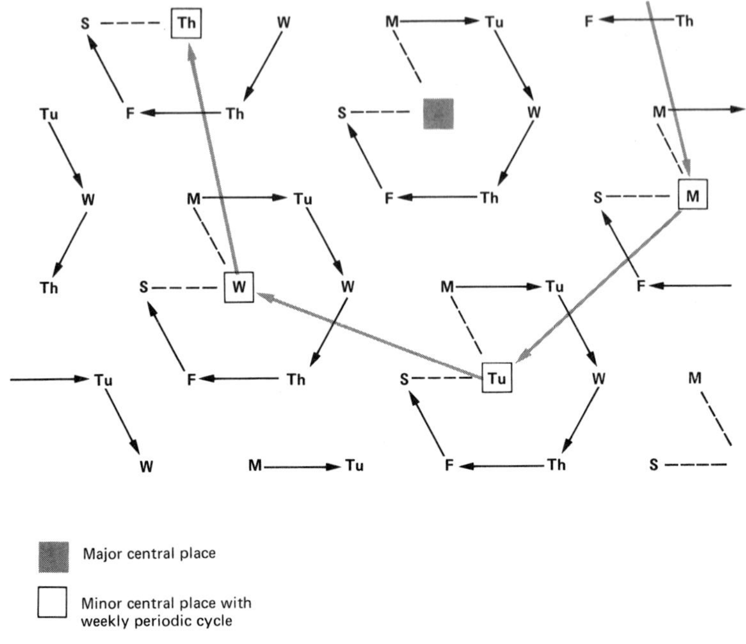


**Figure 5.12** Weekly periodic functions superimposed on a $k = 7$ Christaller landscape.

summer fêtes in adjacent parishes on the same Saturday in June!). An efficient colouring of the set of counties is one in which no two contiguous counties have identical colours. What then is the *minimum* number of colours (days) needed to satisfy this condition for all counties? Map colouring problems have puzzled mathematicians since the work of Möbius in the 1840s (Coxeter, 1961, p. 390). Four colours were found by experience to be the minimum number required to colour any planar map such that no two contiguous counties are the same colour, but theorems to underpin such generalizations have proved elusive. We may conclude, however, that four days (i.e. four colours) will ensure that there are no conflicts between adjacent markets. Figure 5.13 shows some possible four-day periodic systems superimposed on the basic Christaller $k = 4$ lattice. Note that we can conceive of both a closed and an open system, but that greater advantages (in terms of exchange of goods) accrue under the open system. Higher and lower order periodic systems may be linked together (Figure 5.13c) as in the fixed $k$ central place scheme.

The four-colour system is of special interest as a theoretical lower bond. Indeed, as Tinkler (1973, p. 3) speculates: 'Is it too much to suggest that the widely found four-day market week is the natural response to the topology of actual market systems?' In reality this will probably arise from trial and error adjustments of the market system to eliminate same-day conflicts for adjacent markets.' One further advantage of the four-day cycle is that it is relatively easy

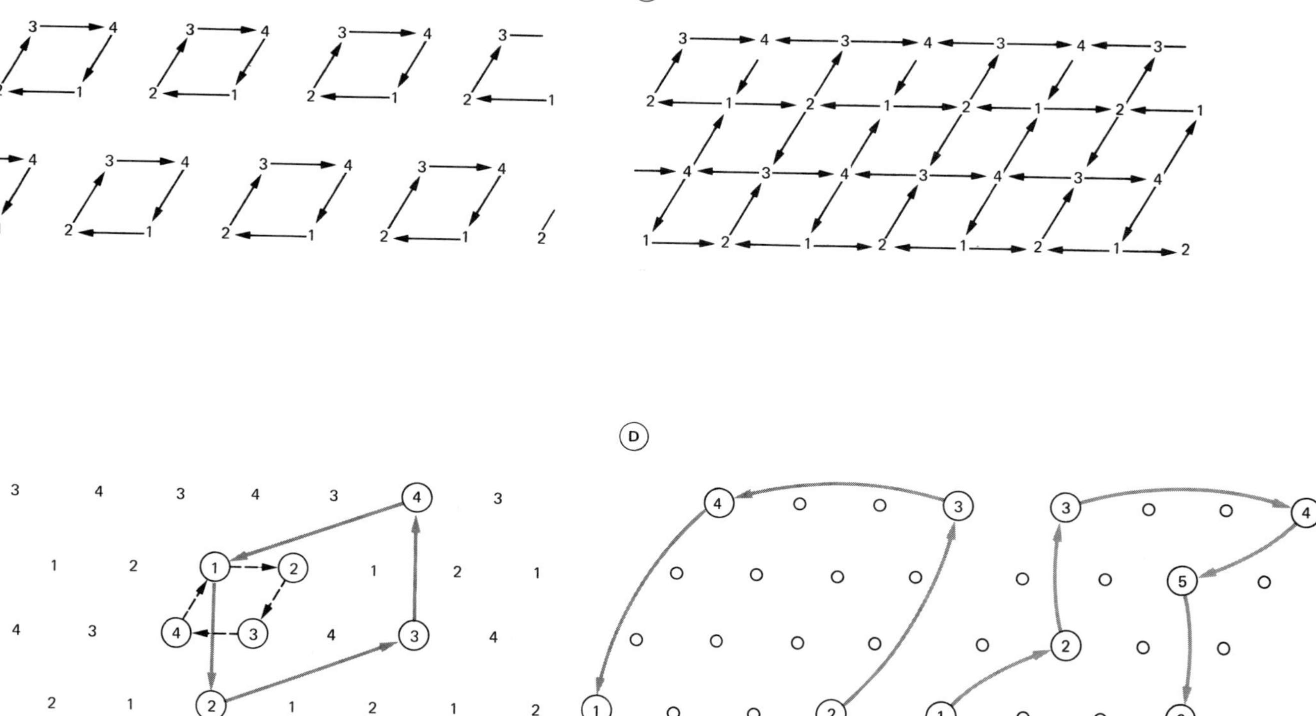


**Figure 5.13** Periodic market cycles in a $k = 4$ Christaller landscape. **A** Closed circuits; **B** Open circuits; **C** Integration of lower and higher-order circuits; **D** Modification to absorb additional centres. Source: Tinkler, 1973.

****

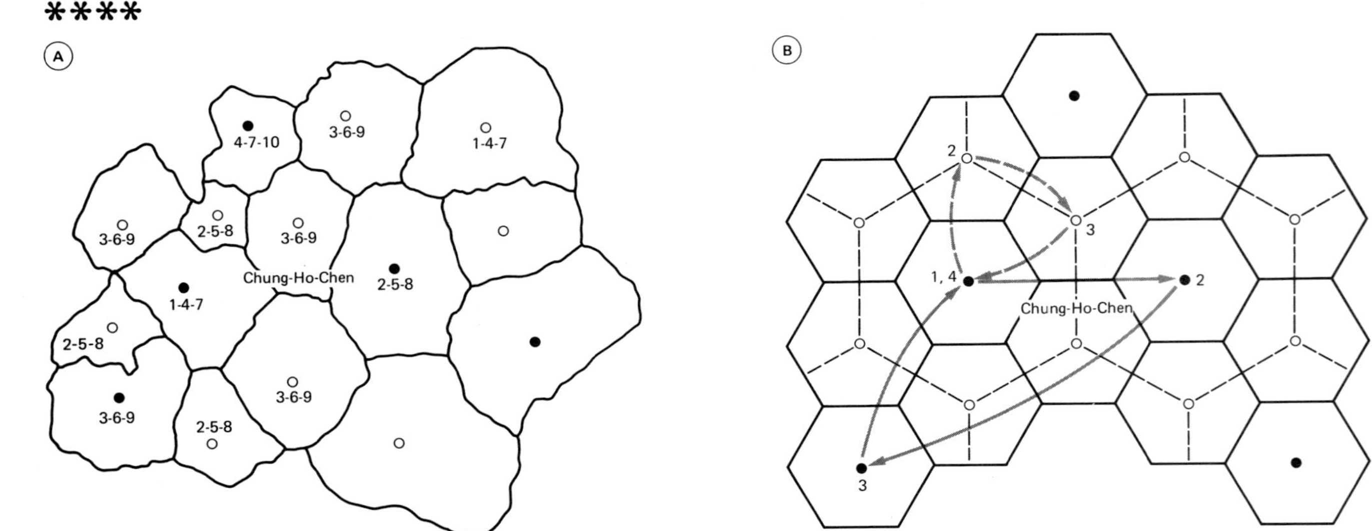


**Figure 5.14** Periodic central places. **A** Map of rural centres in the Chinese province of Szechwan showing days on which markets are held. **B** Transformation to show these centres as part of a $k = 3$ Christaller network. Source: Skinner, 1964, pp. 25–6.

to modify to a six-day cycle by including new markets within the centre of the triangles in the lattice structure (Figure 5.13D). With this modification, it fits readily into the six-working-day calendar common in most countries. As a counterbalance to these theoretical ring studies, Figure 5.14 summarizes the main features of a ten-day cycle described by Skinner (1964–65) for rural areas in the Szechwan province of China. The resilience of these market structures is attested by the breakdown of the more centralized state trading centres superimposed on this area in the early 1950s, and the total re-establishment of the traditional market cycle a decade later.

### 5.3.2 *Evolution of settlement systems*

The formal interlocking shown in Figure 5.13 could clearly not be achieved instantaneously. If local markets arise spontaneously, then we would expect the colouring procedure to be approximately random in the first place. Conflicts of interest between same day markets at adjacent centres would probably lead to *ad hoc* adjustments to bring cycles into phase, with neighbouring rings of different cycle lengths ultimately developing. Rises in population density and/or income would eventually cause local demand to increase to the point where fixed central place functions successively replaced their periodic counterparts.

Among the scholars who have critically analysed the historical bases of central place theory, the most important contribution has been made by Vance (1970). In his *Merchant's world*, Vance argues that the Southern German pattern studied by Christaller was the particular product of the relative geographical uniformity of that area, its economic isolation, and its historical stratification. It was, in effect, a closed system in which higher order places could emerge only with increasing rural productivity and an enlarging hierarchical assembly. Figure 5.15 shows the contrast provided by Vance's more open, mercantile model, in which cities, rather than being the end product of a rural growth process, are themselves the initiators of growth.

Traditionally, economic historians have tended to explain the growth of cities in terms of accepted notions of industrialization and improved nodality (e.g. the coming of the railways). However, while the number of hypotheses and the wealth of special cases studied have proliferated, regional tests have remained unfashionable. Higgs (1969) illustrates one such regional test in his attempt to compare three hypotheses of settlement evolution proposed to account for the growth of cities in four Midwestern American states—Missouri, Iowa, Kansas, and Nebraska—during the late nineteenth century. His regression analyses raise the usual econometric questions of biassed and inconsistent estimates, but appear to show rather strong support for the central place models discussed in Section 5.2.3; *viz.* 'It may be concluded that the direction of causality was from a high rate of agricultural settlement to a high rate of city growth, and that this connection goes farthest in explaining the growth of [these] cities' (Higgs, 1969, p. 375). The importance of nodality to urban growth, as measured by the acquisition of railroad connections, was not fully confirmed, suggesting to Higgs that, although railroad connections might have been a necessary condition for city growth, they were clearly not sufficient. Detailed regional studies such as this are needed to throw more light on the growth processes by which settlement hierarchies both rise and decline.

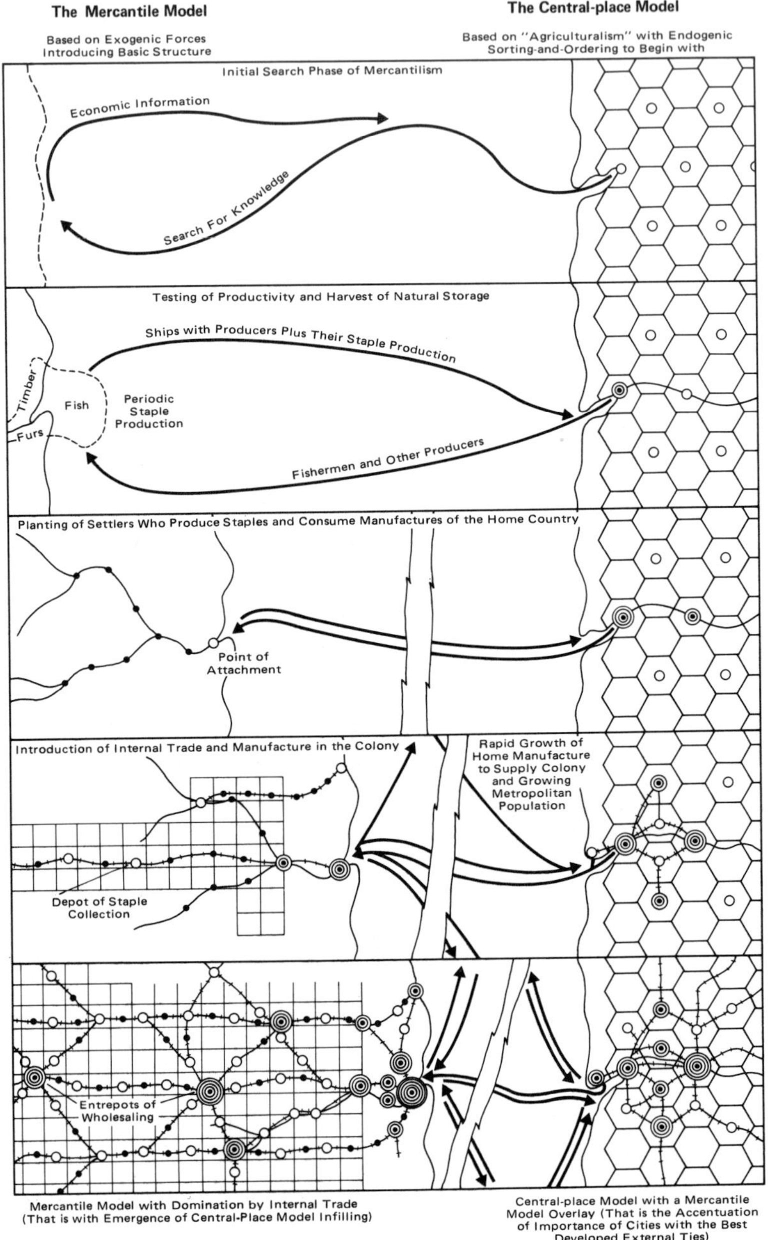


**Figure 5.15** Vance's mercantile model of settlement development. Source: Vance, 1970, p. 151.

### 5.3.3 *City evolution and economic base theory*

An alternative approach to settlement evolution is to examine changes over time within the single city using economic base theory. The employment structure of cities is commonly divided into a *basic* sector, and a *non-basic* or *service* sector (see also Section 5.4.4). The basic or 'city-forming' sector (Alexandersson, 1956) is usually defined as export-oriented employment, covering industries in which the final product is exported out of the particular urban centre of interest. The location of such basic industries is considered to be externally given, and not dependent on other activities within the city. Conversely, the non-basic, or city-serving, sector is concerned with locally oriented employment, and includes industries in which the final product is used within the city of interest. As Massey (1973) shows, the distinction between the two sectors is clearer in theory than in practice, and the categorization may have to be made on the basis of a pragmatic set of rules.

Economic base theory is concerned with the relationships between the two sectors and their presumed significance for urban growth. The population ($P$) of a city may be expressed as some function of total employment ($E$), while service employment ($S$) is some function of total population. These simple relations may be expressed in three equations:

$$\left.\begin{aligned} P &= \alpha E, & \alpha &> 1 \\ S &= \beta P, & 0 < \beta &< 1 \\ E &= E_b + S \end{aligned}\right\} \tag{5.6}$$

where $E_b$ is basic employment. The constants, $\alpha$ and $\beta$, have a rough economic interpretation, so that

$$\alpha = \frac{P}{E} \tag{5.7}$$

is an inverse 'activity rate' measuring the population-employment ratio. In the same way,

$$\beta = \frac{S}{P}, \tag{5.8}$$

is a population-serving ratio. The equations can be rearranged in a reduced form to relate population *directly* to basic employment, namely:

$$P = \alpha E_b (1 - \alpha\beta)^{-1}. \tag{5.9}$$

The term $(1-\alpha\beta)^{-1}$ acts as a multiplier which contains both the direct and indirect effects of basic employment on total population. Using data for the Reading urban region in southern England, Batty (1975) found an activity rate ($\alpha$) of 2.994, a population-serving ratio ($\beta$) of 0.216, and a multiplier of 2.841.

It is useful to split the service sector into the two components, consumer services ($S_1$) and producer services ($S_2$). The service equation must now be rewritten as

$$\left.\begin{aligned} S_1 &= \beta_1 P, & 0 < \beta_1 &< 1 \\ S_2 &= \beta_2 E, & 0 < \beta_2 &< 1 \end{aligned}\right\} \tag{5.10}$$

and

$$E = E_b + S_1 + S_2.$$

Here, $\beta_1$ and $\beta_2$ are the population-serving and employment-serving ratios respectively.

The fitting of economic base models to actual urban systems is usually accomplished through methods such as regression analysis. Thus Isard and Czamanski (1965) regressed population against basic employment for several different size classes of North American city. Although multipliers varied widely between the size classes, more consistent values were found by comparing changes in population and basic employment over a ten year period.

Economists like Paelinck (1970) have suggested that the growth of the city can be modelled in terms of difference equations relating the main elements in its population structure. If, as before, we assume the existence of three components, population ($P$), service activities ($S$), and employment ($E$), with the latter broken down into basic ($E_b$) and non-basic ($E_{nb}$) parts, then a possible model is

$$\left.\begin{aligned} P(t+1) &= a_1 P(t) + a_2 E(t) \\ S(t+1) &= b_1 P(t) + b_2 S(t) \\ E_b(t+1) &= c_1 E_{nb}(t) + c_2 E_b(t) \\ E_{nb}(t+1) &= d_2 P(t) + d_2 E_{nb}(t) \end{aligned}\right\} \tag{5.11}$$

and

$$E(t+1) = S(t+1) + E_b(t+1) + E_{nb}(t+1). \tag{5.12}$$

This system of linear equations can be succinctly represented in matrix form as

$$\begin{bmatrix} P \\ S \\ E_b \\ E_{nb} \\ E \end{bmatrix}_{t+1} = \begin{bmatrix} a_1 & 0 & 0 & 0 & a_2 \\ b_1 & b_2 & 0 & 0 & 0 \\ 0 & 0 & c_1 & c_2 & 0 \\ d_1 & 0 & 0 & d_2 & 0 \\ (b_1+d_1) & b_2 & c_1 & (c_2+d_2) & 0 \end{bmatrix} \begin{bmatrix} P \\ S \\ E_b \\ E_{nb} \\ E \end{bmatrix}_t , \tag{5.13}$$

and summarized as

$$\mathbf{x}(t+1) = \mathbf{Q}\mathbf{x}(t). \tag{5.14}$$

Here $\mathbf{x}$ is an $(n \times 1)$ column vector of activities ($P$, $S$, *etc.*) and $\mathbf{Q}$ is an $n \times n$ matrix of coefficients. In this format, the growth of urban or regional activities over a time period of length $T$, from some origin at time zero, can be expressed as

$$\mathbf{x}(T) = \mathbf{Q}^T \mathbf{x}(0),$$

where $\mathbf{x}(0)$ represents the initial values at time zero and $\mathbf{Q}^T = \alpha_0 1 + \alpha_1 \mathbf{Q} + \alpha_2 \mathbf{Q}^2 + \alpha_3 \mathbf{Q}^3 + \alpha_4 \mathbf{Q}^4$. Here, the $\{\alpha\}$ are the solutions to the equations

$$\begin{bmatrix} 1 & \lambda_1 & \lambda_1^2 & \lambda_1^3 & \lambda_1^4 \\ 1 & \lambda_2 & \lambda_2^2 & \lambda_2^3 & \lambda_2^4 \\ 1 & \lambda_3 & \lambda_3^2 & \lambda_3^3 & \lambda_3^4 \\ 1 & \lambda_4 & \lambda_4^2 & \lambda_4^3 & \lambda_4^4 \\ 1 & \lambda_5 & \lambda_5^2 & \lambda_5^3 & \lambda_5^4 \end{bmatrix} \begin{bmatrix} \alpha_0 \\ \alpha_1 \\ \alpha_2 \\ \alpha_3 \\ \alpha_4 \end{bmatrix} = \begin{bmatrix} \lambda_1^T \\ \lambda_2^T \\ \lambda_3^T \\ \lambda_4^T \\ \lambda_5^T \end{bmatrix} \tag{5.15}$$

and the $\{\lambda_i\}$ are the eigenvalues of **Q**. See Paelinck (1970) for details. Models of this kind form the simplest members of a complex class of forecasting models (see Chapter 16).

## 5.4 Specialized Centres within the Hierarchy

### 5.4.1 *Concepts of specialization*

Despite the evidence discussed in Section 5.2 for the regular arrangement of settlements in hierarchies, we are aware of many cases which seem to contradict these rules. The clusters of coalfield towns in northern England, or of the cotton towns of the Appalachian piedmont, seem to belong to a less regular order, which is grafted on to the 'normal' system of central places. Thomas Hardy sensed this difference when he wrote of Casterbridge '. . . the pole, focus or nerveknot of the surrounding country life; differing from the many manufacturing towns, which are as foreign bodies set down, like boulders on a plain, in a green world with which they have nothing in common' (Hardy, 1886, p. 73).

Contemporary statistics allow some precision to be given to this distinction. Alexandersson (1956) studied a group of United States cities and measured their occupational structure in terms of the 1950 census. For the 864 cities, each with a population of at least 10,000 inhabitants, it was found that some functions were present in all cities (*ubiquitous* types), while others occurred in very few (*sporadic* types). Table 5.3 shows a tentative breakdown of the 36

Table 5.3 Classification of urban industry*

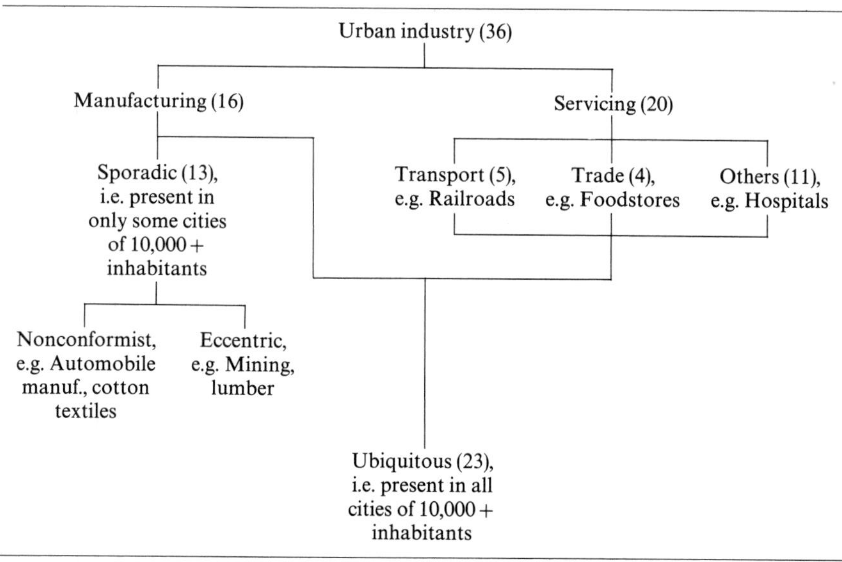


Source: Alexandersson, 1955.

*United States, 1950.

groups on this presence–absence basis, with a further subdivision into conventional divisions—manufacturing and service groups. Although three of the manufacturing groups (construction, printing and publishing, and food-processing) are ubiquitous, the great majority of manufacturing groups are to some degree sporadic, i.e. they occur unevenly throughout the urban system.

An extreme case of a sporadic manufacturing industry is the motor industry, which is absent from over half the towns, but is dominant in a very few, e.g. Flint, Michigan, home of the Buick Motor Corporation. This characteristic distribution is shown by the curve in Figure 5.16 in which the number of towns (*x*-axis) is plotted against the share of the total workforce (*y*-axis). A completely different sort of curve is shown by a typical ubiquitous-type, retail trade (curve B Figure 5.16), which was present in all towns: no town had either less than five per cent or more than 21 per cent of its workforce in this group.

Although Alexandersson's findings apply to one country at one particular point in time, it is significant that the sporadic activity (manufacturing) is a recessive element in urban structure—even in a highly industrial country. In two out of three of the towns in his sample, manufacturing activity employed less than half the total workforce: in no town, however specialized, did it ever account for more than four-fifths of the workforce, and this appears to be an extreme limit.

**Figure 5.16** Distribution of workers in two industries in relation to United States urban structure in 1950. Source: Alexandersson, 1956, pp. 49, 106.

### 5.4.2 *Evidence of accordance*

On the evidence of Alexandersson's work, we should expect that manufacturing, a sporadic activity, would show the greatest divergence from the regularities of city distribution. There is, however, evidence to suggest that manufacturing shows fairly close accordance with the general distribution of urban population, implying that not all specialist activities are located in centres outside the regularities of the central place hierarchy.

(a) *Accordance over space.* Manufacturing was selected by Bogue (1950) as one of the major 'sustenance activities' of the urban population arranged around 67 United States cities (Section 4.2.2). Change in the importance of manufacturing with distance from cities is illustrated by a number of indices taken from the Census of Manufactures, 1940. The absolute distribution is shown in Figure 5.17A through one index (value added in manufacture), while the relative distribution is shown in Figure 5.17B through three indices (value added in manufacture per person, employees per thousand population, and establishments per thousand population). In both graphs, values of the indices ($y$-axis) and distances ($x$-axis) are plotted on logarithmic scales.

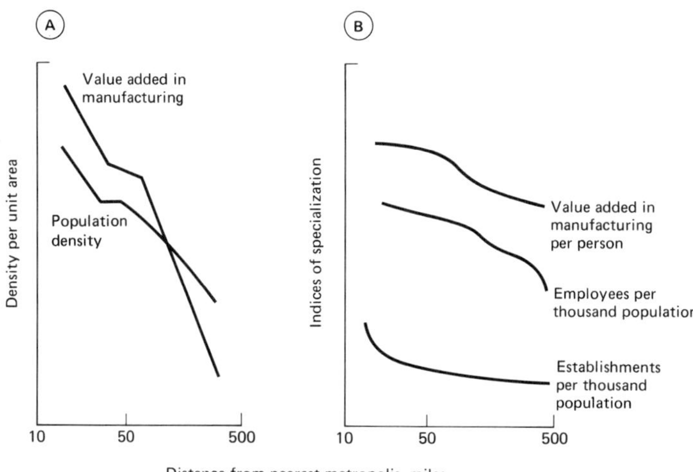


**Figure 5.17** Specialization in manufacturing with distance from the metropolis. United States, 1940. Source: Bogue, 1950, pp. 32, 184.

The fall-off with distance from the city is clear for all four measures of manufacturing, e.g. the first curve displays a rapid decline which is considerably steeper than, but which is of the same form as, that for population density (in Figure 5.17A). There is a steep section to about 30 miles from the metropolis, and a similar steep curve beyond about 65 miles. Between these two points, there is a shelf where large hinterland cities with very strong specialization tend to concentrate.

The *per caput* curves show not only that manufacturing declines in sympathy with population, but that it 'thins out' amongst the population in remoter areas. Comparison of the plant numbers curve with the employees curve suggests that, on average, the size of plant gets smaller away from the metropolis, a trend discussed in Section 5.5.1.

Although central cities themselves are not highly specialized, Bogue found that the size of the central city can have a great effect on the degree of specialization in the hinterland. Larger cities (over 500,000 in 1940) were rather more specialized than the smaller cities, and their hinterlands had a higher level of manufacturing throughout.

In terms of Bogue's threefold classification into route, subdominant, and local sectors (see Section 4.2.2), the indices of manufacturing are clearly lower in the local sectors than in the other two (Table 5.4). However, one significant deviation shows on all the indices; the subdominant sectors are slightly higher than the route sectors. Manufacturing, unlike the other three 'sustenance activities', clusters strongly in the subdominant sectors. At the outer reaches of the metropolis, about 250 miles from the nearest city, the level of manufacturing in the local sector appears to be higher than that in the route sector. The reversal of the general trend at this extreme distance seems to indicate that the metropolis is sufficiently remote and inaccessible to allow local pockets of manufacturing to exist.

Table 5.4 Specialization in manufacturing by sector*

| *Type of sector:* | *Route sector* | *Subdominant sector* | *Local sector* |
|---|---|---|---|
| Indices of manufacturing intensity: | | | |
| Value added per person, dollars | 164 | 171 | 107 |
| Employees/thousand inhabitants | 55 | 65 | 41 |
| Establishments/thousand inhabitants | 1.08 | 1.12 | 0.96 |

Source Bogue, 1950, p. 186.

* United States, 1940.

(b) *Accordance over time.* Instability and eccentricity are more eye-catching than stability and uniformity. Thus it is that the rapid rise of highly specialized centres (e.g. 'boom' mining towns) attracts attention and produces some of the most dynamic studies in historical geography, e.g. McCaskill's study (1962, pp. 143–169) of gold rush centres in the South Island of New Zealand or Goldthwaite's (1927) study of a declining New England town.

Not all specialist centres show such a cycle of activity. More frequently settlements 'mature' as the original source of employment creates other and locationally less-specialized occupations. In one of the earliest of *multiplier* studies, Barford (1938) studied the impact of a new match factory on a small Danish community and suggested ways in which the employment chain reaction it set off could be traced. In multiplier studies (Isard *et al.*, 1960, pp. 189–205), attempts are made to measure the stimulus that the establishment of one type of new employment gives to other sectors of the local economy, in terms of jobs, business, etc. Thus Isard and Kuenne (1953) set out to estimate the effect on the New York–Philadelphia region of a projected integrated steel plant being located at Trenton, New Jersey. Using input–output techniques, they were able to follow the chain of ramifications (steel, steel-using industries, service industries, population) and measure their effects in terms of jobs. For example, expansion in the tin can industry was estimated at one-tenth (an expansion of 923 more workers). This expansion, in its turn, made demands on housing, retail trade, etc. Isard and Kuenne's overall findings, traced through six cycles of expansion, appear in Table 5.5. This demonstrates that the original steel plant, with its 12,000 production workers, was expected to give rise to a total increase in employment of about 159,000; i.e. about thirteen times as many.

Estimates of such multiplier effects are likely to be affected by related chain effects on other regions (e.g. regions outside the New York–Philadelphia area) and the problem of such inter-regional feedback poses more computational difficulties. These are discussed at length in Paelinck and *Nijkamp* (1975, Chapter 5). From the strictly locational viewpoint, we would like to know more about (i) the size of the regional multipliers appropriate to particular types of activities, and (ii) the levels at which a town or region passes the critical 'take-off' threshold. Economic studies into problems of take-off have been carried out for national units (Rostow, 1960, 1963), and they might well be applied to more restricted geographical areas.

Table 5.5 Direct and indirect repercussions of new steel plant*

| *Estimated repercussions:* | *New employees* | *Multiplier effect* |
|---|---|---|
| Sectors affected: | | |
| Primary (iron and steel plant) | 11,666 | 1.0 |
| Secondary (other parts of steel fabricating industry) | 77,014 | 6.6 |
| Tertiary (other sectors) | 70,089 | 6.0 |
| Total effects | 158,769 | 12.6 |

Source: Isard and Kuenne, 1953, p. 297.
* New York–Philadelphia industrial region, United States.

### 5.4.3 *Distortion as a theoretical problem*

Discordance, the existence of centres outside the hierarchy, raises both theoretical and practical problems. With the evidence presented above for the accordance of some specialized activities with the settlement hierarchy, we may reasonably query the need for centres outside that hierarchy. It seems arguable, if the large urban centres may contain all the central functions for the demands of the surrounding territory, that there is no place, in the framework of existing central place theory, within which the specialized manufacturing centre may be fitted. Curry (1962) has shown, however, that the time element, studied in terms of *queuing theory*, may prevent the largest central place from possessing the full range of functions that the dependent territory demands.

In using Curry's model here, we are extending it considerably beyond its original application (which was restricted to service centres within towns), and we are suggesting a more general application than its originator might claim. The theory depends on four basic assumptions: (i) There exists an *order of goods* depending on the size of the population that is required for a market. First order goods require the whole population of the given territory as a market, second order goods require half this population, third order goods one third of this population, and so on. (ii) Corresponding to this order of goods is an *order of centres*. This order, running from large, first order, centres to small, tenth order, centres, forms the $x$-axis of the graphs in Figure 5.18. (iii) There exists a *range of stock* for the order of centres, so that each lower grade of centre supplies one third less than the next highest order of centre. Curry justifies this assumption by mathematical arguments on sections chosen at random from a continuum: it is, as he readily admits, a very rough approximation to reality. The form of the stock-range curve is shown in Figure 5.18A. The relative number of procurement trips in a given time period, the *trip frequency*, is the square of a centre's order. This roughly accords with known movement-behaviour (e.g. the weekly grocery trip, the monthly theatre trip, the occasional furniture buying trip), but the exact form of the curve (Figure 5.18A) is probably more complex. (iv) By multiplying the stock-range by the trip frequency, a *movement index* is produced (Figure 5.18B).

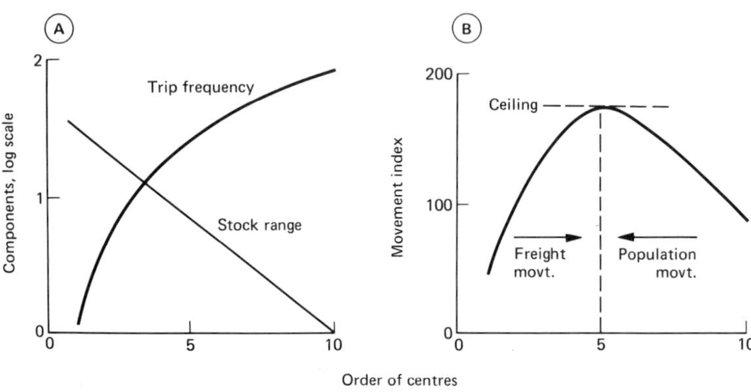


**Figure 5.18** Hypothetical model of movement optimization in a central-place structure. Source: Curry, 1962, p. 41.

The importance of the movement index is shown by the 'humped' nature of the curve in Figure 5.18B. It begins with the lowest point of the curve over the first order centre and reaches its maximum over the fifth order centre before declining slowly towards the tenth order centre. We may argue that the maximum point on the curve represents the *ceiling* for the development of the central place hierarchy in a given territory. Above that point, it is not worth holding stock since the demand (as measured by trip frequency) is too low, and specialized goods (i.e. first to fourth order goods) will be produced in a few centres and shipped to the several fifth order centres as the occasional demand occurs. Below that point, the central place hierarchy extends in an unbroken sequence with sufficient volume of local demand to support it.

It is difficult to say how applicable this model is likely to be. Certainly some of the assumptions on which it is based are untested, but they appear to be reasonable approximations of observed traits in social and economic behaviour. The implications of the theory, that a single large centre may not emerge as the first order central place, but that its functions may be fulfilled by lower order centres drawing on a few specialized (i.e. non-hierarchic) centres is important. It suggests that, even in a theoretical landscape with a regular central place hierarchy, specialized centres are likely to arise outside the regular central place system. Whether these specialized functions will be located in small specialist centres or will be shared between the five fifth order centres is uncertain. Burton (1963b, p. 285) has drawn attention to the *dispersed city*, a group of cities which '... although separated by tracts of agricultural land, function together economically as a single urban unit,' and he has traced their existence in parts of the United States (southern Illinois and the lower Rio Grande), in southern Ontario, Canada, in the Salzgitter area of West Germany, and in the Derby–Chesterfield–Nottingham area of midland England. How far these dispersed cities point to a truncation in the central place hierarchy in these areas, and its replacement by a group of lower level cities with complementary specialist activities, is uncertain. They may equally well be due to entirely local variations in settlement evolution.

### 5.4.4 *Distortion as a measurement problem*

The theoretical case for specialized centres, discussed above, highlights the need for working definitions of the 'specialist' centre. What do we mean by this term and how do we define it? A pioneering study, Moser and Scott's *British Towns* (1961), illustrates the very wide range of characteristics that make up the character of a centre, and the way in which, through principal components analysis, they may be broken down into a few manageable dimensions. Where we are concerned with centre specialization, in the sense of 'discordance' with the central place hierarchy, the problem is somewhat simpler. Two main attempts may be traced to define centres in this way, the first using local data, the second using comparisons between local and regional data.

(i) The first group of studies of centre classification have been based on the idea encountered in Section 5.3.3, *viz.* that the function of a centre can be broken down into two distinct components: (a) the part serving the inhabitants, and (b) the part serving external populations. The first part has been variously termed the 'city-serving', 'self-production', 'secondary', or 'non-basic' element; and the second, the 'city-forming', 'exchange-production', 'primary', or 'basic' element. A useful review of these *basic/non-basic* studies appears in Isard (Isard *et al.*, 1960, pp. 189–205).

Table 5.6 Computation of basic/non-basic ratios*

| *Employment group:* | *Total employment* | *Mining employment* | *Printing employment* |
|---|---|---|---|
| Market served: | | | |
| Basic (national, regional, and world) | 29,250 | 900 | 514 |
| Non-basic (local) | 59,325 | 71 | 1,200 |
| Basic/non-basic ratios | 2.02 | 0.08 | 2.34 |
| Employment multiplier | 3.02 | 1.08 | 3.34 |

Source: Isard *et al.*, 1960, p. 191.

* Wichita, United States, 1950.

To determine how the population of a centre should be apportioned between the basic and non-basic elements presents severe technical problems, and full basic/non-basic studies have been confined to a handful of individual town studies rather than to nationwide comparisons. An example of such a local study is given in Table 5.6 for the town of Wichita in Kansas. The columns show that mining is strongly basic in character, providing mainly for needs outside the town, whereas printing is non-basic, largely serving local needs. Despite the considerable work that has gone into such studies, there remain doubts that many 'mixed' industries can usefully be separated in this way.

(ii) The second group of studies has been based on comparisons of data for a single town against some national or regional benchmark. Alexandersson (1956, p. 16) has reviewed a number of Swedish and American attempts. One typical example is the index of specialization, $s_i$, given by the formula

$$s_i = (k_i - k_j)/k_j \tag{5.16}$$

where $s_i$ is the index of specialization for the *i*th city in industry $k$, $k_i$ is the percentage of the workforce of the *i*th city in that industry, and $k_j$ is the percentage in the nation as a whole. Thus, Detroit with 28.0 per cent of its workforce in the motor industry, compared to a national average of only 1.5 per cent, has a specialization index of 17.6 for that industry. Unfortunately, this approach is very sensitive to changes in the definition of the benchmark area, i.e. whether a national, regional, or state comparison is made.

This difficulty has led to more refined studies, in which the size of a centre has been taken into account in describing its specialization. This derivative of the basic/non-basic approach was developed by Klaasen, Torman, and Koyck (1949) for a Netherlands study, and was taken up by Ullman and Dacey (1962) in the United States. By comparing the workforces of sets of cities in the *same* size range, the lowest proportion found for an industry in any of the towns can be judged to represent the *minimum requirements*, i.e. the lowest level for that industry that a city of a given size must support.

Fourteen industries were analysed in this way for six sizes of American cities by Ullman and Dacey. For the fourteen cities of over one million population, Washington, DC, with 2.3 per cent of its employment in durable manufacturing, formed the 'low' for this box in the table. The minimum

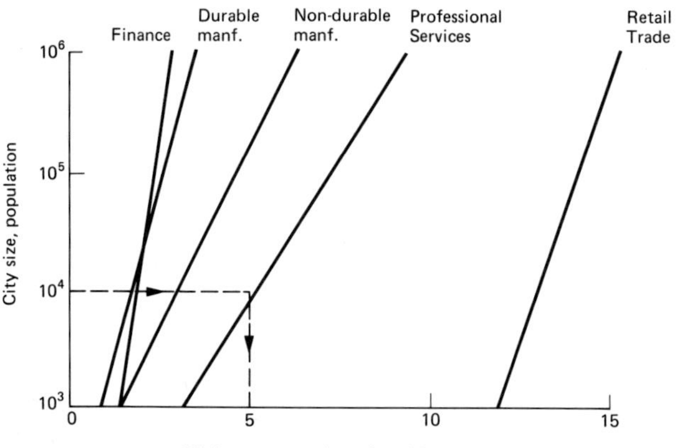


**Figure 5.19** Regression lines for minimum-requirements approach to centre classification, United States, 1950. Source: Ullmann and Dacey, 1962, p. 129.

requirement for a city of over one million was therefore assumed to be 2.3 per cent. Similar lows were calculated for each industry and each population size of city. The two parameters were then plotted against each other, and regression lines fitted to show the average relationships. As Figure 5.19 indicates, the minimum requirements varied with different industries (compare retail trade with manufacturing), but each industry showed a consistent increase in minima with the size of the city. In some cases, the relationship was sharply marked, as with professional services, and in others less significant, as with finance.

The regression lines for the various industry groups were used to compute the 'expected' minimum for a city of a given size: thus, the San Francisco Bay area, with a population of 2.68 millions in 1950, may be expected to have at least 3.6 per cent of its workforce in durable manufacturing: in fact (as Table 5.7 shows) it had 9.6 per cent. The deviations between the expected and observed values for each industry may be combined to give a single index of specialization, $S$, for a city, where

$$S = \Sigma_i\{(P_i - M_i)^2/M_i\}/\{(\Sigma_i P_i - \Sigma_i M_i)^2/\Sigma_i M_i\}. \tag{5.17}$$

Here, $i$ refers to each of the fourteen industrial sectors, $P_i$ is the percentage of the workforce employed in each of the $i$ sectors, and $M_i$ the minimum percentage expected for the size of the city (Ullman and Dacey, 1962, p. 137). Their general findings suggest that there is a strong relationship between size of city and specialization. The sum of all the minima for the fourteen industries ranged from 24 per cent for towns of 2,500 to 3,000 inhabitants to 49 per cent for cities of 300,000 to 800,000 inhabitants. The larger the city, the larger the number of specialities it can support in the 'ecological niches' of its population structure, and thus the more self-contained the city can be. This finding is logically consistent in that at the lowest extreme, the family can sell virtually nothing to itself, while at the upper extreme, the total world population (about four billions) can only sell to itself.

Table 5.7 Estimates of minimum components

| *Activity:* | *Durable manufacturing* | *Non-durable manufacturing* |
|---|---|---|
| Employment parameters: | | |
| San Francisco Bay region (observed) | 9.6% | 10.0% |
| Minimum requirements for region of this size (expected) | 3.6% | 5.5% |
| Excess above minimum requirements | +6.0% | +4.4% |

Source: Ullman and Dacey, 1962, p. 131.

For the 56 cities of over 300,000 population in the United States in 1950, the index varied from a high of 15.2 to a low of 1.4. Cities with high values were highly specialized centres like the steel town of Youngstown (8.5), while more balanced trade centres like Dallas and Denver had low values (around 1.5).

The practical importance of these values in terms of the industrial stability of the towns has been supported by work by Rodgers (1952).

## 5.5 Hierarchic Distortion due to Agglomeration

Despite some evidence for the accordance of industry with the urban pattern, it is clear from the above discussion that we must nevertheless recognize that patterns of specialization remain outside these regularities. These are termed here 'nonconformist' centres (Table 5.3).

We view their problem in a reverse way to that of the German locational theorist, Weber, who in his *Über den Standort der Industrien* (1909; Friedrich, 1929) assumed that specialized industrial activities would be located near their *input sources* (i.e. they would show 'material orientation') unless other forces caused deviations. Here we take the opposite starting point, that industrial activities will be located near their *output destinations* (i.e. 'market orientation') unless other forces cause deviations. Agglomeration is discussed at length by Isard (1956, pp. 172–87), Isard, *et al.* (1960, pp. 400–9), and Smith (1971, pp. 82–8).

### 5.5.1 *Agglomeration within individual plants*

Although the general importance of scale economies in industrial production is well established in theory for industry as a whole, the detailed differences between the various industrial activities is more tentative. Figure 5.20 is based on the findings of an exceptional empirical study of American industry by Bain (1954), and attempts to illustrate the varying importance of scale economies for four different types of industrial activity. In these graphs, the relative increase in cost above an estimated minimum (zero on the $y$-axis) is plotted against a standard measure of plant size, namely share of national capacity in an industry ($x$-axis). The curves for the sample industries show that while, for

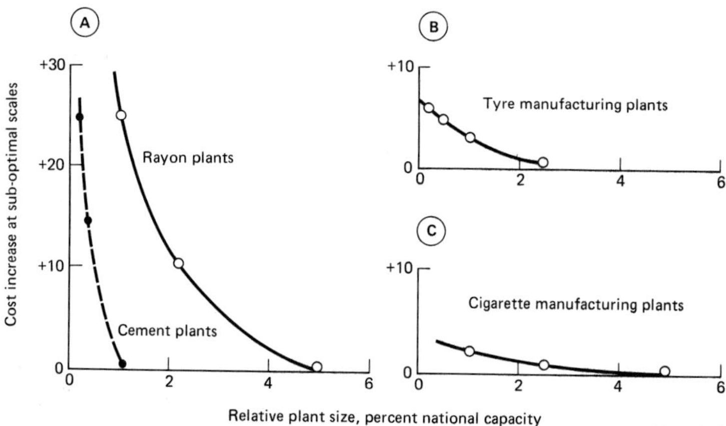


**Figure 5.20** Relation of production costs to plant size. Source: Bain, 1954, p. 25.

an industry like rayon, small plants operate at a very severe cost handicap (production costs a quarter higher if smaller than 1 per cent of national capacity), an industry like cigarette manufacturing is rather lightly affected by plant scale economies.

Isard and Schooler (1955) have shown for the petrochemical industry the overriding importance of scale economies. For two alternative locations, Monroe on the Gulf Coast and Cincinnati in the Industrial Belt of the United States, they compute the cost of three important components—transport, labour costs, and power costs—in the production of a petrochemical product (ethylene glycol) (Table 5.8). The largest of these three items, transport costs by rail, is some five times as great as the maximum labour cost differential and ten times the maximum power differential. However, all three components are dwarfed to insignificance by the enormous difference in production costs between large and small plants, which is over six times as great as the largest other differential. In this situation, regional differences in plant size become the dominant factor and '. . . completely overshadow any other individual or combined regional cost differential' (Isard *et al.*, 1960, p. 240).

Table 5.8 Regional cost differentials on petrochemical production*

| | *Cost differential (cents/100 lb.)*† |
|---|---|
| Transport: | |
| Barge shipments | 0.13 |
| Rail shipments | 0.60 |
| Labour costs, maximum differential | 0.12 |
| Power costs, maximum differential | 0.06 |
| Scale economies, large vs. small plants | 3.98 |

Source: Isard and Schooler, 1955, pp. 19, 22–4.
* Between Monroe (Louisiana) and Cincinnati (Ohio), United States.
† Ethylene glycol.

We may argue that, at its simplest, plant size affects location because the potential number of sites or communities that can accept a very large plant are fewer than those that can accept a small one.

Florence (1953) has found a strong connection between the 'prevailing size of plant' in an industry and the degree of dispersion, such that industries with small plants tend to be dispersed. Table 5.9 illustrates the trend of three sizes of plant (small, medium, and large) against degree of localization as measured by the coefficient of localization for British and American industries in the late 1930s. The conclusion that it is the industries with small plants that are less localized is inescapable. Such industries are dispersed for a number of reasons, but mainly they follow the dispersion over the land of the population itself. The outstanding examples are industries where contact between the factory and customer must be direct, and the job may pass back and forth a number of times: printing is a classic case! Other industries, such as building, demand personal contact and are correspondingly widely spread in small undertakings.

From the viewpoint of industry rather than potential location, Bain (1954) showed that the distribution of large plants is restricted in two ways: (i) by the absolute cost of the smallest economic plant, and (ii) by the relative share of the market such a plant represents. Here the 'smallest economic plant' was estimated from the data on which Figure 5.20 was based. Table 5.10 shows his findings with industries classified into four groups on a logarithmic basis, so that plants in the first category need an investment some hundreds of times greater than those in the third, and so on. The largest investment needed was in steel production, $6.7 \times 10^9$ dollars, compared to shoe production with only $2.0 \times 10^6$ dollars.

Table 5.9 Plant size and localization*

| *Degree of localization:* | *Low* | *Moderate* | *High* |
|---|---|---|---|
| Prevailing size of plant: | | | |
| Large plants | 9% | 10% | 13% |
| Medium plants | 6% | 4% | 11% |
| Small plants | 29% | 8% | 10% |

Source: Florence, 1953, p. 71.
*United Kingdom, 1935; United States, 1939.

When capital supply is severely limited, as in most underdeveloped countries, then this absolute 'threshold' cost may limit the diffusion of high cost plants, and will tend to restrict them to a single specialist centre within the urban system of the country. The slow spread of the integrated steel producing plant (Pounds, 1959), with its large initial thresholds, is a typical example of this restriction, though national prestige reasons have somewhat distorted the expected pattern.

If a single economic plant represents a very small share of the total industrial capacity, then we may argue that its chances of diffusion are greater than one which represents a very large part. We know from Bain's work that the share of national capacity varies greatly from industry to industry. The implications of Table 5.10 are that it needs only three or four really efficient typewriter plants to serve the whole United States market, but that it needs about 500 meat packing plants to serve the same country. There are, of course, more plants than these economic minima, but this is largely due to historical legacy, and the 'squeezing out' process is most acute in just those industries where the efficient plant can serve a very large part of the total market.

It follows from this situation that in certain industries a new plant can be set up only if it can expect to 'capture' a large part of the existing market, and indeed that it must 'go in big' if it is not to produce at costs vastly above its existing competitors. Attempts to enter well-established markets may be met by a series of price-fixing moves by established producers—a process which Rodgers (1952) has traced for the steel industry. By contrast, the industries in which small plants are efficient and need only a small share of the market may show very rapid diffusion as new local population demands build up. Clearly, the locational effect of plant size, whether measured in absolute or relative terms, is either to restrict or to scatter specialist activities through the urban spectrum.

While the chemical process industries studied by Isard and Schooler (1955) may represent an extreme case, there is good empirical evidence to suggest that the average size of production unit throughout the whole of industry is increasing. Chisholm (1962, p. 192) has indicated that, in the period 1924–54, the mean size of manufacturing plant in the United Kingdom employing more than ten workers rose by about one half from 87 to 134; while Florence (1953), in a comparative study of British and American industry, showed an even stronger trend for American industry over a comparable period. The significance of the change is somewhat obscured by employment figures, for with automation a much higher relative production is coming from the very few larger plants. The trend to larger size is not only true of industries in which employment is increasing (automobiles and aircraft manufacture), but also in industries (like flour milling) where the total employment is contracting.

Table 5.10 Estimated minimum size of single efficient plant*†

| *Total capital required for single efficient plant* ( $\times 10^6$ *dollars*): | 1–10 | 10–100 | 100–1,000 |
|---|---|---|---|
| Proportion of national capacity contained in one efficient plant: | | | |
| 0.1–0.5% | Flour milling (3.5)<br>Shoes (2)<br>Canning (3) | | |
| 0.5–1% | | Cement (25) | |
| 1–5% | | Tyres (30) | Petroleum refining (225)<br>Steel (665) |
| 5–10% | | | Rayon (135)<br>Automobiles (500) |
| 10–50% | | Typewriters (?) | Tractors (125) |

Source: Bain, 1954, p. 36.
* Sample of United States industries, *c*. 1951.
† Figures in brackets give the upper estimate in millions of dollars for capital required for single efficient plant.

### 5.5.2 *Agglomeration of groups of plants: regional 'swarming'*

Cutting across the size-localization trend in Table 5.9 is a second trend. The industries with the *highest* localization are not, as expected, those with large plants, but are those with medium scale plants. Certainly the large scale plants are more localized than the small scale, but the outstanding cases of high localization—cotton textiles, woollen textiles, motor-car manufacture—are characterized in general by medium scale plants (Table 5.11). This high localization in one industry may well be due to the fact that the plants between themselves form a single, large, localized producing unit. The difference is that, whereas in the large single plant the economies are internal, in the localized 'swarm' of plants the economies are external.

Table 5.11 Grouping of industries by their locational pattern

| *Coefficient of localization* | *Concentration pattern* | *Locational pattern* | *Industry example* |
|---|---|---|---|
| High | Localized | Swarming | Cotton textile industry |
| Moderate | Moderate localization | Rooted to localized extraction | Iron and steel industry |
| Variable | Variable | (1) Linked | Textile machinery industry |
| | | (2) Footloose | Electric machinery industry |
| Low | Dispersed | (1) Rooted to scattered extraction | Brick industry |
| | | (2) Residentiary | Baking industry |

Source: Florence, 1953, p. 40.

Birmingham and the Black Country conurbation, in central England, provide object lessons in what Florence (1944) has described as 'industrial swarming'. Of the seventeen main manufacturing industries localized in the area, twelve were metal industries with a high degree of linkage. Florence recognized four types of integration between these metal industries: (i) *vertical integration* (e.g. links between the refining of non-ferrous metals and the production of non-ferrous hardware products); (ii) *convergent integration* (e.g. the manufacture of bolts, car bodies, tyres, etc., feeding convergently into the motor assembly industry); (iii) *diagonal integration* (e.g. foundries and tool manufacturers serving a number of local industries); and (iv) *indirect integration* (e.g. food industries which, with their strong preponderance of female workers, tended to balance the preponderance of male employment in the metal industries).

Within this general concatenation still more strongly localized complexes of integrated small plants may be discerned. Wise (1951) has described in detail the evolution of the jewellery and gun quarters in the city of Birmingham. Here, one street may contain a couple of dozen jewellery 'plants', with half as many again integrated plants working in bullion, stone merchants, and so on.

The rationale for this extreme localization does not lie in the present distribution of resources. The natural resources of coal and iron are virtually worked out and the water links are confined to a few constricted canals. As Florence argues, this is a case of localization for the sake of localization for: '. . . the whole of the Birmingham and Black Country complex of linked industries could probably flourish anywhere else, so long as the place was not too far from the centre of the country' (Florence, 1953, p. 88). All the industries hang together like a cluster of swarming bees to form a concatenation or syndrome with little reference to nature.

Similar findings have been suggested for the United States by McCarty, Hook, and Knos (1956). In a study of the machinery industry, they tested three alternative hypotheses by regression analysis and found that an aggregation hypothesis gave the most significant results. They concluded that '... birds of a feather flock together' might be an appropriate summary of the location behaviour of a large part of industry.

Nowhere is this quotation more appropriate than in describing the intra-urban clustering to be seen in many service or tertiary activities. The different kinds of offices, retailing, hotels, personal and specialized consultancy services provide numerous examples. All firms in such swarms are small, and none offers a complete service, so they operate under the paradox that they need, at least in part, to cooperate with neighbours whose throats competition urges them to cut. The agglomerated condition offers the individual units two main benefits; (i) the opportunity of tapping shared facilities and (ii) security. Shared facilities cover the opportunity to specialize minutely within a general field of activity ('fire in tankers' insurance within insurance generally) in the knowledge that neighbours are specializing elsewhere in the field. Success depends heavily on 'flair'. It seems necessary for its generation that firms stay small and flexible, so that the 'calving' of new units is characteristic within the herd. When practices standardize so that reliance on flair diminishes, speed often takes over as the necessary constitutent of success. However much a tyrant speed may be (Illich, 1974), and however wasteful of resources, agglomerated centres are supremely well organized to offer it, especially to the many deadline-dependent activities such as newspaper production and magazine production, which can afford to be nowhere else. Because the whole objective of proximity is to encourage what Haig as long ago as 1926 called 'the transportation of intelligence' and, because the carriage costs of personally conveyed information are so high, these centres offer the further benefit of random contacts and chance information, in addition to the more formal institutional advantages (Thorngren, 1970). So fruitful has this field been that, in addition to the transport cost and land cost-based theories of location, a contact-based location theory has been widely developed by the Swedes (see, for example, Karlqvist and Lundqvist, 1972) and extended by Goddard (1973) from offices in London to settlement strategies in general (EFTA, 1973). Agglomerated centres also develop the advantage of reputation in which all participants share. This automatic accolade of success can run from practising medicine in Harley Street, through wholesaling clothes in Soho, to producing electronics ideas in the science park at Cambridge.

The agglomerations offer security in the sense that it is the human condition to huddle in the face of the unknown. Uncertainty is a powerful welder of bonds, whether induced by acute competition or by the vagaries of changing fashion. Access to the information flows generated by a swiftly changing activity can prevent the economic embarrassment of a warehouse full of unsaleable clothes, a defaulted loan, or an unacceptably ageing product.

Agglomerations are testimonials to success and often grow to the point where a small scale unit cannot afford to be elsewhere. It is interesting to model the spatial growth process of a cluster in terms of vector, distance, specialization and mass. The early growth will be accommodated by marginal accretion which will be either sectoral or concentric depending upon the constraints. Sooner or later, however, the swarming becomes self-defeating, in that the distance information has to move imposes an unacceptably high friction. At this point, a secondary nucleus will appear whose position and distance from the parent swarm will depend upon the attracting nucleus. This can only take place if the secondary nucleus is sufficiently specialized and of sufficient mass to generate more or less instantaneously the kinds of benefits already available in the parent. Such a process means inevitable sorting by type, and sieving by size, of only those units for whom detachment from the swarm does not mean sudden death from exposure.

Heavy agglomerations are not without their penalties which, alarmingly, seem to fall heavily on the public sector as firms externalize some of their important costs. In particular, the assembly and dispersal of a considerable workforce to such centres means that they pay a high price for their commercial leadership in terms of such things as greater commuting distances, congestion and class alienation, considerations that increasingly attract analysis by geographers. It is no coincidence that this interest has grown proportionately to the opportunities for social engineering that governments are beginning to undertake by manipulating tertiary activity to create swarms in places more appropriate than those that arise seemingly as much by chance as by design.

### 5.5.3 *Random nuclei: the problem of 'nonconformist' centres*

Scale economies, whether the internal economies of the plant, or the external economies of the regional 'swarm', may sometimes explain the relative location of specialist activities: they certainly do not explain the absolute location of such activities. Here we come to the essence of the unsolved set of problems that we may characterize as the 'Morris–Oxford', 'Ford–Detroit', or 'Carnegie–Pittsburgh' problem, i.e. the problem of why one, rather than a set of apparently similar cities, proved a successful launching pad for a great industrial venture. The answer probably lies outside the field of human geography and in the study of individualism and industrial opportunism, although only a few of our textbooks, notably Paterson (1975) in a survey of North American industry, hint at the issues. To be sure, we can argue that there are well-trodden limits within which industrial birth rates are likely to be high (Beesley, 1955), but we are unlikely to be able to circumscribe the location much further. The problem of the random nuclei around which so much of our industrial enterprise within developed countries has grown remains an intriguing by-way in locational research which offers as much to the historical geographer as to the locational theorist.

Significant as they are, the net effect of these scale agglomerations is to distort, but not to destroy, the urban hierarchy. Even highly industrial countries like the United Kingdom, which have strong clusters of non-conformist centres, still display a rank-size distribution which, as Berry (1961a) has shown, is not substantially different from that of countries where the population is both more rural and the towns more in accord with the ideal central place hierarchy.

## 5.6 Hierarchic Distortion due to Resource Localization

If we allow that a general urban concentration of industry is the rule, and that random or scale-origin changes in city specialization may cause variations within the hierarchy, problems still remain. We are left with certain stubborn specialized centres that persist in apparently 'eccentric' locations outside the general distribution of urban population. In this section, we consider some of the models put forward to explain the location of these deviant cases.

### 5.6.1 *Movement minimization: Weberian analysis*

One of the classic locational models available for tackling the problem of eccentric locations is that of Alfred Weber. In his *Über den Standort der Industrien* (1909; Friedrich, 1929), he put forward a consistent theory of industrial location which, although it has a number of theoretical and practical drawbacks, provides a useful starting point. It is illustrated here with empirical data drawn from an industry which Weber might have regarded as an outstanding example of the utility of his system, the zinc smelting industry (Cotterill, 1950).

The central argument in Weber's theory of industrial location is that sites will be selected, *ceteris paribus*, so as to minimize unnecessary movement, i.e. that sites will represent minimum-energy positions. We may conceive of movement as being made up of three separate components, the *distance*, $d$, to be moved, the *weight*, $w$, of the material inputs or outputs to be moved, and the *effort* or cost, $c$, of moving given materials over a unit of distance (cf. Isard, 1956, pp. 81–90). We may combine the first two components, distance and weight, to give a *gross movement input* which we can measure conventionally in *ton-miles*; and we may combine this index with cost to give a *net movement input*, $H$, which we can measure in dollar-ton-miles. This may be defined formally as

$$H = \sum_{j=1}^{n} w_j c_j d_j \qquad (5.18)$$

where we sum the movements from all $n$ sources and destinations.

Table 5.12 shows the calculation of net movement inputs for our case industry, and we can see how first tonnage, and then freight costs, modify the cost of movement over standard distances for the four major inputs and the major output of a smelter. The most striking contrast is between heating coal and fireclay; when hauled over the same standard distance as fireclay, heating coal represents a net movement input some 24 times larger, a contrast explicable in terms of its greater importance in the industrial process and its higher freight rates. Clearly, this is an over-simplification: in practice, as Figure 6.11 suggests, freight rates tend to be convex and stepped with distance

(Alexander, Brown, and Dahlberg, 1958), but the net movement input provides a rough guide to the relative movement that we are trying to minimize.

Table 5.12 Derivation of net distance inputs*

| *Parameters:* | *Distance, miles* (*d*) | *Weight, tons* (*w*) | *Freight rate, dollars/ton-mile* (*c*) | *Net distance inputs,* (*H*) |
|---|---|---|---|---|
| Outputs: | | | | |
| Slab zinc | 1.00 | 0.54 | 2.10 | 1.14 |
| Inputs: | | | | |
| Zinc concentrate | 1.00 | 1.00 | 1.00 | 1.00 |
| Reduction coal | 1.00 | 0.37 | 1.10 | 0.41 |
| Heating coal | 1.00 | 1.08 | 1.10 | 1.19 |
| Fireclay | 1.00 | 0.10 | 0.50 | 0.05 |
| Total inputs | — | 2.55 | — | 2.65 |

Source Cotterill, 1950, pp. 62, 78, 87, 110.
* Example of zinc-smelting industry.

(a) *Movement minimization in a two point case.* The concept of net movement inputs may be used very simply in the two point case by separating the movements towards the plant (assembly movements), $H_a$, from the movements away from the plant of finished products after processing (distribution movements), $H_b$, to give an orientation index ($O$). This may be defined as

$$O = \frac{H_a}{H_b} = \frac{\sum_{j=1}^{k} w_j c_j d_j}{\sum_{j=1}^{l} w_j c_j d_j}, \quad (k+l = n) \tag{5.19}$$

where the $k$ assembly movements are separated from the $l$ distribution movements. When the value of $O$ is greater than 1.0 the orientation of the plant is towards its material sources, and when it is less than 1.0, the orientation is towards its product destinations.

In our empirical example (Table 5.12), the sum of the four assembly movements (2.65) and the sum of the single distribution movement (1.14) give an orientation index of 2.32, suggesting that the basic orientation of the industry is towards its sources. The position may be shown very clearly by plotting values of the net movement inputs for the industry over a hypothetical distance of 100 miles. In Figure 5.21A, it will be seen that the total movement increases as the location is shifted from a location, *i*, near the material source to a location, *j*, near the destination. The general relationship between the assembly and distribution components of the net movement input index, *H*, is shown in Figure 5.21B, where the solid line represents the sum of both $H_a$ and $H_b$. This shows clearly that a location at the source is, in this case, the minimum energy position.

Weber (1909) used a simple weight relationship to define his own orientation index, a weight coefficient, as the weight of the assembled material inputs (including coal) divided by the weight of the distributed material outputs. This index, which gave typical values to various industries (e.g. 4.0 to blast furnaces and 1.3 to tube mills in the steel industry), enabled him to divide industries into materials and market oriented, and formed the basis of the convenient, distinction between 'heavy industry' and 'light industry'. This is discussed at length in Friedrich (1929, pp. 48–75) and Smith (1971, Chapter 11).

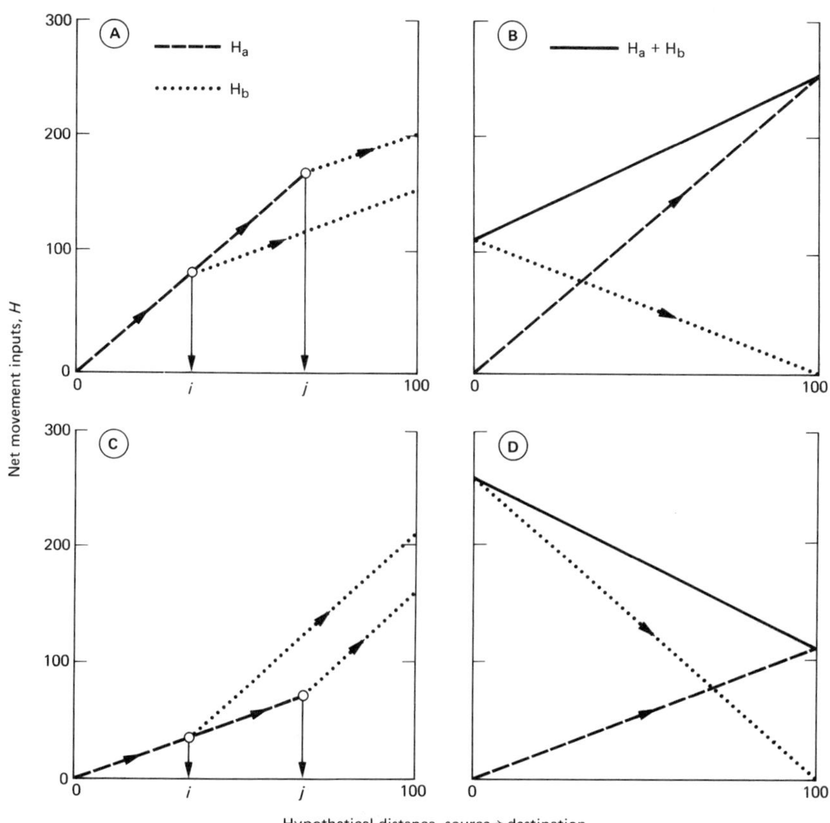


**Figure 5.21** Weberian weight-loss analysis of market or destination orientation (**A, B**) and material or origin orientation (**C, D**).

Smith (1955) has tested the efficiency of Weber's index with respect to 65 British industries. He found that, while the index discriminated reasonably well between those industries located at the materials (e.g. sugar beet processing in the mainly arable areas of England) and those industries which were patently not located at materials, the correlation was by no means a perfect one. The results became clearer when the weight of coal was excluded from the calculations (Table 5.13), but Smith, dissatisfied with the results of the weight index, went on to examine other indices that might be used to separate industrial locations in a helpful way. Three of these indices were at least as discriminating as Weber's index, namely (i) the weight of material per operative (e.g. blast furnaces had values some hundreds of times greater than vehicle manufacture), (ii) the amount of electric power used *per caput*, and (iii) the percentage of male labour in the total workforce. Where values for these indices were very high, strong material orientation in location was observed.

Table 5.13 Weber's material index and characteristic locational patterns*

| *Material index:*† | *Less than* 1.0 | 1.0–2.0 | *Greater than* 2.0 |
|---|---|---|---|
| Number of industries: | | | |
| Located at materials | 2 | 17 | 3 |
| Not located at materials | 16 | 14 | 1 |

Source: Smith, 1955, p. 8.
* Great Britain, 1948. † Excluding coal.

Other workers like Duerr (1960) have suggested alternatives such as specific value (value of a product divided by its weight) to enable locational classification of industrial activities. But, like the Weber and Smith indices, they have proved most valid for the outer extremes of locational behaviour, rather than for cases intermediate between source and destination. Thus, McCarty (McCarty *et al.*, 1956, pp. 81–121) has traced the relationship between the location of the machinery industry in the United States and the location of related metal-using industries. As Figure 5.22 shows, this industry is not strongly associated with either (i) the early stage of metal manufacture (e.g. blast furnaces) nor (ii) with late-stage manufacture (as represented by the motor assembly industry. Between these two extremes it is highly correlated with the middle stages of the metal using chain of industries, with the closest tie ($r = 0.910$) with the 'fabricated steel' industry.

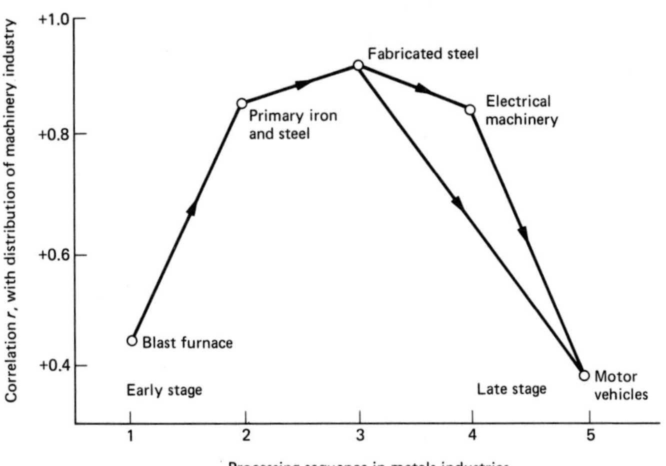


**Figure 5.22** Linkage hypothesis applied to the location of the United States machinery industry. Source: McCarty, Hook and Knos, 1956, p. 109.

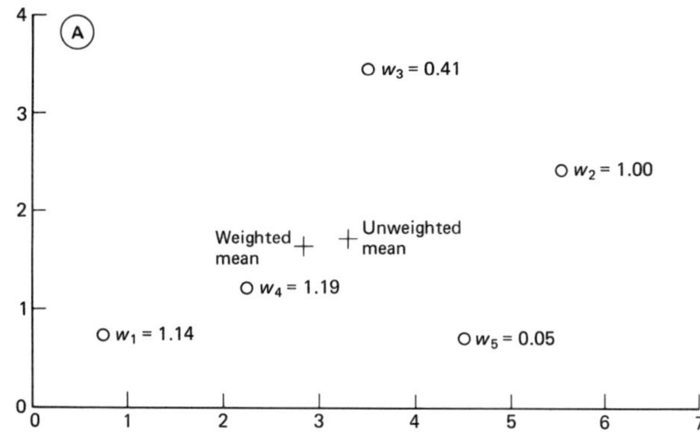

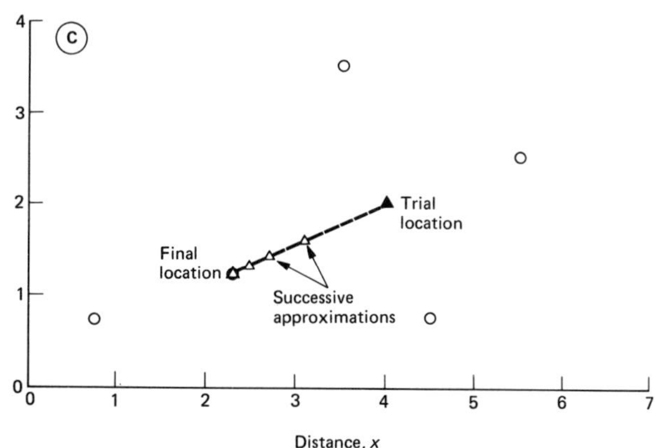


**Figure 5.23** Kuhn-Kuenne algorithm for the optimum location of a single plant given the five weights in Table 5.12.

(b) *Movement minimization in an n-point case.* Multiple sources and multiple destinations are the rule rather than the exception, and the two point cases considered above bear rather little relation to locational reality. Weber, however, was fully aware of this problem and suggested methods for handling general $n$-point situations.

Solution of a five-point problem, illustrating the five components in the zinc smelting industry (Table 5.12), is worked through here. Random locations for the five positions, $a$ (zinc-concentrate source), $b$ (reduction-coal source), $c$ (heating-coal source), $d$ (fireclay source), and $e$ (slab-zinc destination) are shown in Figure 5.23A, which is based upon the values in the last column of Table 5.12. Weber's problem was to find a location in the plane which minimized the total cost (net movement input), $H$, of bringing together the five items for processing, and of shipping the finished product, slab zinc, to its destination. Although Weber proposed a mechanical solution to the problem, a numerical algorithm for the direct solution of the generalized Weber problem is usually credited to Kuhn and Kuenne (1962), although earlier papers had appeared in French mathematical journals in the 1930s. The Kuhn–Kuenne method has four steps.

*Step* 1. Choose an initial location for the plant, $p$, at the orthogonal $x, y$ cartesian co-ordinate position $(x_p, y_p)$, as in Figure 5.23B. This choice may be random, on the basis of the observer's hunch, or use, say, a spatial mean or median (see Section 9.6.2).

*Step* 2. Calculate the total cost, $H$, of this location from equation (5.18). In (5.18), recall that $w_j$ is the weight (or amount) transported at a cost per unit distance, $c_j$, over the distance, $d_j$, from the $j$th ($j = 1, 2, \ldots, n$) source to the trial location.

*Step* 3. Determine an improved location for the plant using the estimating equations for the co-ordinates

$$\left.\begin{aligned} x_p^{(k+1)} &= \frac{\sum_{j=1}^{n} [w_j c_j x_j / d_{j(k)}]}{\sum_{j=1}^{n} [w_j c_j / d_{j(k)}]}, \\ y_p^{(k+1)} &= \frac{\sum_{j=1}^{n} [w_j c_j y_j / d_{j(k)}]}{\sum_{j=1}^{n} [w_j c_j / d_{j(k)}]}, \end{aligned}\right\} \qquad (5.20)$$

where $x_j$ and $y_j$ are the orthogonal $x, y$ cartesian co-ordinate positions of the $j$th source location. The procedure is iterative, and we use the notation $(k+1)$ to denote the revised values of quantities, as opposed to the old values which carry the notation, $(k)$. Thus $d_{j(k)}$ denotes the distance from source $j$ to the initial plant location in the first round of the algorithm, and in later iterations, the distance from source $j$ to the plant location determined in the previous round.

*Step* 4. Recompute the total cost according to equation (5.18) and repeat steps

(3) and (4) until no further improvements can be made in the total cost function. The optimum location, which measures the total cost miles, is now given by the co-ordinate position, $x^{(k+1)}$, $y^{(k+1)}$. Figure 5.23c illustrates a typical approximation sequence.

(c) *Multiple plant location.* The basic Kuhn–Kuenne method is a spatial extension of the Newton–Raphson approximation procedure familiar in many branches of numerical analysis. It can be extended in many ways to accommodate more realistic geographical situations. Non-linearities in transport costs may be incorporated by raising the distance terms, $d_{j(k)}$ in (5.20) by a power term. Eilon, Watson-Gandy, and Christofides (1971, Chapter 4) show how multi-plant location problems may also be encompassed by the same Kuhn–Kuenne equations. The total cost function (5.18) is now rewritten for $m$ plants as well as $n$ sources, *viz.*

$$H = \sum_{i=1}^{m} \sum_{j=1}^{n} w_j c_j d_{ij} \delta_{ij}. \tag{5.21}$$

The new term, $\delta_{ij}$, is a binary 'switch' set at one when plant $i$ draws on source $j$, and is set at zero otherwise. To implement this switch, an initial set of $m$ trial locations is chosen, and each source is allocated to the nearest plant. New plant locations are determined by applying the modified Kuhn–Kuenne equations,

$$\left.\begin{aligned} x_i^{(k+1)} &= \frac{\sum_{j=1}^{n} [w_j c_j x_j \delta_{ij}/d_{ij(k)}]}{\sum_{j=1}^{n} [w_j c_j \delta_{ij}/d_{ij(k)}]} \\ y_i^{(k+1)} &= \frac{\sum_{j=1}^{n} [w_j c_j y_j \delta_{ij}/d_{ij(k)}]}{\sum_{j=1}^{n} [w_j c_j \delta_{ij}/d_{ij(k)}]} \end{aligned}\right\} \tag{5.22}$$

to each plant, $i$, in turn. This step is repeated and $H$ is evaluated until no further reduction in costs can be made. Note that, unlike the single plant problem, the solution obtained is only a *local* optimum conditional upon the $m$ trial locations. There is currently no efficient method which will guarantee that a *global* optimum has been achieved in the multi-plant case. To approximate this, several runs are made with different initial locations, and the best result (as judged by $H$) is taken to approximate the global solution (Figure 5.24).

The question arises as to whether a 'good' choice of initial locations will produce a good suboptimal solution. With high speed computers, successive sets of $m$ random starting points are commonly chosen, but Eilon *et al.* (1972, p. 66) have shown that intelligent guesses for initial locations are useful in improving the chance of getting a good solution.

Given the basic procedures for single and multi-plant locations, extensions may readily be made to accommodate other variables. Variations in production costs, discontinuities in transport costs, locations on a graph (i.e. a transport network rather than a continuous plane), and changes over time have each been explored. Lea (1973) provides a useful review of these location–allocation models; see also the regional applications of linear programming methods discussed in Chapter 15.

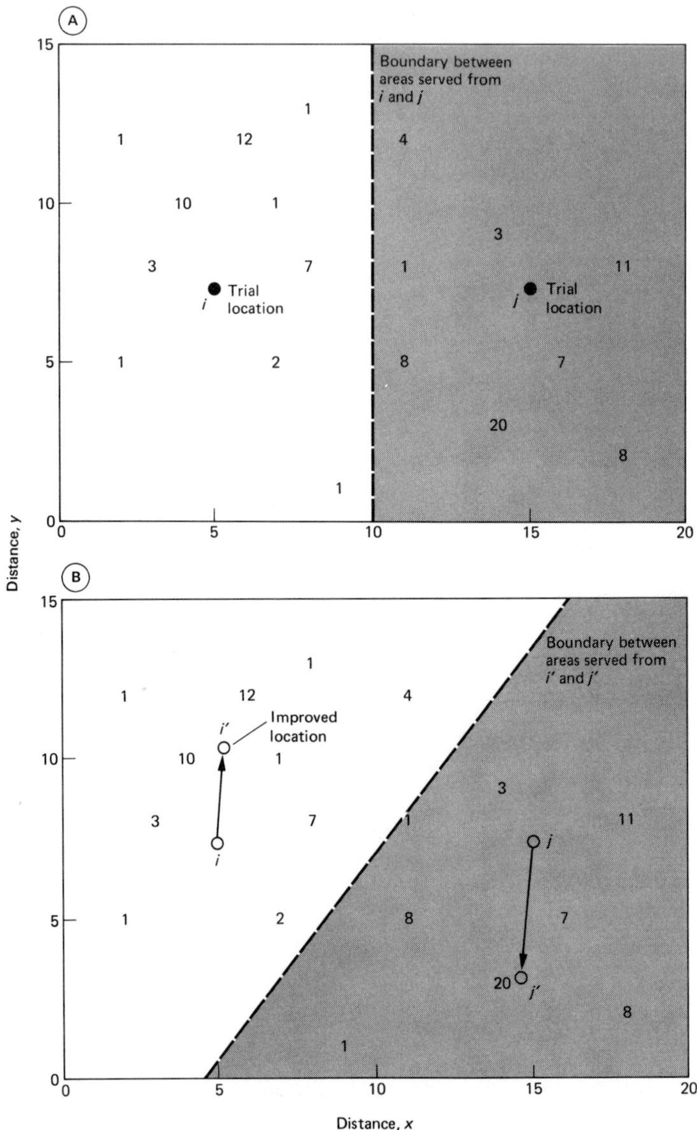


**Figure 5.24** Multiple plant location problem. Illustration of the first (**A**) and second (**B**) steps in the Kuhn-Kuenne algorithm. Numbers indicate the weights ($w$) associated with the particular locations to be served from the two plants ($i, j$).

### 5.6.2 *Variations in the locational surface*

Geographers have shown particular interest in distance costs in determining hierarchical variations in settlement systems. There are, however, a number of technical changes over time which reduce the importance of terms for costs over distance in locational analysis, *viz.* (i) the progressive cheapening of transport costs relative to total production costs; (ii) the progressive reduction in the weight of raw material needed for a given end product brought about by improved technology, so that less has to be moved; (iii) the sharper decline in the costs of moving bulk goods than of finished goods. The net effect of factors (i), (ii), and (iii) is to reduce the need for eccentric locations, and to throw manufacturing still more strongly into the line with the urban hierarchy. This trend is reinforced by two further changes: (iv) the relatively greater expansion in late-stage manufacture (which tends to be market oriented), compared with early-stage manufacture; and (v) the rise of non-economic grounds for locational decision-making, through government, social, or defence policies, in particular. Probably the best way to place movement models in an appropriate position, as compared with the other factors affecting industrial patterns, is through the many studies of individual industries that have been published in the last decade. Smith (1971) provides an excellent review of this work.

In our analysis of movement costs, we assumed that local production costs (labour, power, water are conventional examples) were everywhere the same. Weber was acutely aware that this concept of a uniform location plane was unrealistic and he attempted, through his 'labour coefficient' to introduce the effect of these irregularities. The concept of regional and local variations in our cost surface can be welded on to our earlier discussion of two point movement problems. If we add to our earlier diagram (Figure 5.21), a variable cost surface (stippled) as in Figure 5.25, we can see how the regular changes in the movement inputs are distorted by the local variations. These variations are sufficient in Figure 5.25A to reverse the locational advantages of sites $i$ and $j$,

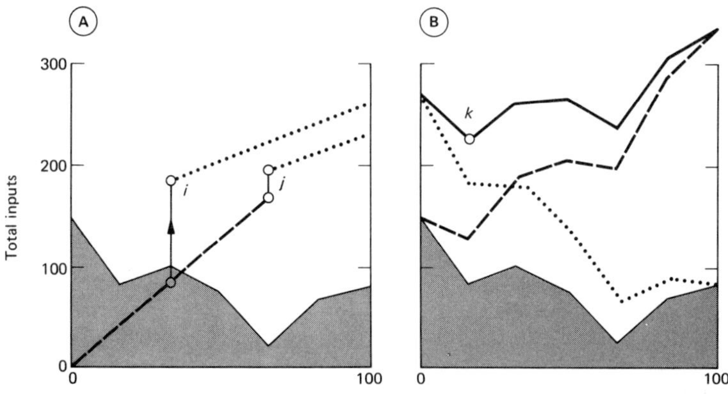


**Figure 5.25** Impact of variations in the local resource surface (stippled) on the market orientation case plotted in Figure 5.21 **A**, **B**.

and to warp the minimum-effort surface in Figure 5.25B so that the optimum location is shifted from the origin to point *k*.

Clearly, the importance of variations in the locational plane will change with (i) the range of the variations in the local cost surface and (ii) the relative importance of these local cost differentials in the total cost structure of the industry. Local variations in processing costs have been extensively reviewed by Greenhut (1956, pp. 123–39), Isard (1956, pp. 126–42), and Smith (1971, pp. 207–35).

### 5.6.3 *Local substitution between inputs*

In reading the standard studies of 'industrial location', it is difficult to avoid thinking in terms of common behaviour within an industry. An 'industry' is, however, as Florence (1953, pp. 15–21) has pointed out, nothing more than a convenient group term for plants which may vary very greatly in their type of product or which may produce similar products by different processes. For example, in the petrochemical industrial complexes, locations with cheap natural gas will commonly use greater amounts of this rather than crude oil; conversely at locations where crude oil is cheap, relative to natural gas, the former may be substituted for the latter. Each separate location may have a local structure of factor loadings, and these may represent a considerable economy over the fixed combinations assumed in an 'industry' analysis (Luttrell, 1962).

(a) *Theoretical example of substitution.* A useful theoretical case of substitution has been provided by Isard (Isard *et al.*, 1960, pp. 415–19). He envisaged a location at which two industrial activities, I and II, are both profitable alternatives. Each activity has a different combination of four basic resource inputs (water, land, labour, and capital), and these resources are in restricted supply. The resource requirements needed per unit of finished commodity produced, and the total resources available, are, for each of the two activities, shown in Table 5.14.

Table 5.14 Hypothetical resources requirements for solution by simple linear programme

| *Resource units required:* | *For Activity I* | *For Activity II* | *Total units available at given location* |
|---|---|---|---|
| Resources: | | | |
| Water (*a*) | 0.5 | 0.6 | 6.0 |
| Land (*b*) | 0.2 | 0.15 | 1.8 |
| Labour (*c*) | 0.4 | 0.2 | 3.0 |
| Capital (*d*) | 3.0 | 2.0 | 24.0 |

Source: Isard, Bramhall, Carrothers, Cumberland, Moses, Price, and Schooler, 1960, p. 416.

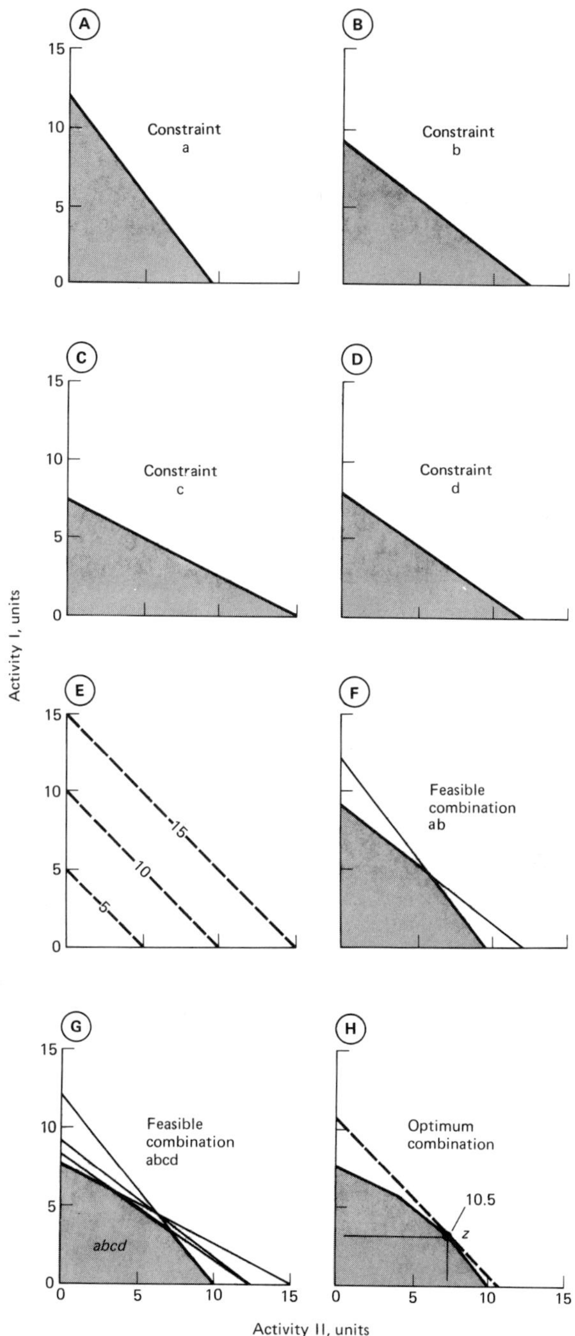


**Figure 5.26** Stages in the graphic solution to a simple four-factor linear program. Source: Isard *et al.*, 1960, p. 417.

The basic substitution problem here is between the two activities. Should the location use all its resources in Activity I, or all in Activity II, or in some combination of I and II? In this simplified situation, Isard suggests that the problem can be solved most simply through linear programming (see Chapter 15). A graphical approach is illustrated in Figure 5.26, in which, on all the graphs, Activity I (*y*-axis) is plotted against Activity II (*x*-axis).

The first four graphs show the solution for single resources. For the water resource, the available six units can be devoted entirely to Activity I to give twelve input units on the *y*-axis (i.e. 6 divided by 0.5), or devoted entirely to Activity II to give ten input units on the *x*-axis (i.e. 6 divided by 0.6). These points are plotted in Figure 5.26A. The line joining them shows all the possible combinations of I and II which just exhaust the available six units of water. All combinations below the line (stippled area) are technically possible, since there is enough water; however, these are inefficient combinations since they do not use *all* the water. Conversely, combinations outside the line are technically impossible in this location because they demand more water than is locally available. Each of the other three resources has its appropriate graph pattern, and these are plotted in Figures 5.26B, C, and D.

It is clear that to solve our problem we must take all four resources jointly into consideration. To do this, the individual resource graphs can be simply superimposed. Figure 5.26F shows the superimposed lines for water (*a*) and land resources (*b*). Here the stippled area (*ab*) represents the feasible combinations when *both* resources are considered, and the heavy line the most efficient combinations. Area *a* on the graph represents combinations which are feasible from the point of view of water resources, but not of land resources; the converse is true of area *b*.

The combination process is continued in Figure 5.26G for all resources to give a convex polygon, or convex hull (Isard *et al.*, 1960, p. 418), on which all efficient solutions lie. Within the hull lie the feasible but inefficient points (area *abcd*), while outside it lie the impossible solutions. We know, however, that all efficient solutions lie somewhere on the convex segmented hull, and the final problem is to determine the most efficient solution.

Equal-income lines for the two activities are plotted as diagonals on Figure 5.26E, with values increasing away from the origin (more production → greater income). The most efficient point on the hull is that which cuts the highest equal-income line, point *z*, on the 10.5 income diagonal (Figure 5.26H). Point *z* is clearly a combination of the two activities, and we can read off its co-ordinates on the *x*-axis as 3.00 and on the *x*-axis as 7.5. In other words, the most efficient course of action for our location with its particular resource suite, is to concentrate on Activity II (7.5 units or 71 per cent) but continue some production in Activity I (3 units or 29 per cent).

Clearly, the example taken by Isard is a simple one, and a much more complex series of resources and activities would need to be solved in practice (Vajda, 1961). Nevertheless, the principle remains that, since locations are likely to differ in the local resources of site and situation, each location is likely to adopt (either scientifically or by trial and error) that 'mix' of activities which enables it make free use of readily available resources and sparing use of scarce resources.

(b) *Empirical example of substitution.* Cotterill (1950) has contrasted the factor-mixes used by two plants in the smelting industry in different locations—one in the 'Gas Belt' of Texas and one in the Illinois coalfield region near Chicago. Both smelters produce substantially the same product but have different cost patterns. Table 5.15 summarizes the main cost components of

Table 5.15 Production costs in two smelting areas*

| *Producing regions:* | *Illinois* | *Gas Belt* | *Source of Gas Belt advantage (% total advantage)* |
|---|---|---|---|
| Cost element, relative cost:† | | | |
| Raw materials costs | 1.70 | 0.59 | 70.0% |
| Labour costs | 1.43 | 0.70 | 22.3% |
| Fuel and power costs | 1.72 | 0.58 | 7.5% |
| Transport costs | 1.02 | 0.98 | 0.2% |

Source: Cotterill, 1950, p. 134.
*Central United States, 1948.
† Equal costs would give both regions a value of 1.0.

the two smelters. With these two plants, the evidence points to a very considerable cost advantage in favour of the Gas Belt smelter on all four cost elements. Two-thirds of this cost advantage stems from its cheaper raw materials, and a further quarter from the advantage in labour costs of a location more remote from the traditional steel making and marketing areas. Since the overall locational advantage of the Gas Belt smelter against the Illinois smelter is of the order of 4:3 we may legitimately ask what keeps the latter in production? Cotterill's study suggests that the answer lies in the sale of by-products, notably sulphuric acid, by the Illinois plant. This by-product is locationally denied to the Gas Belt plant. Sulphuric acid production entails a three times weight gain in water, it cannot be dumped because of its corrosive characteristics, and it is a low value-to-weight product that is very sensitive to distance. On all these counts, it is a strongly market-oriented product that can only be economically produced in or near a large industrial region. Through this sale of local by-products, the net deficit of the Illinois smelter is turned into a profit which allows it to retain its locational equilibrium near the market. Clearly, the *same* product may be produced with a *varying* resource input, so that simple correlations between the location of product $x$ and a standard series of resource inputs is an oversimplification.

## 5.7 Conclusions

In this chapter, we have seen how the population centres examined in Chapter 4 form themselves into a distinctive hierarchical structure. Central place theory represents one attempt to find a regular spatial pattern underpinning this structure, and the only partial success of such models in this task has been described. More recent work has laid special emphasis on the time domain, in both the periodic and the evolutionary sense. Specialization within the hierarchy gives rise to major distortions in the regular hierarchical pattern, and leads into a consideration of industrial location theory.

# 6 **Surfaces**

6.1 **Introduction.** 6.2 **Surfaces and Gradients:** 1 Nature of surfaces; 2 Density surfaces within cities; 3 Density surfaces between cities; Land use 'steps'. 6.3 **Movement-minimization Models: Statement:** 1 Geometry and ring formation; 2 Von Thünen's *Isolierte Staat.* 6.4 **Movement-minimization Models: Evaluation:** 1 Changing distance-decay rates; 2 Changes in distance-movement relations. 6.5 **Distortion of Regular Gradients:** 1 Distortion due to resource localization; 2 Distortion due to spatial concentration; 3 Distortion due to behavioural variations. 6.6 **Surface Change over Time:** 1 Slope development models; 2 Step development models. 6.7 **Conclusions.**

## 6.1 Introduction

The preceding chapters have isolated for study the important constituent elements of the regional system. These elements, the network of routes and the hierarchy of nodal centres, form a regional skeleton articulated by flows. This chapter looks at the ways in which the regional skeleton is given body by being filled out to form coherent surfaces. These surfaces are occupied by differing land uses at differing levels of intensity, characteristically, but not always, arranged as density surfaces around the major urban nodes. In this more abstract form, it is possible to weld together phenomena of apparently diverse kinds and scales, considering them as density decay rates from centre to periphery. Examples include (1) the population-density gradients falling away from city centres, first identified as basically negative exponential in form by Clark (1951); (2) the gradient of economic development expressed in centre–periphery terms by Friedmann (1972); and (3) the land-use intensity rings round both cities and farms developed by von Thünen.

In general, these density decline surfaces around a central node will have one component that is concentric, and one that is sectoral. The former is associated with the economies of spatial polarization, and the latter with the (limited) dissemination of central advantages along the major transport routes. The balance of concentric and sectoral forces controls the overall shape of the density surface, from the symmetrical cone of the classical von Thünen model, to the ribbed and ridged multiple-conic shape of the western city.

## 6.2 Surfaces and Gradients

### 6.2.1 *Nature of surfaces*

Whether we regard phenomena as a series of discrete points in space, or whether we generalize them into a continuous density surface, depends very much upon the degree of spatial generalization that we are prepared to accept. As we demonstrate in Chapters 10 and 12, spatial pattern is largely a function of the scale at which we look. Like height contours on a topographical map, we can regard lines of, say, equal population density as demographic contours. This surface may be thought of statistically as a response surface, in which

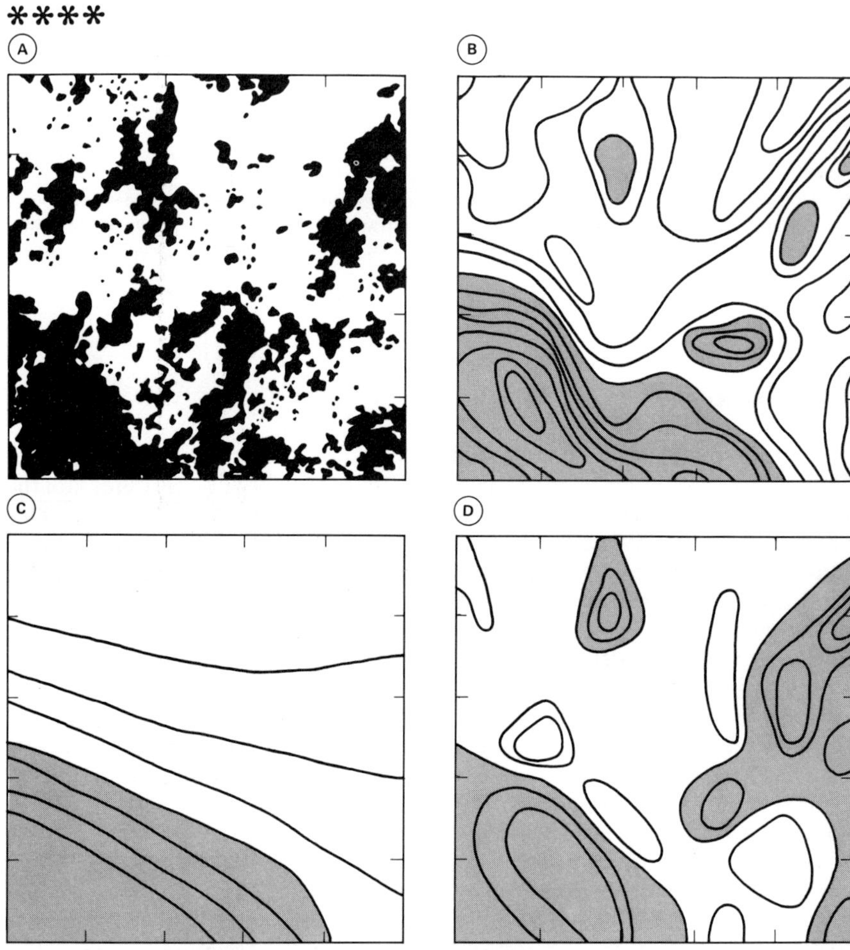


**Figure 6.1** Conversion of a discontinuous land use distribution (**A**) into a continuous isarithmic surface (**B**) with regional trends (**C**) and local residuals (**D**). Sample quadrat of *sobreiro* woodland in the Tagus–Sado basin, central Portugal, with contours at five-degree intervals and areas above the mean shaded. Source: Haggett, 1961b, p. 20.

height (i.e. population density) varies as a response to controlling factors. Ways of depicting geographical distributions depend as much on cartographic convention as on the inherent nature of the phenomena being shown. Thus we may readily convert the land-use pattern shown in Figure 6.1A, which illustrates the distribution of cork oak forests in central Portugal, into the density surface shown in Figure 6.1B or into the still more generalized surface shown in Figure 6.1C, simply by adopting different cartographic techniques.

From an analytical viewpoint, it is easier to work with a two-dimensional cross-section cut into the surface than with the three-dimensional surface itself. Thus we can imagine sections cut diagonally across the first two figures of Figure 6.1, with the first showing a discontinuous sequence of areas (with or without a particular type of forest cover), and the second a continuous but varying slope. In our discussion, we refer to the first type as a *stepped* distribution, with the height of the steps varying with the characteristics (intensity) of the type of land use, and the second type as a density distribution in which distinct *slopes* can be recognized and studied.

Surfaces may be described by statistical trend models (see Section 12.2). For example, population clusters tend to have a nebular structure which bears some comparison with the isotropic bivariate normal distribution (cf. Figure 13.9B). Simpler circular structures have been proposed by Tobler (1969a) to describe population density, such as the conical model,

$$P_d = (3P^*/\pi d_{\max}^2) - (3P^*d/\pi d_{\max}^3), \qquad (6.1)$$

the parabolic model,

$$P_d = (6P^*/\pi d_{\max}^4)(d - d_{\max}^2)^2, \qquad (6.2)$$

and the cosine model,

$$P_d = [\pi P^*/d_{\max}^2(\pi^2 - 4)]\left[1 - \cos\left(\frac{\pi d}{d_{\max}}\right)\right]. \qquad (6.3)$$

Here, $P_d$ is the population density at a distance $d$ from the cluster centre, $P^*$ is the total population of the cluster, and $d_{\max}$ is the outer radius. Clearly, in all the foregoing models, the surfaces are assumed to be symmetrical about a central point. However, Casetti and Semple (1969) have shown how even simple models of this kind may be extended to portray actual density surfaces. Using logarithmic or reciprocal transformations of the distance terms in the conical model, a cone is fitted by regression analysis to an optimum origin ($d_0$) in the study city. This origin is located by trial-and-error procedures to maximize the correlations between measured ($P_d$) and estimated ($\hat{P}_d$) population densities. Values of $\hat{P}_d$ about the optimal centre are regarded as the regional trend, while residuals from this trend ($P_d - \hat{P}_d$) yield a new spatial series (cf. the 'trend' and 'residual' maps in Figure 6.1). By locating a new spatial origin within the residual surface, a second trend and residual surface may be computed, and so on. See the description of Figure 12.4 in Section 12.2.3 for a discussion of the estimation problems involved.

Paralleling the search for appropriate isotropic, single or multiple-centred models are the anisotropic models in which population density is modelled in terms of location on an orthogonal $(X_1, X_2)$ co-ordinate system. These *polynomial* and *Fourier trend models* are treated at length in Sections 12.2 and 12.4.

### 6.2.2 *Density surfaces within cities*

Although the form of density gradients around cities has been a subject of interest since von Thünen's statement in the early nineteenth century, attention has been largely refocussed on the within-city scale only over the last decade or so. The controversial paper published by Clark (1951), postulating a negative exponential decline in population density with increasing distance from a city centre, was essentially a rediscovery of the same regularity noted by Bleicher (1892). Clark's paper stimulated a search for density models that accurately describe the declining rate of concentration of some aspect of population (e.g. density of residences, employment, commuting, or house-plot size) with distance from city centre. Clark studied the residential population density gradients around a group of 36 cities ranging in time from 1801 to 1950 and in space from Los Angeles to Budapest. As noted above, he argued that, within cities, urban population densities decline exponentially with distance away from the city centre, i.e. at a decreasing absolute rate, but a constant proportional rate. We can express Clark's generalization by the model,

$$P_d = P_0 e^{-bd} \tag{6.4}$$

where $P_d$ is the population density at a given distance ($d$) from the centre, $b$ is the density gradient, and $P_0$ is the extrapolated central density. Values of the

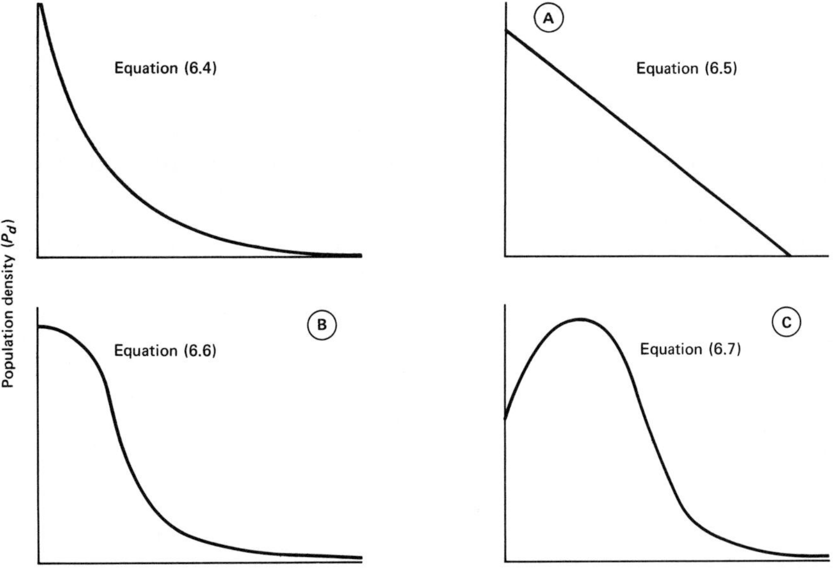


**Figure 6.2** Alternative exponential density gradients.

density gradient can be readily estimated by ordinary least squares by rewriting equation (6.4) as

$$\ln P_d = \ln P_0 - bd. \qquad (6.5)$$

The half-cone of population yielded by model (6.4) is illustrated in Figure 6.2A. Mills (1969) has shown that the exponential decay in residential density is a function of increase in total transport costs with distance from the city centre.

Direct studies of the term, $P_0$, in equation (6.5) have been few, largely because central density has proved so difficult to define. Winsborough (1961) overcame this problem obliquely by demonstrating that central density is a function of the overall population density of a city, regardless of its density gradient. Since the overall population density of a city is significantly associated with the age of dwellings, city size, and the extent of manufacturing employment, so central density will also vary with these attributes.

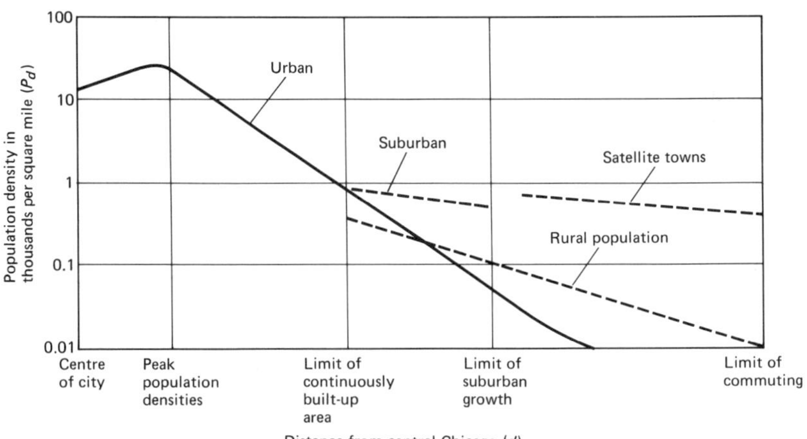


**Figure 6.3** Distance-decay curves for population densities in the Chicago area. Source: Berry and Horton, 1970, p. 280.

The negative exponential appears appropriately to describe the gradient for residential population density within the area covered by a typical Western city. However, two difficulties remain. First, the descriptions of the slopes at the city margins, where urban and rural density gradients meet, must be handled. These may be modelled by compounding curves, as illustrated in Figure 6.3. A second difficulty is how best to accommodate the population density 'crater' at the centre of the city caused by the low residential (night-time) population in what is dominantly a commercial zone. One early modification was to introduce the square of the distance from the city centre (Figure 6.2B) to give

$$P_d = P_0 e^{-bd^2} \qquad (6.6)$$

Newling (1969) and Casetti (1967) have extended this idea to a general quadratic relationship,

$$P_d = P_0 e^{b_1 d - b_2 d^2} \qquad (6.7)$$

(Figure 6.2c). This equation is readily fitted to empirical data by substituting natural logarithms, as in equation (6.5), and solving as a multiple regression equation.

Like Clark, Newling assumed an isotropic situation, so that a concentric pattern within a circular city is produced. But it is difficult to find, or even imagine, a city that is sufficiently lacking in sectoral disturbances (water bodies, transport arteries, secondary centres, etc.) not to produce significant local gradients and a non-circular perimeter. Muth (1962) carried out for the United States a regression study of density gradient against eleven possible controlling variables, of which only two—size of the Standard Metropolitan Area and the proportion of manufacturing outside the central city—yielded statistically significant relationships with the slope parameter (b). Berry *et al.* (1963, pp. 398–9) followed this work with a regression study of the density gradients of 46 United States cities against three variables: size of city, shape distortion from a circular form, and the spatial pattern of manufacturing. Although only city size was significant at the $\alpha = 0.05$ level, and scarcely 40 per cent of the total variance was accounted for by the three variables, there is reasonable doubt as to whether shape distortion and manufacturing employment should be rejected quite as readily as the regression results would suggest.

### 6.2.3 *Density surfaces between cities*

At a larger scale level, city gradients merge into rural ones where, for distances of over 500 miles from city centres, the same negative exponential decline suggested by Clark is found. Although we might expect rural farm population gradients to show little relationship to city-centred organization, Bogue's

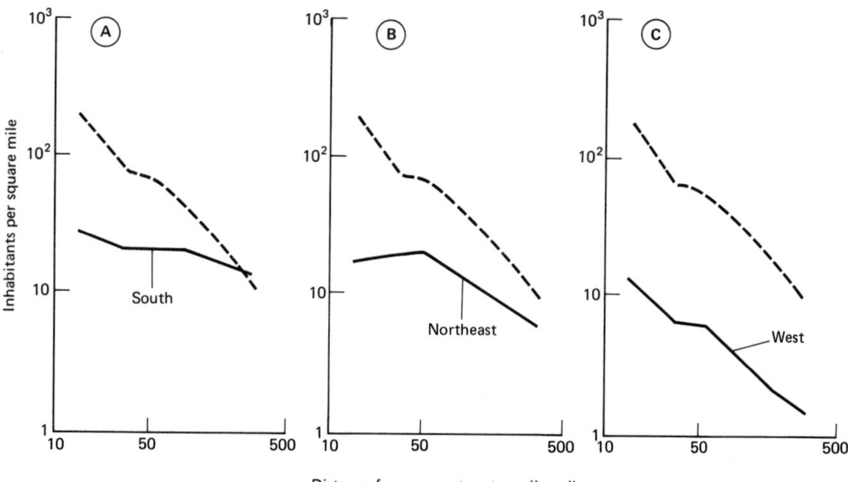


**Figure 6.4** Density-distance relationships for rural farm population in the United States, 1940, by regional divisions. The pecked line is for the USA as a whole. Source: Bogue, 1950, p. 58.

(1950) massive survey of gradients around 67 United States cities suggests otherwise, especially when regional groupings are studied (Figure 6.4).

The general form of the rural farm population density gradient is more convex than that for population density as a whole. For the first 100 miles, the density is around twenty people to the square mile with a rather gentle decline; from 100 to around 300 miles the gradient drops more steeply to around four to the square mile. The gradient is very little altered by the size of the central city (an important factor in urban and manufacturing gradients), and to a lesser extent by the sector. Here the subdominant sector containing the large secondary centres has a higher than average level, while the route and local sectors (as defined in Figure 4.4) are correspondingly reduced.

Perhaps the most striking feature of the density gradients is the variation between the major regions of the United States. The gentle gradients of the South (Figure 6.4A), the sharper fall of the Northeast with its characteristic depression of farm population densities in the near city areas (Figure 6.4B), and the very steep slope of the gradients in the West (Figure 6.4C) underline the basic differences in the agricultural resources of the three areas. To what extent these gradients directly reflect city influence or the passage into less favourable physical environments is difficult to determine.

### 6.2.4 *Land-use 'steps'*

Although the classification of the earth's surface into zones of distinct land use is a traditional geographical pursuit, none of the several schemes developed since 1892 (reviewed by Fox, 1956) has achieved the *ratio* level of measurement (see Section 9.2). Despite the moves of the 1949 Lisbon conference of the International Geographical Union for a world-wide classification system, slow progress has been made in this direction. The most successful works tend to remain the regional monograph on the land-use of a limited area, e.g. Board's (1962) study of the South African Border region.

The fact that land-use data are available in classes (e.g. woodland, arable land) rather than in precise ratios, means that we must view changes from one class to another as a 'break' or 'step', rather than as a gradient. Chisholm (1962) has drawn together a remarkable collection of empirical studies, in which these land-use steps are directly related to continuous ratios (e.g. distance from a settlement). The examples range in scale from the farm to the world-city, in time from the medieval to the contemporary scene, and in space from British Guiana to Soviet Russia.

One of the most interesting examples cited by Chisholm (1962, pp. 61–4) is at the intermediate level for land-use zones around the Sicilian village of Canicatti. Figures 6.5A–C graph the curve of land occupied against distance from the village centre for three important land uses; vineyards, olive groves, and unirrigated arable land. Vines occupy about 6 per cent of the area studied and are strongly concentrated in the inner zone (less than four kilometres out from the centre), while olives are more strongly represented in the middle zone (two to six kilometres out). Unirrigated wheat dominates the landscape of the outer zone but, since it makes up just over half the land area, it is strongly represented in all zones and it occupies half the area of even the inner 'urban zone' within one kilometre of the centre. Other crops which show sensitive reaction to distance are pasture, waste and coppice wood, all characteristic of the outer fringes, and citrus fruit, a characteristic type in the inner zones.

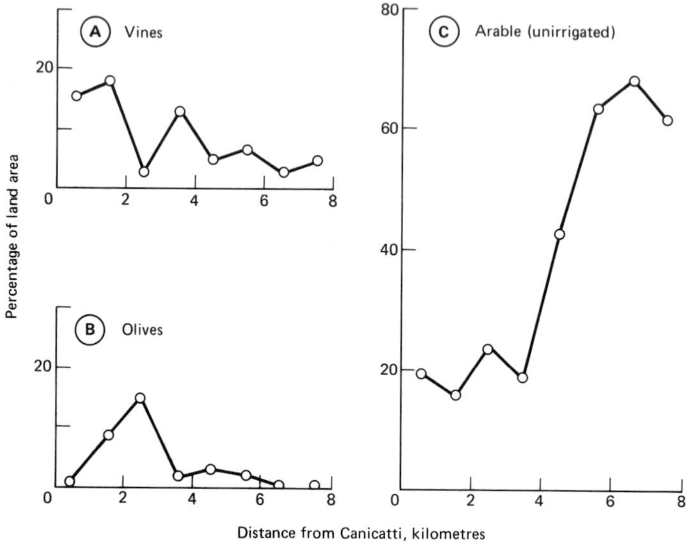


**Figure 6.5** Land use in Canicatti, Sicily, in relation to distance from the village centre, **A** Vines; **B** Olives; **C** Arable land (unirrigated). Source: Chisholm, 1962, p. 63.

To explain this observed pattern, Chisholm has turned to estimates of the annual labour requirements per hectare of the various crops available from the Instituto Nazionale di Economia Agraria in Rome. Table 6.1 summarizes the figures in man-days for the three crops graphed in Figure 6.5. It is clear that those products which are less demanding of labour are located further from the centre; the fallowed wheat fields with their low labour requirements give precedence to the carefully tended and watered vineyards. Even within an individual crop, there is some evidence that methods of cultivation become less intense with more distant crops.

Table 6.1 Land use, labour inputs, and distance from settlement*

| *Type of land use:* | *Vineyards* | *Olive-groves* | *Unirrigated arable* |
|---|---|---|---|
| Average labour input, man-days/hectare | 90 | 45 | 35 |
| Modal distance from Canicatti, kilometres | 1.5 | 2.5 | 6.5 |

Source: Chisholm, 1962, p. 63.

*Canicatti, Sicily.

At a smaller scale, land use varies with distance from the farmstead, and Chisholm cites regularities from Sweden, Finland, the Netherlands, and India to suggest the wide occurrence of this phenomenon. Lapse rates away from the farm suggest falling inputs of both labour and fertilizers with a generally critical level at about one kilometre. An interesting extension of the farm-fields concept comes from the midwestern United States, where Kollmorgen and Jenks (1958) have drawn attention to the phenomenon of 'suitcase' farmers (defined as operators who live more than thirty miles outside the border of the county in which the farmland is located). The fact that these farmers, some of whom are recorded as living as far away as Los Angeles, have to be mobile and travel long distances in their farming has decisive effects on farming practice, and through this on the land-use pattern. As Table 6.2 suggests, the distant 'suitcase' farms devote almost half their smaller acreages to cash crops, particularly wheat. The farms of the suitcase operators stand out as areas of high wheat production in counties in which the established local practice is dominantly a diversified crop and livestock pattern with two-thirds of the land area in pasture and feed crops.

Table 6.2 Land use in relation to the location of farm operator*

| *Locational classification of farmer:* | *Local* | *Non-local* |
|---|---|---|
| Average size of farm, acres | 1,280 | 730 |
| Proportion of farm area, per cent: | | |
| Cash crops | 14 | 60 |
| Feed crops | 25 | 21 |
| Pasture | 56 | 11 |

Source: Kollmorgen and Jenks, 1958, p. 34.
* Sully County, South Dakota, United States, 1950.

Experience in mounting and coordinating the second land-use survey of England at a scale of 1 : 25,000 led Coleman (1969) to develop a step model of land use with increasing distance from urban areas of the form, townscape → farmscape → wildscape. Though a useful heuristic device, the rather wide categories and the difficult assignment problems make the model a descriptive, rather than a programming, tool. Studies in rural areas are paralleled by land-use surveys within urban areas. Dickinson (1964, pp. 125–225) has summarized a number of studies of both the general structure of land use zones throughout the city and of 'natural regions' within specific parts of the city. Although land use studies of individual cities are common enough, comparative studies have been relatively rare. Bartholemew's *Land uses in American cities* (1955) remained one of the few, until supplemented by Niedercorn and Hearle's (1964) survey of land use trends in 48 large American cities.

## 6.3 Movement Minimization Models: Statement

Paralleling the contribution of Weber in the study of industrial location (see Section 5.6) is the earlier contribution of another German, von Thünen, to agricultural location. In his major work, *Der Isolierte Staat in Beziehung auf*

*Landwirtschaft* (von Thünen, 1875) which first appeared in 1826, he put forward a consistent theory of agricultural location which has proved not only the starting point for more refined modern analysis, e.g. Dunn's *Location of agricultural production* (1954), but directly stimulated Weber's work in industrial location. Indeed Thünian and Weberian analyses have much in common in that both are concerned with movement minimization; they differ fundamentally in that, while Weber's problem was to locate *points* in space, von Thünen's problem was to locate *areas* in space.

### 6.3.1 *Geometry and ring formation*

Concern with the location of areas raises the simple, yet fundamental, involvement with plane geometry to which Bunge (1964, pp. 8–11) has drawn attention. If we are concerned with the problem of locating finite areas as near as possible to fixed points, then Figure 6.6 suggests some of the alternative patterns that can emerge. In each case, the total area of each 'ring' ($A$) is the same, and $d_{max}$ is the maximum distance from the fixed point or line to the furthest part of the area.

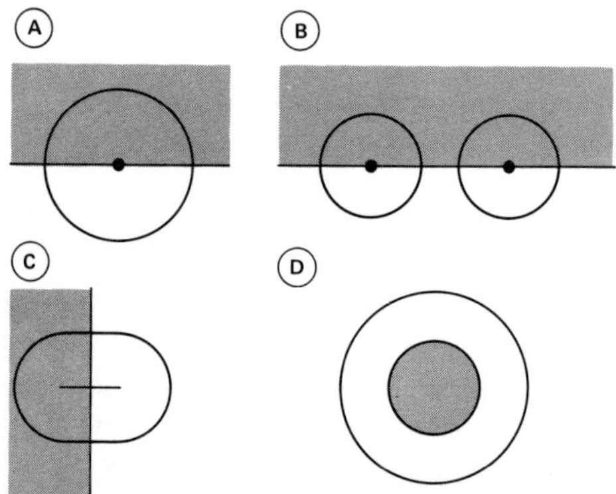


**Figure 6.6** Geometrical variants on the traditional von Thünen ring structure. The shaded areas represent water introduced to illustrate how the natural environment can modify economic symmetry.

The first case considered is that of arranging area nearest to a single point (Figure 6.6A), the classic problem in von Thünen's 'isolated state' with its single market centre, which gives rise to a circular solution. In the succeeding examples, two points are substituted for one (Figure 6.6B), a central line substituted for the two points (Figure 6.6C), and finally a central ring for the line (Figure 6.6D). In each case, the bleak geometric pattern assumes a more familiar geographical aspect when we submerge half the figure with sea (shaded); now we may find parallels between the first two diagrams and agricultural zones around coastal ports; between the third and a zone about a railroad penetrating inland; and between the fourth and population clusters around the continental littorals of a central ocean.

The point we are making here is merely that the von Thünen case of ring development represents only one extreme case in a set of problems in which areas are grouped as near as possible to a point or line. Ring development is discussed in the following section because it is graphically simple and clearly linked to the urban hierarchy, not because it is unique or exclusive.

To understand ring formation, let us consider the simple case of a land-use area to be placed as near as possible to a single point; then a circular form, *ceteris paribus*, is the minimum-movement solution from all parts of the area to the point. Clearly, in this elementary case, the relationship between $d_{max}$ and $A$ is simply $d_{max} = \sqrt{A/\pi}$. This trivial problem becomes considerably more interesting as we differentiate *alternative* land use areas ($A_1$, $A_2$, ... $A_n$) associated with $i = 1, 2, \ldots, n$ different land-use types.

Table 6.3 Derivation of net movement inputs*

| *Parameters:* | *Area required* $km^2$ ($A_i$) | *Maximum radius, km,* $d_{max}$ | *Weight tons/km*$^2$ ($w_i$) | *Cost of movement, units/ton* ($c_i$) | *Net movement inputs at radius,* $H(d_{max})$ |
|---|---|---|---|---|---|
| Land-use activities: | | | | | |
| Type 1 | 100 | 5.64 | 3.0 | 1.0 | 16.92 |
| Type 2 | 200 | 7.98 | 2.0 | 0.5 | 7.98 |
| Type 3 | 300 | 9.77 | 1.0 | 2.0 | 19.54 |
| All types | 600 | 13.82 | — | — | — |

* Theoretical case for three land use types.

Consider the situation summarized in Table 6.3. Here, three types of land use (1, 2, 3) are considered, each associated with a different crop, a different area of production, $A_i$, and a different per acre weight of production ($w_i$). We further assume a unit freight cost ($c_i$) to move the product of each of the three types of land use. For each land-use type, we can now estimate the cost of movement ($H$) at the outer margin using the same Weberian cost functions encountered in Sections 5.6.1, i.e.

$$H(d_{max}) = w_i c_i d_{max(A_i)}, \quad i = 1, 2, \ldots, n. \tag{6.8}$$

In Figure 6.7A, these weighted costs ($H$) are plotted *independently* on the $y$-axis as a function of distance on the $x$-axis.

If we assume that the same piece of land cannot be simultaneously used for more than one crop, then the total crop area required for the three types of land use will be 600 km$^2$ and the corresponding $d_{max} = 13.82$ km (see Table 6.3). What we have yet to determine is: (i) if the three types of land use will form distinct rings or annules about the centre; and (ii) what the sequence of rings will be. For our three types, the zonal sequence could be one of the following six: 123, 132, 213, 231, 312, 321. For $n$ zones, the number of possible sequences is $n!$, so that for von Thünen's seven agricultural zones (i.e., excluding the city market of zone **0** given in Table 6.4 there are 5,040 possible ring sequences. Figure 6.7B plots the six sequences for the three zone case of Table 6.3. Clearly, the *total* effort involved in terms of weighted movement costs at each distance is shown graphically as a cross-section by the shaded areas in Figure 6.7B. This may be defined by the integration

$$H = \int_{\Sigma A_i} w_i c_i d_j \quad i = 1, 2, 3, \tag{6.9}$$

where $j$ is the location of the $j$th point within a circle; the circle is centred on the

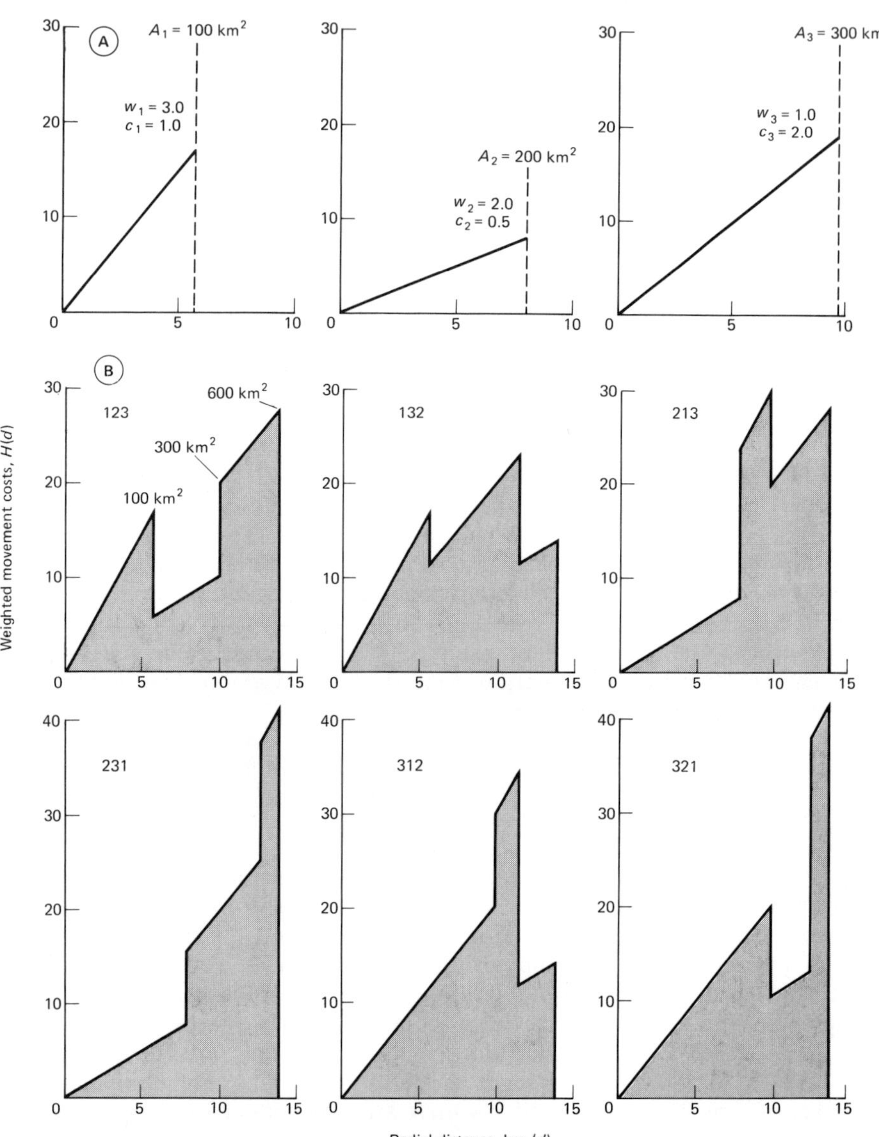


**Figure 6.7** Hypothetical example of the construction of land use rings.

city and has an area equivalent to the sum of areas $A_1$ to $A_3$. The expression given in equation (6.9) is effectively the volume described by a 360° rotation of the shaded cross-sections.

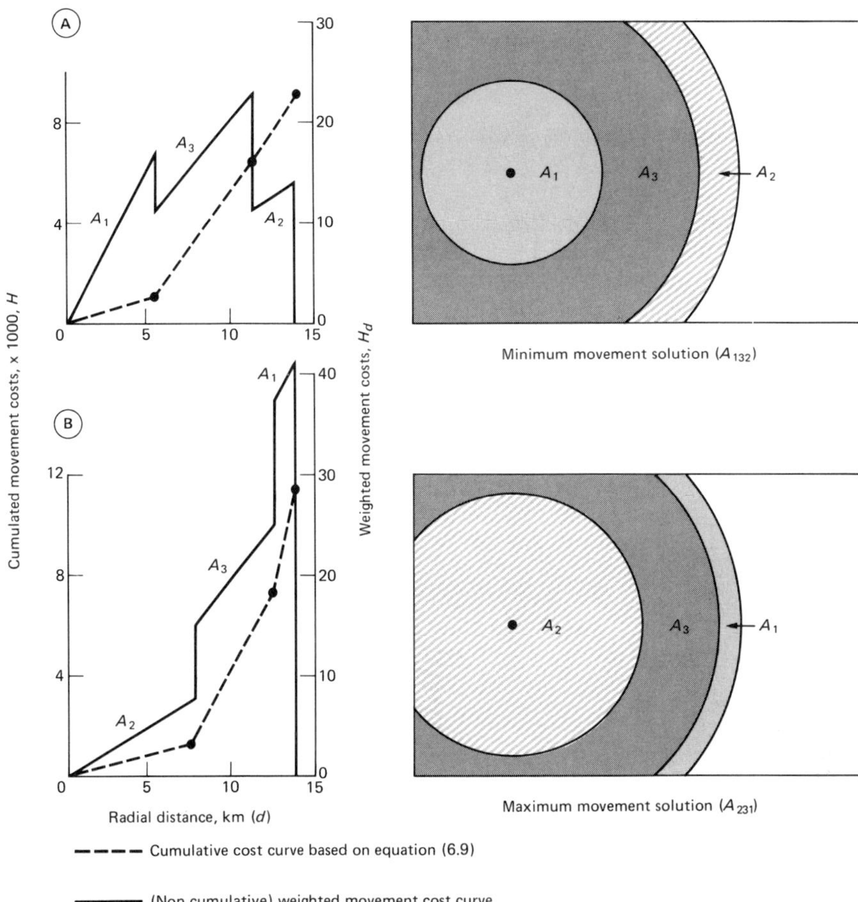


**Figure 6.8** Minimum and maximum solutions to the land use rings example of Table 6.3 and Figure 6.7.

Computation of the $H$ values for each of the six solutions shows that the minimum movement solution is $A_{132}$ (Figure 6.8A). This places the 100 km$^2$ of crop 1 nearest to the city, since it is the costliest to move in terms of its combined weight and cost values ($w_1 \times c_1 = 3.0$). Conversely, the 200 km$^2$ of crop 2 is located furthest from the city, since it is both less bulky and has low freight costs ($w_2 \times c_2 = 1.0$). The most wasteful land-use sequence, $A_{231}$ (Figure 6.8B), reverses that of the minimum solution. Since we have assumed that each type of agricultural activity is homogeneous, there are no grounds at this stage for assuming that the location of any part of any activity further from the centre would bring advantages, and we should expect a circular shaped production zone of 600 km$^2$ immediately adjacent to the centre.

The concepts we have used here are parallel to those of von Thünen. We may set our movement inputs against his concept of locational rent (*Bodenrente*)—sometimes called economic rent—which he derived from the expression,

$$L_{ij} = w_i(r_i - s_i) - w_i c_i d_j, \tag{6.10}$$

where $L_{ij}$ is the locational rent for land use $i$ at location $j$, which is a distance, $d_j$, from the urban market. The per acre yield or generating capacity of a given land use ($w_i$) is combined with the unit transport cost ($c_i$), the market price per unit of commodity at the central urban market ($r_i$) and the production cost per unit of commodity ($s_i$). See Dunn (1954, p. 7). Discussion in terms of ring formation (above) and von Thünen's locational rent is essentially similar, with the assumptions for fixed area demand ($A_i$) replacing the price and cost terms ($r_i$, $s_i$).

Formal analysis of the von Thünen model proceeds by first renumbering crops (or other land uses) according to the steepness of their transport cost functions, i.e., so that

$$w_1 c_1 > w_2 c_2 > \dots w_n c_n, \tag{6.11}$$

(Stevens, 1968). A given crop $i$ will be produced at *some* location if, and only if, the following two conditions are met

$$\left.\begin{aligned} & w_i(r_i - s_i) > w_{i+1}(r_{i+1} - s_{i+1}), \\ & \frac{r_i - s_i}{c_i} > \frac{r_{i-1} - s_{i-1}}{c_{i-1}}, \quad i = 1, 2, \dots, n. \end{aligned}\right\} \tag{6.12}$$

Crops that do not meet these conditions are eliminated from consideration, and the remaining crops are renumbered according to criterion (6.11). The distance from the city centre to the boundary between crop rings can be defined as:

$$\left.\begin{aligned} d_{0,1} &= 0 && \text{(centre)} \\ d_{1,2} &= \frac{w_1(r_1 - s_1) - w_2(r_2 - s_2)}{w_1 c_1 - w_2 c_2} \\ &\vdots \\ d_{i,i+1} &= \frac{w_i(r_i - s_i) - w_{i+1}(r_{i+1} - s_{i+1})}{w_i c_i - w_{i+1} c_{i+1}} \\ &\vdots \\ d_{n,n+1} &= \frac{r_n - s_n}{c_n} && \text{(periphery).} \end{aligned}\right\} \tag{6.13}$$

Clearly, $d_{n,n+1}$ is the outer edge of crop production marking the boundary between the last crop produced ($n$) and the 'waste' beyond ($n+1$). From the foregoing conditions, the form of the rent surface sloping downwards from the city centre to zero at the outer edge is given by:

$$L(d_j) = L_{ij}, \quad (d_{i-1,i} \leqslant d_j \leqslant d_{i,i+1}), \quad i = 1, 2, \ldots, n. \tag{6.14}$$

Here, $L(d_j)$ is the location rent at distance $d_j$ from the city centre.

This somewhat cumbersome procedure for finding equilibrium location and rent patterns in the von Thünen model can be greatly simplified by recasting the problem in a linear programming format (e.g. Stevens, 1968). For a formal discussion, see Section 15.2.3.

### 6.3.2 *Von Thünen's* Isolierte Staat

Diagrams of the concentric rings of land use in von Thünen's hypothetical isolated state are amongst the most common textbook illustrations of locational theory for geographers. The main characteristics of its zones have been summarized by Grotewald (1959) and Chisholm (1962, pp. 21–35), and are reproduced in Table 6.4. It will be seen that the land-use pattern is one of concentric shells ranging from very narrow inner rings of intensive farming (1) and forest (2), through to a broad band of increasingly extensive agriculture (3) and ranching (4) to the waste beyond (5). The outer, circular limit represents the outer margin of production where $L_{ij} = 0$ in terms of equation (6.10).

Table 6.4 Der Isolierte Staat (1926): von Thünen's land use 'rings'

| *Zone* | *Area per cent of state area* | *Relative distance from central city* | *Land-use type* | *Major marketed product* | *Production system* |
|---|---|---|---|---|---|
| **0** | Less than 0.1 | <0.1 | Urban-industrial | Manufactured goods | Urban trade centre of state; near iron and coal mines |
| **1** | 1 | 0.1–0.6 | Intensive agriculture | Milk; vegetables | Intensive diarying and trucking; heavy manuring; no fallow |
| **2** | 3 | 0.6–3.5 | Forest | Firewood; timber | Sustained-yield forestry |
| **3a** | 3 | 3.6–4.6 | Extensive agriculture | Rye; potatoes | Six-year rotation: rye (2), potatoes (1), clover (1), barley (1), vetch (1); no fallow; cattle stall-fed in winter |
| **3b** | 30 | 4.7–34 | Extensive agriculture | Rye | Seven-year rotation system; pasture (3), rye (1), barley (1), oats (1), fallow (1) |
| **3c** | 25 | 35–44 | Extensive agriculture | Rye: animal products | Three-field system: rye, etc. (1), pasture (1), fallow (1) |
| **4** | 38 | 45–100 | Ranching | Animal products | Mainly stock-raising: some rye for on-farm consumption |
| **5** | — | Beyond 100 | Waste | None | None |

In appreciating the remarkable early statement of von Thünen, we should recall its two somewhat paradoxical limitations: (1) the extensive simplifying assumptions necessary in such a partial model and (2) its high empirical content.

(1) The assumptions made by von Thünen may be summarized under six heads: (i) the existence of an 'isolated state' which was cut off from the rest of the world and surrounded by waste on all sides; (ii) the domination of the state by a single large city which served as the single urban market; (iii) the setting of the city in the centre of a broad featureless plain which was assumed to be equal in fertility and trafficability so that production costs and transport costs were assumed to be everywhere the same; (iv) the supplying of the city by farmers who shipped agricultural goods to the city in return for industrial produce; (v) the transporting of farm produce by the farmer himself who hauled his own produce to market along a dense trail of converging roads of equal standard with costs exactly proportional to distance; (vi) the maximizing of profit by all farmers, with automatic adjustment of crops to the needs of the central market, but ignoring cost savings due to economies of scale and complementary production. It might be added that von Thünen's farmers were remarkably insensitive to demand and supply schedules in fixing their prices.

Lösch (1954, pp. 38–48) has pointed out that, even with these simplifying assumptions, ring formations were not inevitable. He argued that for two crops, 1 and 2, there were 17 possible combinations in which one or other crop predominated, or both were grown side by side, and only ten in which rings were formed. To achieve rings in the order, $\{1, 2\}$, about the centre the following conditions had to obtain:

$$1 < \{[w(r-s)_1]/[w(r-s)_2]\} < (w_1/w_2), \tag{6.15}$$

where $w$, $r$ and $s$ are as defined by Dunn (1954) in the preceding section.

(2) The high empirical content of von Thünen's theory can only be understood in terms of his background. Johnson (1962) and Hall (1966) have described the early years of von Thünen's life and its influence on his locational ideas. In 1810 at the age of 27, he acquired his own agricultural estate, Tellow, near the town of Rostock in Mecklenburg on the Baltic coast of Germany. For the next forty years, till his death in 1850, von Thünen farmed this estate and over this period assembled a mass of minutely documented data on the costs and revenue of its operation. His *Der Isolierte Staat* (1926) drew heavily on his farming and estate accounting and many of the assumptions, and all of the empirical constants he used, were based on this localized experience.

Many of the needs of nineteenth-century Mecklenburg now seem quaint and obsolete. Apparently the most serious change in demand affects the location of his second zone, timber and firewood production (Table 6.4), a type of land-use activity which is generally no longer able to bid for high accessibility sites near urban centres in Western countries. [We note, though, that in highly urbanized areas the demand for 'recreational' wooded areas may sometimes lead to its persistence in areas of high accessibility. Gottmann (1961) has illustrated this trend with rising leisure demands in the highly urbanized seaboard areas of the eastern United States.] In the humid tropics, however, rotational timber for firewood and charcoal may still be located in about the position von Thünen suggested, and Waibel (1958) has drawn attention to this arrangement in southeastern Brazil.

## 6.4 Movement Minimization Models: Evaluation

### 6.4.1 *Changing distance-decay rates*

Although direct comparisons are difficult, there is little doubt that the long term trend of real transport costs has been downwards. A succession of technical inventions, the advent of cheap fuels, and the scale economies of ever larger volumes in circulation have generally reduced the relative costs of transport in overall production costs. Chisholm (1962, pp. 185–6) has followed the course of freight rates for one transport medium, ocean shipping, and finds that, when allowances are made for world-wide inflation, the real cost of ocean shipping over the years between 1876 and 1955 had fallen by almost three-fifths.

As the general level of transport costs falls, the relative mobility of products increases, and we should expect to find von Thünen's rings growing wider. Lösch (1954, p. 51) pointed out that, with the growth of a number of closely packed centres, the location of rings around each centre will be distorted outwards. There may simply not be enough room for all the rings, and the outer ones may be displaced toward the periphery of the state. This means that, for the inner rings, the individual town remains the marketing centre, but for the outer rings it is the agglomeration of towns that jointly forms the market centre (Figure 6.9A). This point has been illustrated by Jonasson, who regards northwestern Europe as 'one vast conurbation . . . one geographic centre' (Jonasson, 1925, p. 290). Maps of average decline of yield of eight crops show a remarkable decline with distance from this combined centre (Figure 6.9B).

Peet (1972) has examined the effect on continental European agriculture of the growth of the British market for imported food in the eighteenth and

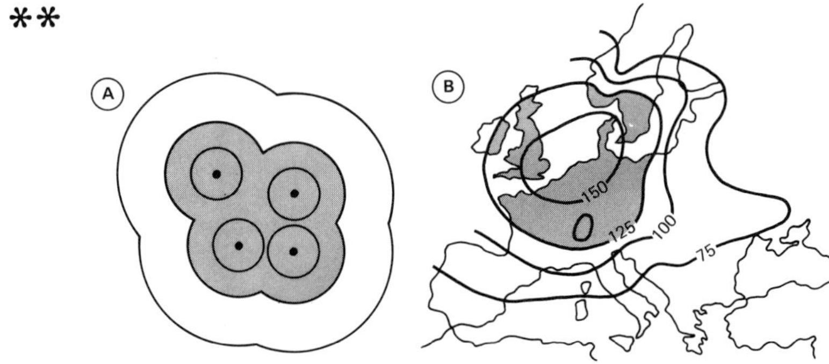


**Figure 6.9** **A** Fusing of ring structure around clusters of centres. **B** Contours of agricultural intensity in Europe. Source: Valkenburg and Held, 1952, p. 102.

nineteenth centuries. Under the more primitive transport conditions before the railways, perishable commodities had to be supplied domestically, even locally. However, Peet identifies a semi-perishable import zone occupying the nearest coastal fringes across the English Channel and the southern North Sea sustained by the opportunity for speedy and cheap delivery to English coastal markets. For non-perishable commodities, cost of transport became the dominant determinant of production site. Figure 6.10 illustrates the great importance of low-cost water transport in encouraging locations for the production of export wheat and dairy produce. Further, this trade led to the proliferation of a host of small ports along the North Sea and Baltic coasts tapping production hinterlands of a radius of 30–50 kilometres. The way in which Ireland's role as a wheat exporter was sustained by the Corn Laws until 1846 was a notable distortion of von Thünen's rings. By the 1860s the international von Thünen rings were clearly to be seen, with inner western Europe and the northeast United States supplying market-garden and dairy produce; southeast Europe, the Ukraine and the American Mid-West supplying grain; and the American West, Argentina, South Africa, Australia and New Zealand sending wool, hides and meat. Table 6.5 illustrates the progressive expansion of the supply rings during the nineteenth century.

Table 6.5 Average distances over which agricultural imports to Britain moved, 1830–1913.

| | *Average distance from London to regions from which each import type derived (miles)* | | | | |
|---|---|---|---|---|---|
| Import type | 1831–1835 | 1856–1860 | 1871–1875 | 1891–1895 | 1909–1913 |
| Fruit and vegetables | 0 | 324 | 535 | 1150 | 1880 |
| Live animals | 0 | 630 | 870 | 3530 | 4500 |
| Butter, cheese, eggs, etc. | 262 | 530 | 1340 | 1610 | 3120 |
| Feed grains | 860 | 2030 | 2430 | 3240 | 4830 |
| Flax and seeds | 1520 | 3250 | 2770 | 4080 | 3900 |
| Meat and tallow | 2000 | 2900 | 3740 | 5050 | 6250 |
| Wheat and flour | 2430 | 2170 | 4200 | 5150 | 5950 |
| Wool and hides | 2330 | 8830 | 10,000 | 11,010 | 10,900 |
| Weighted average all above imports | 1820 | 3650 | 4300 | 5050 | 5880 |

Source: Peet, 1969, p. 295.

Movement of goods at this international scale is clearly part of the same interaction continuum that we noted in Chapter 2. Ohlin (1933), in his classic trade study, *Interregional and international trade*, places these movements within a general framework of locational theory. At this scale it would appear, then, that the effect of reducing transport costs has been to alter the scale of operation of Thünen's rings, rather than their intrinsic value.

At the other extreme, empirical evidence suggests that at the small scale of field and farm, and farm and village, the ring effect remains (Chisholm, 1962, pp. 47–75, 124–53). Here, the movement continues to be measured in terms of time and man-days rather than in freight costs, so that as labour costs rise we

**

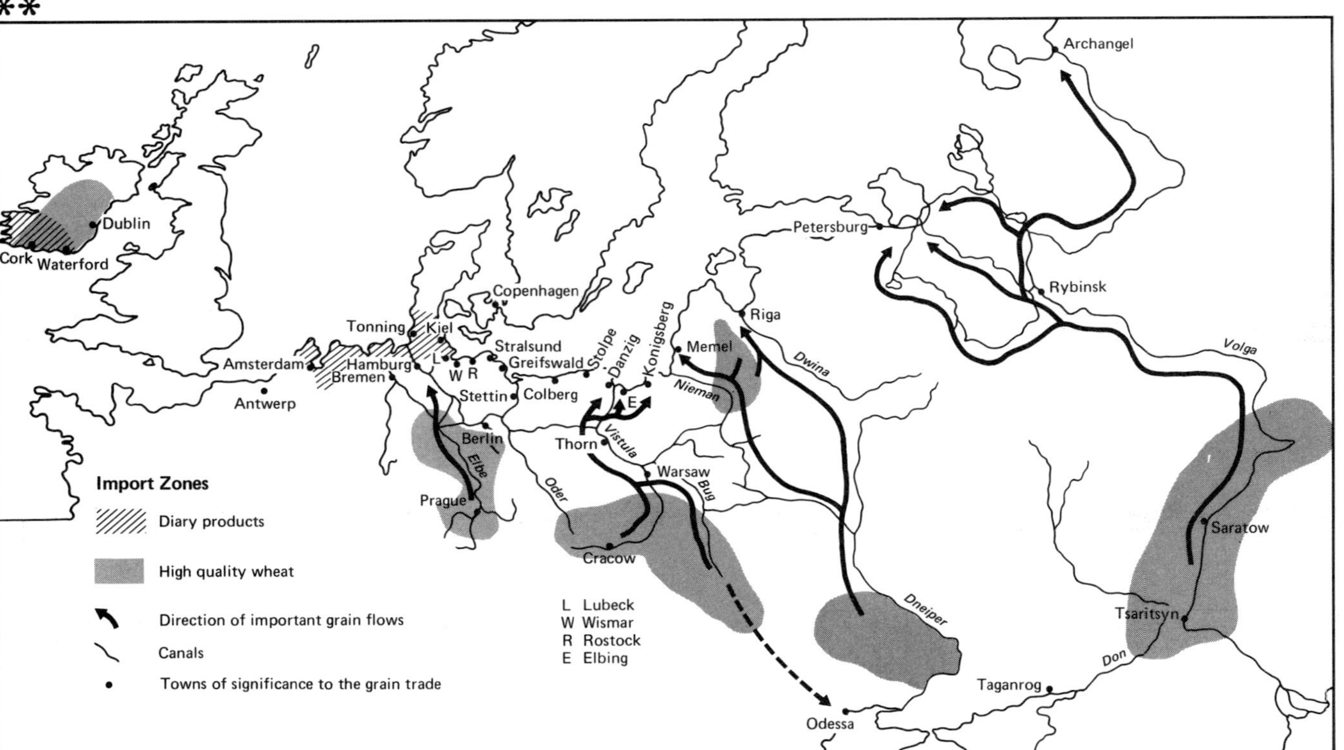


**Figure 6.10** Origins of British imports of dairy products and high quality wheat, *c.* 1830. Source: Peet, 1972, p. 8.

might expect such movement costs to become relatively more important despite being partially offset by more rapid improvements in internal transport (tractors, cross-country vehicles, etc.).

### 6.4.2 *Changes in distance–movement relations*

In the study of movement inputs, the cost of moving over distance was assumed to be linear. We know, in fact, that movement costs are in general: (i) curvilinear (convex) in form; (ii) stepped rather than continuous; and (iii) differentiated by commodity, amount, distance, direction, shipper, season, and related variables (Troxel, 1955). While the detailed discussion of this most complex problem remains outside our immediate field, it is worth illustrating the general form of the cost-distance relationship. For Milwaukee (*a* in Figure 6.11A,B), Alexander (1944) has illustrated the stepped nature of railroad freight rates (Figure 6.11A) and the distortion of the cost surface with directional variations from the city (Figure 6.11B).

Variation in movement costs on different commodities is demonstrated by

***

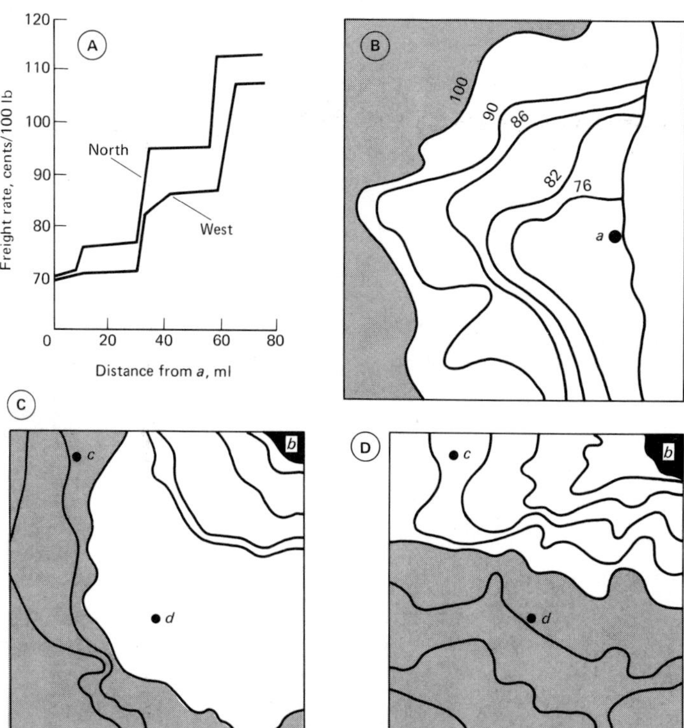


**Figure 6.11** Directional variations in railway freight costs in sample quadrats. **A, B** West of Milwaukee, United States. **C, D** Southwest of Chicago, United States. Sources: Alexander, Brown, and Dahlberg, 1958, p. 9; Alexander, 1944, pp. 26–8.

the pattern of railroad freight rates for grain moved to Chicago, *b* (Figure 6.11C), when compared with livestock rates to Chicago (Figure 6.11D). In both maps, contours are at intervals of two cents per 100 pounds, with areas over thirteen cents stippled in Figure 6.11C and over eighteen cents stippled in Figure 6.11D to emphasize the high cost areas. If we compare the location of two points, *c* and *d*, west and southwest of Chicago, we find that, although both are equidistant from the city (about 110 miles away), the first has a marked locational advantage in livestock production and the second in grain production.

These cases emphasize the dramatic shift from the idyllic picture of von Thünen's state where each farmer took his own product to market by horse and wagon and was therefore directly concerned to minimize his own movements. The shift of transport to independent companies has undermined the logic of this minimization assumption in that we could argue, *ceteris paribus*, that the object of a transport company is to maximize rather than minimize total movement. Troxel (1955) examines some of the restraints that both competition and government place on this maximization urge. We can argue, none the less, that the movement of transport out of the hands of the producer has meant that the economy of the overall movement system rather than that of the individual producer becomes dominant.

## 6.5 Distortion of Regular Gradients

### 6.5.1 *Distortion due to resource localization*

(a) *Variation in resources.* As a practical farmer, von Thünen knew that, in practice, the land-use pattern was modified not only by movement costs but also by the local availability of good soils, growing seasons, management ability, and so on. He produced a modified diagram in which the original rings (Figure 6.12A) were altered not only by competing centres (Figure 6.12B) and cheaper transport routes (Figure 6.12C), but also by different land qualities (Figure 6.12D). A useful example of how the classical von Thünen formulation can be modified to apply to a specific area is provided by Rutherford *et al.* (1966). The assumptions of the model have been relaxed to accommodate three distorting factors: a coastline (Figure 6.13B), terrain oriented parallel to the coast (Figure 6.13C), and multiple instead of single markets (Figure 6.13D). Yet further relaxation to accommodate behavioural assumptions would be necessary to arrive at the actual land-use pattern for New South Wales (Figure 6.13E).

Empirical support for the very close link between physical resources and agriculture is longstanding. For example, Hidore (1963) investigated the relationship between: (i) flat land, defined as slopes of less than 3°; and (ii) cash grain farms. For the sample of 730 counties in the north-central United States, the Pearson product-moment correlation coefficient was statistically significant at +0.652. The only major deviant state was Minnesota where its high percentage of flat land was offset by unsuitable soil conditions, the southern edge of the Laurentian Shield. Studies like that of Hidore are part of a long tradition of environmental studies which have formed a major part of the geographical literature. However, as Found (1971) reminds us in his extensive review of agricultural location theory, we must not allow the fact that land-use variations over large areas can be 'explained' to a considerable extent by variations in land quality (including climate), to persuade us that the role of man as an independent decision maker can be disregarded. Individual environmentally sympathetic decisions at the local scale may be lost when aggregated into land-use zones which conform to the broader sweep of physical circumstances. At the local level, farmers' decisions depend on production functions, and the prices and costs of inputs and outputs; the former is associated with the local environment and the latter with local market conditions, either of which can dominate his decision, at least for a time.

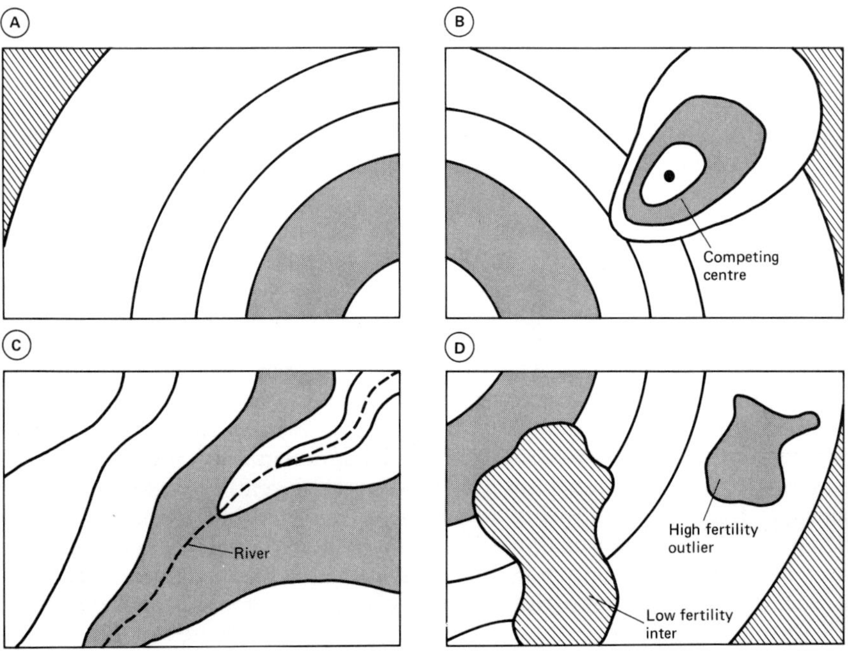


**Figure 6.12** Distortion of the regular annular structure of the von Thünen landscape (**A**) by a second competing centre (**B**), alternative transfer routes (**C**), and areas of different productivity (**D**).

(b) *Substitution between resource inputs.* As with industrial location (Section 5.6.3), substitution modifies any simple relationship between resources and zone location. Von Thünen himself used substitution in his analysis of the distribution of one of his crops, rye, in the 'Isolated State'. Table 6.4 shows that, although rye was grown throughout the outer agricultural zone (3–4), it was shipped to market only within zone 3. This shipping zone nevertheless covers a very wide distance from 3.6 to 44 miles. Despite a common market price for rye and common movement costs per ton, rye from the outer part of zone (3) was able to compete successfully with rye grown about one-tenth this distance from the market in the inner zone (3a).

Using his intensity theory, von Thünen argued that the outer zone can compete with the inner only by substituting a less efficient total production system (*Betriebssystem*), i.e. the outer zone can compete only because it has lower production costs for rye, but these lower costs for this crop are bought at the expense of a wasteful total system in which one-third of the land lies fallow each year. Indeed, if we compare the rotational systems in 3a, 3b, and 3c, we find that the proportion of fallow land rises in the sequence zero, one-seventh, one-third with distance from the market (see Table 6.4).

A similar practical illustration of substitution in the dairy industry in the United States has been provided by Gottman (1961, p. 286). He compares two important dairy farming areas, the Atlantic Coast zone near the Boston–New York–Washington market, and the Wisconsin–Minnesota zone in the midwestern United States. In terms of von Thünen's system, the first zone would be in the intensive inner ring and the second in the extensive outer ring. Although both areas have farm units of about the same size (150 acres) and about the same yield per animal, there are striking contrasts in almost all other inputs in favour of the Atlantic Coast area. Stock per acre and investment in machinery are 40 per cent more, returns are 60 per cent more, per unit output of milk, and investment in lands and buildings is 80 per cent more. Contrasts in land use are slightly less striking, with 30 per cent more hay being grown in the inner zone and with a corresponding decrease in small grains. As with the rye example, the outer zone competes with the inner, and overcomes the additional transport costs, by having a less expensive total production system.

The contrast in output in the two areas partly reflects the returns for liquid milk as opposed to processed milk (butter, cheese, etc.) to which von Thünen drew attention in his Isolated State. A number of studies in both the United States and the British Isles have highlighted the characteristic locational zoning of milk, butter, and cheese production with increasing distance away from the urban-industrial market (Chisholm, 1962). This kind of distinction is shown for New South Wales in Figure 6.13.

In both the rye and dairying examples, the inner zones are the most efficient in terms of overall production, for, as Lösch has emphasized, 'total profits are decisive; there is no additional criterion for individual crops' (Lösch, 1954, p. 61). However, as with our findings for the zinc industry (Section 5.6.1), we must conclude that given crops will be cultivated in a variety of locations where substitutions between local resources make their inclusion in the total crop mix profitable.

Mixing crops in an appropriate combination at a given location may be motivated by the need for diversification as a risk-reducing device, to reap the advantages of complementary production, or to maintain land fertility by conservationist rotations. The problem of which crops to choose has been approached by Gould (1963) using *game theory*. He selects Jantilla, a small village in western Ghana, as typical of the problem of crop mixture in the middle zone of the country, with its very variable rainfall. Here the 'environmental strategy' in game theory parlance is two-fold: it can either be wet or, under Harmattan conditions, dry. To meet this, the 'villagers' strategy' is five-fold: they can grow one or all of five basic crops. However, the yield will vary considerably depending on the particular crop grown and the season (Table 6.6). For example, yams are a speculative crop with high wet-year yields but a poor dry-year yield (only one-eighth as large). By contrast, millet is a very reliable crop which differs rather little between its dry- and wet-year returns. We can see something of the villagers' dilemma: (i) should they hope for a wet season and plant high-yielding (but high-risk) crops; or (ii) play safe with moderate-yielding crops; or (iii) adopt some intermediate strategy?

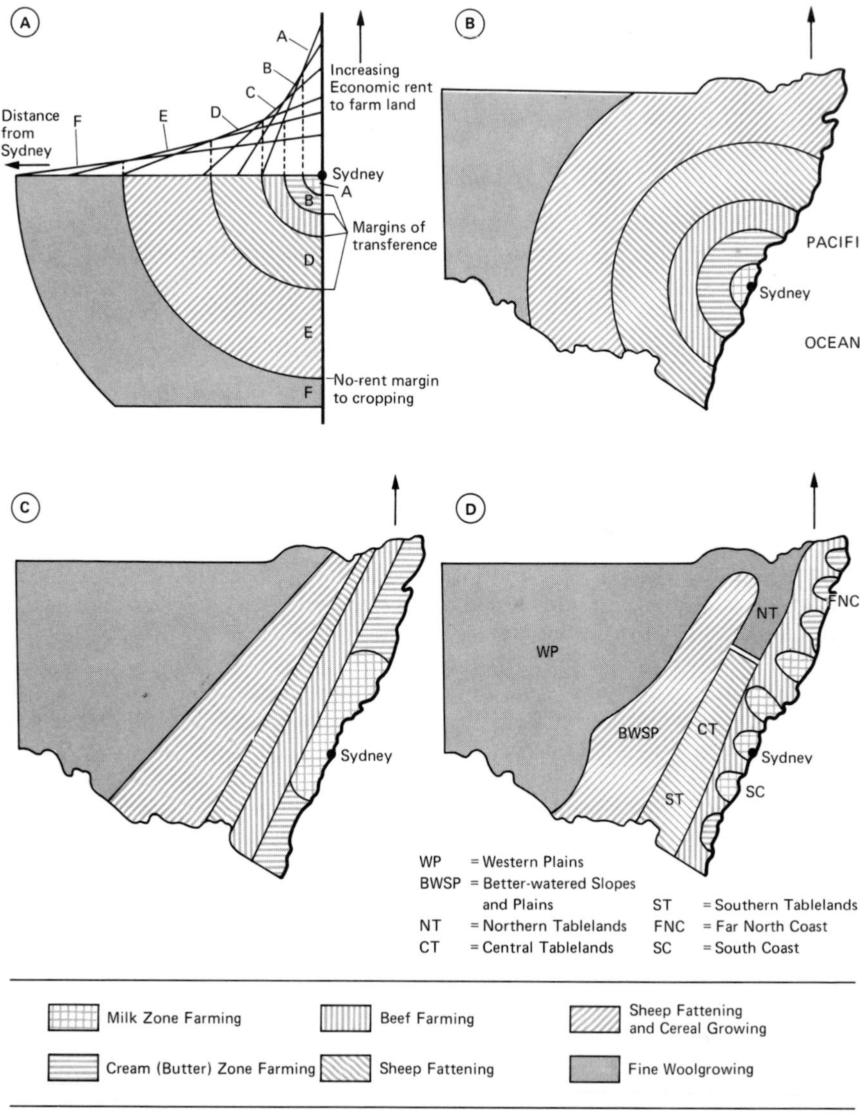

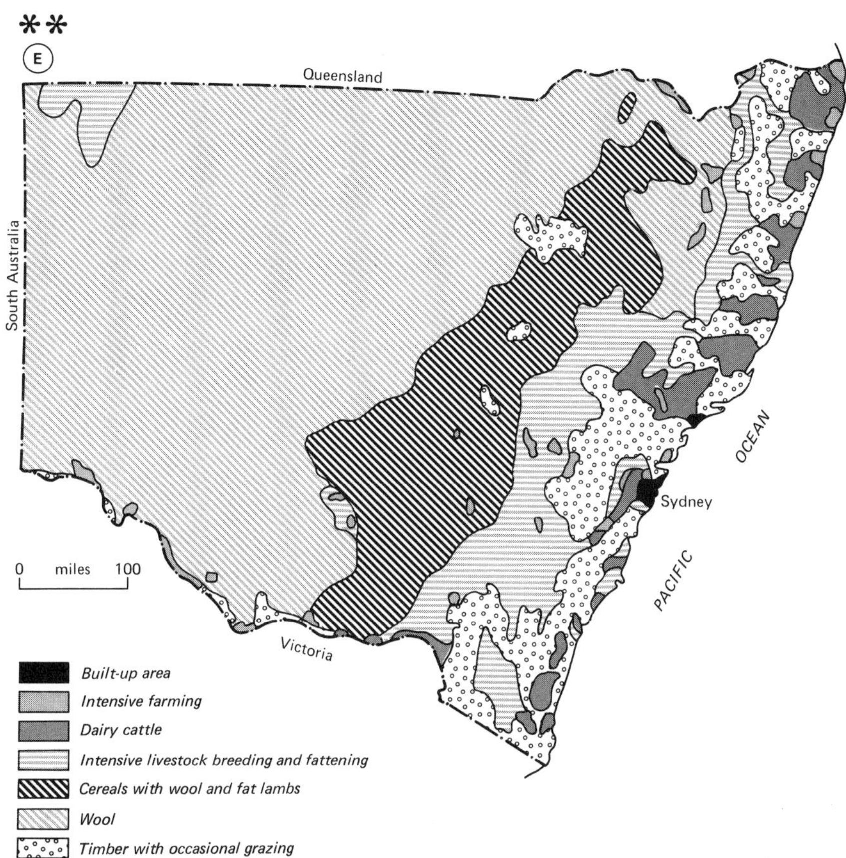


**Figure 6.13** The progressive adaptation of a von Thünen ring pattern to the land use distribution for New South Wales. Source: Rutherford, *et al.*, 1966, p. 46.

Table 6.6 Crop yields under alternative environmental strategies*

| *Environmental strategies:* | *Wet year* | *Dry year* |
|---|---|---|
| Crop yields per unit of area: | | |
| Yams | 82 | 11 |
| Maize | 61 | 49 |
| Cassava | 12 | 38 |
| Millet | 43 | 32 |
| Hill-rice | 30 | 71 |

Source: Gould, 1963, p. 292.
*Jantilla, central Ghana.

Given the simple 2 × 5 table, Gould shows how the optimum solution may be obtained. In Figure 6.14, yield is plotted on separate vertical axes for the wet year (*w*) and dry year (*d*) and the points joined by a diagonal line. The steeper this line, the greater are the contrasts in yield between the two years, and vice versa. Figure 6.14A shows the diagonal for the first crop, yams. In Figure 6.14B, the diagonal for the second crop, maize, is superimposed, and in Figure 6.14C, diagonals for the remaining three crops are added. The intersecting diagonals show the highest yields—yams, maize, and hill-rice—and these are marked as a segmented concave line in Figure 6.14C. On this line, the lowest point (or saddle point), *S*, represents the optimum combination of crops: i.e. those crops which will yield on average the highest returns in a run of good and bad years. This is, in game theory terms, the minimax (minimum risk, maximum profit) solution.

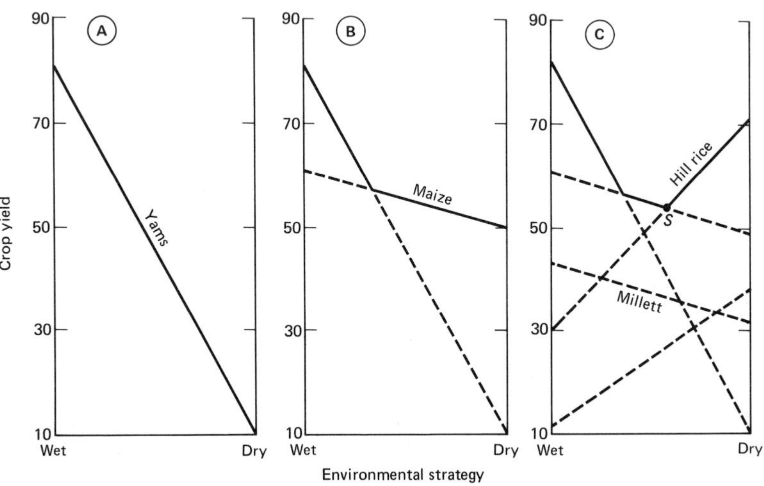


**Figure 6.14** Stages in the determination of the optimum crop mix for a Ghanaian village by game-theory analysis. Source: Gould, 1963, p. 292.

Computation of the relative share of each crop in the minimax solution is shown in Table 6.7. The difference in yield between wet and dry years is calculated for both crops and compared; for each crop the observed difference is transferred to the other; this transferred difference, divided by the comparative difference, gives indices (1.4 and 0.4) which represent the share of each crop and from which percentages may be calculated.

The resulting proportions of 77 : 23 could be interpreted in the long run as planting all the village land in maize for seventy-seven years and all in hill-rice for the remaining twenty-three years of each century! In practice, the short-run solution, planting three-quarters of the area to maize and a quarter to hill-rice each year, would clearly be adopted. Gould finds that the proportions derived by this method are in rough accord with the actual land use patterns in the Jantilla area, suggesting that the solution has been reached there by the rugged path of trial and error. Since error in this case must be translated in human terms into starvation, the potential importance of game-theory approaches to substitution problems is clear. Like the determination of location rents in the von Thünen model, game theory problems of the kind outlined here can also be expressed in linear programming terms. This is done in Section 15.5.2.

Table 6.7 Computation of optimum counter-strategy*

| *Alternative crops:* | *Maize* | *Hill-rice* |
|---|---|---|
| Yield under alternative environmental strategy: | | |
| Wet year | 61 | 30 |
| Dry year | 49 | 71 |
| Difference in yield | 12 | 41 |
| Proportional difference | $\left\lvert\frac{41}{12-41}\right\rvert = 1.4$ | $\left\lvert\frac{12}{12-41}\right\rvert = 0.4$ |
| Optimum counter-strategy | 77% | 23% |

Source: Gould, 1963, p. 293.

*Jantilla, central Ghana.

Although no general account of human geography in recent years is without a well considered and illustrated account of von Thünen's agricultural location model, supported by appropriate decision models of the game theoretic type (see especially Found, 1971), the limitations of the rather simple gaming solutions illustrated are now being recognized. However, the more complex, but more realistic, gaming models, such as those with multiple players, rapidly become intractably difficult to specify. The assumption that a given player knows and understands not only his own range of available strategies, with matching probabilities, but also those of his opponent(s) as well, is a very demanding one. It implies levels of information which are well beyond the reality of most situations, only to be attained (or 'bought') by elaborate search procedures. Aspiration levels can range from maximizing pay-off, down to minimizing the chance of failure or regret, all difficult to quantify precisely. A player's actual choice behaviour might be influenced by a whole range of personal and circumstantial factors. These may include a willingness to gamble recklessly, or, for example, the enjoyment of suffering stoically that Saarinen (1966) rather unexpectedly found in Great Plains farmers.

### 6.5.2 *Distortion due to spatial concentration*

While scale economies have not reached the levels attained by industry, there is evidence that they are increasingly important in understanding rural land use. Harvey's (1963) study of the location of the Kentish hop industry illustrates the link. This specialized activity, possibly located here as much by chance factors as by appropriate physical conditions, became anchored and expanded into a tenacious land-use concentration during the early nineteenth century. Agglomerative forces reinforced its compact form, diminishing returns setting in at its spatial margins. The agglomerating factors amounted to the local availability of willing capital, a pool of skilled, enthusiastic seasonal labour, seaborne fertilizer in quantity, a compatible system of land tenure, and specialized marketing facilities. Above all, the unpredictability of both the demand and supply of hops put market information in pride of place as the spatial precincting factor, a factor that has become widely recognized in agglomerative studies in urban land use (e.g. office location). But even on the hop farms of Kent, the hop acreage rarely exceeded one-fifth, although the remaining acreage was strikingly oriented to complement hop production in one way or another. It is this need for diversification, complementarity and rotation which keeps agricultural agglomeration below the levels reached in industry.

The widespread emergence of cooperatives is another way in which scale economies can be achieved, Denmark probably providing the ultimate example. Not least among the advantages of group marketing is the consumer confidence that can be built up by the exercise of adequate quality standards, and the superior facilities such organizations usually have for the early recognition and adoption of innovations in an activity notorious for its conservatism.

Concentration effects in agriculture can be observed to increase as the city is approached. Partly this is because the specialized crops justified by higher locational returns lend themselves, as we have just seen for hops, to a higher level of scale economies. Partly it is because transport costs here form a much smaller part of the delivered price of a commodity, so justifying more intensive cultivation methods; these in turn ensure an adequate return from the smaller plots that fiercer competition for land produces. The higher costs of land and labour near the city serve to reinforce the need for more intensive methods. The nearer the city, however, the more readily available and cheaper is capital as the distance-imposed uncertainties are diminished, and the more fugitive capital seeks a home in agricultural tax havens. On the immediate rural–urban fringe (Coleman, 1969), the situation suddenly reverses to a position of declining intensity. Sinclair (1967) has shown how land here is held speculatively against imminent urban development by business interests, who either take the land out of farming or let it on short leases to tenants whose investment in the land is minimal. At the same time, urban intrusion is here at its worst, a further discouragement to intensive farming.

Differences in land-use intensities between units of different scales are also apparent. To take one case, Mead (1953), in a review of Finnish farming, finds two important correlates of increasing farm-size: (i) a decline in the amount of cultivated land; and (ii) increasing specialization in 'export' crops. In terms of (i), a survey of farms in the Helsinki area in 1944 showed that about one-third of the area of small family farms (less than 36 hectares) was cultivated, while on larger 250-hectare farms only one-quarter was cultivated. The remainder of the farm area was generally in woodland. For (ii), Mead showed that for small units a large proportion of bread grains was consumed on the farm (90 per cent on farms of less than ten hectares) but that the proportion decreased sharply with size; for farms of over fifty hectares it had fallen to about 5 per cent. In tropical areas, the association between the large operating unit and specialization in export crops is a well-established one. For Ceylon, Farmer (1957) has described the 'dual economy' of the plantation and peasant sectors, and Waibel (1958) has suggested a similar dichotomy in Brazil.

Local scale economies are paralleled by regional advantages. Somewhat akin to Florence's (1953) idea of industrial 'swarming' (Section 5.5.2) is the growth of specialist farm producers who gain economies from common marketing arrangements. California provides a classic case in which an area with marked climatic advantages established itself as the major supplier of citrus fruit to the northeastern United States. The scale of shipment and the standardized product enabled favourable rates to be bargained with the railway companies, so that California was able to undercut nearer but smaller producing areas like Florida. The advent of road transport has permitted Florida to break back into the market since economies of scale appear less important with this form of transport (Chisholm, 1962, p. 191).

Standardized marketing is increasing in Western countries and should allow further scale concentrations of the California type to emerge. Indeed some of the curious concentrations in agricultural production in England—like that of rhubarb cultivation in the West Riding of Yorkshire—may be as well explained as scale concentrations around a random nucleus as by the particular environment of that area.

### 6.5.3 *Distortion due to behavioural variations*

The assumption of a landscape shaped by the profit maximizing rationality of *homo economicus* has been progressively modified over the last few decades. The use of an optimizing assumption is justified by the formidable range of theory and insights that have been achieved by using it. However, the search for alternative modes of explanation and theory-building at the micro-level is now a major concern in human geography. The contrast is illustrated by Wolpert's (1964) study of farm labour productivity for a sample of farms in the Swedish Mellansverige. In this study, he showed that the surface of actual labour productivity (Figure 6.15A) is substantially less than the optimum productivity surface (Figure 6.15B). Optimum values were determined by

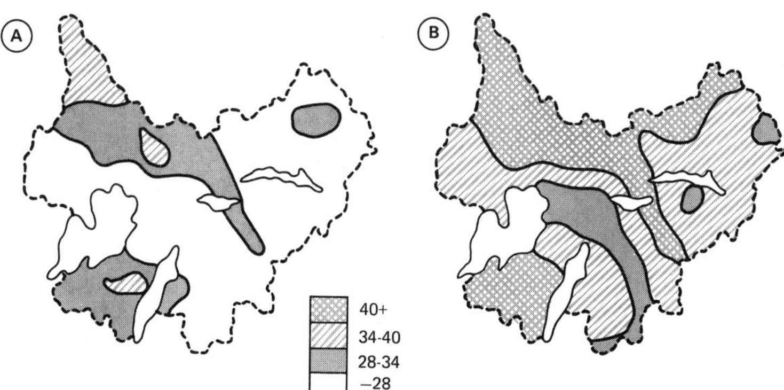


**Figure 6.15** Contrast between the actual (*satisficer*) farm labour productivity surface (**A**) and the potential (*optimizer*) surface (**B**) for the Swedish Mellansverige. Source: Wolpert, 1964, pp. 540, 541.

linear programming (see Chapter 15) for 17 representative farms, and interpolated through regression analysis for the remaining 500 farms. Although such large scale interpolation is not to be recommended under most circumstances, the width of the gap separating the two surfaces was still too great and too consistent at the *control points* to be simply ignored. Less than half the area had performances in excess of 70 per cent of the optimum, and in some pockets, productivity was down to as low as 40 per cent. Wolpert traces the regional incidence of the gap in some detail and concludes that major factors controlling its extent were: (i) the simple fact that Swedish farmers were not aiming at optimum productivity but merely at a satisfactory (but sub-optimal) level; (ii) regional variations in the 'knowledge situation' linked to time lags in the diffusion of information (e.g. of recommended farm practices) from centres like Stockholm and Uppsala; and (iii) uncertainty as to which crop and livestock mixes were likely to prove profitable. These uncertainties were related not only to expected fluctuations of weather or disease, but also to personal uncertainties (e.g. of health or finance) and economic uncertainties about market prices.

Table 6.8 'Expected' production of an agricultural commodity according to a variety of distribution decisions, based on known weather probabilities.*

| *Decision maker* | *Criterion* | Acreage<br>*Steep hills* | *Low hills* | *Plain* | *Valley bottom* | *'Expected' production* (100 *tons*) |
|---|---|---|---|---|---|---|
| Different attributes | gambler | 0 | 0 | 0 | 100 | 23.6 |
| | optimist | 0 | 20 | 0 | 80 | 23.2 |
| | equal-likelihood | 0 | 50 | 0 | 50 | 22.7 |
| | pessimist | 0 | 70 | 0 | 30 | 22.3 |
| Different strategies | maximin | 0 | 65.6 | 0 | 34.4 | 22.4 |
| | minimum regret | 0 | 0 | 100 | 0 | 19.2 |
| Different information levels | knowledge of weather probabilities | 0 | 0 | 0 | 100 | 23.6 |
| | prior knowledge of each year's weather | 0 | 100, 60% of time | 0 | 100, 40% of time | 38.6 |

Source: Found, 1971, p. 122.

* Probability of wet year 0.6. Probability of dry year 0.4.

We assume that wet years incur the risk of flooding, and total crop loss, in the valley bottoms. In dry years, drought is a risk on hill slopes. The valley bottoms have better soils and are assumed to be easier to cultivate than the hill slopes.

We should not be particularly surprised to learn that farmers, in particular, do not maximize utility (that is, do not maximize benefits to themselves) when these benefits are expressed in the economic terms of profit. Many family farms of lower than average size must be close to zero profit after fixed costs have been covered, and we must look to other, possibly psychological, returns to justify their continuance in farming. Although 'satisficing' is an attractive way of describing their behaviour, if this is taken to mean some unknowable level of sub-optimal behaviour, it is an extremely difficult concept to specify precisely. Table 6.8 was devised by Found (1971, p. 122) to give some idea of how different attitudes, strategies and information can lead to different land-use decisions. However, once we recognize that farmers tend to seek collective security by imitative behaviour and that they only make small incremental adjustments, learning as they go if change seems to be necessary, then agglomerative patterns are even more readily expected.

Central and local government interfere increasingly with land-use decisions. Conspicuous is the way in which the designation of Green Belts around the larger British cities led to a pronounced hollow in the curve of residential density, as well as to a displacement and re-ordering of the succession of von Thünen rings around these cities. Zoning regulations in the United States not only control the development of particular land-use types but, by stipulating plot size, determine the style of housing as well. Decisions over urban renewal, as opposed to housing rehabilitation, can alter neighbourhood character and residential density considerably. The way in which the Corn Laws supported the Irish grain trade in defiance of von Thünen's spatial logic has already been quoted, and it is but one example of the massive price support policy many countries use to manipulate agricultural and use and intensity 'in the national interest' (whatever that is). In several of the less developed countries, the government acts as the exclusive buyer of the main agricultural export staples (e.g. cocoa, sugar, coffee), so deriving tax revenues and manipulating production at one and the same time. Selective support for small farms has been a tradition in the United States for well over one hundred years, and the mistaken homestead policies in the southern High Plains put much of the area

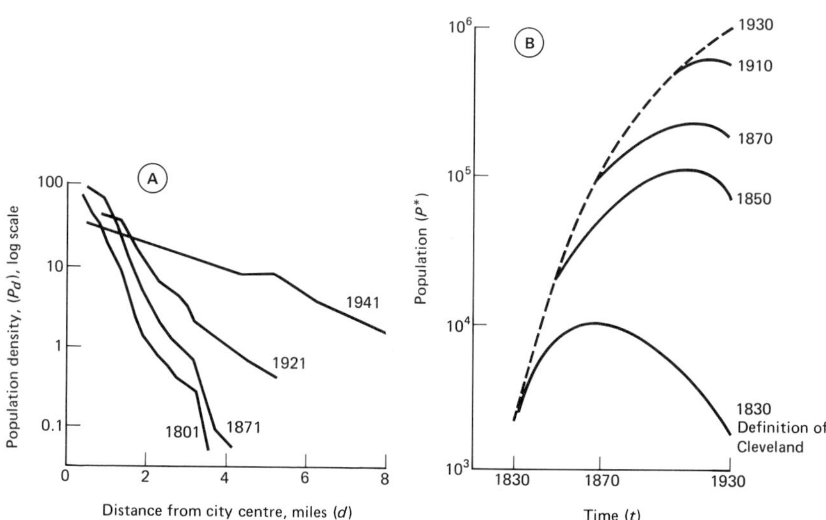


**Figure 6.16** **A** Density-distance relationships for London, 1801–41. **B** Population-time relationships for the city of Cleveland, United States. The *broken* line is the total population curve for Cleveland. Each *solid* line gives the population curve against time for the areas which, in 1830, 1850, 1870, and 1910 were defined as the City of Cleveland. Sources: Berry, Simmons, and Tennant, 1963; McKenzie, 1933.

(and many of the farmers) under increasing strain, until the re-establishment of ranching and dry farming by 1914 brought sanity back to the region (Kollmorgen, 1969). The opposite policy in the USSR and China has resulted in the organization of individual farms into communes, collectives and state farms, with conspicuous effects on land use.

## 6.6 Surface Change Over Time

### 6.6.1 *Slope development models*

(a) *Empirical evidence.* The debate over the nature of the population density gradients around and within cities has covered the ways in which these gradients evolve over time. Two main generalizations can be made on the basis of Clark's studies of the lapse rates around cities when these rates are viewed progressively over time (Clark, 1951). First, he found that the growth of cities was accompanied by a steady *decrease* in density gradient, a 'decompaction' trend. Figure 6.16A reproduces his findings for London for the period 1801–1941, findings which were paralleled for Paris, Berlin, Chicago, New York and Brisbane. Second, he found that the density of central areas, when plotted against time, increased and then decreased. Figure 6.16B illustrates this trend for Cleveland (Ohio, United States). It shows: (i) the overall continuing increase in the total population of Cleveland as indicated by the broken line (from a little under 2,000 in 1830 to near a million by 1930); (ii) continuing expansion of the legal boundaries of the city, implied by the vertical stacking of the solid population curves, as it spread outwards from its centre; (iii) the characteristic rise and then fall in the population of the inner section (for Cleveland, the city, as defined in 1830, reached its peak in population by 1870; thereafter it declined, and by 1930 its population had fallen back to about the same level that it was a century before).

Berry (Berry *et al.*, 1963) corroborated Clark's findings for Western cities, but suggested that they may not be applicable in the case of non-Western

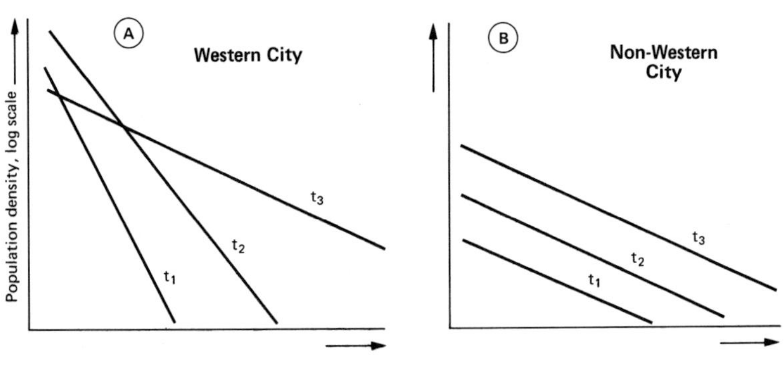


**Figure 6.17** Temporal comparisons of Western (**A**) and non-Western (**B**) cities. Sources: Berry, Simmons, and Tennant, 1963, pp. 400, 403.

cities. From a study of Calcutta from 1881 to 1951, Berry argued that the density gradient remained more or less constant (i.e. there was no 'decompaction' trend) and the central density continued to rise. Thus, while both spatial compactness and crowding diminish over time in Western cities, non-Western cities experience increasing overcrowding, constant compactness, and less expansion of the periphery (Berry and Horton, 1970). See Figure 6.17. If the desire for more spacious living eventually drives the more affluent inhabitants of non-Western cities to residential choices on the edge of city, then we could perhaps regard their present preferences as analogous to those of the affluent in eighteenth-century Western cities. This would imply that non-Western cities are but at an earlier stage in the evolution

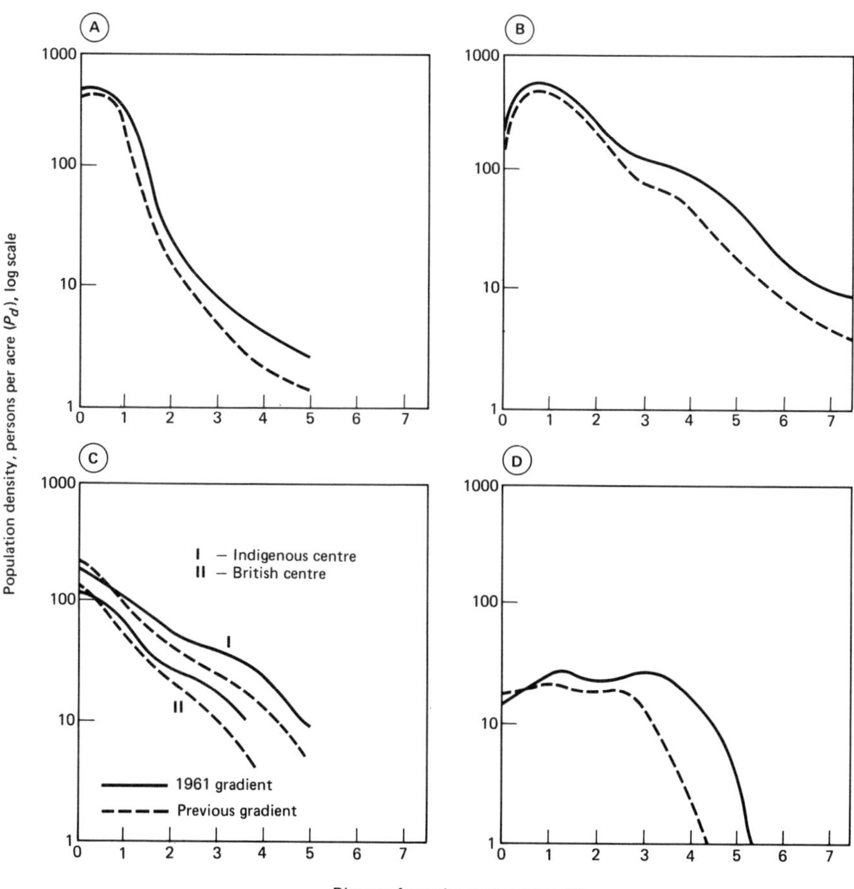


**Figure 6.18** Patterns of change in the density gradients of Indian cities. **A** Central bazaar type. Majority of Indian cities, e.g. Ahmedabad and Poona. **B** Strong British influence. CBD type, e.g. Bombay, Calcutta, Madras. Note the central population crater. **C** Binodal type with bazaar and British centre often 3 miles apart, e.g. Hyderabad, Bangalore. **D** Modern planned cities with no central concentration, e.g. Jamshedpur and Chandigarh. Source: Brush, 1968, p. 373.

of the Western model. In his survey of Indian cities, Brush (1968) found evidence pointing both ways, in that some cities were recognizably indigenously Indian in form, some colonial British, some transitional between the two, and just a few representative of exclusively twentieth-century planning (Figure 6.18).

Clark has attempted a *supply-side* explanation of the spread of a Western city in terms of the twentieth-century availability and lowered cost of rapid transit facilities. In the view of others, however, it is the desire for lower-density living, that only the periphery can provide, which leads the more affluent to the city margin. This results in longer journey-to-work trips which are regarded as an affordable concomitant of what is *demand-based* process. In strong contrast, the more affluent in non-Western cities seek out central city residences, with the result that the least mobile groups occupy the periphery. There they resist as far as they are able the spatial extension of the city and of their journey-to-work trips.

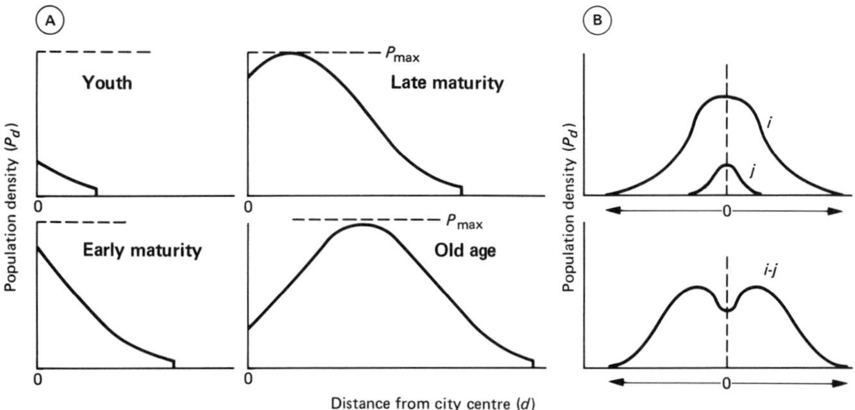


**Figure 6.19** **A** Urban density profiles at successive stages of development under the Newling model. **B** Modelling urban density profiles in terms of differences between normal distribution curves. Source: Newling, 1969, p. 247.

(b) *Statistical generalizations.* Attempts to accommodate the changing pattern of urban population densities over time have led to modifications of the models reviewed earlier in this chapter (Section 6.2.2). For example, Newling (1969) has shown how variations in the parameters of his quadratic exponential model will lead to a characteristic multi-stage succession of density profiles (Figure 6.19A). We could achieve similar results in other ways. For example, if we regard the density surface as a bivariate normal distribution, then the development of the central hollow may be seen simply as the difference between two such distributions (Figure 6.19B). But one heuristic advantage of the Newling model is its notion of a critical population density ($P_{max}$ in Figure 6.19A) to which densities will at first increase, but from which densities will thereafter decrease. Newling specifies this critical density in terms of social costs, speculating that densities above some optimum state cause pathological conditions such as 'intolerable' blight, crime and delinquency; these, in turn lead to a self-regulating fall in density. Some experimental work has been done on the social pathology of humans afflicted by spatial hardship, especially overcrowding, but the evidence is conflicting as yet (Getis and Boots, 1971).

An alternative approach is to substitute city size ($P^*$) as a surrogate for development time. For example, Sanders (1975, pp. 63–4) has shown how Clark's original negative exponential density function [equation (6.4)] can be expressed as a time rate of density growth:

$$\frac{\partial P_d}{\partial P^*} = P_0 e^{-bd}\left(\frac{1}{P_0}\frac{\partial P_0}{\partial b} - d\right)\frac{\partial b}{\partial P^*}. \tag{6.16}$$

$P_d$, $P_0$, $d$ and $b$ are as defined in Section 6.2.2. Solving for distance and city size gives

$$dP^* = \frac{1.\partial P_0}{P_0.\partial b}, \tag{6.17}$$

where $d$ increases in time for a growing city. Sanders is able to show that his distance parameter, $d$, in equation (6.17) marks the 'crest' of the population density wave. This crest represents the dividing line between the central part of the urban area where densities decrease, and the outer part where density is still increasing. Figure 6.20 shows the location of these distance limits for Paris

****

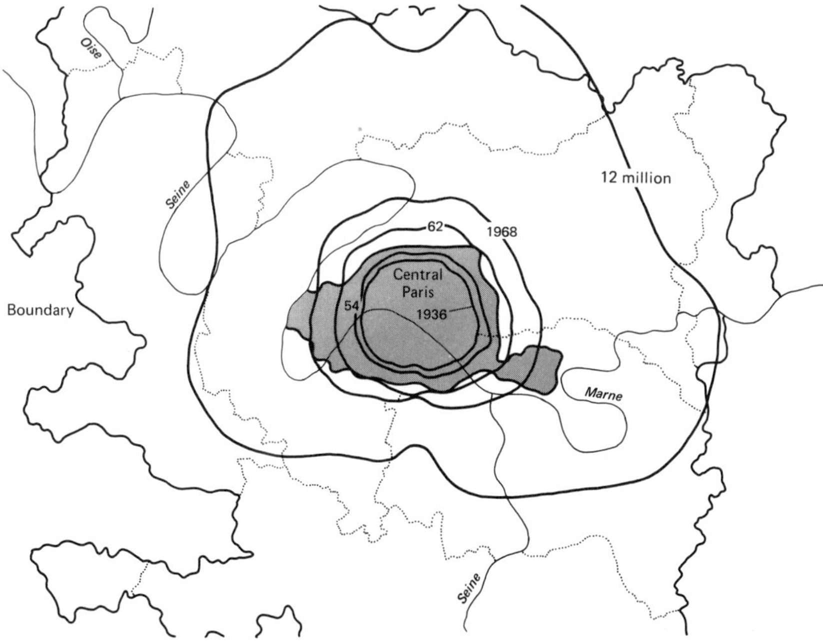


**Figure 6.20** Centrifugal waves of peak population densities in Paris, 1936 to 1968. Source: Sanders, 1975, p. 67.

for 1936, 1954, 1962 and 1968 in relation to the outer limit of the metropolitan area whose total population ($P^*$) in the end period was 12 million inhabitants. Note that the centrifugal wave crests shown in Figure 6.20 are irregular and *not* circular. This is due to Sanders's modifications of equations (6.16) and (6.17) for different azimuthal sectors around the city centre. Evidence of sectoral variation within an urban area is available from empirical work in northwest Glasgow by Whitehand (1972). He emphasizes the wave-like form in which cycles of business boom lead to wave-like emphases on residential building at different points on the margins of the city.

### 6.6.2 *Step development models*

It is a curious paradox that, although the von Thünen model of land use steps (a *static* model) was developed primarily for rural zones, the major models of step development through time (dynamic models) were developed for urban zones. In the same way that von Thünen is applicable to both urban and rural areas, the dynamic models can be likewise extended. Johnston (1971) is the standard work on these urban zoning models, and only three of the simplest are reviewed here:

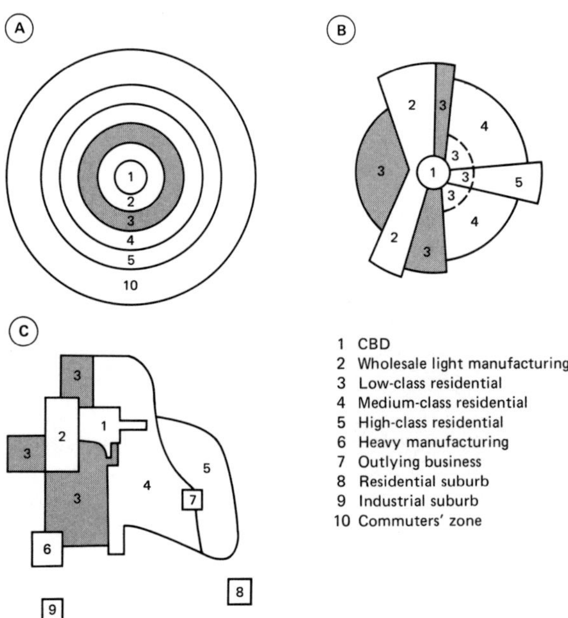


**Figure 6.21** Density-area relationships under the concentric (**A**), sector (**B**), and polynuclear (**C**) models of urban expansion. Source: Pred, 1964, p. 167.

(i) The *concentric-zone* model (Figure 6.21A) was put forward by Burgess (1927) and is based largely on his studies of urban growth in the Chicago area (Dickinson, 1964, pp. 131–44). The theory suggests that a city expands radially from its centre so as to form a series of concentric zones or annules. For

Chicago, the five annules were, in order from the centre outwards: (a) an inner central business district; (b) a transition zone surrounding the central business district with residential areas being 'invaded' by business and industry from the inner core; (c) a 'working class' residential district; (d) a zone of better residences with single-family dwellings; and (e) an outer zone of commuting with suburban areas and satellite cities. Although Burgess acknowledged that this simple annular pattern would be inevitably modified by terrain, routes, and so on, he nevertheless considered that each inner zone extended by colonization of the next outer zone, and that therefore radial expansion along a broad front was the dominant process in shaping the pattern of the city area.

Although the arguments over the Burgess model have been largely confined to urban areas, there is no *a priori* reason why it should not be equally applicable to rural areas. Waibel (1958) has identified a series of semi-concentric zones developing around the areas of early German colonization in southern Brazil, while the history of the colonization of the Argentine Pampas is one in which high-value land use (e.g. wheat farming) progressively pushed lower value uses (e.g. sheep raising) to the outer margins of the area (James, 1959, pp. 324–55). Fusion of the static von Thünen model with the dynamic Burgess model might yield a useful descriptive tool for the analysis of European overseas settlement (Thomas, 1956, pp. 721–62).

(ii) An alternative approach to urban growth patterns was put forward by Hoyt (1939) as the *sector* model (Figure 6.21B). Studies of rent levels in American cities led him to argue that the different types of residential areas tended to grow outwards along distinct radii, with new growth on the outer arc of a sector reproducing the character of earlier growth in that sector. Hoyt's model is clearly an improvement on the earlier Burgess model in that both distance and direction from the city centre are taken into consideration, thereby meeting some of the criticism of the annular model, e.g. on the grounds that cities like Paris (Dickinson, 1964, pp. 144–52) were more star-shaped than circular in their pattern of growth.

Again, the sector model is equally applicable to rural growth processes. Monbeig (1952) has shown how successive periods in the expansion of the 'coffee frontier' in southeastern Brazil were channelled along the valley of the Paraíba river. The sequential regularity of growth, boom, and abandonment led to the development of a variant of the sector hypothesis, the *hollow-frontier* hypothesis, which has bemused so much of the thinking on Brazilian settlement expansion. Sector growth from a base-line, rather than a centre, has been used by Sauer in an interpretation of the development of the major agricultural zones in the eastern United States; here the character of the settlers on the Atlantic base-line (e.g. German settlers in Pennsylvania) was progressively transferred westwards with the 'frontier movement' into the trans-Appalachian areas.

(iii) A *multiple-nuclei model* (Figure 6.21C) was put forward by Harris and Ullman (1945) in a modification of the two foregoing models. They suggested that the pattern of growth is centred on not one, but a series, of distinct urban centres. The number of such growth centres is a function of both the historical development and of the locational forces which aggregate some functions but scatter others. The problem of why some areas become active diffusion centres while others lie dormant has been pursued more actively for rural zones than for urban. Thus Sauer (1952) devoted his Bowman Lectures to the problem of agricultural *hearths* in both the New World and the Old and his findings, controversial though they may be, have stirred up interest and debate on this topic. Spencer and Horvath (1963) have also inquired into the origins of three modern but distinctive agricultural zones, the North American 'Corn Belt', the Philippine 'Coconut Zone', and the Malayan 'Rubber Zone'. It is an

****

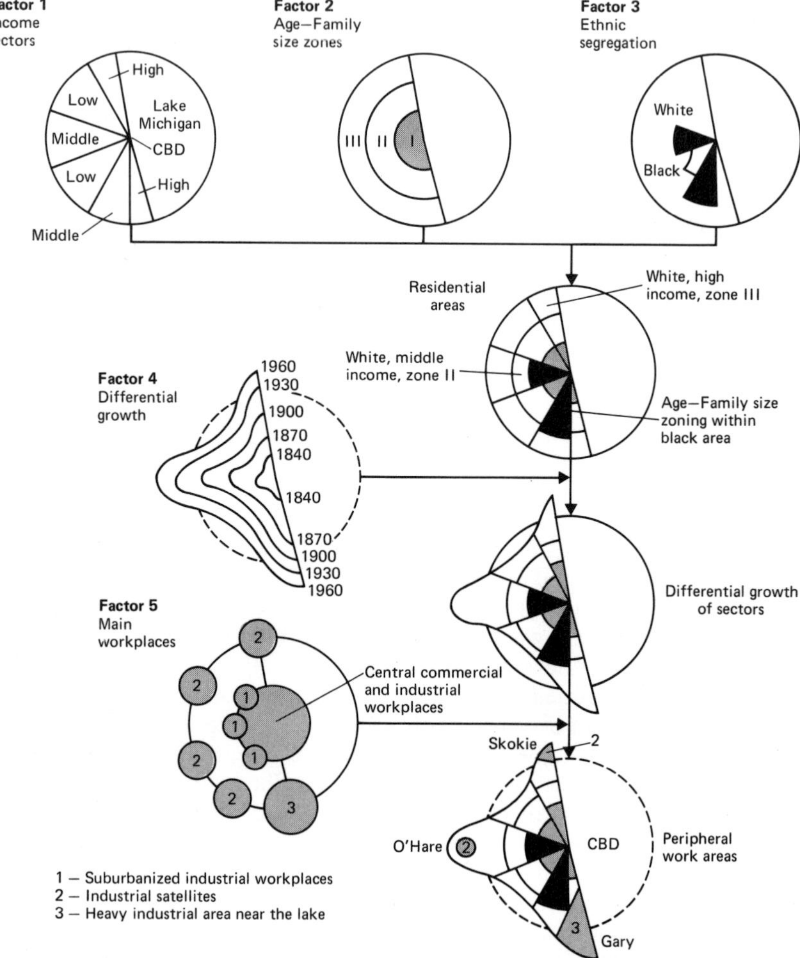


**Figure 6.22** The regional structure of Chicago. Much of the variety within Chicago's semicircular urban structure (itself a product of the lakeshore location) can be explained by the combined effect of five factors. The arrows show the ways in which factors are crossbred together in this simplified model of the city. From P. H. Rees, University of Chicago, unpublished master's thesis, 1968. Reproduced in Berry and Horton, 1970, p. 310.

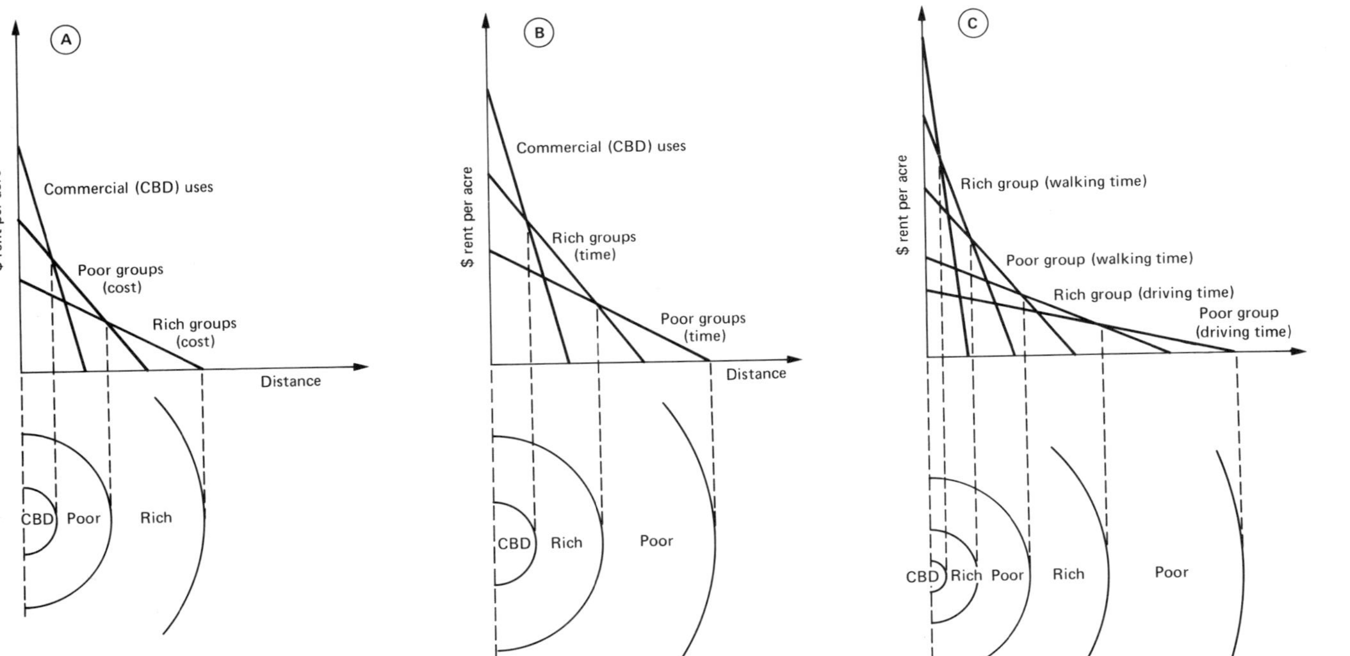


**Figure 6.23** Residential choice by rich and poor under different cost assumptions. **A** Land use patterns based on ability to pay the costs of travel. **B** Land use patterns based on the opportunity costs of travel time to rich and poor. **C** Land use patterns based on the opportunity costs of travel time disaggregated by travel mode. Source: Harvey, 1972, pp. 17 and 18.

interesting but unanswered question whether the diffusion models discussed in Chapter 7, which have so far been applied to spread from known centres, might be reversed (run backwards) so as to give some clue as to the probable location of the nuclei from which growth springs.

The three models—the concentric-zone, sector, and multiple-nuclei—are not, of course, mutually exclusive. Figure 6.22 suggests a fused growth model, in which growth proceeds radially both from the centre and from other sub-nuclei, but which is intersected by axial growth pushing outwards along the transport lines from the main centre. Progressive 'sorting' of industry and residences into distinct social, economic, and technical zones is also assimilated within this general model. The current problems facing urban societies have made it difficult to view with detached academic equanimity such spatial sorting processes, which are imposed upon the population, especially the poor, by their lack of ability both to occupy the high location-rent sites their low travel-capacity demands, and to maintain reasonable levels of living and personal space. Morrill's (1965) study of the Negro ghetto marked for geographers the beginning of a new era of concern for welfare, and of concern for disadvantaged minorities in particular. In general, this concern was accompanied by a willingness to apply conventional analysis to seek fresh explanations and solutions for social problems. Distinctive of this trend in terms of models of residential location and employment opportunities has been the work of Alonso (1964) and Muth (1969), while Bunge (1971) and Harvey (1972, 1973) have carried the reasons for change much deeper into the societal structure of capitalism itself. Their argument is now against the 'exploitation, and appropriation of surplus value by industrial capitalism' and the 'impaction of the poor into environments of inner-city deprivation' by the 'exploitation of the many by the few'. Figure 6.23 puts this kind of thinking into a von Thünian framework.

## 6.7 Conclusions

The study of surfaces has emphasized (i) the regular gradients in population densities and associated attributes both within and between cities and (ii) the spatial sorting processes which lead to them and to the discrete steps in land use zones. The classic von Thünen approach to land-use zoning has been shown to be a geometric variant of the general Weberian location problem of Chapter 5, and therefore capable of being approached via the linear programming formulations of Chapter 15. The introduction of dynamic elements into surface formation as, for example, in Sanders's model of centrifugal density waves discussed in Section 6.6, leads directly to a consideration of diffusion processes in the chapter which follows.

# 7 Diffusion

7.1 **Introduction.** 7.2 **The Hägerstrand Model:** 1 The neighbourhood effect; 2 Formal model structure. 7.3 **The Logistic Curve.** 7.4 **Central Place Diffusion.** 7.5 **Diffusion Barriers and Corridors:** 1 Barriers; 2 Corridors. 7.6 **Goodness-of-fit of Diffusion Models with Reality:** 1 Nature of the comparison problem; 2 Testing procedures. 7.7 **Epidemic Models*:** 1 Types of epidemic model; 2 Results for the simple epidemic model; 3 Results for the general epidemic model; 4 Bartlett's spatial epidemic model; 5 Rapoport's network models; 6 Chain binomial models; 7 Hierarchical and group models. 7.8 **Conclusions.**

## 7.1 Introduction

The Oxford English Dictionary defines *diffuse* as 'to disperse or be dispersed from a centre; to spread widely, disseminate.' Studies concerned with the spread of various phenomena over the earth's surface have accounted for a major portion of geographical research effort over the last 60 years. For example, in the United States the Berkeley School, led by Carl O. Sauer, played a central role in the development of diffusion-type analysis in American geography (Clark, 1954). Sauer and his students were interested in how diffusion processes might help to account for the dispersal of cultural traits from given origins or cultural hearths. This topic has long been of concern to archaeologists as a way of accounting for the widespread dissemination of cultural traits, as opposed to postulating multiple independent origins. Typical studies of this sort are those of Sauer and Brand (1930), who attempted to deduce the culture areas and successions in Southeastern Arizona from archaeological evidence collected at various Pueblo sites, and of Stanislawski (1946), who traced the diffusion of the grid-pattern town in the Americas. Sauer himself considered the cultural diffusion idea at the world scale in *Agricultural origins and dispersals* (Sauer, 1952).

It was in the United States too, that the historian, Frederick Jackson Turner, developed his great theme of the frontier in American history; a theme taken up by Webb (1927) in his classic regional study of the central grasslands of the United States, *The Great Plains*. In geometric terms at least, Turner's frontier thesis was a simple one. He saw the tide of innovations moving remorselessly outwards from the Eastern seaboard: '. . . stand at the Cumberland Gap and watch the procession of civilization, marching single file—the buffalo following the trail to the salt springs, the Indian, the fur trader and hunter, the cattle raiser, the pioneer farmer—and the frontier has passed by. Stand at South Pass in the Rockies a century later and see the same procession with wider intervals between' (Turner, 1920, p. 12).

Gulley (1959) and Mikesell (1960) have shown how Turner's ideas spread rapidly to areas outside North America. They were applied enthusiastically, if indiscriminately, to movements as unlike as the Russian settlement of Siberia and the Roman occupation of Europe, and ranged widely in time and space over human migration. Like the Davisian cycle in geomorphology, the frontier concept was weakened by its extension to explain aspects of historical growth that lay well outside its competence, and in recent years it has come in for severe criticism from historians. Nevertheless it played an important part in the development of human geography in the inter-war years. Isaiah Bowman led a vigorous school in the United States concerned with the frontiers of settlement in various parts of the world, and the findings, published by the American Geographical Society as *The Pioneer Fringe* (Bowman, 1931) and *Pioneer Settlement* (Joerg, 1932), have become classics of that period. Since 1945, the tide of urbanization has begun to run so fiercely that interest in the extension of rural settlement has, with some notable exceptions (e.g. Parsons, 1949; Farmer, 1957), been on the wane.

A second line of approach to diffusion study has come from the field of sociology. Here the concern has been with the spread of concepts through a society, the role of leaders in starting such innovations, and the problem of resistance to change. Rogers (1962) has reviewed some hundreds of such studies, largely concerned with the innovation of new techniques through the farming communities of the United States, but ranging back to include Neolithic diffusion rates (Edmondson, 1961). The bonds between this type of social study with its strong links with market research and sales resistance, the historical study of the Turnerian school, and the geographical studies of diffusion of the Berkeley School were forged in 1952 by a Swedish geographer, Torsten Hägerstrand.

In his 1952 paper, Hägerstrand developed inductively a four-stage model in which he tried to organize existing information about the passage of what he termed 'innovation waves' (*innovationsförloppet*). From isarithmic maps of the diffusion of various innovations in Sweden, ranging from motor-bus routes (Godlund, 1956) to agricultural methods, he constructed a series of cross-profiles. Study of the profiles suggested certain repeating patterns in the diffusion process. Figure 7.1A shows a profile in which the ordinate represents the innovation ratio (that is, the proportion of the population with the introduced item) plotted on a logarithmic scale. The abscissa represents distance. Point $d_1$ is the centre of innovation and points $d_2$ and $d_3$ are at locations increasingly remote from that centre. The four stages are shown by profiles I–IV in Figure 7.1A: Stage I, termed the *primary* stage, marks the beginning of the diffusion process with a strong contrast between the innovating centres and the remote areas; Stage II, the *diffusion* stage, marks the diffusion process proper, in which there is a strong centrifugal effect with the creation of new, rapidly growing centres in the distant areas and a reduction in the regional contrasts of Stage I; in Stage III, the *condensing* stage, the relative increase is equal in all three locations; in Stage IV, the *saturation* stage, there is a general, but slow, asymptotic increase towards the maximum under existing conditions. As an illustration of this process, Figure 7.1B shows the diffusion of a recent innovation (radio receivers) along a profile from Malmö to Hässleholm in southern Sweden in the years between 1925 and 1947. Certainly by 1945 this innovation appeared to be reaching the saturation stage.

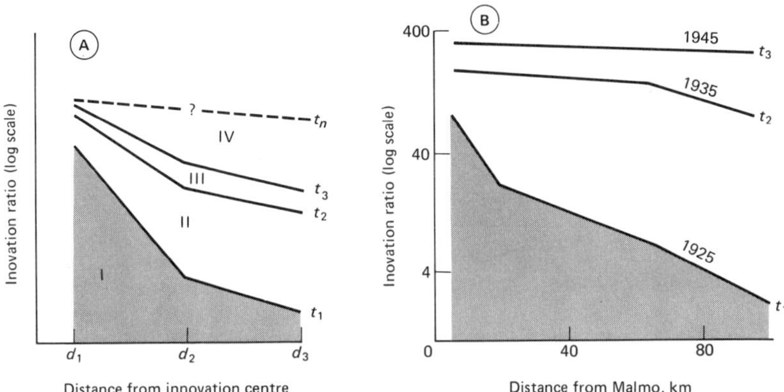


**Figure 7.1** Hypothetical (**A**) and actual (**B**) profiles of innovation waves. Source: Hägerstrand, 1952, pp. 13, 17.

A third research area in which spatial diffusion has been widely considered is epidemiology, where interest has centred upon modelling the spatial pattern of spread of various diseases. Measles epidemics, in particular, have been extensively studied (cf. Section 11.5 and Bailey, 1957). This sort of analysis has also been undertaken recently in veterinary science in an effort to understand the process of spread of animal diseases. Foot-and-mouth epizootics (Tinline, 1972) and fowl pest (Gilg, 1973) have received particular attention.

It is evident from the above discussion that many topics in many disciplines have been looked upon as diffusion phenomena. We have mentioned cultural traits, migration, settlement growth, technological innovations, and human and animal diseases, covering subjects like geography, history, archaeology, communication theory, market research, and epidemiological and veterinary science. Brown (1968) and Brown and Moore (1969) have provided extensive bibliographies on the various research strands, and these authors have also attempted to synthesize the various approaches within a common conceptual framework. In this chapter, a smaller canvas is painted. Our emphasis is upon stochastic models of the diffusion process for the time-space spread of ideas, news, rumours, innovations, diseases, etc., among human (and animal) populations. The literature considered is drawn mainly from geography and epidemiology. Within geography, the work of Hägerstrand and his models of the diffusion process published in the early 1950s are outstanding. Hägerstrand's (1952, 1953) papers have formed the basis of most geographical model building efforts over the last twenty years. Because of the central position of Hägerstrand's work, and because his model raises important issues which have only recently been tackled, we consider Hägerstrand's work in some detail in Section 7.2. The issues raised are discussed in Sections 7.3–7.6. The remainder of the chapter is devoted to epidemiological studies. This literature is not well known among geographers, but the models proposed by some epidemiologists are among the few outside geography which incorporate explicit spatial elements.

## 7.2 The Hägerstrand Model

Hägerstrand selected the Asby district of south-central Sweden to study the spatial pattern of acceptance by local farmers of various agricultural innovations (Figure 7.2). One such was a subsidy which the Swedish government granted from 1928 onwards to farmers of small units ($\leqslant 8$ hectares of tilled land) if they enclosed woodland on their farms and converted it to pasture. The study area was divided into 125, $5 \times 5$ km$^2$, cells. The total number of farms in each cell which had accepted the subsidy by the ends of 1929, 1930, 1931 and 1932 was recorded. Hägerstrand then developed a Monte

**Figure 7.2** The village of Asby in the wooded area of central Sweden provided data for classic early migration and diffusion studies. The 1:10,000 map shows cultivated fields in black. Source: Ekonomisk Karte over Sverige 1:10,000 air photographs, 1945; additional cartographic detail, 1948.

Carlo model to simulate the recorded numbers of acceptors (adopters, tellers or carriers) of the subsidy in each cell up to the end of the three observation years, 1930–32. The model was *stochastic* in the sense that the specification of the system incorporated an element of chance (randomness), as opposed to being *deterministic* (having only one possible outcome).

### 7.2.1 *The neighbourhood effect*

In the developing his model, Hägerstrand assumed that the decision of a potential adopter (any farm $\leqslant 8$ hectares of tilled land which had not yet accepted the subsidy) to accept the subsidy was based solely upon information received orally at face to face meetings between the potential adopter (susceptible) and carriers. It was further assumed that the probability of a potential adopter being paired with a carrier had a strong inverse relationship with geographical distance between the teller and the receiver. This assumption was made because Hägerstrand had noted that the spatial development of many diffusion processes seems to be characterized by the addition of new adopters around the original nuclei of introduction of the innovation (cf. Figure 7.1). This contagious growth has been called the *neighbourhood effect*, and it is one of three empirical regularities commonly noted in diffusion processes (Brown and Cox, 1971). Hägerstrand (1965a, cited in Brown and Cox, 1971) has commented:

> The main spatial similarity is, briefly, that the probability of a new adoption is highest in the vicinity of an earlier one and decreases with increasing distances. Later events seem to be dependent on earlier ones according to a principle for which the term 'neighbourhood effect' would be apt.

### 7.2.2 *Formal model structure*

The Monte Carlo model employed in the Asby study had the following structure:
(1) The input numbers and spatial locations in the model of adopters and potential adopters were the actual configurations in 1929.
(2) A potential adopter was assumed to accept the subsidy as soon as he was told by an adopter.
(3) In each iteration of the model, every adopter was allowed to contact one other person, adopter or non-adopter. The probability, $P_i$, that a carrier would contact an individual located in the $i$th cell of the model plane is shown in Figure 7.3. Each cell in the floating grid is $5 \times 5$ km$^2$, as in the study lattice, and outside the grid $P_i = 0$. These probabilities were estimated from an analysis of migration and telephone traffic data. The floating grid was placed over each existing adopter in turn, so that the adopter was located in the central cell of this *mean information field* (MIF). What Figure 7.3 tells us is that an adopter located in the centre of the central cell of the MIF has approximately a 44 per cent chance of contacting someone within (about) 0–$2\frac{1}{2}$ km of himself, and that this contact probability decays over space to less than

one per cent at a distance of about 14 km (along diagonals) from the adopter and to zero per cent beyond 14–18 km.

| | | | | |
|---|---|---|---|---|
| 0.0096 | 0.0140 | 0.0168 | 0.0140 | 0.0096 |
| 0.0140 | 0.0301 | 0.0547 | 0.0301 | 0.0140 |
| 0.0168 | 0.0547 | 0.4431 | 0.0547 | 0.0168 |
| 0.0140 | 0.0301 | 0.0547 | 0.0301 | 0.0140 |
| 0.0096 | 0.0140 | 0.0168 | 0.0140 | 0.0096 |

**Figure 7.3** Hägerstrand's mean information field.

The location of each carrier's contact was determined in two steps. First, a random number (see Table A6), $r$, $0 \leqslant r \leqslant 1$, from a rectangular distribution located the cell $i$ according to the rule,

$$\sum_{m=1}^{i-1} Q_m < r < \sum_{m=1}^{i} Q_m, \tag{7.1}$$

where $Q_m$, the probability of a contact in cell $m$ with population $n_m$ is

$$Q_m = \frac{P_m n_m}{\sum_{m=1}^{25} P_m n_m}. \tag{7.2}$$

A second random number from a rectangular distribution on $[1, n_m]$ was drawn to locate the receiver in the cell. If the receiver was a potential adopter, he immediately became an adopter by rule (2); if the receiver was an existing adopter, the message was lost; if the receiver was identical with the carrier, a new address was sampled.

(4) To take into account the reduction in interpersonal communication likely to be caused by physical features such as rivers and forests, two simplified types of barrier were introduced into the model plane, namely zero- and half-contact barriers (see also Section 7.5.1). When an address crossed a half-contact barrier, the telling was cancelled with probability 0.5. However, two half-contact barriers in combination were considered equal to one zero-contact barrier.

Using this model, Hägerstrand performed a series of computer runs to simulate the spatial patterns of acceptance of the improved pasture subsidy by farmers in the study area. Hägerstrand (1967, pp. 23–5) gives the results from three runs of the model. See Figure 7.4 for the results of one of these runs. Hägerstrand's model raises several points of interest which we now discuss.

****

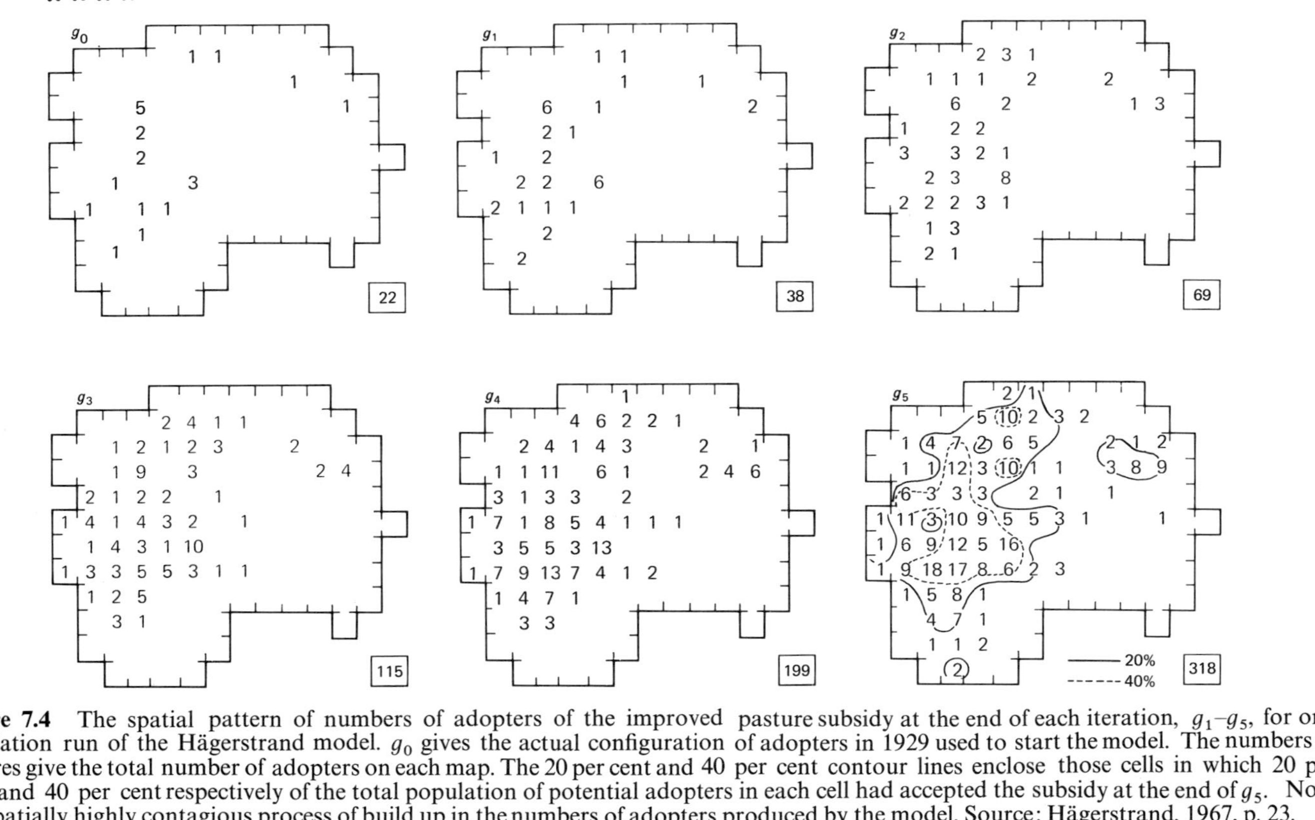


**Figure 7.4** The spatial pattern of numbers of adopters of the improved pasture subsidy at the end of each iteration, $g_1$–$g_5$, for one simulation run of the Hägerstrand model. $g_0$ gives the actual configuration of adopters in 1929 used to start the model. The numbers in squares give the total number of adopters on each map. The 20 per cent and 40 per cent contour lines enclose those cells in which 20 per cent and 40 per cent respectively of the total population of potential adopters in each cell had accepted the subsidy at the end of $g_5$. Note the spatially highly contagious process of build up in the numbers of adopters produced by the model. Source: Hägerstrand, 1967, p. 23.

## 7.3 The Logistic Curve

As we have noted, Hägerstrand believed that the spatial pattern of acceptance of an innovation tends to proceed by the neighbourhood effect. If we consider the temporal build-up in the numbers of adopters in a study area, we encounter the second of three empirical regularities commonly associated with diffusion processes. If the total susceptible population at the start ($t = 0$) of the process is known, then the cumulative proportion of that total who will have become adopters at $t = 1, 2, \ldots$ commonly follows an S-shaped curve when plotted against $t$. See Figure 7.5. We use $p_t$ to denote, at time $t$, the proportion of adopters in the total population at risk. Figure 7.5 implies that acceptance of an innovation is rather slow at first. This is followed by a rapid build-up as the innovation 'takes off'. Ultimately, there is a levelling out as saturation of the susceptible population is approached. The model most commonly fitted to curves of the form of Figure 7.5 is the logistic one. See, for example, Griliches (1957), Mansfield (1961), Casetti (1969), Casetti and Semple (1969) and Cliff and Ord (1975d) for detailed applications.

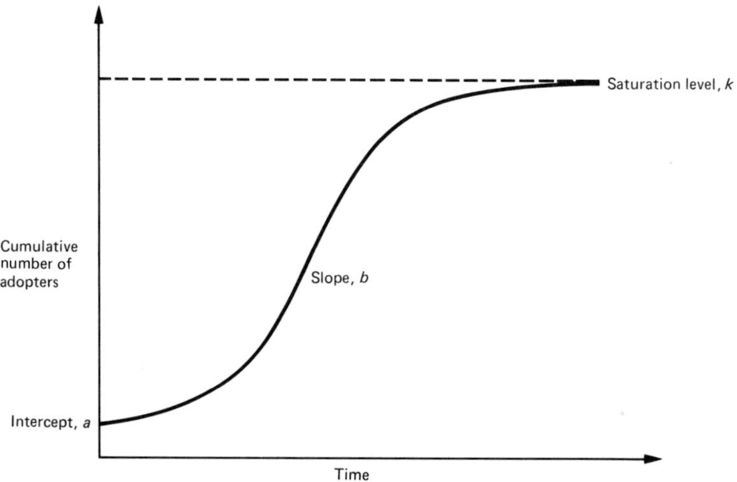


**Figure 7.5** The logistic curve.

The logistic model is given by

$$p_t = (1 + e^{a-bt})^{-1}, \tag{7.3}$$

or

$$y_t = k(1 + e^{a-bt})^{-1}, \tag{7.4}$$

where $p_t$ is defined above, $y_t$ is the *number* (as opposed to *proportion*) of adopters, and $a$, $b$ and $k$ are parameters. The model is readily fitted by ordinary least squares, since both equations (7.3) and (7.4) reduce to simple regressions on taking natural logarithms of both sides. The parameter $k$ is usually interpreted as the maximum possible number of adopters (the saturation level), $a$ is the intercept, and $b$ is the slope coefficient.

The structure of model (7.3) is made clearer by looking at the first derivative, or the rate of change, $r_t$, in $p_t$ with respect to time, where, from Cliff and Ord (1975b),

$$r_t = \frac{d}{dt}p_t = -bp_t(1-p_t). \tag{7.5}$$

Since $p_t$ is the proportion of the susceptible population who have actually adopted by $t$, $(1-p_t)$ is the proportion still at risk. As Cliff and Ord (1975b) have noted, the quantity, $p_t(1-p_t)$, then represents the probability that a random meeting between two individuals is between an adopter and a potential adopter, while the parameter $b$ represents the rate at which meetings take place (the rate of mixing). Note that $b$ is the same *whatever the distance between the adopter and the potential adopter*; that is, (7.5) implies spatially homogeneous mixing between adopters and potential adopters. Hudson (1969) and Cliff and Ord (1975b) have commented that this assumption is apparently in conflict with the neighbourhood effect discussed earlier. Cliff and Ord (1975b) have suggested the following extension of the logistic model which allows homogeneous mixing within $n$ regions ($i = 1, 2, ..., n$), but less mixing between regions [cf. Rapoport's (1951) distance biased net or 'island' model]:

$$r_{it} = (1-p_{it})(b_i p_{it} + \sum_{j \neq i} c_{ij} p_{jt}). \tag{7.6}$$

Here, $c_{ij}$ is the rate of mixing between the $i$th and $j$th regions. Equation (7.6) reduces to (7.5) for each $i$ when all $c_{ij} = 0$. Casetti and Semple (1969) have also considered extensions of the logistic model to handle inhomogeneous mixing as a function of the distance between adopters and potential adopters. Their models may be applied provided that a diffusion pole (that is, the original centre from which the diffusion process started) can be specified. Model (7.6) does not demand this *a priori* specification. Cliff and Ord (1975d) have applied a model of the form of (7.6) to data on the adoption of tractors in the central farming region of the United States, and have shown how the model may be structured to test hypotheses about the existence of diffusion poles.

The suggestion of a conflict between the simple logistic model and the neighbourhood effect may be more apparent than real. As Brown and Cox (1971) have noted, the logistic is but one of several functions (for example, the cumulative normal or ogive) which could be fitted to S-shaped curves of the sort shown in Figure 7.5. The main virtues of the logistic are its ease of fitting and the 'natural' interpretation of the parameters from an empirical point of view. Nor, indeed, is the evidence for a strict neighbourhood effect conclusive. For example, Cliff (1968) was unable to detect such an effect in some of Hägerstrand's original maps, while McClellan (1973) also concluded that there was no simple neighbourhood effect in the spatial pattern of acceptance by farmers of some agricultural innovations in Western Scotland. In addition, in modern industrialized societies, the role of mass media, as opposed to interpersonal communication, in the spread of information about innovations may need some reassessment. Mass media may contribute towards the breakdown of a strict neighbourhood effect by the creation of multiple poles from which the innovation can spread.

## 7.4 Central Place Diffusion

For certain kinds of innovations, for example fashions, we might expect there to be a strong central place hierarchy effect in the adoption régime, as opposed to a simple neighbourhood effect. Thus Hägerstrand (1967; cited in Hudson, 1969, and Cliff and Ord, 1975b) has stated:

> A closer analysis shows that the spread along the initial 'frontier' is led through the urban hierarchy. The point of introduction in a new country is its primate city, sometimes some other metropolis. Then centres next in rank follow. Soon, however, this order is broken up and replaced by one where the neighbourhood effect dominates over the pure size succession.

Table 7.1 Comparison of the speed of different diffusion processes in an idealized landscape.

| | *Number of settlements affected at each period** | | |
|---|---|---|---|
| *Time periods* | *Purely hierarchic process* | *Purely neighbourhood effect* | *Combined hierarchical and neighbourhood process* |
| $t_1$ | 1 (33%) | 1 (33%) | 1 (33%) |
| $t_2$ | 3 (56 %) | 7 (41%) | 9 (63%) |
| $t_3$ | 9 (78%) | 13 (58%) | 27 (100%) |
| $t_4$ | 27 (100%) | 19 (85%) | — |
| $t_5$ | — | 26 (98%) | — |
| $t_6$ | — | 27 (100%) | — |

Source: Christaller $k = 3$ landscape; see Figure 7.6.

* Figures in brackets indicate the proportion of population contacted at each time period where population and hierarchic ranks are related in the following manner: A settlements (27 population units), B settlements (9 population units), C settlements (3 population units) and D settlements (1 population unit).

Diffusion down the central place hierarchy is the third commonly noted empirical regularity for diffusion processes cited in Brown and Cox (1971). Notice, however, that Hägerstrand is arguing for a mixed central-place/neighbourhood-effect process, rather than either alone. An empirical example of such a mixed process is considered in some detail in Section 11.5. Hudson (1969) rejects the idea of pure hierarchical diffusion (that is, no neighbourhood effect) on the grounds that the temporal cumulative build-up of adopters will not follow the logistic curve, and he looks at a mixed hierarchical/spatially contagious process which does yield an S-shaped curve. Alves (1974) has disputed Hudson's suggestion that pure hierarchical diffusion will not produce a logistic build-up, and he proposes a hierarchical model which does. Hierarchical diffusion processes are also considered in Pedersen (1970), Berry (1972) and Hudson (1972). The precise structure of hierarchical models is outlined more fully in Section 7.7.7.

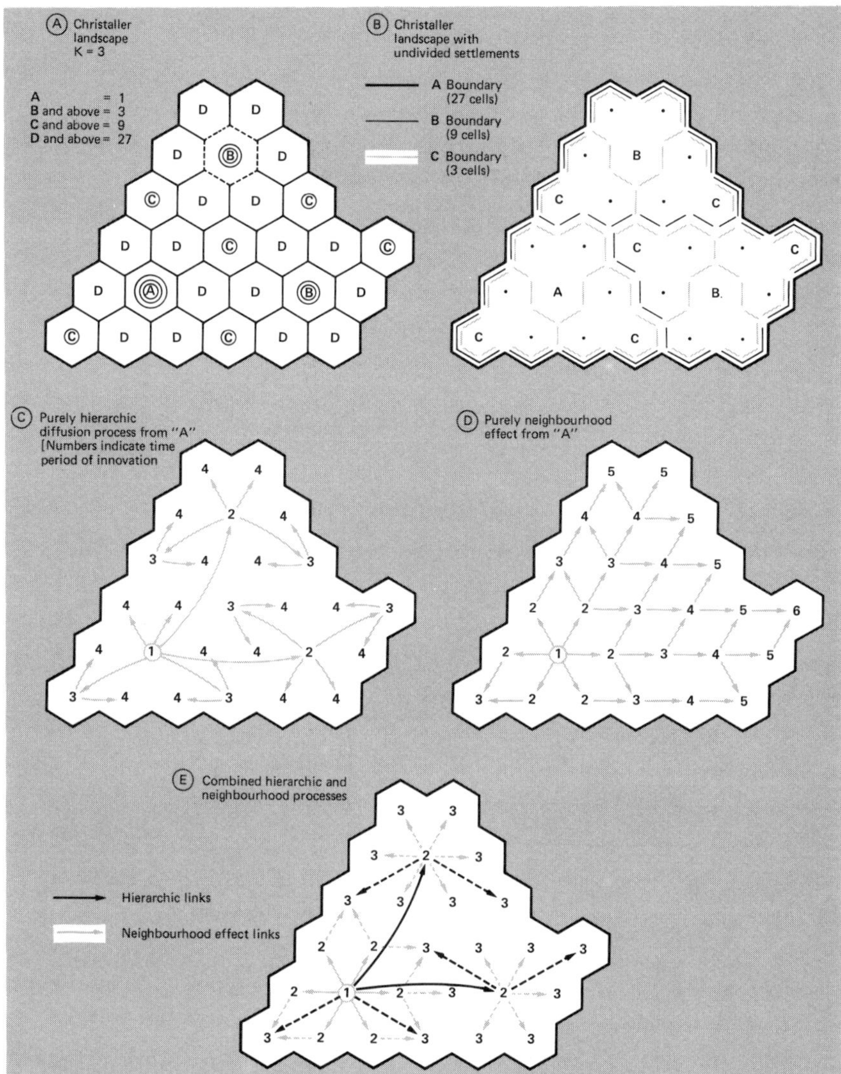


**Figure 7.6** Patterns of diffusion: **A** Christaller landscape $k = 3$; **B** Christaller landscape with undivided settlements; **C** Purely hierarchic diffusion process from 'A' (numbers indicate time period of innovation); **D** Purely neighbourhood effect from 'A'; **E** Combined hierarchic and neighbourhood processes.

It is evident from the discussion in Sections 7.3 and 7.4 that there are many loose ends when any attempt is made to achieve consistency between the neighbourhood effect, hierarchical diffusion and the logistic curve. Probably most diffusion processes are a pot-pourri of all three regularities. See Figure 7.6 and Table 7.1. More work on the consistency problem is required on the lines proposed by Brown and Cox (1971).

## 7.5 Diffusion Barriers and Corridors

### 7.5.1 *Barriers*

Hägerstrand's use of barriers to model the reduction in interpersonal communication caused by physical features such as mountains and rivers gave rise to an interesting Monte Carlo investigation by Yuill (1965) of the detailed effect of different kinds of barriers upon innovation waves. Yuill's study area comprised a 30 × 18 regular lattice of cells, and his MIF was 3 × 3 rather than 5 × 5 as in Figure 7.3. Figure 7.7A gives the MIF, and we assume that two initial adopters (the solid circles) have been located in the central cell. Imagine further

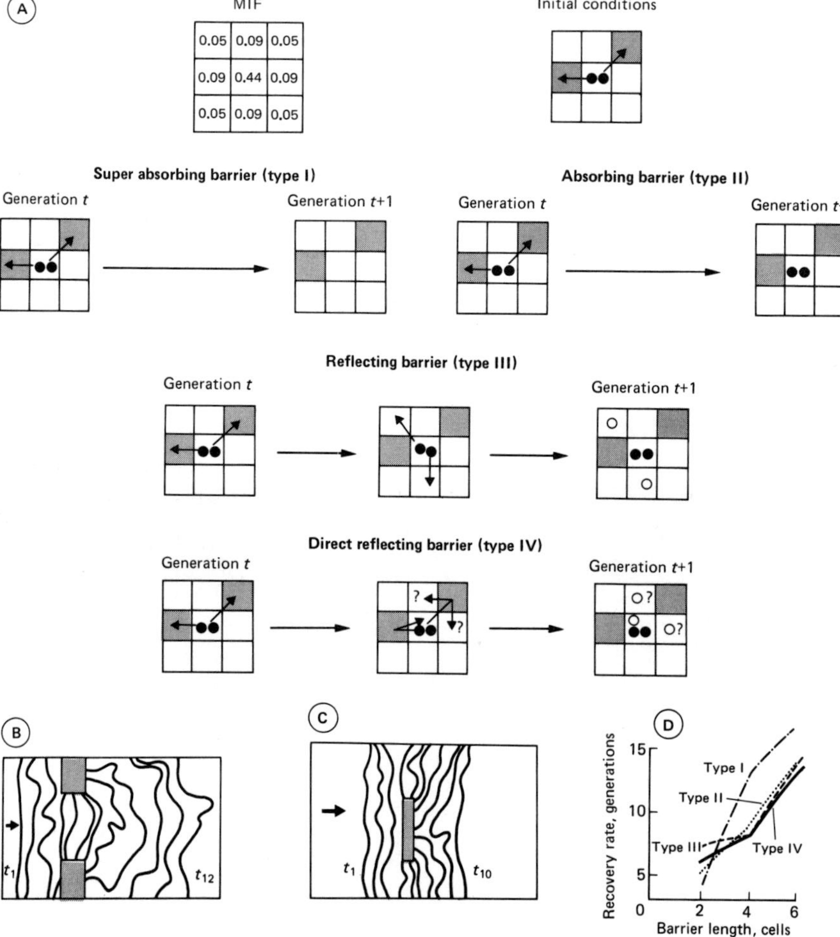


**Figure 7.7** Barrier effects on diffusion waves. **A** MIF and the four types of barrier cells used by Yuill. **B** Diffusion wave passing through opening in a bar barrier. **C** Diffusion wave passing round a bar barrier. **D** Recovery rates around bar barriers. Source: Yuill, 1965, pp. 19, 25, 29.

that centring the grid over those two adopters has caused two cells of the MIF to be occupied by barriers (the stippled cells). The location of each carrier's contact in the next generation of the model (cf. Hägerstrand's Monte Carlo experiment of Section 7.2) is shown by the arrows. Yuill envisaged four types of barrier cell in decreasing order of blocking effectiveness: Type I, *super absorbing*, which absorbed the new contacts and destroyed the transmitters; Type II, the *absorbing* barrier, which absorbed new contacts but did not affect the transmitters; Type III, the *reflecting* barrier, which absorbed the new contacts, but the transmitters were allowed to make a new contact in the same generation (the open circles); and Type IV the *direct reflecting* barrier, which did not absorb the contacts but instead reflected them randomly to the nearest available cell. Each situation was separately programmed and its results plotted. Figure 7.7B shows the advance of a linear diffusion wave ($t = 1$) through an opening in an absorbing bar barrier. The wave front becomes distorted in its passage through the opening because of the loss of contacts at the barrier edge (a frictional drag effect), but it re-forms by about the twelfth generation. Yuill has referred to the number of generations required for the wave to return to its original form after first encountering the barrier as the *recovery rate*. An alternative version of the bar barrier is shown in Figure 7.7C where the diffusion wave passes around a bar and re-forms after about nine generations. Here the recovery rate is directly related to both the barrier length and to the type of barrier, with the curve for the Type I super absorbing barrier showing strong contrasts to those of the other three types (Figure 7.7D).

Although Yuill's results were limited by the range of postulates he tried and by computer capacity, the approach is of direct interest to, among others, historical geographers. The exact impact of the Appalachians, the Blue Mountains, or the Sierra do Mar in holding back the inland spread of settlement from the American, Australian and Brazilian coastlines has long been argued. By using more complex MIFs and environmental weightings for the barriers, different models may be evolved. These can be assessed in a hypothesis-testing sense in much the same way as the experimental hydrological models of estuaries and deltas developed at Wallingford and Vicksburg. As a further example, the technique might be applied to Pyle's (1969) tracks for cholera epidemics in the USA in the nineteenth century, which progressed inland from the Eastern Seaboard and across the Appalachians (see Section 4.6.1).

Yuill's work, by viewing the spread of an innovation as a wave phenomenon, also ties back to Hägerstrand's studies discussed earlier (see Section 7.1). The idea of diffusion waves has been developed further by Morrill (1968, 1970). Morrill has applied various polynomial, sine and cosine waves to innovation situations, and he has considered what happens when waves from different centres meet for the cases of complementary and opposing innovations.

### 7.5.2 *Corridors*

The obverse of a barrier is a corridor of movement, and the identification of such corridors is the theme of a study by Levison, Ward and Webb (1973). These authors constructed a Monte Carlo model to simulate the pattern of settlement of Polynesia by raft voyagers. The drift tracks of the rafts, from a variety of starting points, were determined by sampling from side probability distributions describing factors such as wind frequency, direction and force, ocean currents, and survival rates. Voyages were terminated by either (a) 'contact' with another island or (b) expiry of the voyage as determined by the survival rate probabilities. Mapping of the distribution of voyage-termination points in Polynesia permitted estimates to be made of the probability of reaching the various Polynesian islands from the different starting points. See Figure 7.8.

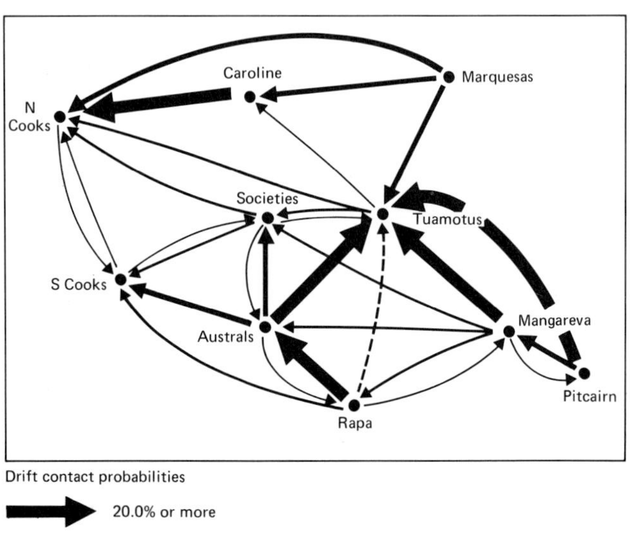


**Figure 7.8** Drift contact probabilities for the Polynesian islands. Source: Levison, Ward and Webb, 1973, p. 51.

## 7.6 Goodness-of-fit of Diffusion Models to Reality

### 7.6.1 *Nature of the comparison problem*

The basic output of the Hägerstrand type models is a series of maps which show, at the end of each iteration of the model, the simulated spatial pattern of acceptance of the innovation being considered. A problem which has exercised a number of workers is how to evaluate the goodness-of-fit of those model maps to the corresponding actual patterns of acceptance. Two kinds of test are required. First, it is necessary to check whether the model has produced the right balance of cells with 0, 1, 2, ... adopters in them. A common way of doing this is to construct the frequency distributions of the numbers of cells with 0, 1, 2, ... adopters in them from the corresponding observed and simulated maps, and then to compare the resulting distributions for systematic departures (e.g. Hägerstrand, 1967, p. 27).

Comparison of the frequency arrays in this sort of way is only part of the task since, in constructing the arrays, the spatial relationships between cells are lost. It is evident that totally different maps can produce the same frequency distributions of counts (cf. the discussion on quadrat count methods in Chapter 13). We also need, therefore, to evaluate the degree of *spatial* correspondence between the real world and the simulated maps. The question we are asking is: can the real world map be regarded as a possible outcome of the stochastic process (i.e. the model) used to produce the simulated map? If the answer to this question is 'yes', we would expect the real world and the simulated maps to differ only by chance. We would not expect there to be areas where the actual numbers of adopters were either consistently over- or consistently under-estimated by the model. Formally, following Cliff (1970) and Cliff and Ord (1973, Chapter 4), we would construct a map of the residual differences between an observed and a simulated map by computing for each cell the quantity (observed–simulated) cell counts. This is analogous to constructing a map of residuals from regression. Zero residuals represent cells in which the simulated and actual map values are identical; positive residuals represent areas of underestimation by the model; negative residuals represent areas of overestimation of the cell values by the model. Interest is centred on the spatial arrangement of the non-zero residuals. If the observed map is a possible realization of the stochastic process used to generate the simulated map, then the non-zero residuals should be randomly located spatially in the residuals map. For this kind of comparison to work, we require the simulated map to be the 'expected' outcome of the process postulated: if a model of the process is specified, rather than the map itself, we can derive an expected map by averaging over several independent realizations of the model (Cliff and Ord, 1973, p. 70).

### 7.6.2 *Testing procedures*

Having outlined our approach to the goodness-of-fit problem, we now need to specify our criterion of fit. This is not straightforward because, as Brown and Moore (1969, cited in Cliff and Ord, 1973, Chapter 4) have noted, the tendency of many diffusion processes to contain some sort of neighbourhood effect means that, once the growth process has moved off in a particular direction, often purely by chance, from the original place of introduction of that innovation, it will tend to retain that orientation. In other words, systematic directional biases may result from chance occurrences. To guard against this difficulty, Cliff and Ord (1973, p. 73) have suggested the following procedure based upon work by Hope (1968):

*Step* 1. Generate $m$ independent realizations of the diffusion model and, from these *and the observed map*, compute an average, expected, map by averaging over the $(m+1)$ realizations.

*Step* 2. For each simulated map and for the observed map, compute a goodness-of-fit statistic between that map and the average (expected) map. For example, Pearson's product moment correlation coefficient, sums of squared differences or $X^2$, would be suitable aspatial criteria, and the spatial autocorrelation measures described in Section 11.2, or Tobler's (1965) method of comparing point patterns, suitable spatial criteria. Under the null hypothesis of no systematic difference between the individual maps and the average map, these $(m+1)$ statistics will be identically distributed and equi-correlated.

****

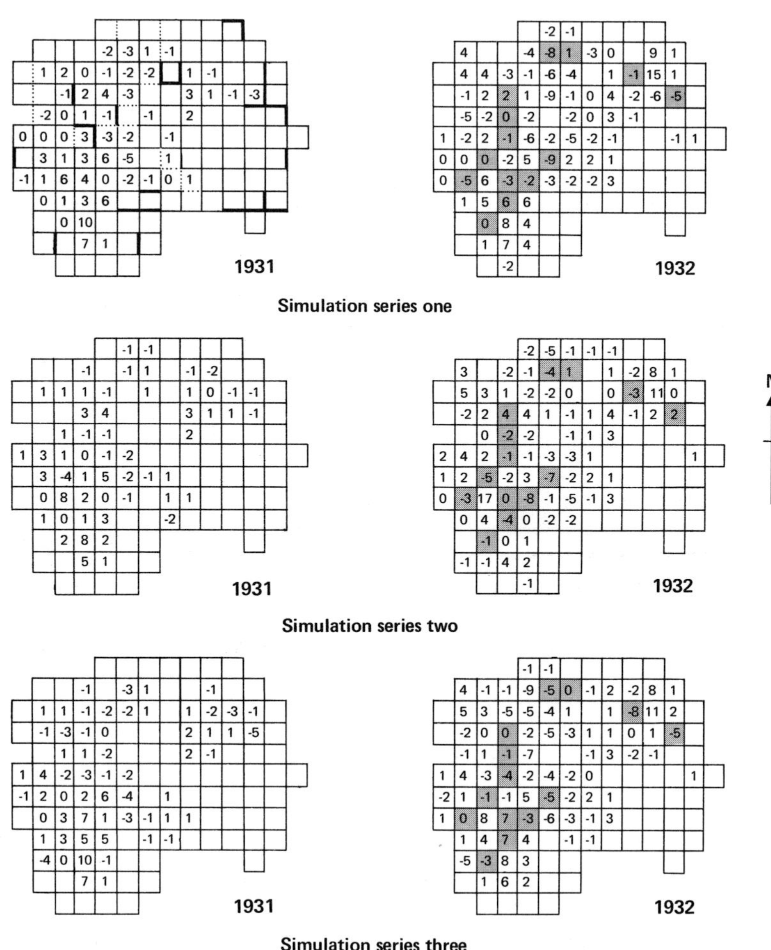


**Figure 7.9** Residuals maps of central Sweden for 1931 and 1932 from the runs of the Hägerstrand model. Source: Cliff and Ord, 1973, p. 77.

*Step* 3. Rank the $(m+1)$ statistics and reject $H_0$ at the $100(j+1)/(m+1)$ per cent level if the statistic between the observed and average map has rank $(m-j+1)$ or worse (one-tailed test). Rules for two-tailed tests may be formulated in a similar manner. In ranking the test statistics, if a measure of correlation is used, call the highest positive value rank 1; if the sum of squared differences or $X^2$ is used, call the smallest value rank 1. In this procedure, we reject $H_0$ only if the difference, including directional bias, between the observed and simulated maps is judged so severe that it could not be regarded as a chance occurrence.

Cliff and Ord (1973, Chapter 4) have used the procedure, with the autocorrelation measure defined in equation (11.7), to evaluate the spatial goodness-of-fit between (1) the observed maps of numbers of adopters of the improved pasture subsidy in the Asby district of Sweden and (2) the simulated maps produced by the Hägerstrand model. They concluded that the observed maps could not be regarded as another possible outcome of the model. Figure 7.9 shows the residuals maps, constructed as described earlier, between the observed maps and the model maps for 1931 and 1932 produced by three runs of the model. The shaded cells indicate the 1929 pattern of adopters used to start the Monte Carlo model (rule 1 on p. 235). It is evident that, by 1932, the model had tended to overestimate the numbers of adopters in these 'seed' cells, possibly at the expense of more distant areas. Thus in the seed cells, the model had overestimated in 8 and underestimated in 3 for simulation series one. The corresponding proportions for series two and three are 9:3 and 9:2. Cliff and Ord (1973, pp. 84–6) have suggested that this might imply that Hägerstrand's MIF given in Figure 7.3 incorporates too rapid a decay with distance in the probability of contact between adopters and potential adopters of the innovation. This result should be compared with that of Tinline (1971) which is discussed in Section 16.2.2.

We have described one way of evaluating the goodness-of-fit of simulation models to reality. Alternative approaches to which the reader is referred are considered in Lankford (1974) and Yapa (1976).

We have now completed our coverage of Hägerstrand's work, some of the issues it has raised, and the models developed in geography as a response to these issues. In the remainder of the chapter, we examine some of the stochastic spatial diffusion models developed in epidemiology.

## 7.7 Epidemic Models*

### 7.7.1 *Types of epidemic models*

Although, as their name indicates, epidemic models were originally developed to study the passage of various diseases through human populations, the results and the models to be described can equally well be applied to the diffusion of innovations. In the epidemiological literature, two basic kinds of model are generally recognized (Bailey, 1957, 1975; Bartholomew, 1973), namely:

1. The *simple epidemic* model. Here, the population in the study area is divided

into two components, susceptibles (≡potential adopters) and infectives (≡adopters). The model describes a pure birth process in which everyone who becomes an adopter continues to transmit information indefinitely. This is exactly the structure of the Hägerstrand model described in Section 7.2. Ultimately, therefore, the whole of the population of potential adopters will become informed, and, as Bartholomew (1973) has noted, the main object of the theory is to study the evolution of the system to that limiting state.

2. The *general epidemic* model. In this model, a three-fold division of the total population into susceptibles, infectives and removals is made. The class of removals comprises those adopters who, after some length of time, cease to pass on information about the innovation. A birth–death process is thus envisaged. The removals are passive adopters, as opposed to the active (transmitting) adopters in the infectives category. In the general epidemic model, questions about the spatial and temporal extent of the diffusion are examined, and the notion of thresholds for an innovation to take off are considered.

### 7.7.2 *Results for the simple epidemic model*

Mollison (1972a, b; cited in Bartholomew, 1973) has considered a stochastic model for the diffusion of an innovation among individuals located at each positive and negative integer on the real line. If a symmetric linear mean information field, MIF, is defined about the source of the innovation (assumed to be located at the integer zero), then the spatial pattern of acceptance of the

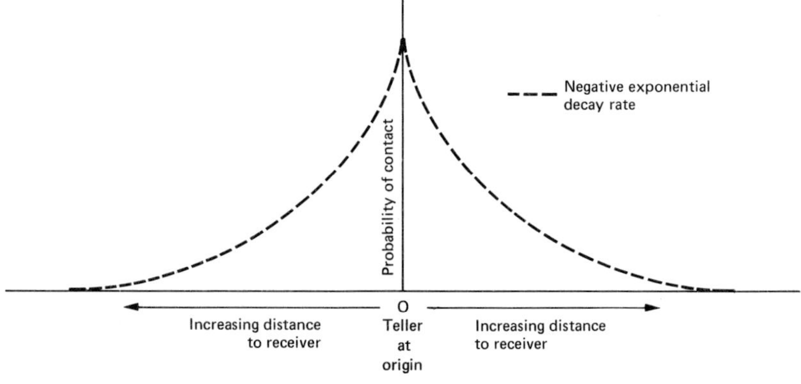


**Figure 7.10** An exponentially bounded MIF.

innovation can be shown to be critically dependent upon the contact probabilities in the MIF. If the linear MIF has exponentially bounded tails (that is, the two tails of the MIF have contact probabilities between an adopter and a potential adopter which approach zero at least as fast as an exponential decay curve with increasing distance between them; see Figure 7.10) then Mollison has suggested that 'contacts are usually made in the neighbourhood of the source and the front of knowers tends to advance outwards from the origin at a steady rate' (Bartholomew, 1973, p. 327). If the boundedness assumption is not met, some contacts will be made a distance ahead of the advancing wave, producing a pattern with a main wave preceded by local clusters. 'If [the MIF] is highly dispersed so as to be almost uniform we are almost back to the case when chance of contact is independent of distance . . . there will be no discernible wave at all—only a gradually merging set of clusters' (Bartholomew, 1973, p. 328). These findings tie back to the discussion of Hägerstrand's model in Section 7.2.2. As noted in Hägerstrand (1967, pp. 165–246), his MIF is, by construction, exponentially bounded. The results of Mollison and Bartholomew now show why the Hägerstrand model builds up a strong concentration of new adopters in areas of original adopters, with very few long distance contacts.

The existence or otherwise of a diffusion wave is also related to the speed with which the innovation spreads spatially. Assume that the probability law describing the MIF is concentrated around the original source of the innovation, so that adopters can only contact potential adopters in their immediate vicinity. Resorting for simplicity to a deterministic approximation of the stochastic process, Bartholomew (1973, pp. 328–31) has shown that there is a minimum velocity, $c$, for the wave, below which no waveform solution is possible. For a waveform to exist, $c$ must satisfy the relation,

$$c \geqslant 2\sqrt{K\beta\sigma}. \tag{7.7}$$

Here, $\beta$ is the rate at which contacts are being made, $\sigma$ is the density of the population per unit area, and $K$ is a constant equal to half the variance of the probability law describing the MIF. Mollison (1972a, b; discussed in Bartholomew, 1973, p. 331) has extended result (7.7) to a more general MIF. If the MIF is exponentially bounded, then the diffusion wave can travel at any steady speed above the minimum necessary for a waveform to exist; if the boundedness condition is not met, then the rate of advance of the wave tends to infinity as $t \to \infty$. Bartholomew argues that this accelerating rate of advance in the deterministic model for a non-exponentially bounded MIF corresponds to the situation where contacts are made in advance of the wave in the stochastic model.

### 7.7.3 *Results for the general epidemic model*

The theory of the general epidemic model dates from a paper by Kermack and McKendrick (1927). A summary of findings since that date appears in Bailey (1957, 1975). Most of the theory for the spatial version of the model is deterministic and is reviewed by Bartholomew (1973, pp. 351–55), the main points of whose account we now describe.

Suppose that the total population of an unbounded region is evenly spread throughout the study area at a density of $\sigma$ individuals per unit area. At time $t$ and location $s$, Bartholomew, following Kendall (1957, 1965) and Bailey (1957, p. 32), divides the total population into:

$x(s, t)$, the proportion of potential adopters (susceptibles),

$y(s, t)$, the proportion of adopters (infectives),

$z(s, t)$, the proportion of adopters who have ceased to pass on information about the innovation (removals), such that the proportions sum to one over all $s$ and $t$. Contacts between adopters and potential adopters are assumed to take place at a rate $\beta$ (the birth or infection rate; cf. Bailey, 1957, section 4.3 and chapter 8), while the distance at which a contact is made is governed by a MIF. The basic differential equations which give the rates of change in $x$, $y$ and $z$ in a closed system with no in and out migration are as follows:

$$\frac{\partial x}{\partial t} = -\beta\sigma x\bar{y}, \tag{7.8a}$$

$$\frac{\partial y}{\partial t} = \beta\sigma x\bar{y} - \gamma y, \tag{7.8b}$$

$$\frac{\partial z}{\partial t} = \gamma y. \tag{7.8c}$$

Here $\gamma$ is the removal or death rate, and $\bar{y}$ is the spatial average of $y$ around $s$.

Equations (7.8a)–(7.8c) are important in the epidemiology literature for the light they throw upon threshold effects. Following Bartholomew (1973, p. 352), it is evident that diffusion is impossible if $\partial y/\partial t$ is non-positive at all locations $s$ (that is, if there is no growth in the adopting population at any location $s$). As an illustration, Bartholomew takes the simplest case, where the innovation starts at $t = 0$ with a very small proportion of adopters, $\varepsilon$, uniformly distributed in the plane. This implies that $y(s, 0) = \bar{y}(s, 0) = \varepsilon$. Since $x(s, 0) = 1-\varepsilon$, diffusion will not occur if

$$\beta\sigma(1-\varepsilon)\varepsilon \leqslant \gamma\varepsilon; \tag{7.9}$$

that is, if the rate at which new adopters are being created (by contacts between adopters and potential adopters) fails to exceed the rate at which existing adopters are joining the population of removals (Bartholomew, 1973, p. 352). Equation (7.9) yields the result that a small number of initial adopters will not start a general diffusion process if $\sigma < \rho$, where $\rho$, the *relative removal rate*, is defined as $\rho = \gamma/\beta$ (Bailey, 1957, p. 22; Bartholomew, 1973, p. 352). Suppose now that the assumption of a spatially uniform distribution of the initial adopters, $\varepsilon$, in the study area is dropped, and is replaced by the assumptions that (a) the initial adopters are concentrated at a particular location and (b) the MIF has a strong distance decay. Under these circumstances Kendall (1957, 1965) and Bartholomew (1973, p. 353) have shown that when

$$\beta\sigma \leqslant \gamma \quad \text{or} \quad \beta \leqslant \rho \tag{7.10}$$

diffusion will *not* occur; if these conditions are not met, general diffusion *will* occur. Thus (7.10) states that there is a threshold population density which must be exceeded, given values for $\beta$ and $\gamma$, for diffusion to take place. If diffusion does take place, then Kendall's *pandemic threshold theorem* (Kendall, 1957; discussed in Bailey, 1957, section 4.5, and Bartholomew, 1973, pp. 353–55) shows that when $\sigma > \rho$, the innovation will ultimately affect all parts of the plane with equal severity, no matter what distance the point is from the original source. Kendall calls this situation a pandemic. From Bailey (1957, Table 4.1), we have the following figures:

| *Proportion of the population ultimately affected* | *k in the relationship* $\sigma = k\rho$ |
|---|---|
| 0.00 | 1.000 |
| 0.20 | 1.116 |
| 0.40 | 1.277 |
| 0.60 | 1.527 |
| 0.80 | 2.012 |
| 0.90 | 2.558 |
| 0.95 | 3.153 |
| 0.98 | 3.992 |

$\sigma/\rho < 1$, no epidemic.
$\sigma/\rho > 4$, everyone ultimately hears.

Kendall (1965, cited in Bartholomew, 1973, p. 354) has also considered whether or not a waveform solution is possible for equations (7.8a)–(7.8c). He has shown that if there is a waveform solution, the wave cannot have a velocity of less than

$$c = 2\sqrt{K}(1-\rho/\sigma)^{\frac{1}{2}}. \tag{7.11}$$

Bartholomew reports the results of a simulation study of a stochastic version of model (7.8a, b, c), in which Mollison (1972b) showed that in an example with $\rho/\sigma = \frac{1}{2}$, the velocity was in fact only about one-fifth of $2\sqrt{K}$ [that is, considerably slower than the value of 0.7 produced from Mollison's figures by equation (7.11)].

So far, we have summarized some general results for simple and general epidemics. We now consider some more specific models. Those dealt with in Sections 7.7.4–7.7.6 are particular examples of the general epidemic model. That considered in Section 7.7.7 is a simple epidemic model.

### 7.7.4 *Bartlett's spatial epidemic model*

Bartlett (1960, chapter 8) has explored the properties of a general epidemic model for an open system which allows limited migration of individuals into and out of the study area. Following Bartlett, the probability rate of infection, $\beta$, of a susceptible in the small element of area $d\mathbf{s}$ by an infective in $d\mathbf{r}$ is assumed to be a function, $\beta(\mathbf{s}-\mathbf{r})$ of the vector displacement (distance), $(\mathbf{s}-\mathbf{r})$. The change of migration, $\alpha$, of an infective from $d\mathbf{r}$ to $d\mathbf{s}$ in the time interval of length $dt$ is assumed to be $\alpha(\mathbf{s}-\mathbf{r})d\mathbf{s}\,dt$. Although the susceptibles may also move, Bartlett replaces them, for simplicity, by the average density of susceptibles, $a$, per unit area. Bartlett then shows that the average (or expected) number of infectives at time $t+dt$ in the element of area $d\mathbf{r}$, which he denotes by $f_1(\mathbf{r}, t+dt)d\mathbf{r}$, is obtained from the equation,

$$f_1(\mathbf{r}, t+dt) = f_1(\mathbf{r}, t)(1-P\,dt)+ \\ dt\left\{\int \alpha(\mathbf{r}-\mathbf{s})f_1(\mathbf{s}, t)d\mathbf{s} + a\beta(\mathbf{r}-\mathbf{s})f_1(\mathbf{s}, t)d\mathbf{s}\right\}, \tag{7.12}$$

where $P \equiv \int \alpha(\mathbf{s}-\mathbf{r})d\mathbf{s}+\gamma$, and $\gamma$ is the death rate among infectives. $Pdt$ is the probability that an infective in area $d\mathbf{r}$ is lost during the time interval of length $dt$ either by out-migration to $d\mathbf{s}$ or by 'death'. The first term in equation (7.12) thus gives the average (expected) number of infectives in $d\mathbf{r}$ at time $t$ who survive to $t+dt$. The two terms in brace brackets give, respectively, the number of new infectives created in area $d\mathbf{r}$ between $t$ and $t+dt$ by (a) migration of infectives from area $d\mathbf{s}$ to area $d\mathbf{r}$ and (b) conversion of susceptibles in $d\mathbf{r}$ by contact with infectives in $d\mathbf{s}$. The new feature of this model, *vis-a-vis* those discussed earlier, is the introduction of the migration terms. It is evident that the model could be extended by including a wide range of such terms to handle inter-area movements.

> . . . the restriction of the discussion to the case of a closed population necessarily ruled out the possibility of recurrent epidemics. If the size of the suseptible population were above the threshold, an epidemic might break out, and if so the susceptibles would drop below the threshold so that no second epidemic could recur (Bartlett, 1960, p. 62).

The extension of model (7.12) to include migration terms for susceptibles would permit the modelling of recurrent epidemic diseases such as measles.

Equation (7.12) yields

$$\frac{\partial f_1(\mathbf{r},t)}{\partial t} = -\gamma f_1(\mathbf{r},t)+a\int\beta(\mathbf{r}-\mathbf{s})f_1(\mathbf{s},t)d\mathbf{s} + \int\alpha(\mathbf{r}-\mathbf{s})f_1(\mathbf{s},t)d\mathbf{s}-f_1(\mathbf{r},t)\int\alpha(\mathbf{s}-\mathbf{r})d\mathbf{s}; \tag{7.13}$$

that is, the rate of change in the number of infectives (adopters) in area $d\mathbf{r}$ is obtained additively from the terms (in order): losses of adopters in $d\mathbf{r}$ by death + gains in adopters by conversion of susceptibles (potential adopters) in $d\mathbf{r}$ as a result of contact with infectives in $d\mathbf{s}$ + gains of adopters in $d\mathbf{r}$ by migration of adopters to $d\mathbf{r}$ from $d\mathbf{s}$ – losses of adopters from $d\mathbf{r}$ by out-migration to $d\mathbf{s}$. We note that model (7.12) is conceptually very similar to that given in Haggett (1975b), where spatial extensions of the Hamer–Soper (1906, 1929) measles epidemic model are considered. In addition, Bailey (1957, pp. 141–53) has also outlined some spatial epidemic models with migration terms which are of essentially the same form as (7.12). Bailey's work draws upon papers by Bartlett published in the 1950s.

### 7.7.5 *Rapoport's network models*

In the late 1940s and early 1950s a whole series of models which could be applied in diffusion situations were developed by Rapoport and his co-workers at the University of Chicago. The models were originally designed to study the transmission of stimuli between nerve endings (neurons) in the human body (cf. nodes or individuals in a graph as in Chapter 3), where the neurons were assumed to be linked by a system of axones (cf. links in a graph or channels of communication). This area of literature was, to a great extent, developed independently of other research work on the diffusion of innovations and epidemiology, and it is reviewed in Brown (1968, pp. 49–65) and Bartholomew (1973, section 10.3). However, as Bartholomew has noted, the Rapoport models are but simple variants of the Kermack and McKendrick model.

> Rapoport's assumptions were the same as those of the general epidemic model except for the one governing the cessation of spreading. He supposed that each spreader told the news to exactly $d$ other people and then ceased activity. . . . The value of studying the model is best seen by considering it as a special case of a more general model in which the number told is a random variable . . . denoted by $\tilde{d}$. . . . The present [Rapoport's] model thus arises as an extreme case when we take the distribution of $\tilde{d}$ as concentrated at the point $d$. Kermack and McKendrick's model is another special case since then $\tilde{d}$ has a geometric distribution (Bartholomew, 1973, p. 355).

See Bartholomew (1973, pp. 356–80) for a discussion of the theory for the temporal behaviour of an epidemic under the Rapoport model. The model is readily 'spatialized' by attaching simple locational accounting tags or identity numbers to the individuals contacted.

### 7.7.6 *Chain binomial models*

The theory of chain binomial models is based upon work by Reed and Frost in 1928 (see Abbey, 1952) and Greenwood (1931), and is described in Bailey (1957, chapter 6). The basic idea of the models is summarized by Bailey (1957, p. 76) as follows.

> At each stage in the epidemic there are certain numbers of infectives and susceptibles, and it is reasonable to suppose that these latter will yield a crop of fresh cases at the next stage distributed in a binomial series. We thus have a chain of binomial distributions, the actual probability of a new infection at any stage depending on the number of infectives and susceptibles at the previous stage.

Assume that the total population under study may be divided at the start of the diffusion process into two categories, infectives, $I$, and susceptibles, $S$. Let $S_t$ be the number of susceptibles at time $t$, and $I_t$ be the number of infectives. If the two groups of people mix homogeneously, with the probability of contact between an infective and a susceptible being given by $p = 1-q$, then $q^{I_t}$ is the chance that a given susceptible will not have contact with any of the $I_t$ infectives. Hence $1-q^{I_t}$ is the probability that a given susceptible will have contact with at least one infective, leading to the conditional probability of $I_{t+1}$ new infectives as

$$P(I_{t+1}|S_t, I_t) = \frac{S_t!}{I_{t+1}!\,S_{t+1}!}(1-q^{I_t})^{I_{t+1}}(q^{I_t})^{S_{t+1}}, \qquad t = 0, 1, \ldots, T \qquad (7.14)$$

(the Reed–Frost model). The process ceases the first time no new infectives are produced, since individuals are allowed to transmit for only one time period. $S_t$

will still be positive at this stage if all susceptibles have not been infected. Greenwood's model is simpler, since he assumed that the chance of infection is not influenced by the number of infectives in the total population, so that the probability of a given susceptible being contacted can be written as $p$. This yields the model

$$P(I_{t+1} \mid S_t, I_t) = \frac{S_t!}{I_{t+1}!\,S_{t+1}!} p^{I_{t+1}} q^{S_{t+1}}, \quad t = 0, 1, \ldots, T. \qquad (7.15)$$

Table 7.2 Values of $t$, $S_t$ and $I_t$ for the chain of infection 1 → 2 → 1 → 1.

| $t$ | $S_t$ | $I_t$ |
|---|---|---|
| 0 | 4 | 1 |
| 1 | 2 | 2 |
| 2 | 1 | 1 |
| 3 | 0 | 1 |
| 4 | 0 | 0 |

*Source: Bailey* (1957, *p.* 78).

The binomial chain is produced by multiplying together the probabilities appropriate to each stage as given by (7.14) and (7.15). Thus from Bailey (1957, pp. 78–79), suppose that in a total population of 5, one initial case at $t = 0$ is followed by 2, 1, and 1 new cases in $t_1$, $t_2$ and $t_3$ respectively. See Table 7.2. Using equation (7.14), the probability of this particular chain of infection is

$$\overset{t\,=\,1}{\left[\frac{4!}{2!2!}(1-q)^2q^2\right]}\overset{t\,=\,2}{\left[\frac{2!}{1!1!}(1-q^2)q^2\right]}\overset{t\,=\,3}{\left[\frac{1!}{1!0!}(1-q)q^0\right]}\overset{t\,=\,4}{\left[1\right]}$$

$$= 12p^2q^4(1-q)^2(1+q) = 12p^4q^4(1+q).$$

A typical pattern of infection in a tracing sense is shown in Figure 7.11. The factorial terms in equation (7.14) cover all possible permutations of the 1 → 2 → 1 → 1 tracing through a population of five. From equation (7.15), application of the Greenwood model to the figures in Table 7.2 yields $12p^4q^3$.

If the available data do not permit the chain of infection to be established, but give instead only the total number of infectives at the end of the epidemic

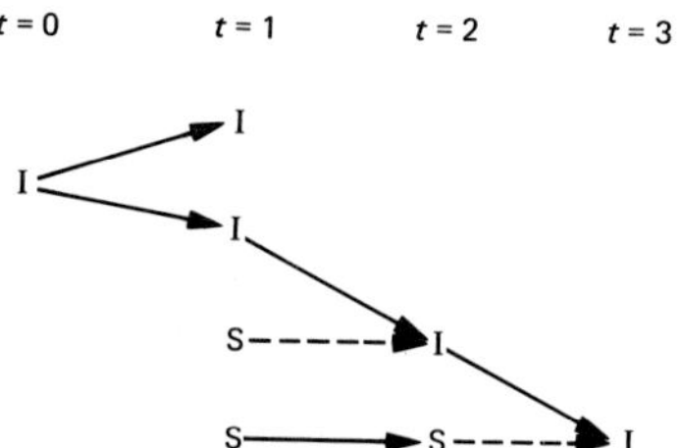


**Figure 7.11** A typical pattern of infection in a tracing sense for a 1→ 2→ 1→ 1 chain of infection.

($I_T$ say), then the overall probability of $I_T$ under the chain binomial models is obtained by adding together the probabilities for the individual chains. Thus in a group of three individuals with one initial infective at $t = 0$, the probability of a total of three infectives by the end of $t_2$ is $2p^2q+p^2 = p^2(1+2q)$ for both the Reed–Frost and Greenwood models. See Table 7.3. Bailey (1957, Chapter 6) gives full details of ways of estimating the parameter, $p$, the probability of infection, from data. He also describes some procedures which can be used to evaluate the goodness-of-fit of the models to given data.

Table 7.3 Individual binomial chains for a group of three.

| | $t_0$ $t_1$ $t_2$ | *Probability* | *Result when* $p = 0.1$ |
|---|---|---|---|
| Chain | $1 \rightarrow 0 \rightarrow 0$ | $q^2$ | 0.810 |
| | $1 \rightarrow 1 \rightarrow 0$ | $2pq^2$ | 0.162 |
| | $1 \rightarrow 1 \rightarrow 1$ | $2p^2q$ | 0.018 |
| | $1 \rightarrow 2 \rightarrow 0$ | $p^2$ | 0.010 |

Chain binomial models may be applied geographically in one of two main ways. First, the individuals in the population may be spatial units. For example, in Section 11.5 and in Cliff, Haggett, Ord, Bassett and Davies (1975) the time–space pattern of spread of measles epidemics among the urban and rural districts of Southwest England is discussed. Here, the infectives at $t = 0$ would be those districts with a measles outbreak, and chain binomials might be used to look at the pattern of spread of the disease to districts without an outbreak (the susceptibles). Alternatively, the individuals in the population may simply be people whose spatial locations are tagged (by grid co-ordinates, for example).

Basic to the chain binomial models so far considered are the assumptions of (a) spatially homogeneous mixing implied in fixed $p$ and (b) independence between the links in the chain. Chain binomials in which $p$ is allowed to vary both within and between chains are considered in Bailey (1957, pp. 91–108). This enables problem (a) to be overcome. Assumption (b), as discussed in Chapter 10, is much more problematical, and is not very plausible when contiguous areal units comprise the individuals in the chain. Situations where independence is more likely to be approximated might be the transmission of some disease or phenomenon from island to island in an island chain, or in central place diffusion.

### 7.7.7 *Hierarchical and group models*

As noted in Section 7.4, Hudson (1972) has considered a series of models for the spread of an item (innovation, disease, etc.) in (a) hierarchical urban (central place) systems and (b) societies with a distinct social clique structure. 'The "space" of such models is usually a social or organizational structure through which the information diffuses. Such a system may be viewed as a network in which information is introduced at the highest level and then spreads downwards through the hierarchy defined by the network' (Bartholomew, 1973, p. 334; cf. the percolation models of Hammersley and Handscomb, 1963, Hammersley and Walters, 1963, and Hammersley, 1966, which are concerned with phenomena such as the percolation of rain down through the pore spaces of rocks on to which the rain falls). Bartholomew indicates that such models are mathematically very similar to *perimeter models*, in which members of the population are immobile and can only communicate with their immediate neighbours. New adopters appear solely at the edges of existing areas of adoption, and the pattern of diffusion follows the density of the susceptible population. Bartholomew argues that such models are of little geographical (spatial) interest:

> For this reason [growth restricted to the perimeter of existing areas of adoption only] the analysis cannot be expected to yield much of interest about the pattern [of spread]. We [are], instead, . . . more concerned with the rate of growth of the total numbers in a situation where contacts are constrained by geography (Bartholomew, 1973, p. 332).

That is, there is a shift of emphasis in these models away from attention to the spatial pattern of growth in numbers of adopters, which has been the main point of interest in the models considered earlier in this chapter, to a consideration of the temporal build-up of the process. The spatial build-up is dictated very much by the structure of the network as, for example, in the case of a central place system where higher order centres dominate lower order ones (see Figure 7.6c).

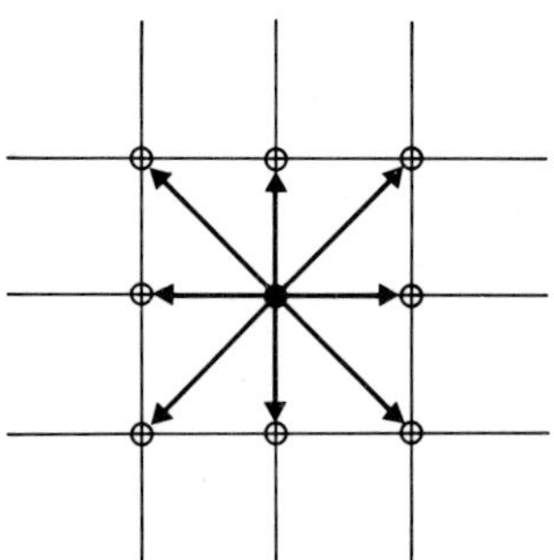

**Figure 7.12** Location of initial adopter and neighbours for the simple perimeter model.

As a simple example of a perimeter model, Bartholomew (1973, p. 332) discusses a model developed by Bailey (1967). Consider a square lattice, and suppose that individuals are located at the vertices of the grid. At $t = 1$, a single adopter located in the centre of the lattice may contact any one of his eight immediate neighbours (see Figure 7.12), but no one else. It is a pure birth process (that is, a simple epidemic situation), so that in subsequent generations of the model, every adopter may make contact with his immediate neighbours. The chance of a susceptible, or potential adopter, hearing from a neighbouring adopter is $p$, and all contacts are assumed to be independent. In the first generation, the number of new adopters, $r$, will have the binomial distribution (Bartholomew, 1973, p. 332),

$$\binom{8}{r} p^r(1-p)^{8-r}, \quad r = 0, 1, 2, \ldots, 8. \tag{7.16}$$

In the next generation, all potential adopters who are neighbours of adopters may be contacted. If a given potential adopter has $a$ adopters as neighbours, the probability that he will become an adopter is $1-(1-p)^a$ [cf. the chain binomial models]. In a study area of finite extent, this kind of model can produce the characteristic sigmoidal growth curve in the total number of adopters. The reader should consult Hudson (1972) for the derivation of binomial expressions analogous to (7.16) for hierarchical and mixed hierarchical/contagious growth central place systems. It is also worth noting that the chain binomial and perimeter models link back to Hägerstrand's work, in that his model can be viewed as a binomial sampling situation.

## 7.8 Conclusions

In this chapter, a series of models for spatial diffusion processes have been described. The classic model in the geographical literature is that of Hägerstrand (1953). We have examined the relationships between Hägerstrand's model and three commonly observed empirical regularities for diffusion processes, namely the neighbourhood effect, the logistic build-up with time in the cumulative number of adopters, and the tendency of some items to spread down the central place hierarchy. In addition, the effect of barriers upon the spread of an innovation, the idea of diffusion waves, and the evaluation of the spatial goodness-of-fit of diffusion models to reality have also been considered.

The Hägerstrand model is a particular example of what is termed the simple epidemic model by the epidemiologists. Hägerstrand's model typically produces a spatially very clustered pattern of adoption, and it has been shown that this is due to the exponentially bounded nature of Hägerstrand's MIF. The general epidemic model provides a more elaborate framework for the analysis of diffusion processes by introducing a class of removals, or adopters who have ceased to pass on news about the innovation. If there is a 'death' mechanism, it can be shown that the density of the population per unit area critically affects the probability that a diffusion process will take off. Some particular examples of the general epidemic model have been described, especially that of Bartlett (1960), which allows migration of individuals into and out of the study area, and chain binomial models.

The models considered in this chapter are stochastic. It is evident from the discussion that the stochastic theory for the spatial spread of innovations is usually intractable, and that frequent recourse has to be made to simplifying assumptions and deterministic approximations. However, as Bartholomew (1973, pp. 354–5) has noted, 'detailed prediction is not . . . a reasonable objective in the present state of the theory. The value of our highly simplified models lies in their ability to suggest broad qualitative features like threshold effects. From the manner of their derivation, one might reasonably hope such effects would survive a good deal of change in the assumptions in the direction of greater realism.' If prediction is the aim, the Box–Jenkins (1970) techniques examined in Chapter 16 may be more helpful. See MacKinnon (1974) and Bennett (1975) for examples of the use of Box–Jenkins methods to predict the spread of diffusion phenomena.

# References and author index

# References and author index

The numbers in brackets after each reference indicate the sections of the book in which the work is cited.


ABBEY, H. 1952: An examination of the Reed–Frost theory of epidemics. *Human Biology*, **24**, 201–33. (7.7.6)

ABLER, R., J. S. ADAMS, and P. R. GOULD. 1972: *Spatial organization: the geographer's view of the world.* Englewood Cliffs, N.J. (15.5.2)

ABRAMSON, N. 1963: *Information theory and coding.* New York. (3.4.2)

ACKERMAN, E. A. 1963: Where is the research frontier? *Annals of the Association of American Geographers*, **53**, 429–40. (1.2.1)

AITCHISON, J. and J. A. C. BROWN. 1957: *The lognormal distribution.* Cambridge. (4.3.3)

AKERS, S. B. 1960: The use of the Wye-Delta transformation in network simplification. *Operations Research*, **8**, 311–23. (3.4.4)

ALEXANDER, J. W. 1944: Freight rates as a geographic factor in Illinois. *Economic Geography*, **20**, 25–30. (6.4.3, 8.2.3)

1963: *Economic geography.* New York. (8.2.3)

ALEXANDER, J. W., E. S. BROWN, and R. E. DAHLBERG. 1958: Freight rates; selected aspects of uniform and nodal regions. *Economic Geography*, **34**, 1–18. (5.6.1)

ALEXANDERSSON, G. 1956: *The industrial structure of American cities.* Lincoln, Nebr. (5.3.3, 5.4.1, 5.4.4)

ALLEN, G. R. 1954: The 'courbe des populations'—a further analysis. *Oxford Bulletin of Statistics*, **16**, 179–89. (4.3.1)

ALONSO, W. 1960: A theory of the urban land market. *Regional Science Association, Papers*, **6**, 149–58. (15.5.1)

1964: *Location and land use.* Cambridge, Mass. (6.6.2, 15.5.1)

ALVES, W. R. 1974: Comment on Hudson's 'Diffusion in a central place system'. *Geographical Analysis*, **6**, 303–8. (7.4)

AMADEO, D. and R. G. GOLLEDGE. 1975: *An introduction to scientific reasoning in geography.* New York. (1.2.1, 1.4.4)

ANDERSSON, T. 1897: *Den Inre omflyttningen: Norrland.* Mälmo. (2.2.2)

ANSCOMBE, F. J. 1950: Sampling theory of the negative binomial and logarithmic series distributions. *Biometrika*, **37**, 358–82. (13.3.1–2)

APPLEBAUM, W. and S. B. COHEN. 1961: The dynamics of store trading areas and market equilibrium. *Annals of the Association of American Geographers*, **51**, 73–101. (2.6.2)

AUERBACH, F. 1913: Das Gesetz der Bevölkerungskonzentration. *Petermann's Mitteilungen*, **59**, 74–6. (4.3.1)

BACHARACH, M. 1970: *Biproportional matrices and input–output change.* Cambridge. (4.4.2)

BACHI, R. 1963: Standard distance measures and related methods for spatial analysis. *Regional Science Association, Papers and Proceedings,* **10**, 83–132. (9.6.2, 13.7)

BAILEY, N. T. J. 1957: *The mathematical theory of epidemics.* New York. (7.1, 7.7.1, 7.7.3, 7.7.4, 7.7.6)

1967: The simulation of stochastic epidemics in two dimensions. *Fifth Berkeley Symposium on Mathematical Statistics and Probability Proceedings,* **4**, 237–57. (7.7.7)

1975: *The mathematical theory of infectious diseases.* London. (7.7.1, 7.7.3)

BAIN, J. S. 1954: Economics of scale, concentration, and the condition of entry in twenty manufacturing industries. *American Economic Review,* **44**, 15–39. (5.5.1)

BAKER, A. R. H. 1969: Reversal of the rank–size rule: some 19th century rural settlements in France. *Professional Geographer,* **21**, 389–92. (4.3.2)

BANNISTER, G. 1975: Towards a model of impulse transmissions for an urban system. *Boston University,* Mimeographed. (4.6.3)

BARFORD, B. 1938: *Local economic effects of a large-scale industrial undertaking.* Copenhagen. (5.4.2)

BARROWS, H. H. 1923: Geography as human ecology. *Annals of the Association ofAmerican Geographers,* **13**, 1–14. (1.2.3)

BARTHOLOMEW, D. J. 1973: *Stochastic models for social processes.* New York. (7.7.1–3, 7.7.5, 7.7.7, 7.8)

BARTHOLOMEW, H. 1955: *Land use in American cities.* Cambridge. (6.2.4)

BARTKO, J. J., S. W. GREEHOUSE and C. S. PATLAK. 1968: On expectations of some functions of Poisson variates. *Biometrics,* **24**, 97–102 (13.2.1)

BARTLETT, M. S. 1957: Measles periodicity and community size. *Journal of the Royal Statistical Society, A,* **120**, 48–70. (11.5.1)

1960: *Stochastic population models in ecology and epidemiology.* London. (7.7.4, 7.8)

1963: The spectral analysis of point processes. *Journal of the Royal Statistical Society, B,* **25**, 264–96. (12.4.3, 13.4.4)

1964: The spectral analysis of two-dimensional point processes. *Biometrika,* **51**, 299–311. (12.4.3)

BASSETT, K. and P. HAGGETT. 1971: Towards short-term forecasting for cyclic behaviour in a regional system of cities. In M. D. I. Chisholm, A. E. Frey and P. Haggett, Editors. *Regional forecasting.* London. 389–413. (4.6.3, 12.5.2)

BASSETT, K. and D. E. HAUSER. 1975: Public policy and spatial structure: housing improvements in Bristol. In R. F. Peel, M. D. I. Chisholm, and P. Haggett, Editors. *Processes in physical and human geography: Bristol essays.* London. 18–66. (9.4.1)

BATTY, M. 1975: *Urban modelling: algorithms, calibrations, predictions.* Cambridge. (5.3.3)

BECKMANN, M. J. 1958: City hierarchies and the distribution of city size. *Economic Development and Cultural Change,* **6**, 243–8. (2.6.2, 5.2.4)

BECKMANN, M. J. and T. MARSCHAK. 1955: An activity analysis approach to location theory. *Kyklos,* **8**, 125–41. (15.4.1)

BEESLEY, M. 1955: The birth and death of industrial establishments: experience in the West Midlands conurbation. *Journal of Industrial Economics,* **4**, 45–61. (5.5.3)

BELFORD, P. C. and H. D. RATCLIFF. 1972: A network flow model for racially balancing schools. *Operations Research,* **20**, 619–28. (14.5.1)

BELL, G. 1962: Change in city size distributions in Israel. *Ekistics,* **13**, 103. (4.4.1)

BENNETT, R. J. 1974: A review of *Spatial Autocorrelation*, by A. D. Cliff and J. K. Ord. *Environment and Planning*, **6**, 241. (11.2.2)

1974a: The representation and identification of spacio-temporal systems: an example of population diffusion in north-west England. *Institute of British Geographers, Publications*, **66**, 73–94. (4.6.3, 7.8, 16.4.1)

1975b, c, d, e: Dynamic systems modelling of the north-west region.
1. Spacio-temporal representation and identification
2. Estimation of the spatio-temporal policy model
3. Adaptive parameter policy model
4. Adaptive spacio-temporal forecasts

*Environment and Planning*, **7**, 525–38, 539–66, 617–36, 887–98. (16.7)

BERRY, B. J. L. 1960: An inductive approach to the regionalization of economic development. *University of Chicago, Department of Geography, Research Papers*, **62**, 78–107. (3.5.2, 4.3.4)

1961a: City size distributions and economic development. *Economic Development and Cultural Change*, **9**, 573–88. (4.3.4, 4.4.1, 5.5.3)

1961b: A method for deriving multifactor uniform regions. *Przeglad Geograficzny*, **33**, 263–82. (14.4.2)

1962: Sampling, coding, and storing flood plain data. *United States, Department of Agriculture, Farm Economics Division, Agriculture Handbook*, **237**. (8.3.2–3, 8.3.5)

1964: Approaches to regional analysis: a synthesis. *Annals of the Association of American Geographers*, **54**, 2–12. (1.4.1)

1966: Essays on commodity flow and the spatial structure of the Indian economy. *University of Chicago, Department of Geography, Research Papers*, **111**. (14.6)

1967: Grouping and regionalization: an approach to the problem using multivariate analysis. *Northwestern University, Studies in Geography*, **13**, 219–51. (14.4.2)

1972: Hierarchical diffusion—the basis of developmental filtering and spread in a system of growth centres. In N. M. Hansen, Editor, *Growth centres in regional economic development*. New York, 108–38. (7.4)

BERRY, B. J. L., H. G. BARNUM, and R. J. TENNANT. 1962: Retail location and consumer behaviour. *Regional Science Association, Papers and Proceedings*, **9**, 65–106. (5.2.1, 5.2.3, 5.2.5)

BERRY, B. J. L. and W. L. GARRISON. 1958a: Alternate explanations of urban rank–size relationships. *Annals of the Association of American Geographers*, **48**, 83–91. (4.3.4)

1958b: Functional bases of the central place hierarchy. *Economic Geography*, **34**, 145–54. (5.2.1)

BERRY, B. J. L. and F. E. HORTON. 1970: *Geographic perspectives on urban systems*. Englewood Cliffs, N.J. (6.6, 6.6.2)

BERRY, B. J. L., R. J. TENNANT, B. J. GARNER, and J. W. SIMMONS. 1963: Commercial structure and commercial blight. *University of Chicago, Department of Geography, Research Papers*, **85**. (6.2.2, 6.6.1)

BERRY, B. J. L. and D. F. MARBLE, Editors. 1968: *Spatial analysis: a reader in statistical geography*. Englewood Cliffs, N.J. (9.5.1)

BERRY, B. J. L. and A. PRED. 1961: Central place studies: a bibliography of theory and applications. *Regional Science Research Institute, Bibliographic Series*, **1**. (5.2.3)

BERTALANFFY, L. von. 1951: An outline of general system theory. *British Journal of the Philosophy of Science*, **1**, 134–65. (1.2.4)

BESAG, J. E. 1974: Spatial interaction and the statistical analysis of lattice systems (with discussion). *Journal of the Royal Statistical Society, B*, **36**, 192–236. (16.7)

BIRD, J. 1956: Scale in regional study: illustrated by brief comparisons between the western peninsulas of England and France. *Geography*, **41**, 25–38. (14.2.2)

BISSELL, A. F. 1972a: A negative binomial model with varying element sizes. *Biometrika*, **59**, 435–41. (13.4.3)

1972b: Another negative binomial model with varying element sizes. *Biometrika*, **59**, 691–93. (13.4.3)

1973: Monitoring event rates using varying sample element sizes. *The Statistician*, **22**, 43–58. (13.4.3)

BLEICHER, H. 1892: *Statistische Beschreibung der Stadt Frankfurt am Main und ihrer Bevölkerung*. Frankfurt. (6.2.2)

BLUMENSTOCK, D. I. 1953: The reliability factor in the drawing of isarithms. *Annals of the Association of American Geographers*, **43**, 289–304. (9.3.2)

BOARD, C. 1962: *The Border region: natural environment and land use in the eastern Cape*. Cape Town. (6.2.4)

BOARD, C., R. J. DAVIES, and T. J. D. FAIR. 1970: The structure of the South African space economy. *Regional Studies*, **4**, 367–92. (14.6.1)

BOGUE, D. J. 1950: *The structure of the metropolitan community: a study of dominance and subdominance*. Ann Arbor. (4.2.2, 5.4.2, 6.2.3, 13.5)

BOOTS, B. N. 1973: Some models of the random subdivision of space. *Geografiska Annaler, B*, **55**, 34–48. (13.5)

BOOTS, B. N. and L. F. LAMOUREAUX. 1972: Working notes and bibliography on the study of shape in human geography and planning. *Council of Planning Librarians, Exchange Bibliography*, **346**. (9.6.1)

BORCHERT, J. R. 1961: The twin cities urbanized area: past, present, and future. *Geographical Review*, **51**, 47–70. (3.5.2)

BOULDING, K. E. 1966: *The impact of the social sciences*. New Brunswick, N.J. (1.4.4)

BOWMAN, I. 1931: *The pioneer fringe*. New York. (7.1)

BOWMAN, K. O. 1973: Power of the kurtosis statistic, $b_2$, in tests of departures from normality. *Biometrika*, **60**, 623–28. (10.5.2)

BOX, G. E. P. 1953: Non-normality and tests on variances. *Biometrika*, **40**, 318–35. (10.5.1)

BOX, G. E. P., and G. M. JENKINS. 1970: *Time series analysis, forecasting and control*. San Francisco. (7.8, 11.5.1–2, 16.1–2, 16.3.1, 16.3.4, 16.4.1)

BRACEY, H. E. 1962: English central villages: identification, distribution and functions. *Lund Studies in Geography, Series B, Human Geography*, **24**, 169–90. (5.2.5)

BRAMS, S. J. 1966: Transactions and flows in the international system. *American Political Science Review*, **60**, 880–98. (14.6.2)

BRILLOUIN, L. 1964: *Scientific uncertainty and information*. New York. (1.2.4)

BROEK, J. O. M. 1932: *The Santa Clara valley, California: a study in landscape changes*. Utrecht. (1.2.4)

BRONOWSKI, J. 1960: *The common sense of science*. London. (1.4.3)

BROOKFIELD, H. C. and D. HART. 1971: *Melanesia*. London. (14.2.1)

BROOKS, C. E. P. and N. CARRUTHERS. 1953: *Handbook of statistical methods in meteorology*. London. (9.3.1)

BROWN, L. A. 1968: *Diffusion processes and location: a conceptual framework and bibliography*. Philadelphia. (7.1, 7.7.5)

BROWN, L. A., and K. R. COX. 1971: Empirical regularities in the diffusion of innovation. *Annals of the Association of American Geographers*, **61**, 551–59. (7.2.1, 7.3–4)

BROWN, L. A. and E. G. MOORE. 1969: Diffusion research in geography: a perspective. *Progress in Geography*, **1**, 119–57. (7.1, 7.6.2)

BRUNHES, J. 1925: *La géographie humaine*. Two volumes. Paris. (1.2.3, 4.2)

BRUSH, J. E. 1953: The hierarchy of central places in southwestern Wisconsin. *Geographical Review*, **43**, 380–402. (4.2.1)

1968: Spatial patterns of population in Indian cities. *Geographical Review*, **58**, 362–391. (6.6.1)

BRUSH, J. E. and H. E. BRACEY. 1955: Rural service centres in southwestern Wisconsin and southern England. *Geographical Review*, **45**, 559–69. (4.5.1)

BRUSH, J. E. and H. L. GAUTHIER. 1968: Service centres and consumer trips. *University of Chicago, Department of Geography, Research Papers*, **113**. (6.6.1)

BUNGE, W. 1962, 1966: Theoretical geography. *Lund Studies in Geography, Series C, General and Mathematical Geography*, **1**. (1.2.2, 2.2.1, 2.4.2, 2.4.4, 3.3.1–2, 5.2.1, 9.8.1, 14.2.1, 14.4.3)

1964: Patterns of location. *Michigan Inter-University Community of Mathematical Geographers, Discussion Papers*, **3**. (6.3.1)

1971: *Fitzgerald—the geography of a revolution*. Detroit. (1.4.5, 6.6.2)

BURGESS, E. W. 1927: The determination of gradients in the growth of the city. *American Sociological Society, Publications*, **21**, 178–84. (6.6.2)

BURGHARDT, A. F. 1959: The location of river towns in the central lowland of the United States. *Annals of the Association of American Geographers*, **49**, 305–323. (13.6.5)

1969: The origin and developments of the road network of the Niagara peninsula, 1770–1851. *Annals of the Association of American Geographers*, **59**, 417–40. (3.5.3)

BURTON, T. 1963a: The quantitative revolution and theoretical geography. *Canadian Geographer*, **7**, 151–62. (1.4.2)

1963b: A restatement of the dispersed city hypothesis. *Annals of the Association of American Geographers*, **53**, 285–9. (5.4.3)

BYLUND, E. 1960: Theoretical considerations regarding the distribution of settlement in inner north Sweden. *Geografiska Annaler*, **42**, 225–31. (4.2.3)

CARELESS, J. S. M. 1954: Frontierism, metropolitanism, and Canadian history. *Canadian Historical Review*, **35**, 1–21. (4.3)

CAROE, L. 1968: A multivariate grouping scheme—association analysis of East Anglian towns. In E. Bowen, H. Carter, and J. A. Taylor, Editors. *Geography at Aberystwyth*. London, 253–69. (14.4.1)

CARTER, H. 1969: *The study of urban geography*. London. (4.4.2)

CASETTI, E. 1964: Classificatory and regional analysis by discriminant iterations. *Office of Naval Research, Geography Branch, Contract 1228(16) Task 189–135, Technical Report*, **12**. (14.2.3)

1966: Optimal location of steel mills serving the Quebec and Southern Ontario steel market. *The Canadian Geographer*, **10**, 27–39. (15.4.1)

1967: Urban population density patterns: an alternative explanation. *Canadian Geographer*, **11**, 96–100. (6.2.2)

1969: Why do diffusion processes conform to logistic trends? *Geographical Analysis*, **1**, 101–105. (7.3)

CASETTI, E. and R. K. SEMPLE. 1969: Concerning the testing of spatial diffusion hypotheses. *Geographical Analysis*, **1**, 154–9. (6.2.1, 7.3)

CHAPIN, F. S., JR., and S. F. WEISS, Editors. 1962: *Urban growth dynamics in a regional cluster of cities.* New York.

CHAPMAN, G. P. 1970: The application of information theory to the analysis of population distributions in space. *Economic Geography*, **46**, 317–31. (4.3.3)

CHAPPELL, J. E. 1975: The ecological dimension: Russian and American views. *Annals of the Association of American Geographers*, **65**, 144–62. (1.2.2)

CHARNES, A. and W. W. COOPER. 1954: The stepping stone method of explaining linear programming calculation in transportation problems. *Management Science*, **1**, 49–69. (15.3)

CHERNOFF, H. and E. L. LEHMANN. 1954: The use of maximum likelihood estimates in $\chi^2$ tests for goodness of fit. *Annals of Mathematical Statistics*, **25**, 579–86. (13.3.4)

CHICAGO AREA TRANSPORTATION STUDY. 1960: *Final report*. Chicago. (2.3.4)

CHISHOLM, M. D. I. 1960: The geography of commuting. *Annals of the Association of American Geographers*, **50**, 187–8, 491–2. (8.4.2, 10.6.1)

1962: *Rural settlement and land use: an essay in location.* London. (2.6.1, 3.3.2, 4.2.3, 5.5.1, 6.2.4, 6.3.2, 6.4.1, 6.5.1–2, 9.3.4)

CHISHOLM, M. D. I. and P. O'SULLIVAN. 1973: *Freight flows and spatial aspects of the British economy.* Cambridge. (2.5.2, 15.2.3)

CHISHOLM, R. K. and G. R. WHITAKER. 1971: *Forecasting methods.* Homewood, Ill. (16.3.3)

CHORLEY, R. J. 1962: Geomorphology and general systems theory. *United States, Geological Survey, Professional Paper*, **500-B**. (1.1, 1.2.4)

1973: Geography as human ecology. Chapter 7. In Chorley, R. J., Editor. *Directions in Geography*. London, 155–69. (1.2.3)

CHORLEY, R. J. and P. HAGGETT, Editors. 1965a: *Frontiers in geographical teaching: the Madingley lectures for 1963.* London. (1.2.3, 1.4.2, 8.2.1, 14.2.1)

1965b: Trend-surface mapping in geographical research. *Institute of British Geographers, Publications*, **37**, 47–67. (12.2.2)

Editors. 1967: *Models in geography: the Madingley lectures for* 1965. London. (1.4.1–2, 3.3.1, 14.7)

CHORLEY, R. J. and B. A. KENNEDY. 1971: *Physical geography—a systems approach.* London. (13.2.1)

CHORLEY, R. J., D. R. STODDART, P. HAGGETT, and H. O. SLAYMAKER. 1966: regional and local components in the areal distribution of surface sand facies in the Breckland, Eastern England. *Journal of Sedimentary Petrology*, **36**, 209–20. (12.3.1–2)

CHOYNOWSKI, M. 1959: Maps based upon probabilities. *Journal of the American Statistical Associations*, **54**, 385–8. (9.5.2)

CHRIST, C. F. 1966: *Econometric models and methods.* New York. (16.1)

CHRISTALLER, W. 1933: *Die zentralen Orte in Süddeutschland: Eine ökonomisch-geographische Untersuchung über die Gesetzmässigkeit der Verbreitung und Entwicklung der Siedlungen mit städtischen Funktionen.* Jena. (2.6.1, 2.7.1, 4.2.1, 4.5.1, 5.2.2–3, 5.2.5)

1966: *Central places in Southern Germany.* Translated by C. W. Baskin. Englewood Cliffs, N.J. (2.7.1)

CLARK, A. H. 1954: Historical geography. In P. E. James, *et al.*, Editors, *American geography: inventory and prospect.* Syracuse. 70–105. (7.1)

CLARK, C. 1940: *Conditions of economic progress.* London. (9.4.1)

1951: Urban population densities. *Journal of the Royal Statistical Society*, A, **114**, 490–6. (6.1, 6.2.2, 6.6.1)

1967: *Population growth and land use.* London. (4.3.1)
CLARK, C., F. WILSON and J. BRADLEY. 1969: Industrial location and economic potential in Western Europe. *Regional Studies*, **3**, 197–212. (2.4.5)
CLARK, P. J. 1956: Grouping in spatial distributions. *Science*, **123**, 373–4. (13.6.5)
CLARK, P. J. and F. C. EVANS. 1954: Distance to nearest neighbour as a measure of spatial relationships in populations. *Ecology*, **35**, 445–53. (13.3.2, 13.6, 13.6.1, 13.6.4)
CLAWSON, M., R. B. HELD, and C. H. STODDARD. 1960: *Land for the future.* Baltimore. (2.6.1, 6.6.1)
CLIFF, A. D. 1965: Residential site selection in urban areas: an application of the Herbert–Stevens model to the city of Evanston, Illinois. *Northwestern University, Dept. of Geography*, M.A. Thesis. (15.5.1)
1968: The neighbourhood effect in the diffusion of innovations. *Institute of British Geographers, Publications*, **44**, 75–84. (7.3)
1970: Computing the spatial correspondence between geographical patterns. *Institute of British Geographers, Publications*, **50**, 143–54. (7.6.1)
CLIFF, A. D. and P. HAGGETT. 1970: On the efficiency of alternate aggregations in region-building problems. *Environment and Planning*, **2**, 285–94. (14.3)
CLIFF, A. D., P. HAGGETT, J. K. ORD, K. BASSETT, and R. B. DAVIES. 1975: *Elements of spatial structure: a quantitative approach.* Cambridge. (4.3.3, 4.6.1, 4.6.3, 7.7.6, 11.5.1–3, 12.2.1–2, 12.3.1, 12.3.3, 12.5.2, 14.3, 16.1, 16.3.1, 16.3.3–4, 16.5.1)
CLIFF, A. D., R. L. MARTIN, and J. K. ORD. 1974: Evaluating the friction of distance parameter in gravity models. *Regional Studies*, **8**, 281–6. (2.4.2, 4.3.3)
CLIFF, A. D., R. L. MARTIN, and J. K. ORD, 1975a: Map pattern and friction of distance parameters: reply to comments by R. J. Johnston, and by L. Curry, D. Griffith, and E. S. Sheppard. *Regional Studies*, **9**, 285–88. (2.4.2)
1975b: A test for spatial autocorrelation in choropleth maps based upon a modified $X^2$ statistic. *Institute of British Geographers, Publications*, **65**, 109–29. (10.2.3, 10.3.1)
CLIFF, A. D., and J. K. ORD. 1969: The problem of spatial autocorrelation. In A. J. Scott, Editor. *Studies in Regional Science.* London, 25–55. (10.5.2, 11.6)
1971: A regression approach to univariate spatial forecasting. In M. D. I. Chisholm, A. E. Frey, and P. Haggett, Editors. *Regional forecasting.* London. 47–70. (16.2.1, 16.5.1–2)
1972: Regional forecasting with an application to school-leaver patterns in the United Kingdom. In W. P. Adams and F. M. Helleiner, Editors. *International geography.* Montreal, 965–8. (12.3.1, 12.3.3, 16.5.1–2)
1973: *Spatial autocorrelation.* London. (4.2.1, 7.6.1–2, 9.3.3, 10.2.1, 10.3.2–3, 11.2.1, 11.3.1–4, 11.4.1–2, 11.5.2, 12.3.2, 13.2.1–2, 13.3.1, 13.4.2–3, 13.5, 16.2.2)
1975a: The comparison of means when samples consist of spatially autocorrelated observations. *Environment and Planning, A*, **7**, 725–34. (10.2, 10.2.1, 10.3, 10.3.1, 10.3.3, 11.6)
1975b: Model building and the analysis of spatial pattern in human geography. *Journal of the Royal Statistical Society, B*, **37**, 297–348. (7.3–4, 10.2.3, 10.4.2–3, 10.6.2, 12.4.2, 13.4.4, 13.6, 13.6.2, 13.7, 16.1, 16.2.1, 16.6, 16.7)
1975c: The choice of a test for spatial autocorrelation. In J. C. Davis and M. McCullagh, Editors. *Display and analysis of spatial data.* New York. (11.2.1)
1975d: Space–time modelling with an application to regional forecasting.

*Institute of British Geographers, Publications*, **64**, 119–28. (7.3)

CLIFF, A. D. and B. T. ROBSON. 1976: An application of a random partitioning model to the urban hierarchy of England and Wales, 1801–1966. Forthcoming. (4.4.1)

COATES, B. E., and E. M. RAWSTRON. 1971: *Regional variations in Britain*. London. (10.6)

COCHRAN, W. G. 1953: *Sampling techniques*. New York. (8.3.5)

COCHRAN, W. G., F. MOSTELLER, and J. W. TUKEY. 1954: Principles of sampling. *Journal of the American Statistical Association*, **49**, 13–35. (8.2.2)

COHEN, J. E. 1966: *A model of simple compeition*. Cambridge, Mass. (4.3.3)

COLE, J. P. 1960: Study of major and minor civil divisions in political geography. *Department of Geography, University of Nottingham*. Mimeographed. (9.6.1)

COLEMAN, A. 1969: A geographical model for land use analysis. *Geography*, **54**, 43–55. (6.2.4, 6.5.2)

CONVERSE, P. D. 1930: *Elements of marketing*. Englewood Cliffs, N.J. (2.3.2)

COOLEY, C. H. 1894: The theory of transportation. *American Economic Association, Publications*, **9** (3). (3.2.3)

COPPOCK, J. T. 1955: The relationship of farm and parish boundaries: a study in the use of agricultural statistics. *Geographical Studies*, **2**, 12–26. (8.2.3)

1960: The parish as a geographical-statistical unit. *Tijdschrift voor Economische en Sociale Geografie*, **51**, 317–26. (8.4.2)

CORMACK, R. M. 1971: A review of classification. *Journal of the Royal Statistical Society, A*. **134**, 321–67. (14.4.2)

COTTERILL, C. H. 1950: *Industrial plant location: its application to zinc smelting*. Saint Louis. (5.6.1,5.6.3)

COURT, A. and P. W. PORTER. 1964: The elusive point of minimum travel. *Annals of the Association of American Geographers*, **54**, 400–6. (9.6.2)

COX, K. R. 1968: On the utility and definition of regions in comparative political sociology. *Ohio State University, Department of Geography*, Mimeographed. (14.4.2)

COXETER, H. S. M. 1961: *Introduction to geometry*. New York. (2.7.1, 5.3.1)

CRESSWELL, W. L. and P. FROGGART. 1963: *The causation of bus driver accidents—an epidemiological study*. London. (13.2.4)

CROWE, P. R. 1938: On progress in geography. *Scottish Geographical Magazine*, **54**, 1–19. (2.2.1)

CROXTON, F. E., D. J. COWDEN, and S. KLEIN. 1968: *Applied general statistics*. New York. (8.3.1)

CURRY, L. 1962: The geography of service centres within towns: the elements of an operational approach. *Lund Studies in Geography, B, Human Geography*, **24**, 31–54. (5.4.3)

1964: The random spatial economy: an exploration in settlement theory. *Annals of the Association of American Geographers*, **54**, 138–46. (4.2.1, 4.3.3, 12.4.2, 13.3.1)

1967: Central places in the random spatial economy. *Journal of Regional Science*, **7**, 217–38. (4.2.1, 13.3.1)

1970: Univariate spatial forecasting. *Economic Geography*, **46**, 241–58. (16.1)

1971: Applicability of space–time moving average forecasting. In M. D. I. Chisholm, A. E. Frey and P. Haggett, Editors. *Regional Forecasting*. London. 11–24. (4.6.3, 10.3.2, 16.6)

1972: A spatial analysis of gravity flows. *Regional Studies*, **6**, 131–47. (2.4.2, 4.6.3)

CURRY, L., and G. BANNISTER. 1974: Forecasting township populations of Ontario from time–space covariances. In L. S. Bourne, R. D. MacKinnon, J. Siegel and J. W. Simmons, Editors. *Urban futures for central Canada: perspectives on forecasting urban growth and form.* Toronto. 34–59. (16.2.2)

CURRY, L., D. GRIFFITH, and E. S. SHEPPARD. 1975: Those gravity parameters again. *Regional Studies,* **9**, 289–96. (2.4.2)

DACEY, M. F. 1960: The spacing of river towns. *Annals of the Association of American Geographers,* **50**, 59–61. (13.6.5)

1962: Analysis of central place and point patterns by a nearest neighbour method. *Lund Studies in Geography, B, Human Geography,* **24**, 55–75. (4.2.1, 13.6)

1963: Order neighbor statistics for a class of random patterns in multidimensional space. *Annals of the Association of American Geographers,* **53**, 505–15. (2.7.2, 13.6.4)

1964: Modified Poisson probability law for point pattern more regular than random. *Annals of the Association of American Geographers,* **54**, 559–65. (4.2.1, 13.4.4)

1965: The geometry of central place theory. *Geografiska Annaler, B,* **47**, 111–24. (4.2.1, 13.5)

1966a: A compound probability law for a pattern more dispersed than random and with areal inhomogeneity. *Economic Geography,* **42**, 172–79. (4.2.1, 13.4.4)

1966b: A county seat model for the areal pattern of an urban system. *Geographical Review,* **56**, 527–42. (4.2.1, 13.4.4)

1966c: Population of places in a central place hierarchy. *Journal of Regional Science,* **6**, 27–33. (5.2.4)

1968: An empirical study of the areal distribution of houses in Puerto Rico. *Institute of British Geographers, Publications,* **45**, 51–70. (4.2.1, 13.3.1, 13.4.2)

1969a: Similarities in the areal distributions of houses in Japan and Puerto Rico. *Area,* **3**, 35–37. (4.2.1, 13.3.1)

1969b: Proportion of reflexive *n*th order neighbors in spatial distribution. *Geographical Analysis,* **1**, 385–88. (13.6.5)

1975: Evaluation of the Poisson approximation to measures of the random pattern in the square. *Geographical Analysis,* **7**, 351–67. (13.6.1)

DACEY, M. F. and T. TUNG. 1962: The identification of randomness in point patterns. *Journal of Regional Science,* **4**, 83–96. (2.7.2, 13.6.4, 13.6.6)

D'AGOSTINO, R. and E. S. PEARSON, 1973: Tests for departure from normality. Empirical results for the distributions of $b_2$ and $b_1$. *Biometrika,* **60**, 613–22. (10.5.2)

DÅHL, S. 1957: The contacts of Västerås with the rest of Sweden. *Lund Studies in Geography, B, Human Geography,* **13**, 206–43. (2.2.2)

DAVIS, D. H. 1926: Objectives in a geographic field study of a community. *Annals of the Association of American Geographers,* **16**, 102–9. (2.6.2)

DAVIS, J. C. 1973: *Statistics and data analysis in geology.* New York. (12.2.2)

DAVIS, J. C. and M. McCULLAGH. 1975: *Display and analysis of spatial data.* New York. (8.4.2)

DAVIS, W. K. and G. W. S. ROBINSON. 1968: The nodal structure of the Solent region. *Journal of the Town Planning Institute,* **54**, 18–22. (14.6.1)

DICKINSON, G. C. 1963: *Statistical mapping and the presentation of statistics.* London. (8.2.3, 8.4.1)

DICKINSON, R. E. 1964: *City and region: a geographical interpretation.* London. (6.2.4, 6.6.2)

DIXON, W. J. 1964: *Biomedical computer programs.* Los Angeles. (12.4.4)

DORFMAN, R., P. A. SAMUELSON, and R. M. SOLOW. 1958: *Linear programming and economic analysis.* New York. (15.2.2, 15.3, 15.5.2)

DUERR, W. A. 1960: *Fundamentals of forestry economics.* New York. (2.6.1, 5.6.1)

DUNCAN, O. D., R. P. CUZZORT, and B. DUNCAN. 1961: *Statistical geography: problems of analysing areal data.* Glencoe. (10.6.1)

DUNN, E. S. 1954: *The location of agricultural production.* Gainesville. (2.4.1, 6.3, 6.3.1–2)

DURBIN, J. 1959: Efficient estimation of parameters in moving average models. *Biometrika,* **46**, 306–16. (16.3.1)

DURBIN, J. and G. S. WATSON. 1950, 1951, 1971: Testing for serial correlation in least squares regression I, II, III. *Biometrika,* **37**, 409–28; **38**, 159–78; **58**, 1–19. (11.3.1, 11.4.1)

EDMONSON, M. S. 1961: Neolithic diffusion rates. *Current Anthropology,* **2**, 71–102. (7.1)

E.F.T.A. 1973: *National settlement strategies: a framework for regional development.* Geneva. (5.5.2)

EILON, S., C. D. T. WATSON GANDY, and N. CHRISTOFIDES. 1971: *Distribution management: mathematical modelling and practical analysis.* London. (3.4.2, 5.6.1).

ESCHER, M. C. 1960: *The graphic work of M. C. Escher.* New York. (1.4)

FANO, P. 1969: Organization, city size distributions and central places. *Regional Science Association, Papers,* **22**, 29–38. (4.3.3)

FARMER, B. H. 1957: *Pioneer peasant colonization in Ceylon.* London. (4.2.3, 6.5.2, 7.1)

FELLER, W. 1943: On a general class of contagious distributions. *Annals of Mathematical Statistics,* **14**, 389–400. (13.2.4)

FENNEMANN, N. M. 1916: Physiographic divisions of the United States. *Annals of the Association of American Geographers,* **6**, 19–98. (14.2.2)

FISHER, R. A. 1941: The negative binomial distribution. *Annals of Eugenics,* **11**, 182–87. (13.2.4)

FISHER, R. A. and F. YATES. 1957: *Statistical tables for biological, agricultural, and medical research.* Edinburgh. (4.2.3, 9.3.1, 10.5.2)

FISHMAN, G. S. 1968: *Spectral methods in econometrics.* Santa Monica. (12.4.4)

FLORENCE, P. S. 1944: The selection of industries suitable for dispersal into rural areas. *Journal of the Royal Statistical Society,* **107**, 93–116. (5.5.2, 10.6.1)

1953: *The logic of British and American industry.* London. (5.5.1, 5.5.2, 5.6.3, 6.5.2)

FOLGER, J. 1953: Some aspects of migration in the Tennessee valley. *American Sociological Review,* **18**, 253–60. (2.6.2)

FOLKE, S. 1972: Why a radical geography must be Marxist. *Antipode,* **4**, 13–18. (1.4.5)

FORD, L. R. JR., and D. R. FULKERSON. 1962: *Flows in networks.* Princeton. (3.4.4)

FORER, P. 1974: Changes in the spatial structure of the New Zealand airline network. *Bristol University, Ph.D. Dissertation.* (9.7.2)

FORGOTSON, J. M. 1960: Review and classification of quantitative mapping techniques. *Bulletin of the American Association of Petroleum Geologists,* **44**, 83–100. (9.4.1)

FOUND, W. C. 1971: *A theoretical approach to rural land-use patterns.* London. (6.5.1, 6.5.3)

FOX, J. W. 1956: Land-use survey: general principles and a New Zealand example. *Auckland University College, Bulletin*, **49**. (6.2.4)

FREUND, J. E. 1967: *Modern elementary statistics.* Third edition. Englewood Cliffs, N.J. (10.1)

FRIEDMANN, J. 1972: A general theory of polarized development. In N. M. Hansen, Editor. *Growth centres in regional economic development.* New York. (6.1)

FRIEDRICH, C. J. 1929: *Alfred Weber's theory of the location of industries.* Chicago. (5.5., 5.6.1)

GARRISON, W. L. 1960: Connectivity of the interstate highway system. *Regional Science Association, Papers and Proceedings*, **6**, 121–37. (3.5.1, 9.7.1)

GARRISON, W. L., B. J. L. BERRY, D. F. MARBLE, J. D. NYSTUEN, R. L. MORRILL. 1959: *Studies of highway development and geographic change.* Seattle. (14.5.3, 15.1)

GARRISON, W. L. and D. F. MARBLE. 1962: The structure of transportation networks. *United States Army, Transportation Research Command, Contract 44–177–TC–685, Task 9R98–09–003–01 Technical Report, 62–11.* (9.7.4)

GATTRELL, A. C. 1975: Complexity and redundancy in binary maps. *Pennsylvania State University, Department of Geography.* Mimeographed. (9.3.3)

GAUTHIER, H. L. 1968: Least cost flows in a capacitated network: a Brazilian example. *Northwestern University, Studies in Geography*, **16**, 102–27. (15.4.2)

GEARY, R. C. 1954: The contiguity ratio and statistical mapping. *The Incorporated Statistician*, **5**, 115–45. (11.4.2)

G.E.C. DEFENSE SYSTEMS DEPARTMENT. 1962: *Tables of the individual and cumulative terms of the Poisson distribution.* New York. (13.3.4)

GETIS, A. 1963: The determination of the location of retail activities with the use of a map transformation. *Economic Geography*, **39**, 1–22. (2.7.3)

1967: Occupancy theory and map pattern analysis. *Department of Geography, University of Bristol. Seminar Paper Series A*, **1** (13.4.2)

1974: Representation of spatial point pattern processes by Polya models. In M. Yeates, Editor. *IGU Commission on Quantitative Geography, Proceedings of the 1972 meeting.* Montreal, 76–100. (13.3.1)

GETIS, A. and B. N. BOOTS. 1971: Spatial behaviour: rats and man. *Professional Geographer*, **23**, 11—14. (6.6.1)

GIBBS, J. P., Editor. 1961: *Urban research methods.* New York. (4.3.1, 4.5.2, 9.6.1)

GILG, A. W. 1973: A study in agricultural disease diffusion. *Institute of British Geographers, Publications*, **59**, 77–97. (7.1)

GINSBURG, N. 1961: *Atlas of economic development.* Chicago. (3.5.2, 8.2.2, 8.4.1, 9.4.3)

GODDARD, J. 1970: Functional regions within the city centre: a study by factor analysis of taxi flows in central London. *Institute of British Geographers, Publications*, **49**, 161–82. (14.6)

1973: *Office linkages and location: a study of communications and spatial patterns in central London.* Oxford. (5.5.2)

GODLUND, S. 1956: Bus service in Sweden. *Lund Studies in Geography, B, Human Geography*, **17**, (7.1)

1961: Population, regional hospitals, transport facilities and regions: planning the location of regional hospitals in Sweden. *Lund Studies in Geography, B, Human Geography*, **21**. (14.1)

GOLDTHWAIT, J. W. 1927: A town that has gone downhill. *Geographical Review*, **17**, 527–52. (5.4.2)

GOODCHILD, M. F. 1972: The trade area of a displaced regional lattice point. *Geographical Analysis*, **4**, 105–7. (5.2.2)

GOLLEDGE, R. G. and G. RUSHTON. 1972: Multidimensional scaling—review and geographical applications. *Association of American Geographers, Commission on College Geography, Technical Papers*, **10**. (9.8.2)

GOODRICH, C. 1936: *Migration and economic opportunity*. Philadelphia. (2.4.4)

GOTTMANN, J. 1961: *Megalopolis: the urbanized northeastern seaboard of the United States*. New York. (6.3.2, 6.5.1)

GOULD, P. R. 1960: The development of the transportation pattern in Ghana. *Northwestern University, Studies in Geography*, **5**. (3.5.3)

1963: Man against his environment: a game-theoretic framework. *Annals of the Association of American Geographers*, **53**, 290–7. (6.5.1)

1965: Wheat on Kilimanjaro: the perception of choice within game and learning model frameworks. *General Systems*, **10**, 157–66. (15.5.2)

1967: On the geographical interpretation of eigenvalues. *Institute of British Geographers, Publications*, **42**, 53–86. (9.7.4)

1970: Is Statistix Inferens the geographical name for a wild goose? *Economic Geography* (*Supplement*), **46**, 439–48. (10.2, 10.3.1, 11.2.1)

1972: Pedagogic review: entropy in urban and regional modelling. *Annals of the Association of American Geographers*, **62**, 689–700. (2.5.1–2)

GOULD, P. R. and T. R. LEINBACH. 1966: An approach to the geographic assignment of hospital services. *Tijdschrift voor Economische en Sociale Geografie*, **57**, 203–6. (15.1)

GOULD, P. R. and R. R. WHITE. 1974: *Mental maps*. Harmondsworth. (2.4.2)

GRANDELL, J. 1972: Statistical inference for doubly stochastic Poisson processes. In P. A. W. Lewis, Editor. *Stochastic point processes*. New York. 90–121. (13.4.4)

GRANGER, C. W. J. 1969: Spatial data and time series analysis. In A. J. Scott, Editor. *Studies in regional science*. London, 1–24. (10.4.1, 10.4.3, 10.6.2, 12.4, 12.4.1, 12.5.1)

GRANGER, C. W. J. and M. HATANAKA. 1964: *Spectral analysis of economic time series*. Princeton. (12.4.4, 12.5.1, 12.5.3)

GRANGER, C. W. J. and A. O. HUGHES. 1968: Spectral analysis of short series—a simulation study. *Journal of the Royal Statistical Society, A*, **131**, 83–99. (12.4.4, 12.5.1, 12.5.3)

GREEN, F. H. W. 1950: Urban hinterlands in England and Wales: an analysis of bus services. *Geographical Journal*, **96**, 64–81. (2.6.2)

GREENHUT, M. L. 1956: *Plant location in theory and practice: the economics of space*. Chapel Hill. (5.6.2)

GREENWOOD, M. 1931: On the statistical measure of infectiousness. *Journal of Hygiene*, **31**, 336–51. (7.7.6)

GREIG-SMITH, P. 1957, 1964: *Quantitative plant ecology*. London. (12.3.1)

GRIGG, D. B. 1965: The logic of regional systems. *Annals of the Association of American Geographers*, **55**, 465–91. (14.2.1, 14.7)

GRILICHES, Z. 1957: Hybrid corn: an exploration in the economics of technological change. *Econometrica*, **25**, 501–22. (7.3)

GROTEWALD, A. 1959: Von Thünen in retrospect. *Economic Geography*, **35**, 346–55. (6.3.2)

GRYTZELL, K. G. 1963: The demarcation of comparable city areas by means of population density. *Lund Studies in Geography, B, Human Geography*, **25**. (8.2.3)

GUELKE, L. 1971: Problems of scientific explanation in geography. *Canadian Geographer*, **15**, 38–53. (1.4.3–4)

GULLEY, J. L. M. 1959: The Turnerian frontier: a study in the migration of ideas. *Tijdschrift voor Economische en Sociale Geografie*, **50**, 65–72, 81–91. (7.1)

GÜLÖKSÜZ, G. 1975: Rank-size distributions for small settlements in Turkey. *Middle East Technical University, Journal of the Faculty of Architecture*, **1**, 145–52. (4.3.2)

GUNAWARDENA, K. A. 1964: Service centres in southern Ceylon. *University of Cambridge, Ph.D. Thesis*. (4.3.2, 5.2.1, 5.2.5)

GURLAND, J. 1957: Sime interrelations among compound and generalized distributions. *Biometrika*, **44**, 265–68. (13.2.2)

HÄGERSTRAND, T. 1952: The propagation of innovation waves. *Lund Studies in Geography, B, Human Geography*, **4**, 3–19. (7.1)

1953: *Innovationsforloppet ur korologisk synpunkt*. Lund. (7.1, 7.8, 13.3.1)

1955: Statistika primäruppgifter, flykartering och data processing maskiner. *Meddelanden Frans Lunds Geografiska Institut*, **344**, 233–55. (9.8.1, 10.5)

1957: Migration and area: survey of a sample of Swedish migration fields and hypothetical considerations on their genesis. *Lund Studies in Geography, B, Human Geography*, **13**, 27–158. (2.3.1, 2.4.2, 2.4.3, 2.6.2, 4.2, 4.2.3)

1965a: Quantitative techniques for analysis of the spread of information and technology. In C. A. Anderson and M. J. Bowman, Editors. *Education and economic development*. Chicago. 244–80. (7.2.1)

1965b: A Monte Carlo approach to diffusion. *European Journal of Sociology*, **6**, 43–67. (13.3.1)

1967: On Monte Carlo simulation of diffusion. *Northwestern University, Studies in Geography*, **13**, 1–32. (7.2.2, 7.4, 7.6.1, 7.7.2)

1971: Regional forecasting and social engineering. In M. D. I. Chisholm, A. E. Frey and P. Haggett, Editors. *Regional forecasting*. London. 1–7. (16.1)

HAGGETT, P. 1961: Multilevel variance analysis of *sobreiro* distribution in the Tagus–Sado basin, central Portugal. Mimeographed. (6.2.1, 10.5.2, 12.3.2)

1963: Regional and local components in land-use sampling: a case study from the Brazilian Triangulo. *Erdkunde*, **17**, 108–14. (8.3.3)

1964: Regional and local components in the distribution of forested areas in southeast Brazil: a multivariate approach. *Geographical Journal*, **130**, 365–80. (8.3.2, 8.4.2, 10.5.2, 12.2.3)

1965: *Locational analysis in human geography*. (First edition) London. (12.2.3)

1972: Contagious processes in a planar graph: an epidemiological application. In N. D. McGlashan, Editor. *Medical Geography*. London. 307–24. (4.6.1, 11.5.1, 11.5.3)

1973: Forecasting alternative spatial, ecological and regional futures: problems and possibilities. In R. J. Chorley, Editor. *Directions in Geography*. London. 219–35. (16.1)

1975a: *Geography: a modern synthesis*. New York. 546–72. (Preface, 1.2.1, 1.2.4, 1.3, 5.2.3, 8.3.4, 8.4.1, 14.5.2, 16.1)

1975b: Simple epidemics in human populations: some geographical aspects of the Hamer–Soper diffusion models. In R. F. Peel, M. D. I. Chisholm, and P. Haggett, Editors. *Processes in physical and human geography: Bristol essays*. London. Chapter 18. (7.7.4)

1976: Measuring instability in the growth of urban systems: a biproportionate index. *Geoforum*. In press. (4.4.2)

HAGGET, P., and K. A. BASSETT. 1970: The use of trend surface parameters in inter-urban comparisons. *Environment and Planning*, **2**, 225–37. (12.2.2)

HAGGETT, P., and C. BOARD. 1964: Rotational and parallel traverses in the rapid integration of geographic areas. *Annals of the Association of American Geographers*, **54**, 406–10. (8.3.3)

HAGGETT, P., and R. J. CHORLEY. 1969: *Network analysis in geography*. London. (3.1, 3.2.2, 3.3.2, 15.3)

HAGGETT, P., R. J. CHORLEY, and D. R. STODDART. 1965: Scale standards in geographical research: a new measure of area magnitude. *Nature*, **205**, 844–7. (1.2.4)

HAGGETT, P., and K. A. GUNAWARDENA. 1964: Determination of population thresholds for settlement functions by the Reed–Muench method. *Professional Geographer*, **16**, 6–9. (5.2.1)

HAGOOD, M. J. 1943: Statistical methods for delineation of regions applied to data on agriculture and population. *Social Forces*, **21**, 288–97. (14.4.4)

HAGOOD, M. J., and D. O. PRICE. 1952: *Statistics for sociologists*. New York. (14.4.3, 14.4.4)

HAIG, R. M. 1925–6: Towards an understanding of the metropolis. *Quarterly Journal of Economics*, **40**, 427. (5.5.2)

HALL, A. D., and R. E. FAGEN. 1956: Definition of system. *General Systems Yearbook*, **1**, 18–28. (1.2.3)

HALL, P. 1962: *The industries of London since* 1861. London. (8.4.1)
1966: *Von Thünen's isolated state*. Oxford. (6.3.2)

HAMER, W. H. 1906: Epidemic disease in England. *The Lancet*, 733–39. (7.7.4)

HAMMERSLEY, J. M. 1966: First passage percolation. *Journal of the Royal Statistical Society*, **B**, **28**, 491–96. (7.7.7)

HAMMERSLEY, J. M., and D. C. HANDSCOMB. 1963 *Monte Carlo methods*. London. (7.7.7)

HAMMERSLEY, J. M., and R. S. WALTERS. 1963: Percolating and fractional branching processes. *Journal of the Society for Industrial and Applied Mathematics*, **11**, 831–39. (7.7.7)

HAMMOND, R., and P. S. McCULLAGH. 1974: *Quantitative techniques in geography*. Oxford. (10.1)

HANNERBERG, D., T. HÄGERSTRAND, and B. ODEVING. 1957: Migration in Sweden: a symposium. *Lund Studies in Geography, B, Human Geography*, **13**. (2.2.1)

HANSON, N. R. 1958: *Patterns of discovery*. Cambridge. (1.1)

HARDY, T. 1886: *The life and death of the mayor of Casterbridge*. London. (5.4.1)

HARMAN, H. 1960: *Modern factor analysis*. Chicago. (9.4.3)

HARRIS, C. D. 1954: The market as a factor in the localization of industry in the United States. *Annals of the Association of American Geographers*, **44**, 315–48. (2.4.2)

HARRIS, C. D., and E. L. ULLMAN. 1945: The nature of cities. *Annals of the American Academy of Political and Social Science*, **242**, 7–17. (6.6.2)

HARRISON, P. J. 1965: Short-term sales forecasting. *Applied Statistics*, **14**, 102–39. (6.3.3)

HART, J. F. 1954: Central tendency in areal distributions. *Economic Geography*, **30**, 48–59. (9.6.2)

HARTSHORNE, R. 1939: *The nature of geography: a critical survey of current thought in the light of the past*. Lancaster. (1.2.2, 1.2.3, 1.2.4, 1.4.3)
1959: *Perspective on the nature of geography*. London. (1.2.1, 8.1)

HARVEY, D. W. 1963: Locational change in the Kentish hop industry and the analysis of land use patterns. *Institute of British Geographers, Publications*, **33**, 123–44. (6.5.2)

1966: Geographical processes and the analysis of point patterns: testing models of diffusion by quadrat sampling. *Institute of British Geographers, Publications*, **40**, 81–95. (13.3.1)

1968a: Pattern, process and the scale problem in geographical research. *Institute of British Geographers, Publications*, **45**, 71–78. (10.6.2)

1968b: Some methodological problems in the use of the Neyman Type A and negative binomial probability distributions for the analysis of spatial point patterns. *Institute of British Geographers, Publications*, **44**, 85–95. (13.2, 13.4.4, 15.4.4)

1969a: *Explanation in geography*. London. (1.2.2, 14.2.1, 14.2.3)

1969b: Conceptual and measurement problems in the cognitive-behavioural approach to location theory. *Northwestern University, Studies in Geography*, **17**, 35–67. (6.5.3)

1972a: Revolutionary and counter revolutionary theory in geography and the problem of ghetto formation. *Antipode*, **4**, 1–13. (1.4.5)

1972b: Society, the city and the space economy of urbanism. *Association of American Geographers, Commission on College Geography, Resource Papers*, **18**. (6.6.2)

1973: *Social justice and the city*. London. (6.6.2, 15.5.1)

HAWLEY, A. H. 1950: *Human ecology*. New York. (1.2.3)

HAYNES, R. M. 1975: Dimensional analysis: some applications in human geography. *Geographical Analysis*, **7**, 51–68. (2.4.3)

HELVIG, M. 1964: Chicago's external truck movements: spatial interactions between the Chicago area and its hinterland. *University of Chicago, Department of Geography, Research Papers*, **90**. (2.2.2, 2.4.3)

HENDERSON, J. M. 1955a: Efficiency and pricing in the coal industry. *Review of Economics and Statistics*, **37**, 50–60. (15.1)

1955b: A short-run model of the coal industry. *Review of Economics and Statistics*, **37**, 224–30. (15.1)

1958: *The efficiency of the coal industry: an application of linear programming*. Cambridge, Mass. (15.1)

HEPPLE, L. W. 1975: Spectral techniques and the study of interregional economic cycles. In R. F. Peel, M. D. I. Chisholm, and P. Haggett, Editors. *Processes in physical and human geography: Bristol essays*. London, 392–408. (4.6.3, 12.5.2)

HERBERT, D. J., and B. H. STEVENS. 1960: A model for the distribution of residential activity in urban areas. *Journal of Regional Science*, **2**, 21–36. (15.5.1)

HERFINDAHL, O. C. 1969: *Natural resources information for economic development*. Baltimore, Md. (8.4.1)

HESS, S. W., J. B. WEAVER, H. J. SIEGFELT, J. N. WHELAN, and P. A. ZITLAU. 1965: Nonpartisan redistricting by computer. *Operations Research*, **13**, 998–1006. (14.5.2)

HIDORE, J. J. 1963: The relations between cash-grain farming and landforms. *Economic Geography*, **39**, 84–9. (6.5.1)

HIGGS, R. 1969: The growth of cities in a Midwestern region 1870–1900. *Journal of Regional Science*, **9**, 369–75. (5.3.2)

HIGHSMITH, R. M., O. H. HEINTZELMAN, J. G. JENSEN, R. D. RUDD, and P. R. TSCHIRLEY. 1961: *Case studies in world geography*. New York. (8.3)

HODDER, B. W. 1966: Some comments on the origins of traditional markets in

Africa south of the Sahara. *Institute of British Geographers, Publications*, **36**, 97–105. (5.3.1)

HODGE, D., and A. GATTRELL. 1975: Spatial constraint and the location of urban public facilities. *Pennsylvania State University*. Mimeographed. (9.3.3)

HOEL, P. G. 1966: *Elementary statistics* (2nd edition). New York. (10.1)

HOLGATE, P. 1965: Some new tests of randomness. *Journal of Ecology*, **53**, 261–66. (13.6, 13.6.1, 13.6.4, 13.7)

1972: The use of distance methods for the analysis of spatial distributions of points. In P. A. W. Lewis, Editor. *Stochastic point processes*. New York, 122–35. (13.6, 13.7, 13.6.1)

HOLMES, J. H. 1973: Population concentration and dispersion in Australian states. *Australian Geographical Studies*, **11**, 150–70. (4.3.1)

1973: Telephone traffic in the Queensland urban system. *University of Queensland*. Mimeographed. (14.6.1–2)

HOLMES, J. H., and P. HAGGETT. 1975: Graph theory interpretation of flow matrices: a note on maximization procedures for identifying significant links. *University of Queensland*. Mimeographed. (9.4.2, 14.6.2)

HOLT, C. C. 1957: Forecasting seasonals and trends by experimentally weighted moving averages. *Carnegie Institute of Technology, Research Memoirs*, **52**. (16.3.3)

HOOVER, E. M. 1936: The measurement of industrial localization. *Review of Economics and Statistics*, **18**, 162–71. (9.3.4)

1948: *The location of economic activity*. New York.

HOPE, A. C. A. 1968: A simplified Monte Carlo significance test procedure. *Journal of the Royal Statistical Society, B*, **30**, 582–98. (7.6.2, 13.5)

HOSKINS, W. G. 1955: *The making of the English landscape*. London. (4.2.3)

HOTELLING, H. 1921: A mathematical theory of migration. *University of Washington, M.A. Thesis*. (2.4.4)

HOUSE, J. W. 1953: Medium sized towns in the urban pattern of two industrial societies: England and Wales—U.S.A. *Planning Outlook*, **3**, 52–79. (4.5.1)

HOWARD, E. 1920: *Territory in bird life*. London. (2.7)

HOWE, G. M. 1963: *National atlas of disease mortality in the United Kingdom*. London. (1.2.2)

HOYT, H. 1939: *The structure and growth of residential neighbourhoods in American cities*. Washington. (6.6.2)

HSU, S. Y., and J. D. MASON. 1974: The nearest-neighbour statistics for testing randomness of point distributions in a bounded two-dimensional space. In M. Yeates, Editor. *Proceedings of the 1972 meeting of the IGU Commission on Quantitative Geography*. Montreal. (13.6.2)

HUANG, D. S. 1970: *Regression and econometric methods*. New York. (16.2.1)

HUDSON, J. C. 1969a: Diffusion in a central place system. *Geographical Analysis*, **1**, 456–58. (7.3–4)

1969b: A location theory for rural settlement. *Annals of the Association of American Geographers*, **59**, 365–81. (4.2.3)

1972: *Geographical diffusion theory*. Evanston, Ill. (7.4, 7.7.7)

HUFF, D. L. 1960: A topographical model of consumer space preferences. *Regional Science Association, Papers*, **6**, 159–73. (2.4.2)

HUNT, L. G. 1974: Recent spread of heroin use in the United States. *American Journal of Public Health*, **64**, Supplement, 16–23. (4.6.1)

HURST, M. E. ELIOT, Editor. 1974: *Transportation geography: comments and readings*. New York. (3.2.3, 3.5)

HURTER, A. P., and L. N. MOSES. 1964: Regional investment and interregional programming. *Regional Science Association, Papers*, **13**, 105–19. (15.4.1)

ILLICH, I. D. 1974: *Energy and equity.* London. (5.5.2)

INGRAM, G. K., J. F. KAIN, and J. R. GINN. 1972: *The Detroit prototype of the NBER urban simulation model.* New York. (15.5.1)

INTERNATIONAL GEOGRAPHICAL UNION. 1964: *Abstracts of papers, 20th International Geographical Congress.* London. (3.3.2, 4.3)

INTERNATIONAL URBAN RESEARCH. 1959: *The world's metropolitan areas.* Berkeley. (4.3, 8.2.3)

INTRILIGATOR, M. D. 1971: *Mathematical optimization and economic theory.* Englewood Cliffs, N.J. (15.5.3)

ISARD, W. 1956: *Location and space-economy: a general theory relating to industrial location, market areas, land use, trade and urban structure.* New York. (1.2.2, 2.2.2, 2.7.3, 4.2.2, 4.3.1, 5.5, 5.6.1–2, 6.5.2)

ISARD, W., D. F. BRAMHALL, G. A. P. CARROTHERS, J. H. CUMBERLAND, L. N. MOSES, D. O. PRICE, and E. W. SCHOOLER. 1960: *Methods of regional analysis: an introduction to regional science.* New York. (1.3, 2.1, 2.4.1, 2.4.3–4, 5.4.2, 5.4.4, 5.5, 5.5.1, 5.6.3, 15.4.1)

ISARD, W., and S. CZAMANSKI. 1965: Techniques for estimating multiplier effects of major government programs. *Papers of the Peace Research Society*, **3**, 19–45. (5.3.3)

ISARD, W., and R. E. KUENNE. 1953: The impact of steel upon the Greater New York–Philadelphia industrial region: a study in agglomeration projection. *Review of Economics and Statistics*, **35**, 289–301. (5.4.2)

ISARD, W., and E. W. SCHOOLER. 1955: *Location factors in the petrochemical industry.* Washington. (5.5.1)

ISBELL, E. C. 1944: Internal migration in Sweden and intervening opportunities. *American Sociological Review*, **9**, 627–39. (2.6.2)

JAMES, G., A. D. CLIFF, P. HAGGETT, and J. K. ORD. 1970: Some discrete distributions for graphs with applications to regional transport networks. *Geografiska Annaler, B*, **52**, 14–21. (9.7.2)

JAMES, P. E. 1959: *Latin America.* New York. (6.6.2)

JAMES, P. E., C. F. JONES, and J. K. WRIGHT, Editors. 1954: *American geography: inventory and prospect.* Syracuse. (1.2.4, 14.2.2)

JANES, E. T. 1957: Information theory and statistical mechanics. *Physics Review*, **106**, 620–30. (2.5.2)

JEFFERS, J. N. R. 1959: *Experimental design and analysis in forest research.* Stockholm. (10.5.2)

JENKINS, G. M., and D. G. WATTS. 1968: *Spectral analysis and its applications.* San Francisco. (12.4.1, 12.4.4, 12.5.1, 12.5.3)

JENKS, G. F. 1963: Generalization in statistical mapping. *Annals of the Association of American Geographers*, **53**, 15–26. (9.3.1)

JENKS, G. F., and M. R. C. COULSON. 1963: Class intervals for statistical maps. *International Yearbook of Cartography*, **3**, 119–34. (9.3.1)

JEVONS, F. R. 1973: *Science observed.* London. (1.4.1)

JOERG, W. L. G., Editor. 1932: *Pioneer settlement.* New York. (7.1)

JOHNSON, H. B. 1941: The distribution of German pioneer population in Minnesota. *Rural Sociology*, **6**, 16–34. (2.6.2)

1957: Rational and ecological aspects of the quarter section: an example from Minnesota. *Geographical Review*, **47**, 330–48. (4.2.1)

1962: A note on Thünen's circles. *Annals of the Association of American Geographers*, **52**, 213–20. (6.3.2)

JOHNSON, W. W. 1892: *The theory of errors and method of least squares.* New York. (9.6.2)

JOHNSTON, J. 1972: *Econometric methods..* (Second edition) New York. (10.2.2, 10.3.1–3, 11.4.2, 12.2.2, 16.2.1, 16.4.2)

JOHNSTON, R. J. 1971: *Urban residential patterns.* London. (6.6.2)

1973: On frictions of distance and regression coefficients. *Area*, **5**, 187–91. (2.4.2)

1975: Map pattern and friction of distance parameters: a comment. *Regional Studies*, **9**, 281–83. (2.4.2)

JONASSON, O. 1925: Agricultural regions of Europe. *Economic Geography*, **2**. (6.4.1)

JONES, E. 1964: *Human geography.* London. (4.2., 4.2.2)

JOHNSON, B. L. C. 1958: The distribution of factory population in the West Midlands conurbation. *Institute of British Geographers, Publications*, **25**, 209–223. (8.4.2)

KAIN, J. F. 1962: The journey-to-work as a determinant of residential location. *Regional Science Association, Papers and Proceedings*, **9**, 137–59. (2.2.1)

KAISER, H. F. 1966: An objective method for establishing legislative districts. *Midwest Journal of Political Science*, **10**, 80–96. (14.5.2)

KANSKY, K. J. 1963: Structure of transport networks: relationships between network geometry and regional characteristics. *University of Chicago, Department of Geography, Research Papers*, **84**. (3.4.3, 3.5.1, 9.7.1)

KARIEL, H. G. 1963: Selected factors areally associated with population growth due to net migration. *Annals of the Association of American Geographers*, **53**, 210–23. (2.4.4)

KARLQVIST, A., and L. LUNDQVIST. 1972: A contact model for spatial allocation. *Regional Studies*, **6**, 401–19. (5.5.2)

KATTI, S. K., and J. GURLAND. 1961: The Poisson Pascal distribution. *Biometrics*, **17**, 527–38. (13.2.4)

KEMP, C. D. 1967: On a contagious distribution suggested for accident data. *Biometrics*, **23**, 241–55. (13.3.1, 13.2.4)

KENDALL, D. G. 1957: La propagation d'une épedémie au d'un bruit une population limitée. *Publications de l'Institut de Statistique de l'Université de Paris*, **6**, 307–11. (7.7.3)

1965: Mathematical models of the spread of infection. In Medical Research Council. *Mathematics and Computer Science in Biology and Medicine.* London. 213–25. (7.7.3)

1971: Construction of maps from 'odd bits of information'. *Nature*, **231**, 158–9. (9.8.2)

KENDALL, M. G. *Time series.* London. (10.4.3, 11.3.1, 12.4.1–2, 12.4.4, 12.5.1–2, 16.1, 16.3.2–3)

KENDALL, M. G., and W. R. BUCKLAND. 1960: *A dictionary of statistical terms.* Edinburgh. (8.2.2, 12.5.1)

KENDALL, M. G., and P. A. P. MORAN. 1963: *Geometrical probability.* London. (4.3.3)

KENDALL, M. G., and A. STUART. 1966: *The advanced theory of statistics*, **3**. *Analysis of variance and time series.* London. (12.3.1, 16.5.1)

1967: *The advanced theory of statistics*, **2**. *Inference and relationship.* London. (10.5.1–3, 16.4.2)

KERMACK, W. O., and A. G. McKENDRICK. 1927: Contributions to the mathematical theory of epidemics. *Proceedings of the Royal Society, A*, **115**, 700–21. (7.7.3)

KERSHAW, K. A. 1964: *Quantitative and dynamic ecology.* London. (8.3.3)

KING, L. J. 1961: A multivariate analysis of the spacing of urban settlements in the United States. *Annals of the Association of American Geographers*, **51**, 222–33. (4.5.2, 10.5.2)

1962: A quantitative expression of the pattern of urban settlements in selected areas of the United States. *Tijdschrift voor Economische en Sociale Geografie*, **53**, 1–7. (4.2.1, 5.2.1)

1969a: The analysis of spatial form and its relation to geographic theory. *Annals of the Association of American Geographers*, **59**, 573–95. (1.2.2)

1969b: *Statistical analysis in geography.* Englewood Cliffs, N.J. (Preface, 10.1, 12.2)

KING, L. J., E. CASETTI, and D. JEFFREY. 1969: Economic impulses in a regional system of cities. *Regional Studies*, **3**, 213–18. (4.6.3)

KLAASEN, L. H., D. H. VAN D. TORMAN, and L. M. KOYCK. 1949: *Hoodfliinen van de sociaal-economische anfwikkeling der gemeente Amerstoort van 1900–1970.* Leiden. (5.4.4)

KLEINROCK, L. 1964: *Communications nets—stochastic message flow and delay.* New York. (3.4.4)

KOLARS, J., and H. MALIN. 1970: Population and accessibility—an analysis of Turkish railroads. *Geographical Review*, **60**, 229–46. (3.4.3)

KOLLMORGAN, W. M. 1969: The woodsman's assaults on the domain of the cattle man. *Annals of the Association of American Geographers*, **59**, 215–39. (6.5.2)

KOLLMORGAN, W. M., and G. F. JENKS. 1951: A geographic study of population and settlement changes in Sherman county, Kansas. *Kansas Academy of Sciences, Transactions*, **54**, 449–94. (4.2.1, 6.2.4)

KOPEC, R. J. 1963: An alternative method for the construction of Thiessen polygons. *Professional Geographer*, **15** (5), 24–6. (13.5)

KRUMBEIN, W. C. 1955a: Composite end-members in facies mapping. *Journal of Sedimentary Petrology*, **25**, 115–22. (9.4.1)

1955b: Experimental design in the earth sciences. *Transactions of the American Geophysical Union*, **36**, 1–11. (10.5.2)

1956: Regional and local components in facies maps. *Bulletin of the American Association of Petroleum Geologists*, **40**, 2163–94. (12.2.3, 12.3.1)

1957: Comparison of percentage and ratio data in facies mapping. *Journal of Sedimentary Petrology*, **27**, 293–7. (10.5.2)

1960: The geological 'population' as a framework for analysing numerical data in geology. *Liverpool and Manchester Geological Journal*, **2**, 341–68. (8.2.2, 8.3.2)

KRUMBEIN, W. C., and F. A. GRAYBILL. 1965: *An introduction to statistical models in geology.* New York. (10.1)

KUHN, H. W., and R. E. KUENNE. 1962: An efficient algorithm for the numerical solution of the generalized Weber problem in spatial economics. *Journal of Regional Science*, **4**, 21–33. (5.6.1)

KUHN, T. S. 1962: *The structure of scientific revolutions.* Chicago. (1.4.1)

KULLDORFF, G. 1955: Migration probabilities. *Lund Studies in Geography, Series B, Human Geography*, **14**. (4.2.3, 10.6.1)

LAKATOS, I., and A. MUSGRAVE, Editors. 1970: *Criticism and the growth of knowledge.* Cambridge. (1.4.1)

LALANNE, L. 1863: Essai d'une théorie des réseaux de chemin de fer, fondée sur l'observation des faits et sur les lois primordiales qui président au groupement des populations. *Comptes Rendus Hebdomadaires des Séances de l'Académie des Sciences*, **42**, 206–10. (3.1)

LAND, A. H. 1957: An application of linear programming to the transport of coking coal. *Journal of the Royal Statistical Society, A*, **120**, 308–19. (15.1)

LANGBEIN, W. B., and W. G. HOYT. 1959: *Water facts for the nation's future: uses and benefits of hydrological data problems.* New York. (8.4.1)

LANGLEY, S. C. 1974: Linear programming applications to school collecting districts. *University of Bristol, Department of Geography, B.Sc. Dissertation.* (14.4.3)

LANKFORD, P. M. 1974: Testing simulation models. *Geographical Analysis*, **6**, 295–302. (7.6.2)

LANGTON, J. 1972: Potentialities and problems of adopting a systems approach to the study of change in human geography. *Progress in Geography*, **4**, 125–79. (1.2.2)

LEA, A. C. 1973: Location allocation models. Part I—Review. Part II—An annotated bibliography. *University of Toronto, M.A. Project.* (5.6.1)

LEARMONTH, A. T. A., and M. N. PAL. 1959: A method of plotting two variables on the same map, using isopleths. *Erdkunde*, **13**, 145–50. (9.4)

LEBART, L. 1969: Analise statistique de la contiguité. *Publications de l'Université de Paris*, **18**, 81–112. (10.3.3)

LEE, D. R., and G. T. SALLEE. 1970: A method of measuring shape. *Geographical Review*, **60**, 555–63. (9.6.1)

LEOPOLD, L. B., M. G. WOLMAN, and J. P. MILLER. 1964: *Fluvial processes in geomorphology.* San Francisco. (4.3)

LEVISON, M., R. F. WARD, and J. W. WEBB. 1973: *The settlement of Polynesia: a computer simulation.* Minneapolis. (7.5.2)

LINSKY, A. S. 1965: Some generalizations concerning primate cities. *Annals of the Association of American Geographers*, **55**, 506–13. (4.3.1)

LINTON, D. L. 1949: The delimitation of morphological regions. *Institute of British Geographers, Publications*, **14**, 86–7. (14.2.2)

LÖSCH, A. 1940: *Die räumliche Ordnung der Wirtschaft.* Jena. (2.7.1)

1954: *The economics of location.* New Haven. (1.4.2, 2.2.1, 2.6.2, 2.7.1, 3.2.2, 3.5.3, 4.2.1, 4.5.2, 4.6.2, 5.2.1–2, 5.2.4, 6.3.2, 6.4.1, 6.5.1)

LOWRY, I. S. 1964: *A model of metropolis.* Santa Monica, Calif. (15.5.1)

LUKERMANN, F. 1965: The 'calcul des probabilités' and the Ecole française de Géographie. *Canadian Geographer*, **9**, 128–37. (1.4.3)

1966: Empirical expressions of nodality and hierarchy in a circulation manifold. *East Lakes Geographer*, **2**, 17–44. (4.4.2)

LUTTRELL, W. F. 1962: *Factory location and industrial movement.* London. (5.6.3)

McCARTY, H. H. 1956: Use of certain statistical procedures in geographical analysis. *Annals of the Association of American Geographers*, **46**, 263. (8.4.2)

McCARTY, H. H., J. C. HOOK, and D. S. KNOS. 1956: The measurement of association in industrial geography. *State University of Iowa, Department of Geography, Report*, **1**. (5.5.2, 5.6.1, 8.4.2, 9.3.4, 12.3)

McCASKILL, M., Editor. 1962: *Land and livelihood: geographical essays in honour of George Jobberns.* Christchurch. (5.4.2)

McCLELLAN, D. 1973: A re-examination and re-consideration of the neighbourhood effect in the diffusion of innovations at the micro scale. Unpublished prize winning essay for the Royal Geographical Society. (7.3)

McCONNELL, H. 1966: Quadrat methods in map analysis. *University of Iowa, Department of Geography, Discussion Papers*, **13**. (13.4.4)

McGUIRE, J. U., T. A. BRINDLEY, and T. A. BANCROFT. 1957: The distribution of the European corn-borer larvae in field-corn. *Biometrics*, **13**, 65–78, (and correction) **14**, 432–44. (13.2.4, 13.4.1)

MACH, E. 1942: *The science of mechanics.* La Salle, Ill. (2.2.1)

MACKAY, J. R. 1953: The alternative choice in isopleth interpolation. *Professional Geographer*, **5**, 2–4. (9.3.2)

1958: The interactance hypothesis and boundaries in Canada. *Canadian* Geographer, **2**, 1–8. (2.6.2)

McKENZIE, R. D. 1933: *The metropolitan community.* New York. (1.2.3, 6.6.1)

MacKINNON, R. D. 1974: Lag regression models of the spatial spread of highway improvements. *Economic Geography*, **50**, 368–74. (7.8)

MacKINNON, R. D., and M. J. HODGSON. 1969: The highway system of southern Ontario and Quebec: some simple network generation models. *University of Toronto, Centre for Urban and Community Studies, Research Report*, **18**. (3.4.3)

MADDEN, C. H. 1958: Some temporal aspects of the growth of cities in the United States. *Economic Development and Cultural Change*, **6**, 143–69. (4.4.2)

MANSFIELD, E. 1961: Technical change and the rate of innovation. *Econometrica*, **29**, 741–66. (7.3)

MARSDEN, B. S. 1970: Urban delimitation on a density basis: Brisbane, 1861–1966. *New Zealand Geographer*, **26**, 151–61. (9.6.1)

MARSH, G. P. 1864: *Man and nature; or physical geography as modified by human action.* New York. (1.2.4)

MARTHE, F. 1878: Begriff, Ziel und Methode der Geographie. *Geographisches Jahrbuch*, **7**, 628. (1.2.2)

MARTIN, R. L. 1974: On autocorrelation, bias and the use of first spatial differences in regression analysis. *Area*, **6**, 185–94. (10.3.2–3)

1975: Identification and estimation of dynamic space-time forecasting models for geographical data. *Advances in Applied Probability*, **7**, 455–56. (16.3.4)

MARTIN, R. L., and J. E. OEPPEN. 1975: The identification of regional forecasting models using space–time correlation functions. *Institute of British Geographers, Publications*, **66**, 95–118. (13.3.1, 16.4.1–2)

MASSAM, B. H. 1975: *Location and space in social administration.* London. (2.7.2, 9.6.1, 14.1, 14.5.3)

MASSAM, B. H., and A. F. BURGHARDT. 1968: The administrative subdivision of Southern Ontario: an attempt at evaluation. *Canadian Geographer*, **15**, 193–206. (9.6.1)

MASSAM, B. H., and M. F. GOODCHILD. 1971: Temporal trends in the spatial organization of a service agency. *Canadian Geographer*, **15**, 193–206. (9.6.1)

MASSEY, D. B. 1973: The basic-service categorization in planning. *Regional Studies*, **7**, 1–15. (5.3.3)

MATÉRN, B. 1960: Spatial variation: stochastic models and their application to some problems in forest surveys and other sampling investigations. *Meddelanden Fran Statens Skogsforsknings-institut*, **49**, 1–144. (13.4.4)

1971: Doubly stochastic Poisson processes in the plane. In G. P. Patil, Editor. *Statistical ecology*, **1**. University Park, Pennsylvania. 195–213. (13.4.4)

1972a: Poisson processes in the plane and related models for clumping and heterogeneity. *NATO Advanced Study Institute on Statistical Ecology.* Pennsylvania State University, Department of Statistics. (13.4.4, 13.5)

1972b: Analysis of spatial patterns and ecological relations: the analysis of ecological maps as mosaics. *NATO Advanced Study Institute on Statistical Ecology*, Pennsylvania State University, Department of Statistics. (13.5)

MATUI, I. 1932: Statistical study of the distribution of scattered villages in two regions of the Tonami plain, Tayama prefecture. *Japanese Journal of Geology and Geography*, **9**, 251–66. (12.3.2, 13.2.1, 13.4.1)

MEAD, R. 1967: A mathematical model for the estimation of interplant competition. *Biometrics*, **23**, 189–205. (11.4.2)

1974: A test for spatial pattern at several scales using data from a grid of contagious quadrats. *Biometrics*, **30**, 295–307. (13.7)

MEAD, W. R. 1953: *Farming in Finland.* London. (6.5.2)

MEAD, W. R., and E. H. BROWN. 1962: *The United States and Canada.* London. (3.3.2, 4.2.1)

MEDAWAR, P. B. 1969: *Induction and intuition in scientific thought.* London. (1.4.2)

MEDVEDKOV, Y. V. 1967: The concept of entropy in settlement pattern analysis. *Regional Science Association, Papers*, **18**, 165–8. (13.7)

MEIJERLING, J. L. 1953: Interface area, edge length, and number of vertices in crystal aggregates with random nucleation. *Phillips Research Reports*, **8**, 270–90. (2.7.2)

MEINIG, D. W. 1962: A comparative historical geography of two railnets: Columbia basin and South Australia. *Annals of the Association of American Geographers*, **52**, 394–413. (1.4.3, 3.2.3)

MEITZEN, A. 1895: *Siedlung und Agrarwesen der Westgermanen und Ostgermanen des Kelten, Römer, Finen und Slawen.* Three volumes; one atlas. Berlin. (4.2.1)

MEYER, J. 1963: Regional economics: a survey. *American Economic Review*, **53**, 19–54. (1.3)

MEYNEN, E. 1960: *Orbis geographicus,* 1960. Wiesbaden. (8.1)

MIEHLE, W. 1958: Link-length minimization in networks. *Operations Research*, **6**, 232–43. (3.3.1)

MIKESELL, M. W. (1960). Comparative studies in frontier history. *Annals of the Association of American Geographers*, **50**, 62–74. (7.1)

MILLS, E. S. 1969: The value of urban land. In H. S. Perloff, Editor. *The quality of the urban environment.* Baltimore. 231–253. (6.2.2, 6.6.1)

MILLS, G. 1967: The determination of local government electoral boundaries. *Operations Research Quarterly*, **18**, 243–55. (14.5.2, 15.4.3)

MINISTRY OF TRANSPORT. 1961: *Rural bus services: report of the committee.* London. (2.6.1)

MINISTRY OF TRANSPORT. 1963: *Traffic in towns: a study of the long term problems of traffic in urban areas.* London. (3.5.3)

MINSHULL, R. 1967: *Regional geography: theory and practice.* London. (14.2.1)

MITCHELL, J. B. 1954: *Historical geography.* London. (4.2.3)

MOELLERING, H., and W. R. TOBLER. 1972: Geographical variances. *Geographical Analysis*, **4**, 34–50. (12.3.1–2)

MOLLISON, D. 1972a: Possible velocities for a simple epidemic. *Advances in Applied Probability*, **4**, 233–57. (7.7.2)

1972b: The rate of spatial propagation of simple epidemics. *Proceedings of the Sixth Berkeley Symposium on Mathematical Statistics and Probability*, **3**, 579–614. (7.7.2–3)

1975: Comments on Cliff, A. D. and J. K. Ord. 1975b: *Journal of the Royal Statistical Society*, **B**, **37**, 334–35. (16.2.2)

MOMBEIG, P. 1952: *Pionniers et planteurs de São Paulo.* Paris. (3.3.2, 6.6.2)

MOMSEN, R. P. 1963: Routes across the Serra do Mar—the evolution of transportation in the highlands of Rio de Janeiro and São Paulo. *Revista Geografica*, **32**, 5–167. (3.2.3)

MONMONIER, M. 1974: Measures of pattern complexity for choropleth maps. *American Cartographer*, **1**, 159–69. (9.3.3)

MOORE, E. F. 1959: The shortest path through a maze. *Annals of the Computation Laboratory of Harvard University*, **30**. (3.4.2)

MOORE, P. G. 1954: Spacing in plant populations. *Ecology*, **35**, 222–27. (13.6.1)

MORAN, P. A. P. 1948: The interpretation of statistical maps. *Journal of the Royal Statistical Society, B*, **10**, 243–51. (11.3.1)

MORGENSTERN, O. 1963: *On the accuracy of economic observations*. Princeton. (8.2.1, 8.2.3)

MORRILL, R. L. 1962: Simulation of central place patterns over time. *Lund Studies in Geography, Series B, Human Geography*, **24**, 109–20. (4.2.3)

1963: The development and spatial distribution of towns in Sweden: an historical-predictive approach. *Annals of the Association of American Geographers*, **53**, 1–14. (1.4.3)

1965: The negro ghetto: problems and alternatives. *Geographical Review*, **55**, 339–361. (6.6.2)

1968: Waves of spatial diffusion. *Journal of Regional Science*, **8**, 1–18. (7.5.1)

1970: The shape of diffusion in space and time. *Economic Geography*, **46**, 259–68. (7.5.1)

MORRILL, R. L., and W. L. GARRISON. 1960: Projections of interregional trade in wheat and flour. *Economic Geography*, **36**, 116–26. (15.1)

MOSER, C. A., and W. SCOTT. 1961: *British towns: a statistical study of their social and economic differences*. Edinburgh. (5.4.4)

MOSES, L. N. 1960: A general equilibrium model of production, interregional trade and location of industry. *Review of Economics and Statistics*, **62**, 373–99. (15.4.1)

MURRAY, M. 1962: The geography of death in England and Wales. *Annals of the Association of American Geographers*, **52**, 130–49. (10.6.1)

MUTH, R. F. 1962: The spatial structure of the housing market. *Regional Science Association, Papers*, **7**, 207–20. (6.2.2)

1969: *Cities and housing*. Chicago. (6.6.2)

NAGEL, E. 1961: *The structure of science*. New York. (1.4.3)

NAGEL, S. S. 1965: Simplified bipartisan computer redistricting. *Stanford Law Review*, **17**, 863–99. (14.5.2)

NAROLL, R. 1961: Two solutions to Galton's problem. In F. Moore, Editor. *Readings in cross cultural methodology*. New Haven. (10.2)

NEAVE, H. 1972: Observations on spectral analysis of short series—a simulation study by Granger and Hughes. *Journal of the Royal Statistical Society, A*, **135**, 393–405. (12.4.4, 12.5.3)

NEFT, D. S. 1966: *Statistical analysis for areal distributions*. Philadelphia. (13.7)

NEWLING, B. 1969: The spatial variation of urban population densities. *Geographical Review*, **59**, 242–52. (6.2.2, 6.6.1)

NEYMAN, J. 1939: On a new class of 'contagious distributions' applicable in entomology and bacteriology. *Annals of Mathematical Statistics*, **10**, 35–57. (13.2.4)

NEYMAN, J., and E. L. SCOTT. 1952: A theory of the spatial distribution of galaxies. *Astrophysical Journal*, **116**, 144–63. (13.4.4)

1958: Statistical approach to problems of cosmology. *Journal of the Royal Statistical Society, B*, **20**, 1–29. (13.4.4)

1972: Processes of clustering and applications. In P. A. W. Lewis, Editor. *Stochastic Point Processes*. New York. 646–81. (13.4.4)

NIEDERCORN, J. H., and E. F. R. HEARLE. 1964: Recent land use trends in 48 large American cities. *Land Economics*, **40**, 105–10. (6.2.4)

NISHIOKA, H. 1975: Location theory in Japan. *Progress in Geography*, **7**, 133–200. (1.1)

NORCLIFFE, G. B. 1969: On the use and limitations of trend surface models. *Canadian Geographer*, **13**, 338–48. (12.2.2)

NYSTUEN, J. D., and M. F. DACEY. 1961: A graph theory interpretation of nodal regions. *Regional Science Association, Papers and Proceedings*, **7**, 29–42. (14.6.1)

OFFICE OF STATISTICAL STANDARDS. 1958: *Criteria for defining Standard Metropolitan Areas*. Washington. (8.2.3)

OHLIN, B. 1933: *Interregional and international trade*. Cambridge, Mass. (6.4.1)

OLSSON, G. 1965: Distance and human interaction: a review and bibliography. *Regional Science Research Institute, Bibliography Series*, **2**. (2.2.2)

OLSON, J. S., and P. E. POTTER. 1954: Variance components of cross-bedding direction in some basal Pennsylvanian sandstones of the Eastern Interior Basin: statistical methods. *Journal of Geology*, **62**, 26–49. (12.3.1)

ORD, J. K. 1967: On a system of discrete distributions. *Biometrika*, **54**, 649–56. (9.7.2)

1972a: *Families of frequency distributions*. London. (10.5.2, 13.2.2, 13.2.4, 13.3.3–4, 13.4.2)

1972b: Density estimation and tests for randomness using distance methods. *NATO Advanced Study Institute on Statistical Ecology*. Pennsylvania State University, Department of Statistics. (13.6, 13.6.1)

1974: Comments of Besag, J. E. 1974: *Journal of the Royal Statistical Society, B*, **36**, 229. (16.7)

1975: Estimation methods for models of spatial interaction. *Journal of the American Statistical Association*. (11.4.2, 16.6)

ORDEN, A. 1956: The transshipment problem. *Management Science*, **2**, 276–85. (15.4.1)

O'SULLIVAN, P. M. 1968: Accessibility and the spatial structure of the Irish economy. *Regional Studies*, **2**, 195–206. (11.4.2)

PAELINCK, J. H. P. 1970: Dynamic urban growth models. *Regional Science Association, Papers*, **24**, 25–37. (5.3.3)

PAELINCK, J. H. P., and P. NIJKAMP. 1975: *Operational theory and method in regional economics*. Farnborough. (5.4.2)

PARK, R. E. 1929: Urbanization as measured by newspaper circulation. *American Journal of Sociology*, **35**, 60–79. (2.6.2)

PARR, J. B. 1970: Models of city size in an urban system. *Regional Science Association, Papers*, **25**, 221–53. (5.2.4)

PARSONS, J. J. 1949: Antioqueño colonization in western Colombia: an historical geography. *Ibero-Americana*, **32**, 1–225. (7.1)

PASSONEAU, J. R., and R. S. WURMAN. 1966: *Urban atlas: 20 American cities*. Cambridge, Mass. (10.6)

PATERSON, J. H. 1975: *North America: a regional geography*. Oxford. (5.5.3, 14.1)

PATIL, G. P., and S. W. JOSHI. 1968: *A dictionary and bibliography of discrete distributions*. Edinburgh. (13.2.2, 13.3.4)

PATTISON, W. D. 1957: Beginnings of the American rectangular land survey system, 1784–1800. *University of Chicago, Department of Geography, Research Papers*, **50**. (4.2.1)

1964: The four traditions of geography. *Journal of Geography*, **63**, 211–6. (1.2.1)

PEDERSEN, P. O. 1967: On the geometry of administrative areas. Copenhagen. Manuscript Report. (2.7.2)

1970: Innovation diffusion within and between national urban systems.

*Geographical Analysis*, **2**, 203–54. (7.4)

PEET, R. 1969: The spatial expansion of commercial agriculture in the nineteenth century: a von Thünen interpretation. *Economic Geography*, **45**, 283–301. (6.4.1)

1972: Influences of the British market on agriculture and related economic development in Europe before 1860. *Institute of British Geographers, Publications*, **56**, 1–20. (6.4.1)

PELTO, C. R. 1954: Mapping of multicomponent systems. *Journal of Geology*, **62**, 501–11. (9.4.1)

PERRING,, F. H., and S. M. WALTERS. 1962: *Atlas of the British flora*. London. (1.2.2, 8.4.2, 9.8.1)

PERROUX, F. 1970: Note on the concept of growth poles. In D. C. McKee, *et al.*, Editors. *Regional economics*. New York. (15.2.3)

PERSSON, O. 1971: The robustness of estimating density by distance measurements. In G. P. Patil, *et al.*, Editors. *Statistical ecology*. University Park, Pennsylvania. 175–90. (13.6.1)

PHILBRICK, A. K. 1957: Principles of areal functional organization in regional human geography. *Economic Geography*, **33**, 299–336. (14.2.2)

PIELOU, E. C. 1957: The effect of quadrat size on the estimation of the parameters of the Neyman's and Thomas's distributions. *Journal of Ecology*, **45**, 31–47. (13.4.4)

1969: *An introduction to mathematical ecology*. New York. (13.1–2, 13.3.1, 13.3.4, 13.5, 13.6.5)

PLATT, R. S. 1942: *Latin America: countrysides and united regions*. New York. (8.3.)

PLATT, R. S. 1959: Field study in American geography: the development of theory and method exemplified by selections. *University of Chicago, Department of Geography, Research Papers*, **61**. (8.3, 8.3.3)

POLLACK, M., and W. WIEBENSON. 1960: Solutions of the shortest-route problem: a review. *Operations Research*, **8**, 224–30. (3.4.2)

POLYA, G. 1931: Sur quelques points de la théorie des probabilités. *Annals de l'Institut de Henri Poincaré*, **1**, 117–62. (13.2.4)

PONSARD, C. 1969: *Un modèle topologique d'equilibre économique interrégional*. Paris. (9.7.4, 14.6.2)

PORTER, P. W. 1960: Earnest and the Orephagians: a fable for the instruction of young geographers. *Annals of the Association of American Geographers*, **50**, 297–99. (13.6.5)

POSTAN, M. 1948: The revulsion from thought. *Cambridge Journal*, **1**, 395–408. (1.1)

POUNDS, N. J. G. 1959: *The geography of iron and steel*. London. (5.5.1)

PRED, A. 1964: The intrametropolitan location of American manufacturing. *Annals of the Association of American Geographers*, **54**, 165–80. (6.6.2)

PYKE, M. 1965: Spacings. *Journal of the Royal Statistical Society, B*, **27**, 395–449. (4.3.3)

PYLE, G. F. 1969: Diffusion of cholera in the United States. *Geographical Analysis*, **1**, 59–75. (4.6.1, 7.5.1)

QUANT, R. E. 1960: Models of transportation and optimal network construction. *Journal of Regional Science*, **2**, 27–45. (3.3.1, 15.4.2)

QUENOUILLE, M. H. 1949a: Problems in plane sampling. *Annals of Mathematical Statistics*, **20**, 355–75. (8.3.2)

1949b: A relationship between the logarithmic, Poisson and negative binomial series. *Biometrics*, **5**, 162–64. (13.2.4)

RAPOPORT, A. 1951: Nets with distance bias. *Bulletin of Mathematical*

*Biophysics*, **13**, 85–92. (7.3)
RAPOPORT, H., and P. ABRAMSON. 1959: An analog computer for finding an optimum route through a communications network. *Institute of Radio Engineers, Transactions on Communications Systems*, **CS-7**, 37–42. (3.4.2)
RAVENSTEIN, E. G. 1885, 1889: The laws of migration. *Journal of the Royal Statistical Society*, **48**, 52. (2.2.2)
RAVETZ, J. R. 1971: *Scientific knowledge and its social problems*. Oxford. (1.4.5)
RAYNER, J. N. 1971: *An introduction to spectral analysis*. London. (12.4.1, 12.4.3, 12.4.4)
RAYNER, J. N., and R. G. GOLLEDGE. 1972: Spectral analysis of settlement patterns in diverse physical and economic environments. *Environment and Planning*, **4**, 347–71. (4.2.1, 12.4.3)
1973: The spectrum of U.S. Route 40 re-examined. *Geographical Analysis*, **5**, 338–50. (4.2.1, 12.4.2)
REED, W. E. 1970: Indirect connectivity and hierarchies of urban dominance. *Annals of the Association of American Geographers*, **60**, 770–85. (9.7.4)
REES, P. H. 1970: The urban envelope: patterns and dynamics of population density. In B. J. L. Berry and F. E. Horton, Editors. *Geographic perspectives on urban systems*. Englewood Cliffs, N.J. 276–305. (6.6.1)
RHYNSBURGER, D. 1973: Analytic delineation of Thiessen polygons. *Geographical Analysis*, **5**, 133–44. (13.5)
RICHARDSON, H. W. 1973: *The economics of urban size*. Lexington, Mass. (4.3.3)
RIDLEY, T. H. 1969: Reducing the travel time in a transport network. In A. J. Scott, Editor. *Studies in Regional Science*. London. 73–87. (15.4.2)
RIMMER, P. J. 1967: The changing status of New Zealand seaports, 1853–1960. *Annals of the Association of American Geographers*, **57**, 88–100. (3.5.3)
ROBINSON, A. H. 1956: The necessity of weighting values in correlation of areal data. *Annals of the Association of American Geographers*, **46**, 233–6. (10.6.1, 10.6.2)
1961: The cartographic representation of the statistical surface. *International Yearbook of Cartography*, **1**, 53–63. (9.3)
ROBINSON, A. H., J. B. LINDBERG, and L. W. BRINKMAN. 1961: A correlation and regression analysis applied to rural farm population densities. *Annals of the Association of American Geographers*, **51**, 211–21. (8.4.2, 9.3.2, 10.6.2)
ROBINSON, A. H., and R. D. SALE. 1969: *Elements of cartography*. New York. (9.1, 9.3.1)
ROBINSON, G. 1970: Some comments on trend-surface analysis. *Area*, **3**, 31–36. (12.2.3)
ROBSON, B. T. 1973: *Urban growth: an approach*. Cambridge. (4.2.3, 4.4.1–2)
RODGERS, A. 1952: Industrial inertia: a major factor in the location of the steel industry in the United States. *Geographical Review*, **42**, 56–65. (5.4.4, 5.5.1)
ROGERS, A. 1965: A stochastic analysis of the spatial clustering of retail establishments. *Journal of the American Statistical Association*, **60**, 1094–1103. (13.2.3, 13.3.1)
1969a: Quadrat analysis of urban dispersion: 1. Theoretical techniques. *Environment and Planning*, **1**, 47–80. (13.1, 13.2.1)
1971: *Matrix methods in urban and regional analysis*. San Francisco. (15.5.2)
1974: *Statistical analysis of spatial dispersion: the quadrat method*. London. (13.3.1–2, 13.3.4)
ROGERS, E. M. 1962: *Diffusion of innovations*. New York. (7.1)
ROSE, A. J. 1966: Dissent from Down Under—metropolitan dominance as the normal state. *Pacific Viewpoint*, **7**, 1–27. (4.4.1)

ROSTOW, W. W. 1960: *The stages of economic growth.* Cambridge. (3.5.3, 3.4.2)
ROSTOW, W. W., Editor. 1963: *The economics of take-off into sustained growth.* London. (5.4.2)
ROUGET, R. 1972: Graph theory and hierarchization modes. *Regional and Urban Economics*, **2**, 263–96. (14.6.2)
RUTHERFORD, J., M. I. LOGAN, and G. J. MISSEN. 1966: *New viewpoints in economic geography.* Sydney. (6.5.1)
SAARINEN, T. F. 1966: Perception of the drought hazard on the Great Plains. *University of Chicago, Department of Geography, Research Papers*, **106**. (6.5.1)
SACK, R. D. 1972: Geography, geometry and explanation. *Annals of the Association of American Geographers*, **62**, 61–78. (1.2.2)
1974: Chorology and spatial analysis. *Annals of the Association of American Geographers*, **64**, 439–52. (1.2.2)
SAMUELSON, P. A. 1952: Spatial price equilibrium and linear programming. *American Economic Review*, **42**, 183–203. (15.1)
SANDERS, E. 1975: Urban population density function of two polar variables. *Regional Studies*, **9**, 63–8. (6.6.1)
SANDNER, G. 1961: Agrarkolonisation in Costa Rica: Siedlung, Wirtschaft und Sozialfüge an der Pioniergrenze. *Schriften des Geographischen Instituts der Universität Kiel*, **19**. (4.2.3)
SAUER, C. O. 1925: The morphology of landscape. *University of California, Publications in Geography*, **2**, 19–53. (1.2.4)
1952: Agricultural origins and dispersals. *American Geographical Society, Bowman Memorial Lectures*, **2**. (6.6.2, 7.1)
SAUER, C. O., and D. BRAND. 1930: Pueblo sites in Southeastern Arizona. *University of California, Publications in Geography*, **3**, 415–48. (7.1)
SAVAGE, L. J. 1954: *The foundation of statistics.* New York. (1.4.3)
SCHAEFER, F. K. 1953: Exceptionalism in geography: a methodological examination. *Annals of the Association of American Geographers*, **43**, 226–49. (1.4.4)
SCHEFFÉ, H. 1959: *The analysis of variance.* New York. (12.3.1)
SCOTT, A. J. 1971a: An introduction to spatial allocation analysis. *Association of American Geographers, Commission on College Geography, Resource Papers*, **9**. (15.1–3, 15.3.2–3, 15.4.1–2)
1971b: *Combinatorial programming, spatial analysis and planning.* London. (3.4.2, 15.4.2, 15.5.3)
SEARS, F. W., and M. W. ZEMANSKY. 1964: *University physics.* Reading, Mass. (3.2.2)
SEMPLE, E. C. 1911: *Influence of geographic environment on the basis of Ratzel's system of anthropo-geography.* New York. (1.2.3)
SEN, A. K. 1976: Large sample-size distribution of statistics used in testing for spatial correlation. *Geographical Analysis*, **8**, 175–84. (11.3.2)
SENIOR, M. L., and A. G. WILSON. 1973: Disaggregated residential location models: some tests and further theoretical developments. In E. L. Cripps, Editor. *Space-time concepts in urban and regional models.* London. 141–72. (15.5.1)
1974: Explanations and syntheses of linear programming and spatial interaction models of residential location. *Geographical Analysis*, **6**, 209–38. (15.5.1)
SHANNON, G. W., and G. E. A. DEVER. 1974: *Health care delivery: spatial perspectives.* New York. (14.5.3)
SHERBROOKE, C. C. 1968: Discrete compound Poisson processes and tables of

the geometric Poisson distribution. *Naval Research Logistics Quarterly*, **15**, 189–203. (13.3.4)

SHUMWAY, R., and J. GURLAND. 1960: A fitting procedure for some generalized Poisson distributions. *Skandinavisk Aktrarietidskrift*, **43**, 87–108. (13.2.4)

SIEGEL, S. 1956: *Nonparametric statistics for the behavioral sciences*. New York. (9.2, 10.5.3, 11.3.1)

SILK, J. A. 1965: Road network of Monmouthshire. *University of Cambridge, Department of Geography, B.A. Dissertation*. (3.3.1)

SILVA, R. C. 1965: Reapportionment and redistricting. *Scientific American*, **213**(5), 20–7. (14.5.2)

SIMON, H. A. 1955: On a class of skew distribution functions. *Biometrika*, **42**, 425–40. (4.3.4)

SINCLAIR, R. 1967: Von Thünen and urban sprawl. *Annals of the Association of American Geographers*, **57**, 72–87. (6.5.2)

SINNHUBER, K. A. 1954: Central Europe–Mitteleuropa–Europe Central: an analysis of a geographical term. *Institute of British Geographers Publications*, **20**, 15–39. (14.2.4)

SKELLAM, J. G. 1952: Studies in statistical ecology, I: Spatial pattern. *Biometrika*, **39**, 346–62. (13.6.1)

1958: On the derivation and applicability of Neyman's type A distribution. *Biometrika*, **45**, 32–36. (13.4.4)

SKILLING, H. 1964: An operational view. *American Scientist*, **53**, 388A–96A. (1.4.1–2)

SKINNER, S. W. 1964–65: Marketing and social structure in rural China. *Journal of Asian Studies*, **24**, 3–399. (5.3.1)

SMITH, D. 1971: *Industrial location*. London. (5.5, 5.6.1–2)

SMITH, W. 1955: The location of industry. *Institute of British Geographers, Publications*, **21**, 1–18. (5.6.1)

SOJA, E. W. 1968: Communications and territorial integration in East Africa: an introduction to transaction flow analysis. *East Lakes Geographer*, **4**, 39–57. (14.6.2)

SOPER, H. E. 1929: Interpretation of periodicity in disease prevalence. *Journal of the Royal Statistical Society*, **92**, 34–73. (7.7.4)

SORRE, M. 1947–52: *Les fondements de la géographie humaine*. Three volumes. Paris. (1.2.3)

SORRE, M. 1961: *L'homme sur la terre*. Paris. (1.2.3)

SPECHT, R. E. 1959: *A functional analysis of the Green Bay and Western Railroad*. Stevens Point. (3.2.2)

SPENCE, N. A. 1968: A multifactor regionalization of British counties on the basis of employment data for 1961. *Regional Studies*, **2**, 87–104. (14.4.3)

SPENCER, J. E., and R. J. HORVATH. 1963: How does an agricultural region originate? *Annals of the Association of American Geographers*, **53**, 74–92. (6.6.2)

SPOONER, R. S. 1975: Local variations in monthly unemployment series: northern England, 1927–36. *Bristol University. B.Sc. Project*. (4.6.2)

SPROTT, D. A. 1958: The methods of maximum likelihood applied to the Poisson binomial distribution. *Biometrics*, **14**, 97–106. (13.2.4)

STAFFORD, H. A., JR. 1963: The functional bases of small towns. *Economic Geography*, **39**, 165–75. (5.2.1)

STAMP, L. D., and S. W. WOOLDRIDGE, Editors. 1951: *London essays in Geography*. London. (14.2.1)

STANISLAWSKI, D. 1946: The origin and spread of the grid-pattern town. *Geographical Review*, **36**, 105–20. (7.1)

STEINER, D. 1965: A multivariate statistical approach to climatic regionalization and classification. *Tijdschrift van het Koninklijk Nederlandsche Aardrijkskundig Genootschap*, **15**, 23–35. (14.4.2)

STEVENS, B. H. 1961: Linear programming and location rent. *Journal of Regional Science*, **3**, 15–25. (15.2.3)

1968: Location theory and programming models: the von Thünen case. *Regional Science Association, Papers*, **21**, 19–34. (6.3.1)

STEWART, C. T., JR. 1958: The size and spacing of cities. *Geographical Review*, **48**, 222–45. (4.3.1)

STEWART, J. Q., and W. WARNTZ. 1958: Macrogeography and social science. *Geographical Review*, **48**, 167–84. (2.4.5, 9.6.2)

STODDART, D. R. 1967: Growth and structure of geography. *Institute of British Geographers, Publications*, **41**, 1–19. (1.4)

1975: Kropotkin, Reclus, and 'relevant' geography. *Area*, **7**, 188–90. (1.4.5)

STOKES, D. E. 1965: A variance components model of political effects. In J. M. Claunch, Editor. *Mathematical applications in political science*. Dallas. (12.3.1)

STOREY, K. J. 1972: Some structural characteristics of the Newfoundland economy. In M. A. Micklewright and P. Y. Velleneuve, Editors. *Problems of slow growth and stagnant areas in developed countries*. St John's, Newfoundland. 165–89. (9.7.4)

STOUFFER, S. A. 1940: Intervening opportunities: a theory relating mobility and distance. *American Sociological Review*, **5**, 845–67. (2.3.4, 2.6.2)

STRAUSS, D. J., and M. ORANS. 1975: Mighty sifts: a critical appraisal of solutions to Galton's problem and a partial solution. *Current Anthropology*, **16**, 573–94. (10.2)

STUART, A. 1962: *Basic ideas of scientific sampling*. London. (8.2.2, 8.3, 8.3.1)

STUDENT. 1914: The elimination of spurious correlation due to position in time or space. *Biometrika*, **10**, 179–80. (10.3.2)

SVIATLOVSKY, E. E., and W. C. EELLS. 1937: The centrographic method and regional analysis. *Geographical Review*, **27**, 240–54. (9.6.2)

TAAFFE, E. J., Editor. 1970: *Geography*. Englewood Cliffs, N.J. (1.2.1)

TAAFFE, E. J., R. L. MORRILL, and P. R. GOULD. 1963: Transport expansion in underdeveloped countries: a comparative analysis. *Geographical Review*, **53**, 503–29. (3.5.2, 3.5.3)

TANNER, J. C. 1967: Layout of road systems on plantations. *Ministry of Transport, Road Research Laboratory Report*, **LR68**. (3.3.2)

TARRANT, J. R. 1973: Comments on the Lösch central place system. *Geographical Analysis*, **5**, 113–21. (5.2.4)

TAYLOR, P. J. 1975: *Distance decay models in spatial interaction*. Norwich. (2.3.1)

THEIL, H. 1965: The analysis of disturbances in regression analysis. *Journal of the American Statistical Association*, **60**, 1067–79. (11.4.1)

1971: *Principles of econometrics*. New York. (10.6.2)

THEODORSON, G. A., Editor. 1961: *Studies in human ecology*. Evanston. (2.6.1)

THOMAS, D. 1963: *Agriculture in Wales during the Napoleonic Wars: a study in the geographical interpretation of historical sources*. Cardiff. (9.4.2)

THOMAS, E. N. 1960: Maps of residuals from regressions: their characteristics and uses in geographic research. *State University of Iowa, Department of Geography, Report*, **2**. (3.3.2)

1961: Towards an expanded central place model. *Geographical Review*, **51**, 400–11. (4.5.2)

1962: The stability of distance–population size relationships for Iowa towns from 1900 to 1950. *Lund Studies in Geography, Series B, Human Geography*, **24**, 13–30. (4.5.2)

THOMAS, E. N., and D. W. ANDERSON. 1965: Additional comments on weighting values in correlation analysis of areal data. *Annals of the Association of American Geographers*, **55**, 492–505. (10.6.2)

THOMAS, F. H. 1960: The Denver and Rio Grande Western Railroad: a geographic analysis. *Northwestern University, Studies in Geography*, **4**. (3.3.2)

THOMAS, M. 1949: A generalization of Poisson's binomial limit for use in ecology. *Biometrika*, **36**, 18–25. (13.2.4, 13.4.1)

THOMAS, W. L., JR., Editor. 1956: *Man's role in changing the face of the earth.* Chicago. (1.2.4, 2.4.4, 2.6.1, 4.2.1, 6.6.2)

THOMPSON, J. H., S. C. SUFRIN, P. R. GOULD, and M. A. BUCK. 1962: Toward a geography of economic health—the case of New York state. *Annals of the Association of American Geographers*, **52**, 1–20. (14.4.3)

THOMPSON, W. R. 1957: The coefficient of localization: an appraisal. *Southern Economic Journal*, **23**, 320–25. (9.3.4, 10.6.2)

THOMPSON, D'ARCY W. 1917; abrid. edit. 1961: *On growth and form.* Cambridge. (1.2.4, 2.2.1, 2.7.1)

THOMPSON, W. R. 1957: The coefficient of localization: an appraisal. *Southern Economic Journal*, **23**, 320–5. (9.3.4)

THORNGREN, B. 1970: How do contact systems affect regional development? *Environment and Planning*, **2**, 409–27. (5.5.2)

THÜNEN, J. H. VON. 1826, 1875: *Der Isolierte Staat in Beziehung auf Landwirtschaft und Nationalökonomie.* Hamburg. (1.2.2, 6.3, 6.3.2)

TINKLER, K. J. 1972: The physical interpretation of eigenfunctions of dichotomous matrices. *Institute of British Geographers, Publications*, **55**, 17–46. (9.7.4)

1973: The topology of rural periodic market systems. *Geografiska Annaler*, **55, B**, 121–33. (5.3.1)

TINLINE, R. R. 1971: Linear operators in diffusion research. In M. D. I. Chisholm, A. E. Frey, and P. Haggett, Editors. *Regional forecasting.* London. 71–91. (7.6.2, 16.2.2)

1972: *A simulation study of the 1967–8 foot-and-mouth epizootic in Great Britain.* University of Bristol. Unpublished Ph.D. dissertation. (7.1, 13.3.1)

TOBLER, W. R. 1963: Geographic area and map projections. *Geographical Review*, **53**, 59–78. (2.7.3)

1965: Computation of the correspondence of geographical patterns. *Regional Science Association, Papers*, **15**, 131–42. (7.6.2)

1967: Of maps and matrices. *Journal of Regional Science*, **7**, 275–80. (16.2.2)

1969a: The spectrum of U.S. 40. *Regional Science Association, Papers*, **23**, 45–52. (6.2.1, 12.4.2)

1969b: Geographical filters and their inverses. *Geographical Analysis*, **1**, 234–53. (16.2.2)

1970: A computer movie simulating urban growth in the Detroit Region. *Economic Geography*, (Supplement) **46**, 234–40. (10.2, 11.2.1, 16.2.2)

TOBLER, W., and S. WINERBURG. 1971: A Cappadocian speculation. *Nature*, **231**, 40–1. (9.8.2)

TROXEL, E. 1955: *Economics of transport.* New York. (6.4.2)

TUKEY, J. W. 1961: Discussion emphasizing the connection between analysis of variance and spectrum analysis. *Technometrics*, **3**, 191–219. (12.3.1)

1962: The future of data analysis. *Annals of Mathematical Statistics*, **33**, 1–67. (11.4.2, 16.4.1)

TURNER, F. J. 1920: *The frontier in American history*. New York. (7.1)

TYLOR, E. B. 1889: On a method of investigating the development of institutions, applied to laws of marriage and descent. *Journal of the Royal Anthropological Institute of Great Britain and Ireland*, **18**, 245–72. (10.2)

ULLMAN, E. L. 1949: The railroad pattern of the United States. *Geographical Review*, **39**, 242–56. (3.3.2)

1957: *American commodity flow: a geographical interpretation of rail and water traffic based on principles of spatial interchange*. Seattle. (2.6.1)

ULLMAN, E. L., and M. F. DACEY. 1962: The minimum requirements approach to the urban economic base. *Lund Studies in Geography, Series B, Human Geography*, **24**, 121–43. (5.2.1, 5.4.4)

UNSTEAD, J. F. 1933: A system of regional geography. *Geography*, **18**, 175–87. (14.2.2)

VAJDA, S. 1961: *The theory of games and linear programming*. London. (5.6.3, 6.5.1)

VALKENBURG, S. VAN, and C. C. HELD. 1952: *Europe*. New York. (6.4.1)

VANCE, J. E., JR. 1960: Labor-shed, employment field, and dynamic analysis in urban geography. *Economic Geography*, **36**, 189–220. (2.6.1)

1961: The Oregon Trail and the Union Pacific Railroad: a contrast in purpose. *Annals of the Association of American Geographers*, **51**, 357–79. (3.2.3)

1962: Emerging patterns of commercial structure in American cities. *Lund Studies in Geography, Series B, Human Geography*, **24**, 485–518. (2.6.2)

1970: *The merchant's world: the geography of wholesaling*. Englewood Cliffs, N.J. (5.3.2)

VIDAL DE LA BLACHE, P. 1917: *La France de l'est*. Paris. (1.2.3)

1922: *Principes de la géographie humaine*. Paris. (1.2.3)

VINING, R. 1955: A description of certain spatial aspects of an economic system. *Economic Development and Cultural Change*, **3**, 147–95. (5.2.4)

VON NEUMANN, J., and O. MORGENSTERN. 1944: *Theory of games and economic behaviour*. Princeton, N.J. (1.4.3)

WAGNER, H. M. 1959: Linear programming techniques for regression analysis. *Journal of the American Statistical Association*, **54**, 206–12. (11.4.2)

1962: Non-linear regression with minimal assumptions. *Journal of the American Statistical Association*, **57**, 572–78. (11.4.2)

WAIBEL, L. 1958: *Capitulos de geografia tropical e do Brasil*. Rio de Janeiro. (6.3.2, 6.5.2, 6.6.2)

WALTERS, S. M. 1957: Mapping the distribution of plants. *New Biology*, **24**, 93–108. (8.4.2)

WARD, J. H. 1963: Hierarchical grouping to optimize an objective function. *Journal of the American Statistical Association*, **58**, 236–44. (14.4.2)

WARNES, A. M. 1975: Commuting towards city centres: a study of population and employment density gradients in Liverpool and Manchester. *Institute of British Geographers, Publications*, **64**, 77–96. (6.6.1)

WARNTZ, W. 1959: *Toward a geography of price*. Philadelphia. (2.4.1, 9.3)

1961: Transatlantic flights and pressure patterns. *Geographical Review*, **51**, 187–212. (3.1)

WARNTZ, W., and D. NEFT. 1960: Contributions to a statistical methodology for areal distributions. *Journal of Regional Science*, **2**, 47–66. (9.6.2)

WARREN, W. G. 1962: Contributions to the study of spatial point processes.

*University of North Carolina, Institute of Statistics Mimeo Series*, **337**. (13.4.4)

WATSON, G. S. 1971: Trend surface analyses. *Mathematical Geology*, **3**, 215–26. (12.2.2)

1972: Trend surface analysis and spatial correlation. *Geological Society of America, Special Paper*, **146**, 39–46. (12.2.2)

WEAVER, J. B., and S. W. HESS. 1963: A procedure for non-partisan districting: development of computer techniques. *Yale Law Journal*, **73**, 288–308. (14.5.2)

WEAVER, J. C. 1954: Crop combination regions in the Middle West. *Geographical Review*, **44**, 175–200. (9.4.2)

1956: The county as a spatial average in agricultural geography. *Geographical Review*, **46**, 536–65. (8.4.2)

WEBB, W. P. 1927: *The Great Plains*. New York. (4.2.3, 7.1)

WEBBER, M. J. 1972: *Impact of uncertainty on location*. Cambridge, Mass. (1.2.2, 5.2.3)

WEBER, A. 1909: *Über den Standort der Industrien*. Tübingen. (1.2.2, 5.5, 5.6.1)

WELLINGTON, A. M. 1886: The American line from Vera Cruz to the city of Mexico, via Jalapa, with notes on the best methods of surmounting high elevations by rail. *American Society of Civil Engineers, Transactions*, **20**. (3.2.1)

1887: *The economic theory of the location of railways*. New York. (3.2.1)

WERNER, C. 1968: The law of refraction in transportation geography: its multivariate analysis. *Canadian Geographer*, **12** (1), 28–40. (3.2.2)

WETHERILL, G. B. 1967: *Elementary statistical methods*. London. (10.1)

WHITE, R. R. 1972: Probability maps of leukaemia mortalities in England and Wales. In N. D. McGlashan, Editor. *Medical geography: techniques and field studies*. London. (9.5.2)

WHITTEN, E. H. T. 1974: Scale and directional field and analytical data for spatial variability studies. *Mathematical Geology*, **6**, 183–98. (12.2.2)

WHITTLE, P. 1954: On stationary processes in the plane. *Biometrika*, **41**, 434–49. (10.3.2, 11.2.2, 11.4.2)

WILLIAMSON, E., and M, H. BRETHERTON. 1963: *Tables of the negative binomial probability distribution*. New York. (13.3.4)

WINTERS, P. R. 1960: Forecasting sales by exponentially-weighted moving averages. *Management Science*, **6**, 324–42. (16.3.3)

WHITEHAND, J. W. R. 1972: Building cycles and the spatial pattern of urban growth. *Institute of British Geographers, Publications*, **56**, 39–55. (6.6.1)

WHITTLESEY, D. 1956: Southern Rhodesia: an African compage. *Annals of the Association of American Geographers*, **46**, 1–97. (14.2.2)

WHITWORTH, W. A. 1934: *Choice and chance*. New York. (4.3.3)

WILLIAMS, W. T., and J. M. LAMBERT. 1959–62: Multivariate methods in plant ecology. *Journal of Ecology*, **47**, 83–101; **48**, 689–710; **49**, 717–29; **50**, 775–802. (14.4.1)

WILSON, A. G. 1967: A statistical theory of spatial distribution models. *Transportation Research*, **1**, 253–69. (2.5.2)

1970: *Entropy in urban and regional modelling*. London. (1.2.4, 2.5, 2.5.1–2)

1972: Theoretical geography: some speculations. *Institute of British Geographers, Publications*, **57**, 31–44. (1.4.2)

1974: *Urban and regional models in geography and planning*. London. (Postscript)

WILSON, A. G., and M. J. KIRKBY. 1975: *Mathematical methods for geographers and planners*. Oxford. (Preface, 1.1)

WINSBOROUGH, H. H. 1961: A comparative study of urban population densities. *University of Chicago, Ph.D. Thesis.* (6.2.2)

WISE, M. J. 1949: On the evolution of the jewellery and gun quarters in Birmingham. *Institute of British Geographers, Publications,* **15**, 57–72. (5.5.2)

WOLFE, R. I. 1963: *Transportation and politics.* Princeton. (3.2.3)

WOLPERT, J. 1964: The decision process in spatial context. *Annals of the Association of American Geographers,* **54**, 537–58. (6.5.3)

WOOD, W. F. 1955: Use of stratified random samples in land use study. *Annals of the Association of American Geographers,* **45**, 350–67. (8.3.2)

WOODWARD, V. H. 1971: Review of *Optimal Patterns of Location,* J. Serck-Hanssen, Amsterdam: North-Holland 1970: *The Economic Journal,* **81**, 396. (15.4.1)

WRIGLEY, N. 1973: The use of percentages in geographical research. *Area,* **5**, 183–86. (16.5.2)

WYNNE-EDWARDS, V. C. 1962: *Animal dispersion in relation to social behaviour.* Edinburgh. (2.7)

YAPA, L. 1976: On the statistical significance of the observed map in spatial diffusion. *Geographical Analysis,* **8**, 255–68. (7.6.2)

YATES, F. 1960: *Sampling methods for censuses and surveys.* London. (8.3, 8.3.1, 8.3.5)

YEATES, M. H. 1963: Hinterland delimitation: a distance minimizing approach. *Professional Geographer,* **15** (6), 7–10. (2.4.2, 14.1, 14.5.1, 15.4.3)

1974: *An introduction to quantitative analysis in human geography.* New York. (10.1)

YEATES, M. H., and B. J. GARNER. 1971, 1976: *The North American city.* New York. (6.3.4)

YUILL, R. S. 1965: A simulation study of barrier effects in spatial diffusion problems. *Michigan Inter-University Community of Mathematical Geographers, Discussion Papers,* **5**. (7.5.1)

YULE, G. U., and M. G. KENDALL. 1957: *An introduction to the theory of statistics.* (Thirteenth edition) London. (10.6.1, 10.6.2)

ZIPF, G. K. 1949: *Human behaviour and the principle of least effort.* Cambridge, Mass. (2.2.1, 2.2.2, 4.3.1)

ZOBLER, L. 1958: Decision making in regional construction. *Annals of the Association of American Geographers,* **48**, 140–8. (14.4.3)

# Further reading

To add a section on further reading to an extended list of references (given on pages 556–88) may appear to be gilding the lily. Nonetheless it is arguable that a list which derives from the reasonable need to document the many and varied sources from which the notes for this book were assembled is not likely to be very helpful to the reader who is looking for some more limited or basic reading or wishes to keep up to date on current trends.

(a) *Basic reading.* If we may assume that the student is already familiar with the traditional literature of regional and human geography then a very good starting point is provided by ABLER, ADAMS, and GOULD (1971)* over the whole range of locational theory and by CHISHOLM (1962) and by SMITH (1971) over agricultural and industrial location respectively. BUNGE (1962) also remains a lively, stimulating and unusual approach to locational analysis from a strongly geometrical viewpoint. Students unfamiliar with more conventional geographical writing will find that HARVEY (1969) and AMADEO and GOLLEDGE (1975) give scholarly reviews of the aims, methods, and problems of the discipline. THOMAS (1956) and HAGGETT (1975a) give examples of substantive studies in human geography.

(b) *Advanced reading.* A number of the classic studies in locational theory—notably those of LÖSCH (1954), CHRISTALLER (1966), von Thünen (HALL, 1966) and HÄGERSTRAND (1967)—are available in translation. Most of the early contributions have been summarized and greatly extended by ISARD (1956) in what is still among the most useful textbooks in the field. WILSON (1974) provides a more rigorous contemporary account with special emphasis on spatial interaction models.

There is no single source for methods in locational analysis, although that by ISARD (*Introduction to Regional Science*, Englewood Cliffs, N.J., 1975) comes nearest. There is a variety of texts on statistical analysis of varying degrees of difficulty and relevance to spatial analysis: that by KING (1969) probably remains the best for geographers. Standard mathematical procedures are outlined clearly in WILSON and KIRKBY (1975). Probably the most important reading here for student geographers is concerned with the whole strategy of scientific method rather than the tactics of individual tests: HANSON (1958) and HARVEY (1969) provide excellent introductions to this field.

* Full titles are given only where books have not been previously mentioned in the text.

(c) *Current research.* The rapid rate of evolution of locational studies and the introduction of wholly new methods (e.g. entropy maximizing methods) means that journals are as important as textbooks if a student is to retain a reasonably contemporary view of the subject. Most of the more traditional geographical journals now carry papers of direct importance in locational analysis. However the key journals, as judged on their content to 1975, are the *Annals of the Association of American Geographers* (Quarterly), *Geographical Analysis* (Quarterly), the *Lund Studies in Geography, Series B and C* (Occasional), the Regional Science Association's *Papers and Proceedings* (Annual), *Regional Studies* (Quarterly), and *Environment and Planning Series A* (Quarterly). In addition to these formal periodicals a few universities publish research theses (the Chicago and California Departments of Geography have outstanding series) and most produce informal discussion papers which are important sources of ideas. (The latter are regularly listed in *Geographical Analysis.*) Most difficult to keep track of are the Contract Reports of research done for government bodies (e.g. the Office of Naval Research in the United States) although these often emerge later as papers in the standard journals. *Progress in Geography* (Vols. 1–9) draws together findings from many of these research sources in regular reviews of developments within the field.

(d) *Research 'readers'.* For the student without access to a periodicals library one useful substitute is the research 'reader'—a collection of research papers on a specific topic drawn from a wide range of journals. Many items of locational interest are included in FRIEDMANN and ALONSO (*Regional development and planning: a reader,* 1975). Urban geography is covered in BERRY and HORTON (1970), economic geography in SMITH, TAAFFE and KING (*Readings in economic geography*, Chicago, 1968), industrial location in KARASKA and BRAMHALL (*Locational analysis for manufacturing: a selection of readings*, Cambridge, Mass., 1969), and transport geography in HURST (1974). Many of the methods of analysis described in the second part of this book are illustrated in BERRY and MARBLE (1968).

# Subject index

# Subject index


Accordance, in industrial location, 162–5
Adaptive forecasting, 524
Administrative principle, in Christaller model, 148
Airline networks, 321–4, 327
Air photo coverage, 285
Agglomeration economies, 102, 217–9
  regional swarming, 173–6
  within individual plants, 170–3
Aggregation problems, in data collecting, 286–90
Agricultural zones,
  location of, 304–5
  output of, 362
    *See also* von Thünen model
Allocation models, 491–516 *passim*
Allometry, 9–10, 121
Amplitude, in spectral analysis, 392
Analyses of variance models, *see* Variance models, analysis of
Anthropogeography, 5
Archaeology, locational analysis in, 541
Areal differentiation, 2
Arc-sine transformation, 347
Association analysis, in region building, 465–7
Autocorrelation,
  alternative measures of, 60, 247, 356–7
  concepts of, 354–6
  distribution theory, 357–9
  hypothesis testing, 347–7
    *See also* Spatial autocorrelation; Space-time models; Temporal autocorrelation
Autoregressive process, 365–7, 396
    *See also* Space-time autoregressive model

Barriers, in diffusion models, 242–3
Bartlett's epidemic model, 251–2
Base theory, *see* Economic base theory
Basic interval, in spectral analysis, 392
Basic sector, in city growth, 159
Basic–nonbasic ratio, 167
Bayesian models, 22
Beckmann–Marschak problem, 505–7
Beckmann model, of city sizes, 151
Behavioural variations, impact on land-use patterns, 219–22
Berkeley school, 6, 231–2
Betti number, 318
Binomial distribution, 346
Biproportionate matrix, 125–6
Bodenrente, 204
Boltzmann's law, 42
Border effects, on network location, 68–9
  on spatial interaction, 52
Boundary cases, assignment in regional classification, 472–7
Boundary overlap, in regional classification, 457–60
Box–Jenkins models, 258, 526
Bunge–Beckmann problem, of network location, 73–4
Bylund model, 106–7

Canals, location of, 67–8, 92
Canberra metric, 471
Capacitated transportation problem, 507
Cartography, in relation to geography, 19
Cascade algorithm, 80
Casey–Huff interaction model, 33
Central goods, in Christaller model, 143
Central limit theorem, 268–70
Central place theory, 143, 165
  diffusion aspects, 240–1
  fixed *k* models, 146–8
  variable *k* models, 148–5
    *See also* Christaller model; Lösch model
Centre-satellite model, 435–6
Centrality measures, in population distributions, 314
Centrography, 312–3
Centuriation, 99
Chain binomial models, 253–5

Chi-squared distribution, *see* $X^2$ distribution
Choropleth maps, 294, 356, 359
Christaller model, 106, 139, 150, 241
*See also* Central place theory
City block metric, 471
City, definitions of, 265–7
Class intervals, on maps, 294–6
Climatic classification, 456
Closed system, 8
Clusters, urban size and function, 139–43
Coefficient of geographical association, 299–351
Cohen model, 117–8
Coherence, in spectral analysis, 408
Collecting areas, irregular, 348–52
impact on statistical measures, 349–51
standardization of, 351–2
Combination mapping, 304–6, 489–90
Compactness, of spatial distributions, 310, 482
Compage, 453
Complementarity, in gravity models, 38
Compounding distributions, 418
Concentric-zone land use model, 226–7
Cone of dependencies, 356
Conical model, of population distribution, 193
Connectivity measures, in networks, 86, 314–5
Conservation condition, in linear programming problems, 507
Contact patterns, 175
Contagion, in point patterns, 418–20
Contours, spacing of, 294–6
Control points, arrangement of, 296–7
Coordinate systems, 324–8
Correlogram analysis, 299, 367–74
in space, 369–72
in time, 367–9
regional applications of, 372–4
*See also* Martin–Oeppen procedure
Corridors, in diffusion models, 243–4
Cosine curve, 391–7
Cosine model, for population distributions, 193
Crop combinations, 216
Cycles, in periodic markets, 153–7
Cyclomatic number, 318

Data, collecting, 260–90 *passim*
coverage problems, 282–90
matrix, 15
spatial variations in quality of, 282–5
Degeneracy, in linear programming problems, 502–3
Delta-wye transformation, 83
Density gradients, 194, 221, 223
between cities, 196–7
within cities, 194–6
Dependent places, in central place theory, 143
Depression, economic, 132
Deterministic models, in geography, 19–22
Diffusion models, 231–58, 530
barriers in, 242–4
central place systems, 240–1
corridors in, 242–4
rural settlements, 106–9
*See also* Bylund model; Epidemic models; Hägerstrand model
Dimensional analysis, 37
Disease, spatial aspects of, 233, 518
*See also* Epidemics
Distance component, in gravity model, 34–6
Distance-decay rates, 31, 195, 207–11
Distance grouping in *n*-dimensional space, 467–72
Distributions, statistical, *see* Gamma function; *F* distribution; Normal distribution; *t* distribution; $X^2$ distribution
Distribution-free procedures, 348
Dispersed city, 166
Dirichlet regions, 436–9
Domain, in spectral analysis, 400
Drift contact, in diffusion, 244
Duals, in linear programming, 493, 500, 511
Durbin–Watson statistic, 357
Dyads, 485
Dynamic programming, 515

Ecological fallacy, 10
Ecology, traditions in geography, 5–6
Ecosystem, 5–6
Economic-base theory, 159–61
Economic development, 90–92, 119, 191
Einzelhof, 105
Electoral districts, boundaries of, 509
optimization of, 479–85
Elimination solutions, to irregular data problems, 287–8
Employment fields, 49–50
*See also* Unemployment
Entropy function, in interaction, 40–2
in linear programming, 512
in mapping, 302
in settlement arrangement, 116–7
*See also* Maximum entropy models
Environmental determinism, 20
Environmental information, 283
Epidemics, 132–3, 233, 247–58, 372–4
general epidemic model, 249–51
hierarchic models, 255–7
simple epidemic model, 248–9
types of, 247–8
*See also* Bartlett model; Chain binomial model; Rapoport model
Epizootics, 233
Equifinality, 431–2

Euclidean space, 78, 82, 471
Event array, in spectral analysis, 402
Exponential growth, 13, 435–6

*F* distribution, 245, 329, 336
  table of values, 553
Facies mapping, 302–4
Factor combination sampling, 275
Factor analysis, 306–336
Fields, shape of, 51–4
  size of, 47–50
Finite population, statistical, 263
Floating-point location problems, in networks, 69–73
Forecasting models, 161, 517–40
  identification problems, 525–6
  parameter variation in, 534–9
  purely spatial, 539–40
    *See also* Adaptive forecasting; Martin–Oeppen procedure; Space–time autoregressive models
Fragmentation index, for maps, 299
Freight, flows, 28–9
  rates, 66, 210
Frequency, in spectral analysis, 392–3, 405
Fourier analysis, 390–406
    *See also* Spectral analysis
Functional range, in settlement studies, 140

Gain, in spectral analysis, 408
Galton's problem, 330
Game theory, 213–7, 512–5
Gamma distribution, 346, 420
  tables of, 554
Geographical association, measures of, 299–301
Geographical data, coding of, 324–5
  sources of, 261–2
  types of, 262–4
Geography, 1–24
  as critical science, 23–4
  definitions and traditions, 2–3
  external relations of, 10–12
  internal dialogues in, 2–10
  paradigm shifts in, 13–17
  trends within, 12–24
Geometry, role in geography, 3–4, 19
Geometric programming, 515
Generalizing distribution, in point pattern analysis, 418
General Register Office (GRO) districts, 367–7, 372
Ghetto formation, 229–30
Goodness-of-fit models, 244–7
Graph theory, 313–24
Gravity models, basic, 30, 81–2
  refinements of, 38–40
    *See also* Interaction
Greenwood model, for epidemics, 254–5
Grid solutions, to irregular data problems, 288–9
Gross national product, 86, 354
Grouping, hierarchic, 470
  procedures for, 454–7
Growth pole theory, 497–8

Hägerstrand model, 17, 234–7, 247, 249, 257
    *See also* Diffusion models
Hamiltonian circuit, 76, 78
Haufendorf, 105
Herbert–Stevens model, 510–2
Hexagonal fields, 60–3, 143–6
Hierarchic sampling, 274
Hierarchic organization, of settlements, 7, 139–90 *passim*
Historical geography, 164, 541
Hollow frontier hypothesis, 227
Holt–Winters model, 525
Household tenure, mapping of, 303–4
Hudson model, of settlement spread, 109–10
Hypotheses, statistical testing of, 329–52

Independence assumption, in nearest-neighbour models, 440–1
  in statistical analyses and modelling, 327–42, 374–77
Infinite population, in sampling, 263
Innovation waves, 232–3
    *See also* Diffusion models
Instabilities, in urban systems, 121–38
Integration, in industrial structure, 174
Interaction, spatial, 7, 26–63
  elementary models of, 30–3
  fields, 47–54
  interpretation of, 33–40
  relation to spatial form, 26–30
  territories, 55–63
    *See also* Gravity models
Interest levels, spatial change in, 132
Intervening opportunity model, 33
Interval scale, in mapping, 292
Isarithmic maps, 293–4
Island model, diffusion, 239
Isolierte Staat, 205–7

*k*-values, in settlement models, 146–53
  empirical evidence on, 151–3
  relation to lattices, 143–6
Kalman filters, 540
Kermack–McKendrick model, 253
Kuhn–Kuenne algorithm, 72, 182–4
Kulturlandschaft, 6
Kurtosis, 345–6

Lapse rates, regional studies of, 28–30
Labour coefficient, 185

Lagrangian multipliers, 44, 72, 512
Land use, intensities, 191–2, 198, 218
 development models of, 226–30
 ring formation, 202–3, 205, 521
 step structures, 197–9
  *See also* von Thünen model
Latent structure, in networks, 320–4
Latin square designs, 279
Lattices, distortion over space, 102–6
 distortion over time, 106–10
 settlements as, 98–102
Leads and lags, in spectral analysis, 406–7
Le Châtelier's principle, 8
Lex parsimoniae, 27
Likelihood ratio, 345
Linear programming methods, 17, 44, 184, 186–8, 311, 365, 477–9
Line samples, 276–7
Linkage analysis, 486–90
Link-length analysis, 70–1
Location, traditions in geography, 3–5
Locational quotient, 301
Locational surface, in industrial location, 185–6
Logistic curve, 13, 238–40
Log normality, 346
 in settlement models, 121–4
 regional evidence for, 115
Löschian model, 106, 139, 148–52
  *See also* Central-place models
Lowry-type models, 541

Macrostates, in Wilson model, 45
Maps, colouring problems, 153–4
 complexity measures, 297–9
 coordinate systems for, 324–8
 multicomponent, 301–6
 progressive coverage, 284
 redundancy measures, 299
 scale of, 284
Marketing principle, in Christaller model, 148, 152
Market rings, 153
Martin–Oeppen procedure, 526–34
Markov models, 19, 366
Marschufendorf, 105
Mass component, in gravity model, 33–4
Maximum entropy models, 8, 40–7, 116–7, 510
Mean information field (MIF), 235–6, 242–3, 247–9, 521
Measles, spread of, 367–8, 373, 377
Measurement levels, relation to mapping, 291–3
Migration, 27–8, 37–8, 252, 330
Minimum absolute deviation (MAD), 365, 521
Minimum requirements approach, to urban growth, 168–9
Minkowski metric, 471
Missing data problem, 518
Morphometric analysis, 293
Moments, method of, 429–30
Monte Carlo models, 234–5, 247, 331, 333, 354, 360
Mosaics, *L* and *S*, 439
Movement costs, 26–8, 48, 51
Movement-minimization models, 177–85, 199–211
Multidimensional scaling, 326–8
Multiple-nuclei model, of urban growth, 227
Multipliers, employment, 164–5
Multistage sampling, 274
Multivariate data, mapping of, 306

Nearest neighbour methods, 100–1
 boundary problems in, 441
 extensions of, 441–3
 reflexive, 443–6
 sectoral, 442–6
Negative binomial distribution, 418, 420–32 *passim*
Neighbourhood effects, in Hägerstrand model, 235
Nesting, of regions, 454
 of sampling designs, 274–5
 variance models, 352
Net, distance biased, 239
Networks, 7, 64–96, 319
 combinatorial aspects, 76–8
 geometry of, 86–7
 location of, 69–76
 routes through, 76–86
 structure of, 86–96
Newtonian concepts, 19, 30–1
Newton–Raphson approximations, 183
Neyman type A distribution, 421–31 *passim*
Nodal regions, 7–8, 453
 as graphs, 485–90
Nodes, *see* Settlements
Non-basic sector, 159
Non-Euclidean space, 79, 82
Non-normality, problems of, 345–6
Normality, concepts of, 345–52
 transformations to, 346–8
  *See also* Normal distribution
Normal distribution, 129, 346, 358, 440, 540
 maps based on, 306–7
 table of areas under, 550
Nonconformist centres, in industrial location, 176–7
Northwest corner rule, in linear programming, 497
Nyquist frequency, 405

Ordinary least squares (OLS), 17, 31, 36
Open system, 8

Operational definitions, in data collecting, 265–7
Opportunity cost, 499
Order-neighbour distances, 441–2
*See also* Nearest neighbour methods
Ordinal scales, 292
Orientation index, in industrial location, 178

Packing, elementary models, 55–7
regional studies of, 57–60
Pandemic threshold theorems, 250
Pareto distribution, 111, 121
Parsimony, principle of, 526
Partitioning procedures, in region building, 454–7
Paul Revere network, 73
Payoff matrix, 513
Percentage data, mapping of, 302–6
Percolation models, in diffusion, 256
Perimeter model, 256
Phase, in spectral analysis, 393, 408
Phenomenology, 22–3
Planning regions, 453
Point patterns, 4, 276–7, 414–47
*See also* Nearest-neighbour methods; Quadrat counts
Poisson–binomial distribution, 421–31 *passim*
Poisson distribution, compound, 418–21
maps based on, 307–9
model comparisons, 421–3
processes in space, 100, 344, 346, 418
simple, 416–8
Poisson–Pascal distribution, 421–31 *passim*
Pólya–Aeppli distribution, 421–31 *passim*
Polygon techniques, 436–9
Populations, geographical, 261–7
Population density, 36, 191, 194–5, 225, 289, 294, 349, 518
concentration, 349, 519
formal models of, 397–8
potentials, 39–40, 312
regional lapse rates, 103
Ports, 66–7, 69
development model of, 92–5
Positivism, 22–3
Possibilism, 20
Primacy, in urban settlements, 111–2, 116, 121–4
Primal problem, in linear programming, 499–500, 510
Principal components analysis, 306, 336, 476
Probability, maps, 306–9
matrix, 107–8
models, 19–22
regional applications, 458–60
Productivity surface, 219
Pseudo-random numbers, table of, 554
*See also* Random numbers

Quadrant counts, in settlement studies, 102
model fitting, 429–30
probability distributions, 110, 415–30
regional applications, 430–6
Quadratic models, 36, 364
Quantification, in geography, 17–9
Queuing theory, 165

Railways, 20, 64–9, 74, 86–7
density of, 87–92
development models for, 92–5
simulation models, 82–4
Rank-size regularities, 44, 108, 111–5
Range of a good, in central place theory, 142–3
Random numbers, 100, 358, 554–5
*See also* Pseudo-random numbers
Random sampling, 280–1
Random spatial economy, 100–102, 118, 398–9
Random splitting process, 117–8
Rapoport model, 252–3
Ravenstein migration model, 31–2
Reed–Frost epidemic model, 253–5
Refraction laws, applied to route location, 66–8
Regional correlation bonds, 476
Regional geography, 6–10
Regions, as assignment problems, 465–77
as combinatorial problems, 460–5
as districting problems, 477–85
concepts of, 450–60
types of, 450–3
Regional science, 11–12
Reilly-converse model, 32–3
Regression models, 31, 35, 89, 160, 168–9, 379–83
autocorrelation in, 360–1
solutions for, 361–7
spatial distortion in, 334–6
Rents, spatial variation in, 204, 496–7, 499
Resources, locational impact of, 177–89, 211–7
Retail gravitation, law of, 32
Rings, in market structures, 153–7
in von Thünen model, 200–7
Roads, 64, 68–9, 71, 81–2
density of, 88–92
development model of, 92–5
in plantations, 75–6
in rural areas, 74–5
Routes, location of, 64–9
density of, 87–92
development model of, 92–6
Rundling, 105
S-I Index, 317–9, 428
Sampling, efficiency of, 274–7
frames, 286
size considerations, 279–82
space-time, 277–9
spatial configuration, 270–4

Scale, components, 378–413 *passim*
  concepts in geography, 6–10
  in regional hierarchies, 453–4
School districts, 477–9, 509
Sector model, of urban growth, 227
Set theory, 310, 454–60
Settlements, classification of, 98
  evolution of, 153–61
  hierarchies of, 139–53, 161–70
  spatial patterns of, 97–110, 401–3, 430–6
  size considerations, 97–138 *passim*
    *See also* Central place theory
Shadow prices, in linear programming, 503
Shape, measurement of, 309–12
Share-size model, 117–8
Shen Lin algorithm, 80
Shocks, in urban systems, 132
Short distribution, 421–31 *passim*
Shortest-path distribution, 84–6, 319–20
Simplex algorithm, 497
Simulation models, 85, 107
    *See also* Monte Carlo models
Slack variables, in linear programming, 503–5
Snell's law, 66
Soap-film methods, 70–1
Space, *n*-dimensional, 467–72
Spacing of settlements, 128–32
Space–time autocorrelation, 355–6
Space–time autoregressive model, basic (STAR), 518–21
  exponential smoothing, 522–5
  STARIMAR, 522–5
  STIMA, 522–5
Space–time spectral analysis, 406–13
    *See also* Fourier analysis; Spectral analysis
Spanning-tree problems, 76, 80–4, 462–4
Spatial autocorrelation, 35, 330, 332, 336–7, 353–77 *passim*, 432–4
Spatial independence, problem of, 329–36
  solutions to, 336–42
Spatial interaction, *see* Interaction, spatial
Spatial lags, 365, 372, 374
Spatial stationarity, concepts of, 161–2, 342–3
  consequences of, 344–5
  formal definitions of, 343–4
Spectral analysis, 101, 299, 390–406
  estimation problems, 404–6, 413
  principles of, 390–9
  two-dimensional, 399–404
    *See also* Fourier analysis; Space–time spectral analysis
Standardization problems, in data collecting, 285–90
Standard Metropolitan Area (SMA), 266
Stationarity, 399, 409, 521
    *See also* Spatial stationarity
Statistical distributions, tables of, 549–55
Steady states, 8
Stepping-stone algorithm, 497
Strassendorf, 105
Stratification, in sampling designs, 271–4
Student's *t*-distribution, *see* *t*-distribution
Surfaces, 7, 191–230 *passim*
    *See also* Density surfaces
Swarming, in industrial location, 173–6
Systematic sampling, 271, 273
Systems, concepts of, 5–6

*t*-distribution, 329–336, 345, 376–7
  table of values, 549
Target population, 264
Telephone traffic, 64, 85, 488
Thiessen polygons, 436–9
Thomas's distribution, 421–31 *passim*
Threshold, population, 141–3
Time-space trajectories, 17
Topology, 3, 313–6
Townships and range, 99
Traffic principle, in Christaller model, 148
Transformations, of data, 193
Transportation problems, 480, 492–7
  algorithm, 497–505
  extensions of, 505–10
  formal model, 492–3
  network problems, 507–9
  region building, 509
    *See also* linear programming
Trans-shipment problem, 505–7
Travelling salesman problem, 76, 78–80
Trend surface analysis, 299, 352–3
  scale components in, 383–4
  limitations of, 382–3
  polynomial models, 379–84
  spatial forms, 379–82

Unbiased estimator, 36
Uncertainty principle, 21
Unemployment, forecasting of, 518–9, 522, 540
  spatial variations in, 17–18, 132, 134–8, 263, 343, 390–1, 408–13
Uniform regions, 451–3
Urban density profiles, *see* Density gradients
Urbanization hypotheses, of city-size distribution, 119
Urbandschaft, 6

Variance, analysis of, 384–90
  Model I, 385
  Model II, 385–90
  nested model, 385–7
  region-building, 475
Variate differencing, spatial, 338–42

Venn diagrams, 454–6
Von Thünen model, 66, 205–7, 230
Voronoi polygons, 436–9

Waldhufendorf, 105
Wavelength, in spectral analysis, 392
Weberian models, 139, 170, 177–85
Wellington model, of network location, 65–6
Wheat belts, location of, 209
White noise, 397
Whitworth model, 117–8

$X^2$ distribution, 329, 336–7, 349, 417, 429, 440, 442, 465–7
table of values, 552

Yields, spatial variations in, 350
*See also* von Thünen model

Zinc smelting industry, location of, 177–8, 182, 189
Zipf model, of settlement-size distribution, 117–18